The Right to a Speedy and Public Trial

Recent Titles in
Reference Guides to the United States Constitution
Jack Stark, Series Editor

Prohibited Government Acts
Jack Stark

State Sovereign Immunity
Melvyn R. Durchslag

Constitutional Remedies
Michael Wells and Thomas A. Eaton

Privileges and Immunities
David Skillen Bogen

Searches, Seizures, and Warrants
Robert M. Bloom

The Supremacy Clause
Christopher R. Drahozal

Procedural Due Process
Rhonda Wasserman

Double Jeopardy
David S. Rudstein

Freedom of the Press
Lyrissa Barnett Lidsky and R. George Wright

The Taxing Power
Erik M. Jensen

Freedom of Speech
Keith Werhan

The Religion Guarantees
Peter K. Rofes

Limits on States
James M. McGoldrick, Jr.

The Full Faith and Credit Clause
William L. Reynolds and William M. Richman

The Right to a Speedy and Public Trial

A Reference Guide to the United States Constitution

Susan N. Herman

Foreword by ERWIN CHEMERINSKY

REFERENCE GUIDES TO THE
UNITED STATES CONSTITUTION, NUMBER 16
Jack Stark, *Series Editor*

PRAEGER

Westport, Connecticut
London

Library of Congress Cataloging-in-Publication Data

Herman, Susan N.

The right to a speedy and public trial: a reference guide to the United States Constitution/ Susan N. Herman; foreword by Erwin Chemerinsky.

p. cm.—(Reference guides to the United States Constitution, ISSN 1539-8986; no. 16)

Includes bibliographical references and index.

ISBN 0-313-32108-6 (alk. paper)

1. Speedy trial—United States. 2. Publicity (Law)—United States. 3. Conduct of court proceedings—United States. 4. Criminal justice, Administration of—United States. 5. United States. Constitution. 6th Amendment. I. Title. II. Series.

KF9223.4.H47 2006

345.73'056—dc22 2006015395

British Library Cataloguing in Publication Data is available.

Library of Congress Catalog Card Number: 2006015395
ISBN: 0-313-32108-6
ISSN: 1539-8986

First published in 2006

Praeger Publishers, 88 Post Road West, Westport, CT 06881
An imprint of Greenwood Publishing Group, Inc.
www.praeger.com

Printed in the United States of America

The paper used in this book complies with the Permanent Paper Standard issued by the National Information Standards Organization (Z39.48–1984).

10 9 8 7 6 5 4 3 2 1

Contents

Series Foreword

Jack Stark

One can conceive of the United States Constitution in many ways. For example, noting the reverence in which it has been held, one can think of it as equivalent to a sacred text. Unfortunately, most of its devotees have had less knowledge and even less understanding of the document than they have had reverence for it. Sometimes it is treated as primarily a political document and on that basis has been subjected to analysis, such as Charles Beard's *An Economic Interpretation of the Constitution of the United States.* One can plausibly argue that the Constitution seems most astounding when it is seen in the light of the intellectual effort that has been associated with it. Three brief but highly intense bursts of intellectual energy produced, and established as organic law, most of the Constitution as it now exists. Two of these efforts, sustained over a long period of time, have enabled us better to understand that document.

The first burst of energy occurred at the Constitutional Convention. Although some of the delegates' business, such as the struggle between populous and non-populous states about their representation in Congress, was political, much of it was about fundamental issues of political theory. A few of the delegates had or later achieved international eminence for their intellects. Among them were Benjamin Franklin, Alexander Hamilton, and James Madison. Others, although less well known, had first-rate minds. That group includes George Mason and George Wythe. Many of the delegates contributed intelligently. Although the Convention's records are less than satisfactory, they indicate clearly enough that the delegates worked mightily to constitute not merely a polity but a rational polity—one that would rise to the standards envisioned by the delegates' intellectual ancestors. Their product, though brief, is amazing. William Gladstone called it "the most wonderful work ever struck off."

Despite the delegates' eminence and the Constitution's excellence as seen from our place in history, its ratification was far from certain. That state of affairs necessitated the second burst of intellectual energy associated with that document: the debate over ratification. Soon after the Convention adjourned, articles and speeches—some supporting the Constitution and some attacking it—began to proliferate. A national debate commenced, not only about the document itself, but also about the nature of the polity that ought to exist in this country. Both sides included many writers and speakers who were verbally adroit and steeped in the relevant political and philosophical literature. The result was an accumulation of material that is remarkable for both its quantity and its quality. At its apex is *The Federalist Papers*, a production of Alexander Hamilton, James Madison, and John Jay that deserves a place among the great books of Western culture.

Another burst, not as impressive as the first two but highly respectable, occurred when the Bill of Rights was proposed. Some delegates to the Constitutional Convention had vigorously asserted that such guarantees should be included in the original document. George Mason, the principal drafter of the Virginia Declaration of Rights, so held, and he walked out of the Convention when he failed to achieve his purpose. Even those who had argued that the rights in question were implicit recognized the value of adding protection of them to the Constitution. The debate was thus focused on the rights that were to be explicitly granted, not on whether any rights *ought* to be explicitly granted. Again many writers and speakers entered the fray, and again the debate was solidly grounded in theory and was conducted on a high intellectual level.

Thus, within a few years a statement of organic law and a vital coda to it had been produced. However, the meaning and effect of many of that document's provisions were far from certain; the debates on ratification of the Constitution and the Bill of Rights had demonstrated that. In addition, the document existed in a vacuum, because statutes and actions had not been assessed by its standards. The attempt to resolve these problems began after Chief Justice John Marshall, in Marbury v. Madison, asserted the right of the U.S. Supreme Court to interpret and apply the Constitution. Judicial interpretation and application of the Constitution, beginning with the first constitutional case and persisting until the most recent, is one of the sustained exertions of intellectual energy associated with the Constitution. The framers would be surprised by some of the results of those activities. References in the document to "due process," which seems to refer only to procedures, have been held also to have a substantive dimension. A right to privacy has been found lurking among the penumbras of various parts of the text. A requirement that states grant the same "privileges and immunities" to citizens of other states that they granted to their own citizens, which seemed to guarantee important rights, was held not to be particularly important. The corpus of judicial interpretations of the Constitution is now as voluminous as that document is terse.

As the judicial interpretations multiplied, another layer—interpretations of interpretations—appeared, and also multiplied. This layer, the other sustained intellectual effort associated with the Constitution, consists of articles, most of them published in law reviews, and books on the Constitution. This material varies in quality and significance. Some of these works of scholarship result from meticulous examination and incisive thought. Others repeat earlier work, or apply a fine-tooth comb to matters that are too minute even for such a comb. Somewhere in that welter of tertiary material is the answer to almost every question that one could ask about constitutional law. The problem is finding the answer that one wants. The difficulty of locating useful guidance is exacerbated by the bifurcation of most constitutional scholarship into two kinds. In "Two Styles of Social Science Research," C. Wright Mills delineates macroscopic and molecular research. The former deals with huge issues, the latter with tiny issues. Virtually all of the scholarship on the Constitution is of one of those two types. Little of it is macroscopic, but that category does include some first-rate syntheses such as Jack Rakove's *Original Meanings*. Most constitutional scholarship is molecular and, again, some fine work is included in that category.

In his essay, Mills bemoans the inability of social scientists to combine the two kinds of research that he describes to create a third category that will be more generally useful. This series of books is an attempt to do for constitutional law the intellectual work that Mills proposed for social science. The author of each book has dealt carefully and at reasonable length with a topic that lies in the middle range of generality. Upon completion, this series will consist of thirty-seven books, each on a constitutional law topic. Some of the books, such as the book on freedom of the press, explicate one portion of the Constitution's text. Others, such as the volume on federalism, treat a topic that has several anchors in the Constitution. The books on constitutional history and constitutional interpretation range over the entire document, but each does so from one perspective. Except for a very few of the books, for which special circumstances dictate minor changes in format, each book includes the same components: a brief history of the topic, a lengthy and sophisticated analysis of the current state of the law on that topic, a bibliographical essay that organizes and evaluates scholarly material in order to facilitate further research, a table of cases, and an index. The books are intellectually rigorous—in fact, authorities have written them—but, due to their clarity and to brief definitions of terms that are unfamiliar to laypersons, each is comprehensible and useful to a wide audience, one that ranges from other experts on the book's subject to intelligent nonlawyers.

In short, this series provides an extremely valuable service to the legal community and to others who are interested in constitutional law, as every citizen should be. Each book is a map of part of the U.S. Constitution. Together they map all of that document's territory that is worth mapping. When this series is complete, each book will be a third kind of scholarly work that combines the macroscopic and the molecular. Together they will explicate all of the important constitutional topics. Anyone who wants assistance in understanding either a topic in constitutional law or the Constitution as a whole can easily find it in these books.

Foreword

Erwin Chemerinsky[1]

The Sixth Amendment, like all of the Bill of Rights, was ratified 215 years ago in 1791. One would think after so much time that there would be settled understandings as to what the government must do to comply with the requirements of providing a speedy and public trial. Yet, just recently, a federal court of appeals acknowledged that there is a secret docket for certain drug cases, and apparently these matters are handled entirely in secret.[2] There have been repeated accounts of completely secret trials and appeals in terrorism cases. And only a few years ago, two federal courts of appeals considered, and came to opposite conclusions about, whether completely closed immigration proceedings violate the First Amendment.[3]

As this is written in May 2006, there are individuals who have been incarcerated by the United States without trial for more than four years and for whom any trial would be in secret. More than 650 individuals have been imprisoned at Guantanamo, obviously without a speedy trial and without any prospect of a public trial. Additionally, the government is holding an unknown number of individuals as enemy combatants without providing either a speedy or a public trial. Jose Padilla, for example, was apprehended in May 2002 and was not criminally charged until 2005.[4]

All of this requires thinking again about why the rights to a speedy and public trial are so vital. As I read Professor Susan N. Herman's wonderful book, I kept thinking about how much these basic rights, accepted as essential to fair proceedings since even before the ratification of the Constitution, are at issue today.

What is the origin of these rights? What policies are served by them? What are the legal doctrines that the Supreme Court has developed with regard to each of these rights? These are the questions on which Professor Herman focuses.

Professor Herman carefully details the origins of the rights. She shows that, contrary to the common understanding, neither provision is a response to systematic abuses that occurred in England or in the colonies. For example, even the infamous Star Chamber trials were held in public. Instead, both rights can be traced to developments in English law. Each came to be recognized as basic to ensuring a fair proceeding for criminal defendants. Each thus came to be included in the Sixth Amendment when the Bill of Rights was added to the Constitution.

Professor Herman also explores in detail the justifications for these rights, both at the time of ratification and today. In discussing the right to a public trial, Professor Herman shows that it was defended by Blackstone as a way to prevent torture and decrease the likelihood of "malicious, oppressive, partial, or corrupt proceedings." Public trials were thought to be a way of keeping judges and juries more honest. Although all of these justifications remain just as powerful today, other explanations for the Sixth Amendment also have emerged. For example, Professor Herman discusses the contemporary emphasis on the trial as a form of public education and even catharsis.

Professor Herman's presentation of the doctrines in each area is masterful and will be an invaluable resource to anyone seeking to understand the law in this area. As to each of these rights, Professor Herman describes the cases and then examines the contemporary law in each area.

Until reading the book, I had never focused on how there are many Supreme Court decisions defining the requirement for a speedy trial, but virtually none interpreting the "public trial" requirement of the Sixth Amendment. With just a couple of exceptions, all of the Supreme Court discussion about public trials has come in the context of the First Amendment right to attend criminal proceedings. As Professor Herman shows, this has crucial significance. A defendant can waive his or her rights, including those under the Sixth Amendment. But a First Amendment right, belonging to the press and the public, cannot be compromised even if the defendant and the prosecutor wish to do so.

The coverage of these two rights together also raises other interesting comparisons. The speedy trial right is embodied in statutes, such as the federal Speedy Trial Act, as well as in the Constitution.[5] As Professor Herman shows, many states have speedy trial requirements in their constitutions, statutes, and rules. In contrast, statutes in the area of the right to a public trial are more about defining circumstances for closure than about ensuring openness.[6]

In reading Professor Herman's discussion of the two rights, it was striking to see that no exceptions have developed to the right to a speedy trial. The case law is about defining when the right attaches and about the factors that courts are to consider in deciding whether the right has been violated.[7] But significant exceptions have emerged allowing some criminal proceedings to be closed to the press and the public.

Reading about the two rights together also highlights an interesting similarity between them: neither has been the focus of recent reexamination by the Supreme Court. By contrast, some of the Supreme Court's most important decisions in the past several years have concerned other aspects of the Sixth Amendment. In Apprendi v. New Jersey (2000),[8] the Supreme Court held that the Sixth Amendment rights to trial by jury and proof beyond a reasonable doubt mean that any factor, other than a prior conviction, that leads to a sentence greater than the statutory maximum must be proven to a jury beyond a reasonable doubt. *Apprendi*, of course, has created an enormous amount of litigation and has engendered great and continuing uncertainty as to the meaning of these Sixth Amendment rights.

In Crawford v. Washington (2004), the Court dramatically changed the law of the confrontation clause of the Sixth Amendment.[9] The Court held that an out-of-court statement which is "testimonial" cannot be used against a criminal defendant on the grounds that the declarant is unavailable. In the two years after *Crawford*, there have been hundreds of published decisions interpreting and applying it.

The reexamination of these parts of the Sixth Amendment in *Apprendi* and *Crawford* raises the possibility that other aspects of the Sixth Amendment, notably the requirements for a speedy and public trial, might also be reconsidered in the years ahead. When lawyers and judges engage in this reexamination, they should begin their work by reading Professor Herman's comprehensive and engaging book.

NOTES

1. Alston & Bird Professor of Law and Political Science, Duke University.
2. United States v. Ochoa-Vasquez, 428 F.3d 1015 (11th Cir. 2005).
3. Detroit Free Press v. Aschroft, 303 F.3d 681 (6th Cir. 2002); North Jersey Media Group v. Ashcroft, 303 F.3d 198 (3d Cir. 2002), cert. denied, 538 U.S. 1036 (2003).
4. See Padilla v. Hanft, 432 F.3d 582 (4th Cir. 2005) (describing the Padilla proceedings).
5. 18 U.S.C. §922.
6. See, e.g., Classified Information Procedures Act, 18 U.S.C.App. 3, §1-18. For a recent discussion of the procedures followed under the Act, see United States v. Moussaoui, 382 F.3d 453 (4th Cir. 2005).
7. 407 U.S. 514 (1972) (balancing factors such as the length of the delay, the reasons for the delay, the defendant's assertion of the right, and prejudice).
8. 530 U.S. 466 (2000).
9. 541 U.S. 36 (2004).

Acknowledgments

To my family—my husband Paul Gangsei, my daughter Erica Herman Gangsei, my mother Frances Pickus Herman Cohen, and my brother George Herman—for their love and support, and to my father, Nathan H Herman, the first lawyer I knew and still my inspiration. I would like to thank Michele Kenney, Jessica Gary, Andrew Gefell, and Brandon Johnson for their excellent research assistance and Brooklyn Law School for the support of its generous research stipend program.

Introduction

Speedy and public trial are the first rights enumerated in the Sixth Amendment's list of rights that the Constitution guarantees in a criminal prosecution. The Sixth Amendment, in its entirety, says:

> In all criminal prosecutions, the accused shall enjoy the right to a speedy and public trial, by an impartial jury of the State and district wherein the crime shall have been committed; which district shall have been previously ascertained by law, and to be informed of the nature and cause of the accusation; to be confronted with the witnesses against him; to have compulsory process for obtaining witnesses in his favor, and to have the assistance of counsel for his defence.

The rights to speedy and public trial, unlike the other rights the Sixth Amendment prescribes, are conjoined and even grouped as a single "right," although the reasons for this pairing are not immediately apparent. At first glance, the rights listed in the Sixth Amendment appear to share a concern for fairness to any person accused of a crime. The Supreme Court has listed the functions of the right to a speedy trial as being (1) to prevent a criminal defendant from undue and oppressive incarceration before trial, (2) to minimize anxiety and concern accompanying public accusation, and (3) to limit the possibilities that a long delay will impair the ability of the accused to defend himself (United States v. Ewell, 1966). The functions ascribed to the right to a public trial also feature protections for the accused. The Supreme Court has said that "the purpose" of the right is "to guarantee that the accused would be fairly dealt with and not unjustly condemned" (In re Oliver, 1948). Various historians and Supreme Court Justices have identified many ways in which a defendant might benefit from holding a trial in public: preventing the possibility of the use of torture by exposing the proceedings to public scrutiny, promoting truthful evidence by requiring witnesses to testify in public, controlling jurors by preventing them from hearing extrajudicial evidence, encouraging the appearance of otherwise unknown defense witnesses, and ensuring that the verdict will be based only on evidence submitted in open court, among other explanations.

Some Justices have described each of these rights as also serving the interests of the public. The speedy trial guarantee has been said to belong in part to the public (Barker v. Wingo, 1972), which has its own interests in ensuring that defendants will be tried speedily: to eliminate the possibility that defendants will commit other crimes in the interim, to minimize the chance that guilty defendants will escape justice because the prosecutor's evidence has deteriorated over time, and to avoid the expense and injustice of unnecessary pretrial incarceration of an innocent defendant.

The right to public trial can also serve public purposes beyond an individual defendant's interests. In our constitutional scheme, the right to punish belongs to the public, the Constitution's "we the people," rather than an aloof sovereign. The right to trial by jury ensures that members of the public will participate in the criminal justice system; the right to attend trials enables the public to serve as a jury of the whole. Public observation of trials allows the people to evaluate the laws their legislative representatives have enacted and the application of those laws by prosecutors, judges, and even jurors. An informed public can ensure that the criminal justice system does not serve only the passions and interests of a few rather than of the public generally. Chief Justice Warren Burger described public trials as cathartic public rituals, helping the community to absorb horrific criminal events without resorting to vigilantism. Public observation of trials can generate public confidence in the fairness of the criminal justice system, a necessary precondition to the agreement of the community, as well as the accused and the victim, to yield to that system and to honor its verdicts and sentences.

These explanations may all be described as benefits of holding speedy and public trials, but it is difficult to say that any of these benefits are the "purposes" of either right, in the sense that an originalist might seek the intent of the framers of the guarantee. History does not reveal any ascertainable reason for the institution of the public trial in England or for its adoption by the framers of the Constitution. Most commentators refer to the public nature of trials as having been an historical accident. The framers of the Constitution did not include this guarantee in the Constitution in reaction to any actual abuse they had suffered as colonists or deplored in English history. Commentators generally agree that there had never, or virtually never, been any tradition of secret proceedings either in England or the colonies for the framers to deplore. Even the infamous Star Chamber seems not to have held its proceedings in secret. That the public trial right slipped into the law casually in its adoption, insertion into the Constitution, and incorporation against the states makes it difficult to interpret. There is not much to be gleaned from the language or placement of the right. This lack of guidance has left the Court divided on some significant issues about the scope of the public trial right. Some Justices have concluded that the Sixth Amendment right was intended to provide a right for the public to attend trials, to serve a republican as well as an instrumental function. Others have viewed the Sixth Amendment as belonging only to the defendant and any public right of access to judicial proceedings as emanating from the First Amendment.

Similarly, the speedy trial guarantee was not a reaction to any particular event in England or the colonies. The colonists may have expressed fear of "transportation"—being transported to distant England to be tried for actual or trumped up crimes—but this burdensome practice does not seem to have been used. The Supreme Court has relied on history in deciding cases limiting the scope of the speedy trial right. A divided Court found, for example, that the right does not come into play until a defendant has been formally arrested or charged with a crime (Marion v. United States, 1971). Defendants who find themselves charged with an offense years after the conduct allegedly occurred cannot raise claims under the Sixth Amendment because of the Court's construction of the "purpose" of the guarantee.

On the other hand, the fact that the Supreme Court has not decided whether the purposes of a public trial include education of the public makes it difficult for the lower courts to decide issues like whether it is a denial of a defendant's Sixth Amendment rights to wrongfully exclude some members of the public if others are present.

The two rights, speedy and public trial, have another feature in common. Depending on the circumstances, a defendant might believe that it would be to his/her advantage to forego the right and instead demand its opposite: a delayed or closed proceeding. While some defendants would be disadvantaged if their trial were delayed for so long that favorable witnesses' memories faded, others would be delighted if those faded memories belonged to damning prosecution witnesses. And so while some defendants will actively seek a speedy trial and genuinely resist and regret belated prosecutions, others will be inclined to stall. Similarly, some defendants will welcome the public's attendance at their trials, perhaps as insurance against tyrannical prosecution or as a platform to explain their situation; others will prefer to be tried without the glare of publicity, possibly to avoid embarrassment or to prevent unfairness, possibly to shield themselves from public anger over an incendiary crime, or possibly just to conceal their guilt.

The Supreme Court's jurisprudence in the speedy trial area is more fully developed than its public trial jurisprudence. The Court has decided only two cases directly interpreting the Sixth Amendment right to a public trial (In re Oliver, 1948; Waller v. Georgia, 1984). In both cases, defendants who demanded an open trial won. In a series of other Supreme Court cases, defendants objected to various forms of publicity, claiming that their right to a fair trial had been compromised. Although the Court easily decided that defendants do not have the right to demand the opposite of an open trial, the Court had considerably more difficulty deciding when to rule that publicity had impaired the fairness of a particular proceeding. For years, the Court evaded the question of whether the public had a countervailing right of access to trials. When the Court finally decided that such a right does exist (Richmond Newspapers v. Virginia, 1980), it nevertheless recognized that the public's right could be overcome if publicity would compromise a particular defendant's fair trial rights. Once the Court had recognized a First Amendment right, Sixth Amendment public trial law was destined to remain stunted. Most of the cases the Court considered involved defendants who resisted publicity, opposing their fair trial rights against the public's interests. The Court did not reach any final resolution of the question of whether the public shares the Sixth Amendment right.

Advancing technology has added an increasing level of urgency and interest to questions about the scope of the right to a public trial. At some points in time, concern with public attendance at trials could have seemed "quaint."[1] In the dense and expanding society of twentieth-century America, trials could no longer approximate the common law and colonial model in which everyone in a community knew about significant judicial proceedings and was likely to congregate in the courtroom. Most trials occurred without many disinterested spectators, other than perhaps a few retired courtwatchers. Courtrooms empty of all but a few friends or relatives of the people involved may have appeared strange to those familiar with court proceedings primarily through Hollywood movies or television shows, like Perry Mason, in which the galleries are typically full of eager spectators.

But in the era of expanded media coverage, modern trials have once again become community events. Through increasingly national reporting by the print media, radio and television broadcasting, and the Internet, the courtroom has been expanded to create a virtual nationwide stage. The entire country can serve as the jury of the whole. Given that defendants, as noted above, do not always thrive at this level of exposure, many of the key cases interpreting the right to a public trial have followed highly notorious trials: a con man known as Murph the Surf, politician and scam artist Billie Sol Estes, Doctor Sam Sheppard (the model for the television series and film *The Fugitive*), the Lindbergh kidnapping defendant, and so on, all sought to have their convictions reversed because of the impact of the extravagant publicity surrounding their trials. The Supreme Court's ruling in Chandler v. Florida (1981) that broadcasting court proceedings is permissible but not required engendered national debate on the subject of cameras in the courtroom. The trial of O.J. Simpson, which took place daily in homes, bars, and airports around the world, led to extensive analysis of the impact of cameras in the courtroom.

The right to a speedy trial, on the other hand, has not galvanized public attention. The speedy trial cases, too, tell strange stories: Captain Jeffrey MacDonald, who either killed his family or became another victim of a bizarre murderer, was prosecuted by military authorities, released, and then reprosecuted and convicted years later for the same offense. The Court, however, found that he had not been denied a speedy trial because, in between the two prosecutions, no charge was technically pending against him (United States v. MacDonald, 1982). But the Court's intricate speedy trial doctrine, balancing multiple factors and parsing periods of time, is more interesting to an individual defendant whose freedom is at stake than it is to the general public.

As this book is being written, the country is still in the initial stages of reacting to the events of September 11, 2001, and to the proposition that we are waging a war against terrorism. New questions about the scope of all the rights of the Sixth Amendment have been raised, as the U.S. government has proposed alternative models to Sixth Amendment "prosecutions" to serve different functions. The Bush administration's argument has been that the Sixth Amendment model does not apply when what is at issue is not a "criminal prosecution" but an incident of war. Therefore, the government claims the right to detain people designated as "enemy combatants" without charges, without allowing them to see counsel, and without any right to speedy or public trial. The courts have not yet decided to what extent to allow the government to circumvent the guarantees of the Sixth Amendment by the simple expedient of not bringing criminal charges. Issues about the constitutionality of procedures used in the alternative forum of military tribunals have been raised. In criminal prosecutions, other issues will be raised concerning government claims that national security demands closure of all or part of a trial. As has been typical of the history of both of these Sixth Amendment rights, it is consideration of proposed exceptions that will lead to a clearer definition of their scope.

The first chapter of this book will cover the right to a public trial, discussing what we know of the history of the right, beginning in England and moving through the Colonial Era to the adoption of the Sixth Amendment. This section will conclude with a discussion of the rationales commentators have offered for the right to public trial, to ground further discussion of the purposes of the right. The second chapter will discuss the development of the right, beginning with the Supreme Court cases. Because the public trial right is so deeply intertwined with cases on prejudicial pretrial publicity and with cases finding and implementing a First Amendment right of public access to trials, principal cases in those areas will be included. This analysis continues by discussing the state of the law of public trial in the lower federal and state courts, considering such issues as what proceedings must be open under the Sixth as opposed to the First Amendment, how partial or temporary closures are handled, permissible exceptions allowing closure of all or part of a proceeding, and procedures for raising and litigating public trial claims. Two discrete issues will be discussed at the end of the chapter: the dilemma of cameras in the courtroom and the challenge posed to the Sixth Amendment by military commissions and the demands of national security.

The third chapter will discuss the right to a speedy trial, again beginning with a history of the right from England through the colonies through adoption of the Sixth Amendment. The fourth chapter will provide an analysis of the speedy trial right, beginning by recounting the Supreme Court's struggles to define the scope of the right and then commenting on the speedy trial statutes and rules that have eclipsed much constitutional litigation. After offering some reflections on the Supreme Court's doctrine, this section will discuss the state of the law in the lower courts, including a discussion of when the right attaches and how the lower courts have applied the Supreme Court's template for speedy trial analysis in Barker v. Wingo (1972).

A bibliographic essay is provided at the end of each part.

NOTE

1. H. Richard Uviller, *Criminal Justice: Investigation and Adjudication,* 2d ed. (St. Paul, MN: West, 1979), 946.

PART I

The Right to a Public Trial

1

History: The Origins of the Right to a Public Trial

PREAMBLE: CLASSIC ARCHETYPES

On a hill in ancient Athens stood three buildings: the assembly, the court, and the theater. From occasional contemporary accounts we have reason to believe that Athenian trials, like Athenian theater, were highly public affairs. The trial of Socrates in 399 B.C.E., for example, took place before a jury of 501 representative Athenian citizens and a crowd of additional spectators.[1] The public was heavily represented on the jury as well as in the audience. Other accounts confirm this picture of heavy public involvement in the justice system, with members of the public serving both as jurors and as spectators.[2] While there is little evidence that Athenian law directly influenced English practice,[3] the image of a theatrical public trial, especially when trial involved some form of jury, recurs like an archetype in cultures the English admired.

In ancient Rome, pleadings occurred in open arenas, open not only to the public but to scorching sun and disease. Outdoor trials were not always a boon to the participants. One sixteenth-century English author tells the story of Cato's negative response to the practical suggestion that the trial arena should be covered with protective canvas: the pleaders, he said, "should feel so much paine of those prickles in going thither as their heades does of sunne in tarrying there."[4] Public trial, in Cato's account, might promote speedy proceedings, if only to end the physical discomfort of litigation. Although public trial seems to have been a feature of Roman law too, we again have little reliable information on Roman criminal procedure and little evidence that Roman procedural law directly influenced the English.

The trial of Jesus Christ, in the description of the gospels, was highly public, although the crowd did not play a creditable role. According to Luke, Pontius Pilate called together "the chief priests, the leaders and all the people" and told them "I have examined [Jesus] in your presence" before announcing his verdict.[5] Matthew and Mark describe Pilate's questioning of Jesus, the verdict, and the crowd's lynch mob reactions in demanding that Jesus be crucified.[6]

These classical images of public participation in critically important proceedings are as revealing in their differences as they are in their common thread of public involvement. The Athenian proceeding evokes an idealized image of the public jury trial as the apotheosis of democracy. Members of the public are the decision makers and the observers. Whether the conviction of Socrates is considered just or unjust, it is clearly the verdict of the community, both because so many members of the community served on the jury and because so many others appear to have attended the proceeding to judge the testimony and the jury's verdict for themselves. The Roman proceeding evokes an image of the public trial as a form of ordeal. Litigants had to be hardy enough to withstand the elements as well as public scrutiny. And the gospels offer a darker view of community involvement. Pontius Pilate may be cast as the villain, but the public does not dispute his verdict and may have led or at least encouraged him to reach the popular conclusion. Some students of history and literature studying these proceedings might characterize public attendance at trial proceedings as serving one particular purpose: the Athenian public as practicing democratic ideals, the Roman public as seeking a brutally entertaining alternative to circuses, and the biblical public as goading Pilate to a brutally intolerant result. But more thoughtful students might well glean an impression that the members of the polity have used trial proceedings, both at the time of the trial and in later historical or literary accounts, for their own divergent purposes, whether cathartic, political, deterrent, educational, or for sheer entertainment. It would be impossible to ascribe one particular purpose to the presence of "the public" at any of these proceedings in any of these eras, because we lack sufficient historical accounts of what members of the public actually did and because trials may have been used by different people or subgroups within each society for different purposes over time.

Similarly, there are only tidbits of history recording the extent to which trials were held publicly in England before the eighteenth century and even less history recording how the observers of public proceedings would have described their interest or role in attending those proceedings. There are several explanations for this persistent lack of documentation. First, criminal procedure was rarely a subject of legislation or any other form of rules or written pronouncements, so documents attesting to trial processes simply were not generated. Because there was no body promulgating criminal procedure rules, no one was making official decisions about processes in a manner that could be explained; thus, even if written accounts of trial processes survived, no one could provide any relevant description of the intent behind a particular process. There were no counterparts to our contemporary judicial conferences and commissions reporting on why the authors of rules selected one among a number of procedural options, and no legislative history revealing debates or explanations of what a particular procedural choice might mean.

It may also be, as some commentators maintain, that the right to public trial was not discussed because it was simply assumed to be an inherent part of the Anglo-American criminal justice system. It only seems to have been at times when some authority was perceived as likely to hold all or part of a criminal procedure in secret that the people involved, or commentators, asserted that there was such a thing as a right to public trial. These eruptions are most easily explained if, indeed, public proceedings were the assumed norm and deviations therefore seemed shocking. However, history also reveals that there were few, possibly no, occasions for the public to express outrage at secret proceedings held in colonial America or in England. Even the Star Chamber, sometimes proffered as a deplorable example of secret proceedings, seems to have held its proceedings, unfair as they may have been in other respects, openly. Commentators' reactions to the evil of closed proceedings usually seem to have been engendered not by events in England itself, but by English disdain for what was understood to be inferior continental criminal procedure in places like France and Turkey, including such uncivilized horrors as secret proceedings.

Finally, the criminal trial in its current form emerged over a period of centuries. The right to a public trial is linked to the right to trial by jury, historically as well as in its location in the Sixth Amendment. The public trial right is, in some respects, a logical corollary of the decision to employ lay jurors, rather than professional judges, as decision makers. Evidence disclosed to a jury at trial has already been published to some representative members of the community. It might well prove difficult as a matter of practice to keep such proceedings secret, even if that were considered desirable. The jurors themselves may discuss what happened at the trial with other members of the public, whom they are representing. More fundamentally, the two rights are both manifestations of the same theory of governance. It is not surprising that a structure like the U.S. Constitution that values decision making by members of the community would also value community awareness of the workings of the criminal justice system, even if the values served are variously described. Whether the purpose of the jury is described in Blackstonian terms as providing a "bulwark" against government oppression, or in more structural terms as allowing the people to own the criminal justice system, that function will be served best if jury trials are held in public. The visibility of the proceeding will enable people to assess whether a jury proceeding is indeed a judgment of the peers of the accused or whether the proceeding has been corrupted

Thus, one way to trace the development of the public trial right is to trace the development of the criminal jury trial. How did it happen that in England, as in ancient Athens, criminal trials became a community affair rather than an inquisitorial process held by authorities with the potential to act in secret? English historians trace their right to trial by jury not to the Greeks or Romans, but to their own ancestors. Some claim that jury trials exist in a clear line of succession going back to the Anglo-Saxons and even the early Britons; others contend that the true progenitor of jury trials arrived in England as a result of the Norman Conquest. In either case, the jury trial, with twelve members of the community sitting in judgment and others invited to attend while the jurors heard testimony, was certainly in place in England by the era of the influential commentator William Blackstone and the framing of the Sixth Amendment.

But the history of public proceedings in England is not fully coextensive with the history of trial by jury or communal courts. The proceedings that predated criminal jury trials, like the trial by ordeal, also seem to have taken place in public. The types of proceedings that lend themselves to secrecy do not seem to have been favored or even tolerated during any period of English history.

This history will describe what we know of the chronological development of the criminal jury trial, focusing on the role of the community in the criminal proceeding. Different elements of the jury trial developed during different eras, but this account will focus on whether proceedings during various eras were held in public and on what role the public played, so far as documentation exists.

ENGLISH HISTORY

Pre-Norman Conquest

Frederic Maitland and Francis Montague, among others, argue that the origin of the English trial by jury is Frankish and that it was imposed by royal prerogative rather than created by popular will, despite tenacious English mythology to the contrary. The English regard for the jury trial as the "palladium of English liberties" and a "bulwark of the British Constitution" (phrases used by Blackstone in his celebration of the English jury) need not be diminished, they maintain, by "any modern discoveries of ancient facts, even though they may have to learn that in its origin trial by jury was rather French than English, rather royal than popular, rather the livery of conquest than a badge of freedom."[7]

The extent to which the public participated in or observed criminal proceedings before the Norman Conquest is unclear. Many English historians point to the use of trial by jury, or at least by members of the community, in some form, before 1066. "[T]he trial by jury of twelve men, was the USUAL trial among the Normans in most suits," said Sir Matthew Hale. "And that trial was in use here in England before the conquest."[8] A form of jury trial, contends Sir John Hawles, was practiced by the first inhabitants of Britain.[9] Blackstone described jury trial as "a trial that has been used time out of mind in this nation, and seems to have been coeval with the first civil government thereof. Some authors have endeavored to trace the original of juries up as high as the Britons themselves, the first inhabitants of our island; but certain it is, that they were in use among the earliest Saxon colonies."[10] Not only did the Saxons employ trials by jury for some purposes, reports Hawles, but a right to jury trial was incorporated into King Ethelred's laws.[11] King Alfred is said to have hanged judges for imposing verdicts without jurors' consent.[12] Maitland and Sir Frederick Pollock speculate that the Scandinavians had also developed something very like the jury, and conclude: "We can not say a priori that there is only one possible origin for the jury, we can not even say that England was unprepared for the introduction of the institution; but that the Norman duke brought it with him as one of his prerogatives can hardly be disputed."[13]

The Anglo-Saxons employed courts as one among a number of methods of resolving disputes and avenging crimes.[14] While direct evidence about the constitution of Anglo-Saxon courts is scanty,[15] in Saxon England from about 449 to 800 there were "courts" for the political subdivisions called the shires and the hundreds, which were composed of various members of the community. It was the duty of certain people to attend these courts; there were no professional judges, lawyers, or clerks.[16] In the hundred court, the responsible people were the parish priest, the reeve, and four men of each township in the hundred. Together, these men formed the court.

Saxon courts were far less formal than modern courts[17] but evidently no less public. Pollock and Maitland describe Anglo-Saxon courts as "not surrounded with such visible majesty of the law as in our own time, nor furnished with any obvious means of compelling obedience."[18] Law was still struggling to replace more primitive systems of blood feud and vengeance.[19] And "[p]robably the public courts were always held in the open air."[20] These public courts, the open-air hundred and county courts, stand in contrast to lord's courts, or "halimotes" (hall-moots), which would have been held in the house of the lord having jurisdiction over the matter in question. But Pollock and Maitland find no evidence of such halimotes occurring before the Norman Conquest.[21] Court evidently was not held in churches.[22] Thus, it would seem that anyone who wished could attend Anglo-Saxon "court" proceedings of any type, because they would have been held out of doors. Holding court in open air is consistent with the growth of the modern idea that crimes were an offense not just against the individual who had been harmed or that individual's family or clan, but against the entire community.

Anglo-Saxon law also provided methods of judging the guilt of an accused that had nothing to do with the judgment of members of the community—principally, the trial by ordeal. Blackstone describes the various forms of the trial or purgation by ordeal at considerable length.[23] If an accused could withstand the water ordeal (plunging one's arm into boiling water) or the fire ordeal (lifting or walking on red-hot metal), he was adjudged innocent, having been cleared by divine judgment. Although condemning this practice as primitive, barbaric, and superstitious, Blackstone does not describe whether the ordeals took place in public. He does remark that such ordeals were to be performed in a church or on other consecrated ground.[24] But he does not say who could attend these proceedings. Communities did not sit in judgment, but did they sit in attendance? Plucknett's account goes further in describing a community role in the choice of proceeding, as well as a community presence: Anglo-Saxon criminal proceedings, he says, were "oral, personal, accusatory, and local. One person publicly charged another before the community, which in turn decided what form of proof—compurgation, ordeal, or battle—the trial should take. . . . Whichever method was chosen, certain features of this primitive system would become hallmarks of English justice. There was a definite and known accuser who publicly confronted his antagonist, trials were open, and judges acted as arbiters to enforce the rules of fairness."[25] Plucknett maintains that the compurgators were not early incarnations of jurors, because their appearances were voluntary and not a matter of duty.[26]

Given the decentralized nature of law enforcement and the relative lack of royal involvement in preserving the peace, it seems credible that much if not all of the range of criminal law enforcement would have taken place in public. As described above, Pollock and Maitland find no evidence of trial-like proceedings in any private venue, royal venue, manor-house, or church. In the absence of a strong lord or centralized executive authority, would anyone have benefited by excluding members of the public from proceedings that usually seemed to involve individual complaints about another individual's alleged crimes of violence or property? One could, as later commentators do, ascribe many functions that would have been served by holding trials and ordeals in public—ranging from the use of such proceedings for their educational or deterrent value, to the desire to ensure that the proceedings be conducted in a manner considered fair—but there is no reason to think that any or all of these post hoc justifications actually led to any decision about whether to allow members of the public to attend such proceedings. It seems more likely that the public simply attended such proceedings at will because there were no walls and no reason to exclude them.

From the Norman Conquest to Magna Carta

The Frankish kings used juries for a number of purposes. "[The King] uses it in order that he may learn how he is served by his subordinates: —the neighbours are required to say all that they know about the misconduct of the royal officers. He uses it in order that he may detect those grave crimes which threaten his peace: —the neighbours must say whether they suspect any of murders or robberies."[27]

It was this sworn inquest of neighbors that the Normans introduced to England.[28] William the Conqueror guaranteed continuation of the rights the English enjoyed under Edward the Confessor.[29] Whether or not that guarantee would have included a right to jury trial depends on whether one is willing to characterize the Anglo-Saxon communal courts as sufficiently like jury trials, a matter not without controversy. The Norman inquest added a new feature to Anglo-Saxon practice, which resembled grand jury indictment.

The inquest as it developed in the eleventh and twelfth centuries became an important part of a new system of government and royal justice.[30] The function of the jury during this era, at least in the Pollock and Maitland description, was the function the king wanted filled—to secure the king's peace and to find out about misdeeds committed by his servants or his citizens. The interests of the king's people were also served, incidentally, to the extent that they shared the king's desire for peace and for honest royal servants. There does not seem to have been any thought that such a jury would protect citizens against the king. It would indeed be surprising if jury trial was considered to be a "right" in the modern sense of that word during an era in which there would have been no means of enforcing that right. In the early communal courts, attendance at trials was characterized as a duty of freemen, not as anyone's right.[31]

Early Norman juries did not try crimes. Juries handed down the verdicts that were gathered in the fiscal records of the Domesday Books. Their verdicts served purposes of governance more than of litigation.[32] Local juries provided the king with information about his possible sources of revenue.[33] Pollock and Maitland describe the earliest known case that could properly be described as a trial by jury. The jurors, including royal justiciars, the count of Martain and the Bishop of Coutances, found facts to settle a land dispute between the abbot of Ely and others. At the same time, the Normans introduced trial by battle which, according to Blackstone, disrupted the English tradition of trial by jury.[34]

Earlier kings had shared jury use with the church. It was not until the reign of Henry II (1154–89) that the king conceded to his subjects the royal prerogative of using juries.[35] Henry, more than his predecessors, "regarded breaches of the peace or threats to life or limb as offenses of a public nature, warranting more than merely private retribution."[36] During his reign, his subjects were given an opportunity to present certain questions of fact, albeit in civil cases, to "a jury of twelve sworn knights of the vicinage summoned for that purpose by the sheriff."[37] The Assize of Clarendon, in 1166, which provided instructions for itinerant justices throughout the land, provided the remedy of a royal writ in connection with property claims. A jury would be summoned and, in the presence of the king's justices, would decide who owned contested property. This concept of protection of a right to enjoy possession of land, enforceable by the king and ultimately even against the king, furthered the notion of public law, and enhanced the role of juries.[38] The procedure was a predecessor of the right to grand jury indictment.

The sworn inquest first grew in civil proceedings, in which the power and authority of the king grew as kings intervened more frequently in matters of justice. Henry II consulted with diverse groups of people before reaching judgments and held public hearings in a variety of matters. In an 1157 case involving papal claims, Henry sat in the chapter house of monks, joined by two archbishops, three bishops, his chancellor, two chief justiciars, and several other barons. The hall was described as "filled by no small multitude of people."[39] At some point, the king seems to have given the parties a private audience, accompanied by a few councillors, his chancellor, two justiciars, constables of England and Normandy, a chamberlain, and a clerk. But then the public session was resumed.[40] This is one of only a very few extant descriptions of any aspect of any proceeding having been held in private in England during any era. Henry did not adopt the procedures of canon law.[41] Instead, he gradually adopted the sworn inquest. In 1164, Henry even attempted to require the ecclesiastical courts to use an accusing jury, so that laymen could not be accused on the basis of an unsworn accusation.[42] Henry had an interest in criminal justice, generally distrusting evidence produced by ordeal[43] and favoring the centralization of justice. All of these attitudes contributed to the development of the common law jury trial.[44] But neither Henry nor his predecessors would have "intended [or] expected the jury to become a bulwark of popular liberty and the strongest protection against any attempt to tamper with the principle of publicity."[45]

By the time of Magna Carta in 1215, although the civil jury was established, crimes were still subjected to trial by battle rather than by jury.[46] The trial by ordeal is believed to have ended during the reign of King John.[47] But the right to jury trial was not, contrary to some popular belief, directly guaranteed by Magna Carta. Holdsworth replied to those who read Magna Carta as embodying the principle of a right to a jury trial in criminal cases:[48] "It is not difficult to show that, taken literally, these interpretations are false. Trial by jury was yet in its infancy. . . . But there is a sense in which these interpretations are true. These clauses do embody a protest against arbitrary punishment, and against arbitrary infringements of personal liberty and rights of property: they do assert a right to a free trial, to a pure and unbought measure of justice."[49]

In Pollock's description, twelfth-century trials would seem to us more "like a rather disorderly public meeting than a court of justice."[50] Pollock speculates that if Bracton were to visit modern England, he would admit that twelfth-century justice was still essentially barbaric, but would ask, "Is it nothing that we did keep it public?"[51]

Post–Magna Carta

Over the next several centuries, royal power was consolidated, and the trial by jury was adopted for use in criminal cases. During the fourteenth century, Edward III replaced local sheriffs with justices of the peace who represented the king, thus moving toward a centralization of the justice system.[52] In the face of this centralization, jurors represented a form of local control as well as local information. Jurors were required to come from the vicinage where a crime had taken place. "Living in the neighbourhood, they were most unquestionably the very county, or *pais*, to which both parties had thought proper to appeal; and thus circumstanced, were supposed to have had a prior and a perfect knowledge, as well of the characters of the parties themselves, as of the witnesses . . . from whence it was concluded, that they the better knew what credit to give to the facts in evidence before them."[53] By the fifteenth century, as social interactions became more complex, the roles of jurors and witnesses had diverged,[54] as had the roles of the grand and petit juries, which evolved into two distinct bodies.[55]

Public opinion was also coalescing behind the idea that public trial was an independent virtue. By the thirteenth century, English judges were expressing their horror over the presumed continental approach to criminal justice, particularly deploring the role of torture.[56] And by the mid-1400s, Chief Justice John Fortescue was proclaiming that, in England, the innocent would not be found guilty because evidence was given "in open court" and the accused tried by twelve men of good character.[57] According to Pollock, jury trials during the Tudor period "permanently secured the publicity of judicial proceedings."[58] From the sixteenth century on, "publicity [was] essential."[59]

The public nature of jury trial, first in the civil and later in the criminal context, is often described as requiring evidence to be given in open court. In discussing the section of Magna Carta, chapter 29, which provides that "[n]o freeman shall be taken, or imprisoned, or be disseised of his freehold, or liberties, or free customs, or be outlawed, or exiled, or any otherwise destroyed; nor will we not pass upon him, nor condemn him, but by lawful judgment of his peers, or by the law of the land," Coke describes the *per legale judicium* (a manner of trial by law) before this provision as entailing a presentation of evidence against a prisoner "in open court in his presence."[60] "All Causes ought to be heard, ordered, and determined before the judges of the kings courts openly . . . and in no chambers or other private places: for judges are not judges of chambers, but of courts, and therefore in open court."[61] Similarly, Sir Thomas Smith notes that trials involving inquests were open to the public. "Evidences of writinges be shewed, witnesses be sworne, and heard before them [the jury], not after the fashion of the civil law but openly, that not only the xii, but the Judges, the parties and as man as be present may hear what ech witnesse doeth say. . . . "[62]

Blackstone's rhapsodic tribute to the English jury tradition, mocked by Pollock and Maitland, focuses more on the advantages of the jury trial to the citizen, and on the adjudicating petit jury rather than the investigating grand jury. Blackstone described "[t]he trial by jury, or the country, *per patriam*, which, as the grand bulwark of his liberties, is secured to him by the great charter" as most valuable in criminal cases.[63] Blackstone also focused on disputes between the king and a subject rather than between subjects. "[I]n times of difficulty and danger, more is to be apprehended from the violence and partiality of judges appointed by the crown, in suits between the king and the subject, than in disputes between one individual and another."[64] Blackstone ascribes the need for such a jury bulwark to the growth of the centralized executive power: "It was necessary, for preserving the admirable balance of our constitution, to vest the executive power of the laws in the prince: and yet this power might be dangerous and destructive to that very constitution, if exerted without check or control, by justices of *oyer* and *terminer* occasionally named by the crown; who might then, as in France or Turkey, imprison, dispatch, or exile any man that was obnoxious to the government. . . . "[65]

It is Blackstone's jury, the bulwark and palladium of protection against the monarch, that would need, more than the Frankish royal prerogative inquest, to be accompanied by a right to have juries operate in public. Blackstone grandly declared: "all our accusations are public, and our trials in the face of the world; where torture is unknown, and every delinquent is judged by such of his equals."[66] Blackstone also describes the process of an English trial, stressing that all evidence is given "in open court," that all objections are "publicly stated, and by the judge are openly and publicly allowed or disallowed, in the face of the country" and that a party or counsel who misstates the law may be required "publicly to seal a bill of particulars."[67]

While the length of the historical pedigree of the jury trial is in doubt, it is clear that by the time of Blackstone, the double jury system had replaced alternative systems for addressing criminality. It is also clear that the history of open trials in England extends back beyond the jury system. As Pollock has summarized, public trials are "one tradition . . . which has persisted through all changes" in English criminal procedure.[68]

There is less agreement on why public proceedings occurred or were valued. Blackstone's explanations of the function of public attendance may be in part anachronistic, simply his own analysis of the current value of the public trial. Given that Blackstone's views were well known to the framers of the Sixth Amendment, however, one may well question whether the earlier history should matter in interpreting the constitutional provision. It is likely to have been Blackstone's extrapolations rather than the actual history that influenced the framers of the Constitution.

There is also incomplete agreement about whether there were any significant exceptions to open proceedings at all, outside canon law.

Historical Exceptions—Challenges to the Public Trial Model?

The Star Chamber

The infamous Star Chamber is described by some authors and judges as having been the site of secret proceedings. While it is not at all clear that the Star Chamber actually deviated from the ideal of the public trial, it certainly did challenge the romanticized ideal of the jury trial. The Star Chamber began as an antidote to corrupt jury proceedings.[69] Early juries operated within a feudal system, where powerful landowners could and did bribe or intimidate individual jurors. The initial Star Chamber proceedings, providing an alternative to the corrupt jury system, were praised for their fairness.[70] Some notorious politically motivated Star Chamber proceedings in the early seventeenth century, generally considered to be abuses of the Star Chamber rather than its raison d'etre, led to its abolition in 1640.[71] Typically, there are few descriptions of what Star Chamber proceedings looked like or who was present. A few authors maintain that secret proceedings were conducted in the Star Chamber, but they do not cite any evidence for this contention.[72] Others characterize Star Chamber proceedings as having been open, although sometimes with just as little support. According to Leonard Levy, interrogation may have occurred in secret, both in the Star Chamber and its predecessor Privy Council, which was instituted in the mid-1500s under the Tudors and employed inquisition and torture. But "the trial itself, even before the Star Chamber, remained public."[73]

There is simply not enough reliable information to base a conclusion on how Star Chamber proceedings, or other proceedings during this era, were conducted. The law concerning trial procedure continued to be unwritten. Max Radin, author of a leading article on the Sixth Amendment right to public trial, takes the lack of contemporary complaints about secret proceedings in the Star Chamber as fairly persuasive evidence that no such proceedings took place. He notes that the opponents of the Star Chamber did not mention secret proceedings among their other complaints in the English Petition of Rights of 1621, or in the Bill of Rights of

1689, as they might have been expected to do if secret proceedings had indeed occurred.[74]

Whatever the failings of the Star Chamber, the period following its abolition led to "great changes" in procedure,[75] which included promotion of the independence of the jury. Trial rights later included in the Sixth Amendment became a matter of course. As of 1640, "[i]n every case, so far as I am aware, the accused person had the witnesses against him produced face to face," and had the right to cross-examine the witnesses as well as to call witnesses on his own.[76] And, whatever had occurred in the Star Chamber, trials were held in public.

Treason Trials

The High Court of Justice, which tried Charles I and his adherents and sentenced them to death for treason, is said by Sir Fitzjames Stephen to have been the only case in English history in which judges sitting without a jury (other than the members of courts-martial) were entrusted with the power of life and death.[77] And even these proceedings appear to have been held in public. In any event, divergence from public trial was clearly rare, if it occurred at all, highly unpopular, and hence politically loaded.[78] Blackstone tells us that confessions of treason had to be made in "open court."[79] During the Tudor period, the Crown's concern with maintaining power led to a number of treason trials, some of which may have strayed from the ideal of a public trial. Under Henry VIII, an act of Parliament provided that a person could be declared guilty of treason without any trial at all.[80] During the late-fifteenth and sixteenth centuries, at least, treason trials were held in public.[81] These trials generated considerable public attention; one notorious trial is described as having drawn 2,000 spectators. In 1586, Queen Elizabeth considered limiting the public's access to the trial of Mary Queen of Scots, given the "obvious fear of disturbance."[82] In general, however, "the government encouraged people to attend treason trials for the purpose of publicizing the offences and the names of the miscreants."[83]

One of the most notorious and best-documented treason trials was that of John Lilburne, who was put on trial three times and became the first quotable champion of a personal right to a public trial—his own. At his first trial, Lilburne reported, the Chief Justice "stood up and in the face of all the country present there" told him that "we will not take advantage of [your insurrection], to try you by the rules of arbitrary Martial laws, or any other arbitrary ways; but we will try you by the rules of the good old laws of England. . . . "[84] One of these rights, according to Lilburne himself, was the right to a public trial. After Lilburne was acquitted in that first proceeding, he reported that he was summoned by a committee of Parliament to appear before it in a secret proceeding. He "refused to proceed" before the secret committee "till by special order they caused their doors to be wise thrown open, that the people might have free and uninterrupted access to hear, see and consider of what they said to me. . . . For no trial in such cases ought to be in any place, unless it be public, open and free. . . . if I be denied this undoubted privilege, I shall rather die here than proceed any further."[85] At the outset of his third treason trial, in 1649, Lilburne reported that he "found the gates [of the courthouse] shut and guarded, which is contrary both to law and justice."[86] Lilburne delivered an impassioned speech demanding the right to a public trial, identifying that right as "the first fundamental liberty of an Englishman . . . and my inheritance and birthright."[87] When he concluded, presiding Judge Keble is quoted as having anticlimactically replied, "Mr. Lilburne, look behind you, and see whether the door stands open or no."[88] These politically motivated proceedings were widely discussed, and Lilburne claimed that "thousands of my friends (well wishers to the freedoms of England . . .) with abundance of cordial honest men in several countries" took an interest in the fairness of his trial.[89]

Several decades later, the treason trial of a Mr. Cornish for conspiring to kill Charles II was shrouded in controversy, mostly centering on whether the evidence in the case was contradictory and incomplete, and whether Cornish had been given adequate time to prepare a defense. Here, Sir John Hawles, who was Solicitor General, invoked the right to a public trial in what may have been a defense against these accusations, introducing justifications for the right.

> The reason that matters of law are, or ought to be transacted publicly, is, [t]hat any person, unconcerned as well as concerned, may, as *amicus curiae*, inform the court better, if he thinks they are in an error, that justice may be done: and the reason that all trials are public, is, that any person may inform in point of fact, though not *subpoena'd,* that truth may be discovered in civil as well as criminal matters. There is an invitation to all persons, who can inform the court concerning the matter to be tried, to come into the court, and they shall be heard.[90]

Discussing another treason trial, Throckmorton's case, Pollock describes how jurors were "reprimanded and some of them fined" for refusing to convict the accused of treason. He then reports that "[f]rom that time the power of juries, and their function as the voice of public feeling, began to be understood."[91]

Ecclesiastical Courts

According to Pollock, most exceptions to the English norm of public trials were "derived from the essentially Roman and canonical procedure of the spiritual courts."[92] The battle in England over the power and independence of the ecclesiastical courts was lengthy and fervent. The story of to what extent trials were public within the ecclesiastical courts is not relevant here, however, because the English rejected so many of the premises of continental canon law. Undoubtedly, public reactions to real or perceived injustices in the ecclesiastical courts served to reinforce the horrified reaction many Englishmen had to the real or perceived injustices of inquisitorial systems and to their smug reiterations of the decency and superiority of the English accusatorial system.

Limited exceptions to open trials were available to protect the privacy of particular evidence during otherwise public proceedings. A trial might be temporarily closed, for example, while the victim of a sexual offense was testifying.[93] The history and status of such exceptions will be discussed infra.

This is what is known of the actual history of public trials in England. What English commentators said about public trials and their functions is a separate story, to be discussed at the end of this section, because their discussion, in the absence of illuminating primary sources, has become the received history.

COLONIAL PRACTICES AND CHARTERS

The tale of the evolution of colonial criminal justice systems in America mirrors, to some extent, English history: the community involvement inherent in the development of a double jury system, a challenge to the common law system from religion, and an assumption rather than a declaration or decision that criminal trials, like criminal punishments, would be public.[94] One telling example is the 1642 trial of Thomas Granger, who was accused of stealing farm animals. He confessed to magistrates in private, but then "repeated his confession publicly, first to ministers and later to the court and the jury."[95] In a better-known example of a public colonial proceeding, when William Penn was tried in 1670 for illegally preaching at a Quaker ceremony, a court officer at the trial placed Penn's hat and that of his codefendant, William Mead, on the defendants' heads and then declared them to be in contempt for wearing their hats. Mead is quoted as having announced, "I desire the jury, and all the people, to take notice of the injustice of the recorder,"[96] suggesting that "all the people" would have been available to take notice of this purported injustice.

Colonists assumed that they enjoyed the "basic rights of Englishmen," including the public jury trial.[97] While colonists did not generally enjoy all of the other rights later codified in the Sixth Amendment, like the right to counsel or the right to call witnesses, the customary public trial before a jury was considered a very fair proceeding for its time.[98] While some thought it superfluous to prescribe that English common law included the right to a public trial by jury,[99] some colonies nevertheless broke with common law tradition and codified these rights in charters and laws.[100] The prototypical 1641 *Massachusetts Body of Liberties* does not specifically mention the right to a public trial, although it does provide for jury trials and in several sections makes reference to "open court."[101] The *Concessions and Agreements of West New Jersey*, drafted in 1677 by either William Penn or Edward Byllynge, explicitly recognized the right to a public trial in its final chapter.

> That in all publick courts of justice for tryals of causes, civil or criminal, any person or persons, inhabitants of the said Province may freely come into, and attend the said courts, and hear and be present, at all or any such tryals as shall be there had or passed, that justice may not be done in a corner nor in any covert manner, being intended and resolved,

by the help of the Lord, and by these our Concessions and Fundamentals, that all and every person and persons inhabiting the said Province, shall, as far as in us lies, be free from oppression and slavery.[102]

Penn himself certainly drafted the 1682 Pennsylvania Frame of Government, which provided for a right to trial by a jury which was to have final judgment and that "all courts shall be open."[103] While some historians warn that it is anachronistic to describe the colonists as concerned about individual rights rather than about ordering society,[104] Penn certainly seems to have interpreted his own experience as showing the benefit of public trials to the accused. "And since there can be nothing more reasonable than a right information, especially of public acts; and well knowing how industrious some will be to misrepresent this trial, to the disadvantage of the cause and prisoners; it was thought requisite, in defence of both, and for the satisfaction of the people, to make it more public."[105] Other charters, like those of New York, Virginia, and Maryland, simply provided that the common law was in force, or that the colonists were to enjoy the "rights of Englishmen,"[106] probably as remembered by the colonists or gleaned from the works of writers like Coke or, during the Revolutionary Era, like Blackstone.[107]

Not all colonies consistently held jury trials, however. Rhode Island was one of several colonies that created exceptions to the rule of jury trial.[108] One historian notes a divergence in criminal procedure in the northern colonies, where the Bible rivaled common law as a source of law and where—because criminal proceedings aimed to reform and redeem criminals—religiously fanatical magistrates might have distrusted juries.[109] So although it is difficult to find any evidence of examples of secret trials in the colonies during the pre–Revolutionary Era, the framers of the Constitution might have been aware of colonial deviations from the Englishmen's right to trial by jury. Some colonists, like the firebrand Samuel Adams, were also outraged about two acts of Parliament that authorized the royal government to try colonists without juries and outside their vicinage.[110]

The Declaration of Independence in 1776 inspired new Declarations of Rights in the states. The Declaration of Independence itself did not mention the right to public trial, but it did complain about failure to afford colonists jury trials. The 1776 Pennsylvania Declaration of Rights, following on Pennsylvania's colonial charter, guaranteed a "speedy public trial, by an impartial jury of the country. . . ."[111] The North Carolina Declaration of Rights provided that "no freeman shall be convicted of any crime, but by the unanimous verdict of a jury of good and lawful men, in open court, as heretofore used."[112] Other declarations did not mention the right to a public trial, perhaps assuming that their references to the law of the land or their guarantees of the right to trial by jury encompassed this right. In the 1779 Committee Draft of the Massachusetts Declaration of Rights, Article XII explicitly provided for a "speedy and public trial by an impartial jury," but this provision was not included in the final 1780 Declaration.[113]

Explicit or not, the common understanding was that public jury trials were the norm, and even a right. In 1774, the First Continental Congress wrote a letter to

English subjects in Quebec, encouraging Canadian resistance to the continued use of civil law in their country. The letter explained and endorsed the rights of Englishmen, including the right to trial by jury, which provided that neither life, liberty, nor property could be taken from an accused until twelve men from the neighborhood, who "may reasonably be supposed to be acquainted with [the accused's] character, and the characters of the witnesses, upon a fair trial, and full enquiry, face to face, in open Court, before as many of the people as chuse to attend, shall pass their sentence upon oath against him."[114] Even the trial of the English soldiers charged with murder for their alleged roles in the Boston Massacre, held under highly charged circumstances, was open to the public.[115]

Public attendance at trials was more than a boon for defendants. It was an integral part of the life of many colonists. Several sources describe "court day" as a ritual in which virtually everyone in the community would come together in the courthouse to watch the proceedings and leave with a sense that they had witnessed important decisions and transactions, observed the workings of government, and participated in shaping and ratifying communal affairs.[116]

THE CONSTITUTIONAL CONVENTIONS

Article III of the United States Constitution itself provides: "The Trial of all Crimes, except in Cases of Impeachment; shall be by Jury; and such Trial shall be held in the State where the said Crimes shall have been committed; but when not committed within any State, the Trial shall be at such Place or Places as the Congress may by law have directed."[117] Although the framers did not leave legislative history explaining why this provision was inserted and worded as it was, embodying the right to jury trial in the Constitution seems to have been responsive to the concerns expressed in the Declaration of Independence: that colonists were vulnerable to being denied jury trials, or transported "beyond Seas to be tried for pretended offenses."

In Federalist Paper No. 83, Alexander Hamilton described two discrete rationalizations for requiring trial by jury: "The friends and adversaries of the plan of the convention, if they agree in nothing else, concur at least in the value they set upon the trial by jury; or if there is any difference between them it consists in this: the former regard it as a valuable safeguard to liberty; the latter represent it as the very palladium of free government." Hamilton explained that he thought it pointless to choose between the instrumental and the republican justifications for esteeming the jury. "For my own part, the more the operation of the institution has fallen under my observation, the more reason I have discovered for holding it in high estimation; and it would be altogether superfluous to examine to what extent it deserves to be esteemed useful or essential in a representative republic, or how much more merit it may be entitled to, as a defense against the oppressions of an hereditary monarch, than as a barrier to the tyranny of popular magistrates in a popular government."[118] Thus, from the beginning, the constitutional right to trial by jury itself could be described as serving a structural/republican function, creating a democratic branch of the judiciary;[119] an instrumental function, as a right protecting defendants against unjust prosecution or punishment; or both.

Article III did not include the range of trial rights ultimately located in the Sixth Amendment, to the concern of some. Virginia's George Mason sparked a debate about adding a Bill of Rights to the U.S. Constitution because the Article III reference to a right to jury trial did not include civil juries or provide an adequate vicinage requirement.[120] During the state ratifying conventions, several states proposed adding amendments to the Constitution. Unlike the right to trial by jury, the right to a public trial did not play a significant part in any of these discussions. It may simply have been assumed that trials, especially if they were jury trials, would be public, perhaps because a right to proceedings in open court was already guaranteed in so many of the state declarations and constitutions, or perhaps simply because public trial had always been a feature of trials at common law. An amendment proposed by New York would have included the right to a "speedy, public" trial by an "impartial Jury of the County where the Crime was committed."[121] A minority of the Pennsylvania delegation proposed adding an amendment to guarantee "a speedy trial, by an impartial jury of the vicinage,"[122] which did not mention public trial at all.

THE SIXTH AMENDMENT

When the Bill of Rights was actually added to the Constitution,[123] the right to a public trial, once again, was not a subject of debate or discussion. Controversies before the drafting of the Sixth Amendment centered on the scope of the right to jury trial and the right to a trial in the vicinage where the crime had taken place.[124] Perhaps because of the incidents described above in which states like Rhode Island had subjected their citizens to punishment without jury trial, an early draft of what was to become the Sixth Amendment would have prohibited the *states* from infringing rights, including the right to trial by jury. This version was passed by the House of Representatives but, for reasons not recorded, was rejected by the Senate,[125] and so the Sixth Amendment as written was only expected to govern federal trials.

It was on June 8, 1789, that James Madison gave the speech before the House of Representatives in which he introduced amendments for consideration, including the right to a speedy and public trial.[126] James Madison's draft of nine amendments to be inserted into the Constitution was submitted to a Committee of Eleven with one delegate from each state that had already ratified the Constitution. This Committee forwarded the amendments to the House, which passed them and appointed a Committee of Three to edit the amendments and forward them, now numbering seventeen, to the Senate. A conference then reduced the number of amendments from seventeen to twelve, which were then sent to the states, which ratified all but two. All ten of the states that sent in returns agreed to the text of what became the Sixth Amendment, effective in 1791.[127] The language guaranteeing the right to a speedy and public trial had not been debated and had not changed since Madison's original proposal. The Annals of Congress show that when Congress first addressed the language that became the Sixth Amendment, on August 11, 1789, there was some debate about the right of a defendant to delay a trial, but none about the right to public trial.[128]

Throughout these proceedings, there was little informative debate about most of the rights included in the Sixth Amendment, and none at all about the right to a public trial. The House and Senate debates contain no argument about why the Constitution should secure this right.[129] Therefore, it would be sheer speculation to ascribe to the framers of the Sixth Amendment particular reasons for including the right. It seems clear that the framers of this amendment were not reacting to any particular abuse that anyone was known to have suffered in recent memory, either in colonial America or even in England. Although the Declaration of Independence cited threats to the right to jury trial and the vicinage right, there is no indication that any secret proceedings had been held. Including the right to a public trial in the Constitution seems to have been more a codification than a change of direction or an act of defiance.

The absence of legislative history detailing why the right to public trial was included in the Bill of Rights poses a challenge to those who would interpret the scope of the right. The language and placement of the Sixth Amendment can be regarded as providing some clues to the thinking of the framers. The right to a public trial appears in an amendment that begins "In all criminal prosecutions. . . ." So modified, the right to a public trial seems to be tied to criminal proceedings and not to civil, although as the English history described above suggests, civil matters were tried just as publicly as criminal. The right to public trial is linguistically tied to the right to a jury trial: "[T]he accused shall enjoy the right to a speedy and public trial, by an impartial jury of the State and district wherein the crime shall have been committed. . . ." The Seventh Amendment, which provides a parallel guarantee of jury trial in civil cases ("In Suits at common law, where the value in controversy shall exceed twenty dollars, the right of trial by jury shall be preserved, and no fact tried by a jury shall be otherwise re-examined in any Court of the United States, than according to the rules of the common law"), makes no mention of a right to a public trial. A reader might infer from this difference that the framers did not intend for there to be a right to public civil trials.

The Sixth Amendment provides that in all criminal prosecutions there is a right to a speedy and public "trial." This language too could be taken as limiting, guaranteeing a right to public attendance only at those parts of a criminal prosecution that can be designated part of the "trial." This narrow interpretation initially attracted the Supreme Court, which once held that preliminary criminal proceedings, like a pretrial motion to suppress evidence, were not covered by the Sixth Amendment guarantee. As will be described, the Court ultimately chose a more expansive definition of the Sixth Amendment public trial right, holding that the amendment guarantees public attendance at pretrial hearings on motions to suppress evidence.

Finally, the amendment provides that, in all criminal prosecutions, "the accused shall enjoy" the right to a speedy and public trial. On its face, the language suggests that the right is for the benefit of the accused. The Supreme Court has never accepted the argument that the Sixth Amendment public trial guarantee confers any independent right on the public and press, although individual Justices have taken that position. This may be regarded, as the cases discussed will describe, as an open question. Nevertheless, the Court has held that the functions the Sixth Amendment serves may go beyond the interests of the defendant. The Court has held, for example, that a criminal defendant may not make a unilateral decision to waive the right to a public trial, any more than a defendant may make a unilateral decision to waive trial by jury.

Within the Sixth Amendment, the right to public trial is lumped together with the right to a speedy trial. Indeed, the two rights are listed as a single "right." Yet as the discussion of the two rights will show, the rights have been interpreted quite differently with respect to their scope, their remedies, and so on.

Reading the language of the Sixth Amendment against the background of the Article III guarantee of jury trials is a challenging but potentially instructive exercise. Why does the Sixth Amendment reiterate some aspects of Article III, like the right to trial by jury and the vicinage requirement; articulate other rights that might have been presumed to be inherent in the guarantee of criminal jury trial, like public trial; and add other rights not enjoyed by defendants at common law, like the right to counsel and the right to confront witnesses? Nineteenth-century constitutional commentator Joseph Story believed that it was superfluous to require that criminal trials be public when trials at common law were always public, and thus no one would have understood the Article III guarantee to provide for anything other than a public trial.[130]

The focus of the debates over the Sixth Amendment language was on the rights of the accused not embedded in the common law, particularly the right to counsel, the right to call or confront witnesses, and the more precise vicinage requirement.[131] If Article III already guaranteed a common law criminal jury trial and the Sixth Amendment added additional rights not recognized at common law, why would the framers have wished to add a specification that the criminal trial take the form it already would have been presumed to take? One possible interpretation is that the framers were proceeding cautiously, consistent with Madison's concern that the Bill of Rights was not only superfluous but dangerous because the enumeration of some rights might be taken to deny the other rights not listed. The framers might have wished to ensure that the list of new trial rights in the Sixth Amendment not be construed to eliminate other valued trial rights never explicitly listed. Another possible interpretation is that the new rights the Sixth Amendment conferred changed the nature of the criminal trial sufficiently that the framers wanted to address newly aggravated concerns that trials might be delayed (because counsel might prolong proceedings) or held in secret (because prosecution witnesses being cross-examined by a defense attorney might prefer closed-door proceedings).[132]

A third possibility is that, considering Hamilton's description of the dual functions of the criminal jury trial as both a locus of democracy and a bulwark against oppression, the framers were making the choice Hamilton had found unnecessary at the time. If the framers viewed the Sixth Amendment as conferring a right to the features of a common law criminal jury trial upon "the accused," then the Article III jury trial provision might now be understood, at least in retrospect, as guaranteeing the public's right to trial by jury. Article III could be interpreted as a structural rather than an individual right, and the Sixth Amendment as creating personal instrumental rights for the accused to "enjoy." The essential purpose of the Sixth Amendment might have been to ensure that criminal defendants could claim a remedy for denial of the rights listed. This interpretation is consistent with the Seventh Amendment guaranteeing a right to jury trial in certain civil cases without specifying that civil jury trials need to be either speedy or public. The jury trial as developed at common law was expected to be speedy and public, but it was only criminal defendants who were given a "right" that they might enforce if their own trials were not speedy or public. Civil litigants were left to the mercy of the courts and legislatures to vindicate their own interests in speedy or open justice, and the public was left to argue that the First Amendment might create a right to attend civil proceedings.

There is no documentation favoring any one of these interpretations, but the third interpretation may make the most sense analytically. Under this interpretation, the public does not have any stake in the Sixth Amendment right to public trial in criminal cases because the public's interest is expressed elsewhere—in Article III and ultimately, in the Supreme Court's analysis, in the First Amendment. The public's much-vaunted interest in the right to jury trial may be attributed not to the Sixth Amendment right to trial by an impartial jury, which may be viewed as belonging only to the defendant, but to Article III. If the public does not have an interest in the public trial right created by the Sixth Amendment and the purpose of the Sixth Amendment was to confer the newly listed rights on "the accused," then a defendant might be permitted to decide unilaterally to waive that right, just as a defendant is permitted to waive the new, instrumental right to counsel and proceed pro se (Farretta v. California, 1975). But if the Article III jury trial is the common law jury trial, including features like proceeding in open court, then the public would have its own countervailing interest in attending criminal proceedings, even without reference to the First Amendment. Additionally, the defendant might be prevented from making a unilateral decision about waiver in the same way defendants are prevented from making a unilateral decision to waive a jury trial, an Article III structural right belonging at least in part to the public (Singer v. United States, 1965). The relationship of the Article III guarantee and the Sixth Amendment right, and the relative scope of their guarantees, can have practical consequences.

A HISTORY OF RATIONALIZATION

In choosing its relatively expansive interpretations of the Sixth Amendment public trial right, the Supreme Court has not paid much attention to either the language or placement of the Sixth Amendment. There is no legislative history of the Sixth Amendment right. So for authority, the Court has routinely cited the English tradition of open proceedings, an argument that has seemed to some Justices to prove too much because judicial proceedings in England, as the previous history shows, were generally open even in civil cases. When confronted with questions of interpretation like whether or not the Sixth Amendment would permit closing part of a proceeding to protect the identity of an undercover informer or of a rape victim, the Court frequently has had little useful history to fall back on. Because of these gaps, judicial opinions interpreting the Sixth Amendment public trial right tend to invoke not the history of the public trial guarantee itself, but the history of commentary effusing about the functions served by public judicial proceedings. As the history above shows, there is no document, no debate, and no point in time at which public trials were ordained, and so these commentators, from Coke to Blackstone and beyond, provided post hoc rationalizations, describing functions served by public proceedings or benefits that might be derived, rather than "the purpose" of the public proceeding. Speeches and debates before the adoption of the Fourth Amendment, by way of contrast, show that the framers wished to include a warrant requirement to constrain executive discretion to search and seize citizens because of their negative experiences as colonists with oppressive searches by royal agents. In light of this history, it is plausible to say that "the purpose" of the warrant requirement can be ascertained and distinguished from other functions that the requirement might serve.[133] In an oddly postmodern twist, what commentators have said in describing the right to a public trial has become the history of that right.

Therefore, it is worth looking at what commentators have had to say about the functions of public trials, particularly before the drafting of the Sixth Amendment, because the reputation of the public trial right during the eighteenth century, more than its actual history, may have been familiar to the framers of the amendment. In addition, in the cases to follow, courts disagree about interpretation of the scope of the public trial right in ways that ultimately can be traced to their identification of different functions as governing their analysis.

PRE-CONSTITUTIONAL COMMENTARY

William Blackstone, the commentator who would have been best known to the framers of the Sixth Amendment; the historians on whom he relied (primarily Matthew Hale); and their predecessors all stressed the instrumental functions of public trial that may benefit defendants (although not in every case) and a limited number of additional functions that serve various public interests.

Abjuring Torture and Canon Law

Many commentators, including Blackstone, express pride in the English institutions that avoid the perceived continental sins of the use of torture and inquisitorial courts. Holding a trial in public rather than behind closed doors is viewed by these commentators as a method of insuring that the accused is not being tortured. "[A]ll our accusations are public, and our trials in the face of the world; where torture is unknown, and every delinquent is judged by such of his equals."[134] Open trials, Sir Thomas Smith smugly observed, may seem "strange to all nations that doe use the civill Lawe of the Roman Emperours, that for life and death there is nothing put in writing but the endictement onely. All the rest is done openlie in the presence of the Judges, the Justices, the enquest, the prisoner, and so manie as will or can come so neare as to heare it, and all depositions and witnesses given aloude, that all men may here from the mouth of the depositors and witnesses what is saide."[135]

Preventing Oppression

As early a commentator as Sir John Hawles in his 1680 paean to jury trials identified jury trials as a means of addressing concerns about despotism, arbitrariness, and malicious, oppressive, partial, or corrupt proceedings.[136] Public jury trials avoid the prospect of the criminal justice system serving the "passions or interests of a few."[137] Blackstone believed that the jury was especially important in criminal cases to protect an accused against the power of the king, who appointed the judges.[138] Although it may be anachronistic to describe public trial as a "right" during many of the earlier proceedings Blackstone and Hawles describe, Blackstone's readers would have understood public trial to have served the instrumental function of protecting defendants against biased judges.

Truth Seeking

One of the earliest champions of public jury trial, Chief Justice John Fortescue in the mid-1400s, remarked that in England innocent people would not be found guilty because evidence is given in open court and the accused is tried by twelve people of good character.[139] The connection between open trials and discovery of the truth has been variously described. Some commentators explained that when witnesses must testify in public, they will have a greater incentive to testify honestly because it is more likely that perjurious testimony will be discovered and repudiated. Sir Matthew Hale, in his treatise published posthumously in 1713, opined that having witnesses testify in open court increases the likelihood of full and truthful testimony, because personal and open examination "beats and boults out the truth much better."[140]

In addition, various commentators opine that valuable witnesses who have not been called by the parties are more likely to come forward if they know that a trial is taking place and they are able to attend. Sir John Hawles commented, in the context of commentary on John Lilburne's treason trial, "The reason that matters of law are, or ought to be transacted publicly, is, [t]hat any person unconcerned as well as concerned, may, as *amicus curiae*, inform the court better, if he thinks they are in error, that justice may be done. . . . There is an invitation to all persons, who can inform the court concerning the matter to be tried, to come into the court, and they shall be heard."[141]

While a representative sample of the public may serve the functions described previously—exposing government oppression or corruption of the process by either party—it could be reasoned that the truth-promotion function is best served when as many members of the public as possible observe the proceeding. The wider public knowledge of a trial, the more likely it is that critical witnesses will learn of the proceedings and come forward to supplement or correct the evidence given in court.

One may also question the validity of the assumption that greater publicity will lead to more accurate testimony. When trials took place in small communities where both jurors and spectators could be expected to know about the events in question, it may have been more likely that public knowledge would have kept witnesses (and jurors) honest, or that members of the public would come forward to dispute a witness's testimony. A principal function of the jury and other members of the public, as described by such commentators as Hawles, was to provide a source of information. A member of a local community could not be railroaded with false accusations because the members of the jury, as well as the members of the community, were likely to know the defendant and be present. Today, the entire community does not attend criminal trials, which are held inside courtrooms that limit attendance. It might be argued that, to promote this function, trials should be disseminated as broadly as possible—an argument for televising trials. However, most media coverage of trials is selective, showing or describing only tidbits of today's longer proceedings, and so the likelihood that erroneous or perjurious testimony will reach the ears of someone who can correct the record is reduced.

It is also plausible, especially in an emotionally charged case, that a witness testifying in public might be tempted to say what the public wishes to hear, even if it is not truthful. If a witness has something to say that is embarrassing, the witness might be more forthcoming in a closed proceeding. Opponents of televising trials also argue that emotions ranging from stage fright to vanity are more likely to affect the accuracy of a witness's testimony if the witness is facing a large audience.

Keeping Jurors Honest

All defendants have an interest in avoiding torture and oppressive or baseless prosecutions. To the extent that public jury trials promote honest proceedings aimed at discovering the truth, individual defendants might or might not benefit. If having a critical number of jurors is an effective means of ensuring that the crown cannot bribe or threaten jurors to reach a verdict, a corrupt defendant will also be stymied in any attempt to influence or intimidate jurors. Just as the public will be able to expose jurors who are overly partial to the prosecution, so too will the public be able to stymie defendants who have colluded with the prosecution to fool jurors, or who have bribed or threatened jurors. If public jury trials promote the integrity of the trial system against juror corruption or misconduct, the interests of some defendants may begin to diverge from the public's interest in fair proceedings.

Open trials provide a popular check on the jury itself. If proceedings take place in public, members of the public can judge whether or not the jurors are deciding cases on the basis of the evidence presented to them. Hale thought that having public trials would prevent jurors from hearing extra, unauthorized evidence.[142]

If jurors are the democratic branch of the judiciary, public proceedings can be an effective method of providing some measure of political accountability. Jurors are representatives of the public and so the public must be able to evaluate how well they are doing their jobs. On the other hand, the negative side of democracy is that jurors might also be influenced by the passions and prejudices of the community in an emotionally charged case, or in a case involving a delicate issue like race, even if they could have surmounted their own biases in the more sheltered and exalted environment of a courtroom.[143]

The Jury of the Whole

Another rationalization for the right to public trial, closely tied to the right to a jury trial, also endorsed by Blackstone, is that the entire public may participate in a criminal prosecution directly, rather than only being represented by petit jurors. Once crimes began to be viewed as implicating society and not just an individual victim, criminal prosecution became a community affair. Crimes, Blackstone said, are a "breach and violation of the public rights and duties, due to the whole community, considered as a community, in its social aggregate capacity."[144] Jurors represent the community when they decide guilt or innocence, but the entire community is still interested in the prosecution and therefore must be permitted to attend, just as they might have been on the jury itself. It is not surprising that Blackstone, a vigorous champion of the value of trial by jury, took the idea of public representation in the jury system a step further by considering the jury trial to be not just the jury's but the public's. This idea, too, does not necessarily promote every defendant's self-interest. An unpopular defendant might stand a chance of winning over a carefully selected jury subject to the controls of a judge in the courtroom, but be fated to lose in the court of public opinion.

This concludes the range of recorded explanations for public trial available at the time of the framing of the Constitution. Since that time, others have weighed in, adding to this list of rationales and discussing the values and functions that can be served by public trial.

POST–SIXTH AMENDMENT RATIONALIZATIONS

Influential commentators in the nineteenth century included Jeremy Bentham who, not surprisingly, emphasized the utilitarian role of holding judicial proceedings in public, elaborating on the theory of Hale and Blackstone that publicity enhances the ability of a judicial proceeding to discover the truth. Publicity, he argued, is "the most effectual safeguard of testimony."[145] "Falsehood may be bold in a secret examination; it is difficult for it to be so in public." Publicity "awakens all the mental faculties" of witnesses, leading toward a "faithful statement." Witnesses will know that spectators can correct their untruthful statements and, if they are lying, will feel "shame in the presence of a crowd of spectators." Publicity also allows evidence to be "brought to light, which would have remained buried, if nothing had been known about the transaction." Bentham also seconded the argument that public trials prevent oppression, arguing that publicity ensures the integrity of judges, prevents abuses, and raises public confidence in judges. Public trials are necessary for "the integrity of the people" and present "the strongest of all securities." Bentham tells of Frederick of Prussia and Catherine of Russia, both of whom attempted to reform their criminal justice systems, but who failed "[b]ecause they did not admit publicity into their courts; and without it, all imaginable precautions are but cobwebs."[146]

Arguing that judicial proceedings should presumptively be open, Bentham said of would-be inquisitors, "[i]f they have nothing to fear from the public eye, why wrap themselves up in darkness? Why convert the temple of justice into a cavern as secret as a den of robbers?"[147]

The Trial as Education

Bentham also articulated a new idea, that of the trial as a form of civic education. Publicity of judicial proceedings elevates public discourse, he maintained. When members of the public hear testimony, "[d]iscussions on judicial matters then enter into the course of ordinary ideas; and the public becomes accustomed to take a deeper interest in their result." Part of Bentham's argument is that open proceedings will contribute to public confidence in those proceedings. "[W]henever the temple of justice is thrown open to all the world, it becomes a national school, in which the most important lessons are taught with a degree of energy and authority, which they would not otherwise possess."[148] Of course, the public's confidence in the justice system will only increase if the public deems what it has seen to be fair. "The audience is the true court of appeal, in which the decisions of the tribunal are judged and estimated according to their worth." Bentham recognized that public evaluation of the worth of a court's decisions will not always be reliable. But, he said, "[i]t is a thousand times better, that the people should judge wrong, than that they should lose all interest in public affairs."[149]

Bentham also embraced, at least metaphorically, the idea of trials as a form of theater: "the courthouse is a 'theatre of justice,' wherein a vital social drama is staged; if its doors are locked, the public can only wonder whether the solemn ritual of communal condemnation has been properly performed."[150]

American Commentary

There is not very much early American commentary on the right to public trial. Commentators tended to follow the lead of Blackstone in describing mostly the instrumental role of public attendance at trial, but some commentators also endorsed the type of public functions described by Bentham.

Joseph Story in his Commentaries on the Constitution, published in 1833, waxes eloquent about the role of the jury in preventing tyranny and oppression on the part of rulers and violence and vindictiveness on the part of the people,[151] but he has nothing to say about why, in his pronouncement, "[t]he trial is always public."[152]

John Henry Wigmore, in his treatise on evidence, divides the reasons for holding public trials into two categories. First, based on the explanations of Hawles, Blackstone, and Bentham, is to secure "the trustworthiness and completeness of the testimony."[153] The second category, "independent of evidential service," includes first, preventing abuses; second, allowing the public to hear what is going on; and, third, following on Bentham, promoting the "educative effect of public attendance," which also leads to confidence in judges.

The American Bar Association (ABA), in a 1968 report entitled "Advisory Committee on Fair Trial and Free Press," summed up as follows: "The historical origins of the right to public trial are obscure. . . . But whatever its origins, it is clear that the tradition became an important one and, when incorporated in American constitutions, was principally motivated by a desire to protect the accused from proceedings of an inquisitional character, particularly those involving religious or political persecution."[154]

The Trial as Theater

Wigmore describes early American trials as having been used as a form of entertainment.[155] Chief Justice Earl Warren, in his concurring opinion in the case of Estes v. Texas (1965) (declaring televising of trials to effect a denial of due process), was highly critical of members of the public who attend trials for their entertainment value, commenting that, by the twentieth century, American society should have moved beyond the barbaric use of trials as a form of sensationalism. To him, the idea of the trial as a form of theater was anathema. He also disagreed with Bentham's notion of trials as a form of public education, announcing bluntly that the purpose of a trial is not to educate. A later Supreme Court Justice, Ruth Bader Ginsburg, was quoted as echoing Warren's disdain for those who would watch trials as a form of entertainment: "a society that makes entertainment out of the administration of criminal justice is sick."[156]

Justice William Brennan, who dissented in the *Estes* case, believed that trials could properly serve multiple purposes, including a theatrical function. "[T]he theater metaphor is legitimate, I think, because criminal trials are and are intended to be richly symbolic and educational—that is part of their function in a society governed by the rule of law. . . . "[157] In that respect, his vision of the role the public may legitimately play was very different from Earl Warren's view. Brennan also believed that attendance at trial is an important component of democracy. (As will be discussed, Brennan expressed some of his views on the propriety of permitting trials to be used for different functions in the context of cases interpreting the First Amendment right of the public and press to attend trials, which may serve a different set of purposes than the Sixth Amendment right.) A desire to be entertained may attract some members of the public who otherwise would not pay attention to the criminal justice system, but who may then use what they have observed in productive ways. Bentham posited that it is better for the people to be wrong than to lose interest in public affairs.

The Greek custom of citizen involvement in the justice system and the Greek understanding of the relationship of trials and theater provide an interesting point of comparison in the debate about the metaphorical or actual use of trials as theater. Trials are similar to classical drama both in form (the *agon* or contest) and in function. The audience in both forums hears two sides of the story.[158] Trials, like drama, were viewed as reassessing social position between particular members of society and reestablishing social order.[159] Keeping law in the hands of amateurs was a quick and cheap method of dispensing justice.[160] And Athenian trials, like plays in an outdoor arena, took place before an enormous audience.

Trials that take place in a large arena rather than a constricted courtroom, a practice Earl Warren describes pejoratively in his concurring opinion in *Estes* as "show trials," might be considered the ideal if one purpose of the trial is to educate. The term "show trial" bears the pejorative connotation that the trial is literally only a form of theater because the state is using a proceeding with a preordained end—a guilty verdict—to deter certain conduct. Warren does not distinguish an unfair, scripted trial, intended to repress or oppress, from a fair trial, aimed at deterring criminal conduct, attended by a large audience. A large audience in and of itself does not render a proceeding unfair.

A "show trial" might pander to those seeking entertainment, or it might seek to deliver a message. The message may be that of either prosecutor or defendant. When Justice Robert Jackson developed protocols for the Nuremberg trial, he set out to design what he hoped would be not just a legal proceeding, but a way to engrave Nazi atrocities into the memory of the world. To accomplish this creation of history and memory, he insisted that all proceedings be open to the press and the public and had transcripts translated into four languages.[161] A very different message and a very different viewpoint on the majesty of the justice system was offered by the defendants in the Chicago 8 Conspiracy Trial, who clowned their way through their criminal trial for antiwar activities to demonstrate to the public and to history their view of the absurdity of the charges.[162]

Warren's suspicion of large audiences has practical consequences. His view would lead to the conclusion that the right to public trial is satisfied as long as some representative members of the public or press are present; Brennan's view would promote accommodating as many members of the public as wanted to attend.

The Trial as Social Control

As the "show trial" concept suggests, the public may use its observations of trials to judge and react to its governing officials, but the governing officials may also make use of trials to educate the public in the consequences of lawbreaking, to deter crime, or to intimidate. Recall the enormous attendance at early English treason trials.

Thurman Arnold, writing in the 1930s, describes the function of public jury trials more cynically, as serving the purposes of government in preserving its own image and power, rather than serving the purpose of truly empowering the people.[163] Arnold describes juries as convenient scapegoats. If jurors are perceived as reaching an incorrect result, the government may deflect blame for the perceived mistaken decision and thus avoid being held responsible. It was not the government that acquitted O.J. Simpson, or the officers the public believed had brutalized Rodney King, but representatives of the people themselves. Even as the government appears to be ceding power to the people, it is in fact securing its own power by creating a safety valve.

Holding jury trials in public is a necessary element of this self-interested process. The jury trial cannot truly serve the function of legitimating the verdict and the proceedings if the public does not know what has happened or believes that important events have occurred behind the scenes. It is the apparent transparency of the proceedings that builds public trust and enables the government to use trials to deter certain forms of behavior, as was the case with English treason trials. In this sense, all trials are "show trials," and Warren's desire to avoid allowing the government to use trials for educational purposes, or to avoid allowing the public to use trials for their own purposes, whether political or theatrical, must be unavailing. Some judges who oppose allowing cameras in the courtroom complain of the potential breakdown of decorum because they do not wish to cede control of their own image. Public trials can serve the purposes of the government in controlling the populace; they can also serve to radicalize the populace by taking control of the appearance of a trial away from trial judges, just as jury trials take away judicial control of the verdict.

The Trial as Catharsis

Chief Justice Warren Burger, in his opinion for the Court in the *Richmond Newspapers* case described public trials as serving a therapeutic value for the community, placing this function high on his own list of the purposes of open trials. Burger believed that members of the community who watch a trial in an upsetting case and see justice being done will thereby be more inclined to suppress vengeful vigilante reactions and be better prepared to move on. This idea of community "therapy" is not far removed from the Greek notion of catharsis, which can be achieved in the theater as well as the court.[164] Burger's concept won endorsement from a majority of Supreme Court Justices.

Because there are so many functions that a public trial might be viewed as serving, judges must sometimes choose which interests will govern their analysis. If, for example, a judge believes that the Sixth Amendment reflects a structural decision to enable the community to act as a jury of the whole and to use trials to educate and empower themselves to speak back to the government, then the Sixth Amendment should be interpreted as creating a presumption in favor of as much public participation as possible. Trials should be televised, for example, to maximize the number of people who can view the workings of the criminal justice system. If, on the other hand, a judge believes that the purposes of the Sixth Amendment are circumscribed by the instrumental functions articulated by Blackstone—contributing to the fairness of the trial by ensuring that trials do not occur in secret—then the public trial right will be satisfied, as Earl Warren believed it should be, as long as some number of representatives of the public have the opportunity to attend. If the public is to serve as a jury of the whole, ensuring that the jurors in a particular case are serving as their true representatives, then it seems appropriate to allow the public only to observe those aspects of a trial that take place in the presence of the jurors. But if the public's role is to provide a check on the fairness of the proceedings in general, public presence might be most necessary when the jury is absent. If the Sixth Amendment is viewed as encompassing the democratic values described by Justice Brennan, then defendants should not have a veto over publicity. But if those public benefits inhere only in the First Amendment right to public access, and the purpose of the Sixth Amendment is exclusively to benefit defendants, then the Sixth Amendment right of a defendant who welcomes public participation should weigh more heavily against the prosecutor's desire to close a proceeding for the benefit of the public interest in, for example, juror privacy.

The above history does not provide any firm foundation for making those choices, beyond showing that holding trial in public has been a tradition.[165] As the next chapter will show, the Supreme Court has adopted a broad view of the role of the public in the criminal justice system, but mostly in the context of its First Amendment case law. Few Supreme Court cases interpret the Sixth Amendment, so many of the key choices about the meaning of the Sixth Amendment have thus far been made only in lower federal or state courts, or not at all.

2

The Right to a Public Trial: Analysis

DEVELOPMENT OF THE RIGHT

The Supreme Court Cases

Many of the rationales for the right to public trial described above posit that defendants can benefit from the publicity of a trial in a variety of ways. Some defendants will wish to claim these benefits by invoking the Sixth Amendment right and arguing for a broad interpretation of its scope. But other defendants will wish to avoid publicity which, in some cases, may compromise the fairness of their trial. A trial might become a media circus, distracting the trier of fact, as the Supreme Court believed had happened in several cases it considered (Estes v. Texas, 1965; Sheppard v. Maxwell, 1966). Prejudicial pretrial publicity assuming a defendant's guilt may make it difficult to select an unbiased jury, as the Court thought had happened in the case of Irvin v. Dowd (1961). Evidence not intended for the jury may be disclosed to the public at large, creating a risk that the jury's decision will be tainted if the inadmissible evidence reaches one or more jurors, as also happened in *Irvin.* A publicized trial might lead witnesses unfavorable to the defendant to come forward, or might foster a lynch mob atmosphere if the defendant or the crime charged is unpopular. In such circumstances, defendants may wish to foreswear their Sixth Amendment right to an open proceeding and instead seek a closed proceeding, perhaps arguing that excessive publicity denies them due process.

Most of the criminal defendants in the Supreme Court's public trial cases fell into this latter category, resisting some degree of publicity. In only two of the Supreme Court cases had the defendants invoked their Sixth Amendment right and resisted closure of a proceeding (In re Oliver, 1948; Waller v. Georgia, 1984). The Court has never ruled against a defendant raising a claim for open proceedings under the Sixth Amendment. In cases in which defendants have opposed publicity, pitting defendants' interests against the interests of the public, the Court's results have been mixed. In the majority of cases, whether under the Sixth or First Amendments, the Court's decisions have favored open proceedings. In only one case (Gannett Co. v. DePasquale, 1979), did the Court rule that closing part of a criminal proceeding (a pretrial suppression hearing) did not violate the Sixth Amendment, and *Gannett* was subsequently superseded by the Court's later decision in *Waller* that a defendant does have a presumptive right under the Sixth Amendment to have the public attend a pretrial suppression hearing. The only other case in which the Court actually allowed a limitation on the publicizing of criminal trials was *Estes*, during which the Court held that televising trials presumptively denied defendants due process of law. *Estes*, in turn, was superseded by the Court's subsequent decision in Chandler v. Florida (1981), allowing the states to experiment with televising trials.

While the Court has consistently favored open proceedings, the Justices have differed vigorously in their interpretations of the Sixth Amendment right to a public trial on many key issues: Where does the Sixth Amendment right to public "trial" apply—that is, how can "trials" be distinguished from proceedings that may take place in secret, like grand jury proceedings, and how should pretrial hearings and other ancillary proceedings be categorized? Should a defendant have a right to waive the Sixth Amendment right and insist on a closed proceeding? If both parties to a criminal proceeding, the defendant and the government, agree to closure, may a proceeding then be closed? Do the press and public share the Sixth Amendment right with the accused?

The Supreme Court cases described below answer many but not all of these questions and frequently provide an array of opinions as to whether the Court's answers are correct. The sequence of cases in which the Court struggled with these issues is interesting not just for the results the Court reached, but for the choices made along the way: What cases the Court chose to hear and when, the debates among various Justices about the scope and nature of the Sixth Amendment right, and the Court's struggles with the question it avoided answering until its affirmative answer finally eclipsed much of the discussion of the Sixth Amendment: Is there a right under the First Amendment for the public and press to attend judicial proceedings?

The Justices also applied their views on general issues of constitutional interpretation. Some believers in the tenets of federalism were squeamish about depriving states of the opportunity to experiment with their own procedures; others were more willing to require nonconforming states to adapt their procedures to those used in the majority of states. The Justices also differed about the nature of the relative roles of trial and appellate courts—when should an appellate court set forth general rules for the conduct of trials and when should trial judges be allowed to decide on a case-by-case basis how to handle the conflicting demands of defendants, the public, and the press?

In re Oliver—Distinguishing Open Trials from Secret Grand Jury Proceedings

The U.S. Supreme Court's first serious examination of the Sixth Amendment public trial right came in the case In re Oliver (1948), in which a defendant claiming the right to an open proceeding prevailed, setting a strong precedent for later cases. This case required the Court to deconstruct an unusual state grand jury proceeding that melted into a contempt trial in order to separate the trial, where the Sixth Amendment public trial right would apply, from the traditionally secret grand jury proceeding, where it would not.

Oliver appeared pursuant to a subpoena as a witness before a Michigan circuit judge who, under a unique Michigan law, was conducting a "one-man grand jury" investigation into various gambling and official corruption offenses. The session was closed to the public, although several people other than the judge/grand juror appear to have been present. After hearing Oliver's testimony, the judge/grand juror, evidently considering his statements in the context of other testimony that Oliver had not heard, told him that his story did not "jell." The judge/grand juror then proceeded to charge Oliver with criminal contempt, convict him then and there, and sentence him immediately to sixty days in jail.

Three days later, a lawyer acting on Oliver's behalf filed a habeas corpus petition challenging the conviction, asserting that Oliver had been denied many rights, including the Sixth Amendment rights to the assistance of counsel, to cross-examine the other grand jury witnesses, to summon other witnesses to refute the charges against him, and to sufficient notice of the nature and cause of the accusation against him. Oliver did not challenge the constitutionality of Michigan's unusual decision to vest grand jury powers in a single judge. On hearing his appeal, the Michigan Supreme Court upheld the contempt conviction, reasoning that it would have been "an idle gesture" to require the judge to adjourn as a grand jury and reconvene as a court in what the state supreme court seemed to regard as one proceeding, given the state law's hybridization of the role of grand jury and judge.

The U.S. Supreme Court disagreed that allowing the one-man grand jury system necessitated allowing a procedural hybrid. The Court began by separating the grand jury proceeding, where testimony was taken, from the contempt adjudication on the ground that "grand juries do not adjudge the witnesses guilty of contempt." It did not matter to the Court that the same individual filled both grand jury and trial judge functions—those discrete functions had to be separated for the purpose of determining what rights the witness/defendant had. After declaring that the contempt proceeding must "be measured not by the limitations applicable to grand jury proceedings, but by the constitutional standards applicable to court proceedings in which an accused may be sentenced to fine or imprisonment or both," the Court went on to say, "[t]hus our first question is this: Can an accused be tried and convicted for contempt of court in grand jury secrecy?"

It is notable that the Court elected to begin with the question of whether Oliver's right to a public trial had been violated rather than with questions about the right to counsel, the other Sixth Amendment rights at stake, or the due process issue the petitioner had actually asserted.[166] Secrecy, to the Court, was the hallmark of a grand jury proceeding. And if the contempt finding was properly part of the grand jury proceeding, then Oliver would presumably have had no more Sixth Amendment right to the assistance of counsel than any other grand jury witness. The Court's decision to address the issue of secrecy as the primary issue in the case is even more noteworthy in light of the fact that this choice drew a dissent from Justices Frankfurter and Jackson on the ground that the constitutionality of the secrecy of the contempt proceeding was not within the arguments alleged in Oliver's petition for *certiorari* to the Supreme Court, and had not been raised in the state court habeas corpus petition. The dissenters complained that because this question had not been litigated below, there was no record made with respect to this claim, and therefore the issue should have been remanded.

Having made the choice not only to hear but to give primacy to the claim to a public tribunal, Justice Hugo Black, writing for seven members of the Court, relished the opportunity to paint the claim as obviously meritorious. Beginning with history, Black asserted that "Counsel have not cited and we have been unable to find a single instance of a criminal trial conducted in camera in any federal, state, or municipal court in the history of this country. Nor have we found any record of even one such secret criminal trial in England since abolition of the Court of the Star Chamber in 1641, and whether that court ever convicted people secretly is in dispute."[167]

Black described the public trial right as an "accompaniment of the ancient institution of jury trial," and traced its appearance in state constitutional provisions, noting that "almost without exception" every state, either by constitution, statute, or court decision, required that criminal trials be open to the public. Black then went on to comment on the possible reasons for the Anglo-American distrust of secret proceedings. That right, he said, "has always been recognized as a safeguard against any attempt to employ our courts as instruments of persecution." He also listed in a footnote other "benefits" ascribed to public trials: (1) public trials will come to the attention of key witnesses who might otherwise have been unknown to the parties, and who may then voluntarily come forward to offer their testimony, and (2) spectators learn about their government and develop confidence in judicial remedies.

Taking a rather unnecessary pass at defining the limit of the right of the public to attend trials, the Court observed that the lower federal and state courts had differed over when particular spectators could be excluded from a criminal trial. The instant proceeding, of course, where everyone but the judge and his "attaches" was excluded, was clearly overly exclusive by any standard. An accused, announced the Court, is "at the very least" entitled to have his friends, relatives, and counsel present. A footnote to this sentence, citing to several lower court cases and two commentaries on the right to a public trial, made clear who was omitted from the Court's initial list of who "at the very least" must be permitted to attend: the press. The commentaries cited had spoken approvingly of the right of the press to attend criminal trials, including a statement that no court had ever gone so far as to affirmatively exclude the press.[168]

Because *Oliver* involved a state court proceeding and the decision came in the days before the Court had clarified its position on incorporation of rights like the Sixth Amendment right to a public trial (that is, whether rights specified in the Bill of Rights apply in state as well as federal courts),[169] the holding of the case was that Oliver had been denied due process of law by being tried and sentenced in a secret proceeding. "In view of this nation's historic distrust of secret proceedings, their inherent dangers to freedom, and the universal requirement of our federal and state governments that trials be public, the Fourteenth Amendment's guarantee that no one shall be deprived of his liberty without due process of law means at least that an accused cannot be thus sentenced to prison." Therefore, the Court held that the right to a public trial is an aspect of due process of law sufficiently fundamental that states may not to choose to hold nonpublic trials. In this section of the opinion, the Court focused exclusively on the potential benefits of publicity to a defendant and did not allude to any interests of the public, although one of the rationales cited as undergirding the Sixth Amendment right was the public's interest in educating itself about the criminal justice system.

The Court's first explication of the Sixth Amendment right to a public trial, thus, bore the stamp of Hugo Black's characteristically expansive enthusiasm for the provisions of the Bill of Rights as he interpreted them, in his frequently absolutist manner, to protect criminal defendants against government overreaching.

Oliver, other than procedurally, was an easy case for the Supreme Court for several reasons. As is frequently the case when the Supreme Court interprets a Bill of Rights provision to preclude a state's procedural choice, the state in question, Michigan, had made a choice different from most other jurisdictions. By blending the functions of the grand jury and judge, the state had also blended the inherently secret grand jury with a proceeding (a contempt trial) traditionally held in open court. That Michigan was the only state to merge these procedures made it easier for the Court to reject the state's argument that both functions—investigation and the contempt finding—could be served in a single proceeding under whichever set of rules the state selected.

Once the Sixth Amendment right to a public trial was held to be an essential element of due process, applicable to the states (even before other Sixth Amendment rights), the Court was now obligated to address other more difficult questions that would arise in the future about the meaning and scope of that right.

Irvin v. Dowd—The Price of Publicity

For the next several decades, the Supreme Court's view of the value of a public trial was far less affirmative. A series of notorious cases inspired extensive media coverage and, in each instance, the defendants challenged their convictions on the ground that the publicity had deprived them of a fair trial. The Court thus began to consider the issue it had left open in *Oliver*—does the press have a right to attend and publicize criminal trials? And when might such a right be subject to limitation if publicity compromised a defendant's right to a fair trial?

In three of the four cases the Court heard during the 1960s and 1970s (Irvin v. Dowd, 1961; Estes v. Texas, 1965; Sheppard v. Maxwell, 1966), the Court held that the defendants had indeed been denied due process because of some aspect of the press coverage of their trials. In *Irvin*, the focus was on the impact of prejudicial pretrial publicity on the impartiality of the jurors, who had been exposed to the publicity. In *Estes* and *Sheppard*, the problem was the indecorous atmosphere at the trial itself. In the course of evaluating these defendants' claims, the Court began to limn the right to a public trial as a right belonging only to criminal defendants and not, despite some discussion of the public functions served by open trials, to the public or press. The Court also began to address the question of whether it could or should impose limits on publicity beyond reversing convictions in particular cases in which the press had gone too far.

In *Estes*, the Court set an important limit by ruling that television coverage of a criminal trial presumptively prejudiced criminal defendants in every case (a holding the Court was to overrule only fifteen years later). But by the time it decided the last of these four cases, Murphy v. Florida (1975), the Court seemed to retreat, upholding Murphy's conviction and leaving the job of preventing and curing prejudicial publicity to the trial courts.

The first of the prejudicial publicity cases (Irvin v. Dowd, 1961), involved petitioner Leslie Irvin's conviction and death sentence for a murder committed in Indiana. Shortly after Irvin's arrest, the prosecutor issued press releases announcing that Irvin had confessed to six murders. Because press coverage of these confessions was so extensive, Irvin's counsel moved for a change of venue but then concluded that the inflammatory pretrial publicity had also heavily prejudiced the inhabitants of the new trial site against his client. The jury panel at trial consisted of 430 people, of whom 268 were excused for cause on the ground that they had already formed fixed opinions about Irvin's guilt on the basis of media accounts. Ninety percent of the prospective jurors who were examined on the point admitted having an opinion about Irvin's guilt, ranging from a mere suspicion to absolute certainty. Eight of the twelve people who served as jurors at trial admitted that they thought Irvin was guilty, but stated that they nevertheless believed that they could keep an open mind as to his guilt.

Although the Indiana state courts had affirmed the petitioner's conviction and the lower federal courts hearing his habeas corpus petition had ruled against him, Irvin succeeded in getting his conviction reversed in the Supreme Court. The Court began by stressing the importance of the right to trial by an impartial jury, and then recounted the "buildup of prejudice" in the case.

When one's life is at stake, wrote Justice Tom Clark for a unanimous Court, "it is not requiring too much that petitioner be tried in an atmosphere undisturbed by so huge a wave of public passion and by a jury other than one in which two-thirds of the members admit, before hearing any testimony, to possessing a belief in his guilt."

While the majority emphasized the extreme and what a reader might have understood to be the unusual nature of the publicity in this case, Justice Felix Frankfurter, concurring, noted that "unfortunately, this is not an isolated case." He said, "[o]f course I agree with the Court's opinion," but not a Term passed without the Court being asked to review convictions from states throughout the country of people whose jury trials had been distorted because of inflammatory newspaper accounts, or who decided to forego trial by jury altogether rather than face jurors subjected to such extraneous prejudicial influences. "For one reason or another," he said, the Court does not undertake to review all such "envenomed" state convictions. But again and again, he said, the Court is compelled to reverse convictions "in which prejudicial newspaper intrusion has poisoned the outcome. . . . This Court has not yet decided that the fair administration of criminal justice must be subordinated to another safeguard of our constitutional system—freedom of the press, properly conceived. The Court has not yet decided that, while convictions must be reversed and miscarriages of justice result because the minds of jurors or potential jurors were poisoned, the poisoner is constitutionally protected in plying his trade."

Once again, as in *Oliver*, the Court left for another day the question of whether there might be any limits on press attendance at and publications about criminal trials. Irvin's conviction was reversed because of the adverse impact of the publicity on his trial, but the Court did not provide rules or even suggestions to trial court judges trying to balance the due process claims of defendants with the claims asserted by the press. If Justice Frankfurter was right in observing that a large number of defendants suffered the same fate as Irvin—being tried by jurors whose impartiality was suspect—then the Court would continue to be confronted with decisions about which cases to pluck out the pile of *certiorari* petitions for a hearing, and whether, as Frankfurter suggested, to set out rules to limit the "poisoners."

Estes v. Texas—Cameras out of the Courtroom

In the case of Estes v. Texas (1965), the Court confronted the question of limitations on the press as well as the question of whether a particular defendant had been denied a fair trial because of massive publicity. The defendant in this case, Billie Sol Estes, was a highly notorious figure throughout the state of Texas and throughout the nation. At his trial for swindling, in Tyler, Texas, evidence was presented to show that Estes, through false pretenses and fraudulent representations, had sold farmers fertilizer tanks and other related equipment that did not exist and then induced the farmers to sign and deliver to him chattel mortgages on the imaginary property. The press and public were outraged by the nature of the scams charged as well as by their sheer scale.

As in the *Irvin* case, defendant's counsel could not avoid the impact of massive pretrial publicity through a change of venue. Among the questions petitioner brought to the Supreme Court in his *certiorari* petition was the question of whether he had been denied a fair trial because, as in *Irvin*, his jurors had been infected by prejudicial pretrial publicity and assumed his guilt. The Court did not grant *certiorari* on this issue, and left standing a state appellate court ruling that the members of the jury were not prejudiced by pretrial publicity (Estes v. Texas, 1965) (Stewart, J., dissenting). As in the series of cases Justice Frankfurter described in his opinion in *Irvin*, the Court "for one reason or another" decided not to hear this typical claim, perhaps because its discussion of this claim would not have been likely to add much new law to the analysis of the same issue in *Irvin*. Instead, the Court agreed to hear Estes's claim that he had been denied due process by media coverage *during* his trial. The focal point of this complaint was the impact of television cameras on the proceeding. The *Estes* trial was one of the first such trials to be televised.

Defense counsel had objected to televising the trial, as well as to radio broadcasting and news photography. The judge held a hearing on this defense motion, which was itself the subject of massive publicity. He then denied the motion, attempting instead to supply rules to prevent the media from disrupting the proceedings.

In the trial courtroom, the presence of the reporters and cameras led to what a majority of Supreme Court Justices described as a "carnival atmosphere," even before the judge had ruled on whether the cameras were to be permitted. According to a newspaper account of the September 24 hearing on whether to allow televised proceedings, "a television motor van, big as an intercontinental bus, was parked outside the courthouse and the second-floor courtroom was a forest of equipment. Two television cameras had been set up inside the bar and four more marked cameras were aligned just outside the gates. . . . Cables and wires snaked over the floor."[170] As defense counsel argued his motion to exclude cameras, "a cameraman wandered behind the judge's bench and snapped his picture."

In his order allowing the televising of the proceedings, the trial judge set out specific rules designed to limit the intrusiveness of the cameras. A booth was constructed at the back of the courtroom, painted to blend in with the rest of the courtroom, to house television cameras and newsreel photographers. The booth had an aperture for the lens of the camera. As one reporter put it, the "snouts" of four television cameras protruded through an opening of the booth. Four television cameras, representing three major networks and a local station, were permitted, and their film was made available to other stations on a pooled basis. As a result of restrictions imposed by the judge, only the prosecution's opening and closing arguments and the jury's return of its verdict were broadcast live with sound. Videotaping without sound was permitted during testimony, and the cameras filmed intermittently to prepare footage to be shown during newscasts. As defense counsel requested, the trial judge prohibited any coverage of defense summations. Cameras were required to be noiseless, and the use of flood lights or flash bulbs was prohibited. Microphones were not permitted to intrude on conversations between Estes and his lawyers. Witnesses and jurors were permitted to ask not to be televised, although in practice none made such a request. As a result, live telecasting of the trial was limited but film clips were frequently shown, with commentary added, during regularly scheduled news programs. On one night, videotapes of the September hearing on whether to allow cameras in the courtroom were rebroadcast on television in the time slot of the "late movie."

In the Supreme Court, the trial court's decision to allow cameras in the courtroom unleashed the most extensive debate about the nature of a public trial the Court had yet held. Estes did not assert a Sixth Amendment right to a public trial, but rather opposed the overly public nature of the proceeding on due process grounds, setting up a classic fair trial–free press conflict. Four dissenting Justices, Potter Stewart, Hugo Black, William Brennan, and Byron White, argued that Estes had not been denied due process by this coverage of his trial. Under Texas law, they noted, the jurors were sequestered, and thus could not have been exposed to any telecasts or pictures of anything that happened during the trial. The jurors were not permitted to watch television at all, except for one occasion on which a portable television was brought in so that the jurors could watch election returns for a circumscribed period of time. And the jurors received only newspapers which had been purged of all references to the trial. Thus, unlike the situation in *Irvin*, the jurors could not have been affected by the content of the contested publicity.

A majority of the Court nevertheless reversed Estes's conviction on finding that the very presence of the cameras had presumptively prejudiced his ability to receive a fair trial. Justice Tom Clark, who had written the majority opinion in *Irvin*, acknowledged that ordinarily, in a due process claim, "we require a showing of identifiable prejudice to the accused. . . . Nevertheless, at times a procedure employed by the State involves such a probability that prejudice will result that it is deemed inherently lacking in due process." Clark then went on to list possible sources of prejudice to a defendant that televising trials might engender. First, there might be an impact on jurors, the "nerve center of the fact-finding process." Even if the jurors are sequestered and cannot watch the filmed product of the cameras, a trial assumes a different status once it is televised, Clark maintained. Jurors aware of the fact that a trial has been selected for broadcasting will, like other members of the community, carry with them the knowledge that the trial is a *cause celebre,* because the economics of the entertainment business will dictate that only notorious trials will be broadcast. In addition to feeling the impact of their awareness of the special nature of a televised trial, jurors might also feel more obligated to return a guilty verdict when they know that their neighbors have been following all the morbid details of the case and probably believe that the defendant is guilty and should be punished. Thus, Clark reasoned, even if the jurors are not actually infected by the content of prejudicial publicity, the act of publicizing itself may create a bias toward conviction because jurors may anticipate difficulty in explaining a vote for acquittal to their friends and neighbors. In addition, the jurors might be distracted by the mere presence of the television cameras. Furthermore, in the majority of states, where juries are not sequestered, jurors might be exposed to prejudicial and extrajudicial material because of publicity.[171] Finally, retrials would be jeopardized because potential jurors would have been exposed to the prejudicial publicity unleashed during the coverage of the first trial, and so it would be difficult to garner an untainted jury if a retrial were to become necessary—either after a hung jury or other form of mistrial, or if the defendant's conviction were to be reversed on appeal.

Next, the Court outlined ways in which televising a trial might adversely affect the trial testimony. Witnesses, on becoming aware that they are being televised, might react in any one of a number of unpredictable ways. "Some may become demoralized and frightened, some cocky and given to overstatement; memories may falter, as with anyone speaking publicly, and accuracy of statement may be severely undermined." Witnesses, who are not sequestered, might be approached on the street by cranks or busybodies who critique their testimony. Because they are not sequestered, witnesses, even in the face of admonitions by the trial judge, could watch coverage of the trial at home and might be tempted to tailor their testimony in light of what they heard—perhaps to make their own testimony more important. The traditional exclusion of witnesses from the courtroom during testimony becomes ineffectual if the courtroom is expanded to the witnesses' living rooms. Finally, the fact that a proceeding is being televised might make a prospective witness more reluctant to testify at all, whether because of shyness or fear of adverse public reaction to their testimony.

The trial judge was also portrayed as susceptible to the influence of the television cameras. The judge might be distracted from the key job of running a fair trial by the necessity of supervising the cameras, or by self-consciousness about his or her own appearance on television. Judges who are elected, as was the case in the majority of states at the time of the *Estes* decision, would be particularly vulnerable to a desire to play to the crowd with respect to their trial rulings and even with respect to deciding whether to permit cameras in the courtroom. Clark hypothesized that where one judge in a state that elects judges permits broadcasting of trials she or he is supervising, another judge will probably feel compelled to follow suit to gain approval of the electorate.

The Court then listed the possible adverse effects of television coverage on the defendant. The camera's presence is "a form of mental—if not physical—harassment, resembling a police line-up or the third degree." Close-ups might invade a defendant's privacy, affect his sense of dignity, undermine his ability to concentrate on the proceedings against him, and deprive him of effective assistance of counsel by intruding into the confidential attorney-client relationship. The cameras might also compromise the defendant's prospects of fair adjudication by infecting the defense attorney, like the prosecutor, judge, jurors, or witnesses, with a desire to "play to the public audience."

All of these possible consequences of televising trials were speculative, as Clark acknowledged. "There is little wonder that the defendant cannot 'prove' the existence of such factors. Yet we all know from experience that they exist." The majority's willingness to deviate from the usual rule of requiring a defendant to prove prejudice and instead to presume prejudice based on these speculative effects was clearly based on the view of the Sixth Amendment right to public trial that Clark, on behalf of four Justices, espoused. "A defendant on trial for a specific crime is entitled to his day in court, not in a stadium, or a city or nationwide arena." The purpose of a public trial, said Clark, was to guarantee that the accused would be fairly dealt with and not unjustly condemned. Because the cameras might actually detract from this goal, the Sixth Amendment public trial right, which is the right of the accused, could not provide a basis for the press to argue a right to use cameras in a courtroom. And so the defendant's right to a fair trial did not conflict with the right to a public trial, as the latter right was deemed to be only an instrument to serve the former.

The majority also concluded, in a brief discussion, that the First Amendment did not confer a right for the media to televise from the courtroom. The freedom of the press to inform the citizenry about public events, including judicial proceedings, must "necessarily be subject to the maintenance of absolute fairness in the judicial process." Thus, according to the Court's account, the First Amendment freedom of the press did not conflict with defendants' interests—that freedom simply did not exist if the defendant was prejudiced, as he presumptively was here. The Court made no attempt to impose a typical First Amendment balancing test in evaluating the media's claim, although that approach might have tipped the balance toward the media in the absence of any proof that the defendant had actually been prejudiced.

The Court then hedged its holding by confining it to the current state of the media arts. "When the advances in these arts permit reporting by printing press or by television without their present hazards to a fair trial we will have another case."

As in *Oliver*, the Court's decision was made easier by the fact that virtually every other state disagreed, at that time, with the choice made by the Texas trial court here. When the *Estes* decision was written, only two states allowed televising or photographing of a criminal trial.[172]

Chief Justice Warren, in a concurring opinion joined by Justices William Douglas and Arthur Goldberg, supported the Court's decision to make a "definitive appraisal" of television in the courtroom, in this case, by articulating his own narrow view of the focus of the Sixth Amendment right to a public trial. "Trial," said Warren, is a term of art with an identifiable meaning, and that meaning includes an atmosphere of calm and dignity. The criminal trial has only one purpose, he maintained, and that purpose is to provide a fair and reliable determination of guilt. Televising trials detracts from that proper purpose in that it has an inevitable impact on all the trial participants, and also gives the public the wrong impression about the purpose of trials, thereby detracting from the dignity of court proceedings and lessening the reliability of trials.

Warren recounted the history of public trials in early frontier America, deploring the fact that "the entertainment a trial might provide often tended to obfuscate its proper role." Before the days of television, criminal trials were the "theater" of old rural America.[173] "I had thought," said Warren, that "these days of frontier justice were long behind us, but the courts below would return the theater to the courtroom."

It was important to Warren that the theater and the courtroom remain two distinct venues, with distinct purposes. He talked about the wave of horror that had met Fidel Castro's decision to conduct prosecutions before an audience of 18,000 in Havana Stadium. He hypothesized that if trials were publicized, the public would equate trials with other subjects of television coverage, leading them to disrespect the justice system. Furthermore, he warned that the public might attribute shortcomings of the television industry to the trial process itself. He even warned that television's attempt to rig quiz shows could be replicated as to trials, which might be fixed with an eye toward improving the ratings.

"The function of a trial is not to provide an educational experience; and there is a serious danger that any attempt to use a trial as an educational tool will both divert it from its proper purpose and lead to suspicions concerning the integrity of the trial process." Here, Warren used another cold war horror story—the Soviet Union's "show trial" of alleged spy Francis Gary Powers. The Soviet legal system, he wrote, unlike ours, uses the trial and indeed the very safeguards of justice themselves as "instruments of the social and political objectives of the state."

Toward the end of his opinion, Warren announced that his opinion was not inconsistent with the Sixth Amendment right to a public trial, which had as its purpose safeguarding against any attempt to employ our courts as instruments of persecution. The right to a public trial is "a necessary component of an accused's right to a fair trial and the concept of a public trial cannot be used to defend conditions which prevent the trial process from providing a fair and reliable determination of guilt." Warren did not say whether the ease with which he could find the Sixth Amendment right satisfied was contingent on the fact that Estes himself, far from invoking that right, had objected to the extent of the publicity surrounding his case. Warren did assert, however, that "the publicity of trial proceedings is not an end in itself."

Justice John Harlan wrote a separate concurring opinion, agreeing with Warren and the majority that "the right of 'public trial' is not a right belonging to the public, but an instrumental right belonging to the accused. . . . A fair trial is the objective, and 'public trial' is an institutional safeguard for attaining it." According to Harlan, no particular member of the press or public has a right to attend, no less publicize, a trial. "Attendance by interested spectators in the courtroom will fully satisfy the safeguards of 'public trial.' " The public trial guarantee is obviously not violated, he reasoned, if an individual member of the public cannot attend a trial because there are not enough seats in the courtroom. "The guarantee will already have been met, for the 'public' will be present in the form of those persons who did gain admission." In other words, members of the public attending a trial are representative, in the same way that jurors are representative of the public, and are included only to promote the interests of the defendant in receiving a fair trial. Harlan argued that no additional relevant function would be served by expanding the size of the audience. "[T]he addition of masses of spectators would, I venture to say, detract rather than add to the reliability of the process."

Like Warren, Harlan also discounted the public education function of the public trial right, although his conclusion, unlike Warren's, was limited to notorious cases. "Whatever force such arguments might have in run-of-the-mill cases, they carry little weight in cases of the sort before us, where the public's interest in viewing the trial is likely to be engendered more by curiosity about the personality of the well-known figure who is the defendant (as here), or about famous witnesses or lawyers who will appear on the television screen, or about the details of the particular crime involved, than by innate curiosity to learn about the workings of the judicial process itself."

Harlan's analysis of how television in particular, and publicity in general, work in a highly notorious case became important because his was the fifth vote for the majority's conclusion that television presumptively denies due process, and his rationale was more limited than that of the other four Justices in the majority. Because the *Estes* trial was so sensational and heavily publicized, and because of his customary attentiveness to the dictates of federalism,[174] Harlan "put aside all other types of cases." Harlan was not willing to say that he would draw a distinction in the scope of permissible coverage based on the notoriety of the case involved, but wished, unlike the four Justices voting with him to reverse Estes's conviction, to defer the question of whether such a line was feasible until a case arose that was more routine. In the *Estes* case, he argued, the potential for prejudice was severe because of the nature of the case and, on the other side of the balance, the interesting and credible "policy" arguments the press made as to why television coverage of the trial would serve the public interest were, to him, not arguments of constitutional dimension. The possibilities for prejudice, he suggested, might be fewer in a less notorious case, and therefore might not rise to constitutional proportions. "[T]he Court should proceed only step by step in this unplowed field. The opinion of the Court necessarily goes no farther, for only the four members of the majority who unreservedly join the Court's opinion would resolve those questions now."

The significance of Harlan's qualification was underscored by dissenting Justice William Brennan, who wrote a separate opinion for the sole purpose of emphasizing that Harlan's limiting concurrence rendered Justice Clark's opinion a four-Justice plurality and not, as the opinion described itself, a majority opinion of the Court. "[T]oday's decision is *not* a blanket constitutional prohibition against the televising of state criminal trials." It would be fifteen years before the Court revisited the issue and agreed with Harlan and Brennan's characterization of *Estes*, opening the door of some courtrooms to television cameras.

Potter Stewart, in his dissent on behalf of four Justices, including Justice Brennan, would not have declared any rule at all. While concerned that the introduction of television into a courtroom was unwise, at least in the "present state of the art," he did not believe that anything unconstitutional had happened to Estes, and declared himself unwilling to "escalate this personal view into a *per se* constitutional rule." "I cannot say at this time that it is impossible to have a constitutional trial whenever any part of the proceedings is televised or recorded on television film." Stewart declared himself troubled by "intimations" in the opinions filed by the Justices in the majority "disturbingly alien to the First and Fourteenth Amendments' guarantees against federal or state interference with the free communication of information and ideas."

Of course, Stewart's conclusion that free expression rights were being improperly limited was contingent on his own conclusion that Estes had not been denied a fair trial. Conversely, the majority's conclusion that Estes had been denied a fair trial through presumptive prejudice was contingent on its assumption that no freedom protected by the First Amendment was actually at stake. The First Amendment, the issue not formally raised in *Estes*, was clearly identified as a battleground for future cases.

Sheppard v. Maxwell—Applying *Irvin* and *Estes*

One year later, the Court selected another infamous case for a full hearing. The Supreme Court decision reversing the murder conviction of Dr. Sam Sheppard did not really make any new law, but the facts were riveting. Dr. Sheppard, the model for the television show and movie *The Fugitive*, claimed that his pregnant wife had been bludgeoned to death by an intruder in the upstairs bedroom of the Sheppards' suburban home. In his own nightmarish account, he had struggled with the intruder, was struck on the back of the neck and rendered unconscious, regained consciousness to find his wife dead, chased the intruder to the lake shore and again grappled with the intruder who again left him unconscious, this time with his body partly submerged in the lake. The Cleveland police constructed a different account of Marilyn Sheppard's murder—that her husband was the killer and had invented the story of the mysterious intruder. Ever since Dr. Sheppard's conviction, his guilt or innocence has been debated.[175] In the publicity before his trial, Dr. Sheppard was generally portrayed as a murderer and adulterer.

When Sheppard's trial began, all prospective jurors but one testified at the voir dire (jury selection) that they had heard about the case through newspaper or broadcast coverage. Intense anti-Sheppard coverage continued, according to Justice Clark's account for an eight-member majority of the Court, throughout the trial, and resulted in some outrageous incidents detailed in Clark's opinion.

As in *Irvin*, the Court made the requisite remarks about the value of public trials, followed by the maxim that such publicity could not be permitted to deny a defendant a fair trial. As in *Estes*, the Court did not require the defendant to prove that the publicity surrounding his trial had adversely affected the fairness of the proceeding. The totality of circumstances in this case, the Court announced, warranted taking the approach of *Estes*, because the law "has always endeavored to prevent even the probability of unfairness." The "Roman carnival" atmosphere of the trial was described as even more sensationalistic than the *Estes* trial. As one judge had remarked, "[m]urder and mystery, society, sex and suspense were combined in this case in such a manner as to intrigue and captivate the public fancy to a degree perhaps unparalleled in recent annals" (quoting the Ohio Supreme Court in State v. Sheppard, 1956).

The Supreme Court shied away from considering the question of "what sanctions might be available against a recalcitrant press," following their practice in *Irvin* of deflecting the issue of what to do about the "poisoners" rather than the *Estes* approach of setting out prophylactic rules. Instead, the Court focused on failure of the trial judge to control the press coverage as the basis for the reversal of Sheppard's conviction. The Court described its holding in *Estes* as requiring the trial judge to restrict the press when it is apparent that the accused might otherwise be prejudiced or disadvantaged, and suggested various measures the trial court might have taken to minimize the possibilities of prejudice.[176]

It is notable that Sheppard's petition, for a writ of habeas corpus, was not heard by the Court until twelve years after his trial. The Court, in its final paragraphs, provided some explanation of why the Justices had decided to hear the provocative Sheppard case when what was at stake seemed to be only Sheppard's fate and not any significant new issues of constitutional law. "From the cases coming here we note that unfair and prejudicial news comment on pending trials has become increasingly prevalent. . . . The trial courts must take strong measures to ensure that the balance is never weighed against the accused. . . . Reversals are but palliatives; the cure lies in those remedial measures that will prevent the prejudice at its inception. . . . Collaboration between counsel and the press as to information affecting the fairness of a criminal trial is not only subject to regulation, but is highly censurable and worthy of disciplinary measures." In this statement, the Court seemed to be announcing that it could not hope to solve the problem of prejudicial publicity by after-the-fact reversals. Thus, the Court identified the trial judges as the first line of defense.[177]

Justice Hugo Black dissented, without opinion. One can only speculate whether he was becoming concerned about the undeclared boundaries of the First Amendment.

Murphy v. Florida—The Tide Turns

As if to confirm its delegation of the problem of prejudicial publicity to the lower courts, the Supreme Court granted *certiorari* to hear about another case of an allegedly unfair trial nine years later, but declined to reverse the petitioner's conviction. Jack Murphy, another notorious defendant, had become famous for taking part in a cinema-worthy theft of the Star of India sapphire from a New York museum, as well as for his flamboyant lifestyle. The newspapers dubbed him "Murph the Surf" and covered his exploits even before he was tried for the robbery of a Miami Beach home. Like Irvin and Sheppard before him, Murphy submitted volumes of press clippings and raised a particular claim about how the jurors in his trial might have been affected by the publicity: the jurors had been exposed to information, inadmissible at trial, about Murphy's prior felony convictions. Justice Thurgood Marshall, writing for eight members of the Court, was not impressed. The reasons given by the Court for presuming prejudice in *Estes* and *Sheppard*—the presence of television cameras in the courtroom in the former, and the overwhelming amount of publicity in the latter—were found not to apply in this case. And so this state court defendant was required to demonstrate, under the totality of the circumstances, that his trial was unfair. According to the Court's analysis of the record, the jurors who had been aware of Murphy's prior conviction had not been influenced by their knowledge of it. "Indeed, four of the six jurors volunteered their views of its irrelevance, and one suggested that people who have been in trouble before are too often singled out for suspicion of each new crime—a predisposition that could only operate in petitioner's favor."

The Court's opinion features a close examination of the facts, particularly of statements made during voir dire. The decision not to reverse Murphy's conviction, however, may have been effectively made when the Court decided not to presume prejudice, which may not have been any easier to prove in this context than in *Estes*.

Justice William Brennan, dissenting, thought the case was like *Irvin* and *Sheppard*—both in the risk that the prejudicial publicity had infected the trial and in the failure of the trial judge to insulate the jurors from prejudicial material. Brennan described the facts quite differently from the majority, observing that at least one juror had admitted his predisposition to convict Murphy, even if others had denied any such predisposition. According to Brennan, "the risk that taint of widespread publicity regarding [Murphy's] criminal background, known to all members of the jury, infected the jury's deliberations is apparent, the trial court made no attempt to prevent discussion of the case or petitioner's previous criminal exploits among the prospective jurors, and one juror freely admitted that he was predisposed to convict petitioner."

After the *Murphy* case, the Court only rarely agreed to hear a prejudicial publicity claim. Having set out a few rules—providing a standard of review in *Irvin* (whether the totality of circumstances showed the jurors could not be impartial) and a heightened standard presuming prejudice in cases involving television coverage, in *Estes*—the Court seemed content, for the most part, to leave it to the lower federal and state courts to determine whether each individual claim of prejudice was more like *Irvin* and *Sheppard*, warranting a presumption of prejudice or reversal, or more like *Murphy*, in which prejudice was not presumed and not deemed proven. In the few cases in which the Court did agree to hear a case about the impact of publicity on a jury, its rulings followed the pattern set in *Murphy*. In Patton v. Yount (1984), for example, the Court refused to reverse a murder conviction on the ground that the jury was not impartial, relying on the statement in Irvin v. Dowd that the trial court's findings of juror impartiality should be reversed only for "manifest error." The Court also added to the law by ruling that a lapse of time—four years in this case—between the bulk of the publicity and petitioner's retrial served to rebut any presumption of partiality or prejudice that might have existed at the time of the initial trial.[178] And in the 1991 case of Mu'Min v. Virginia, a sharply divided Court again declined to second-guess a trial judge's conduct of voir dire in a case involving massive and hostile pretrial publicity.[179] Justice Frankfurter's description of the Court as not hearing such cases, despite their proliferation, for "one reason or another" no longer seemed apt. A majority of the Court seemed to have settled on one particular reason for declining to hear such cases: avoiding the problems generated by publicity surrounding a trial was the job of the trial judge, under the general rules the Supreme Court had already sketched out, and monitoring the exercise of the trial courts' discretion was the job of lower state and appellate courts. Future prejudicial pretrial publicity cases would be regarded as cases about facts, not law.

The substantial legal issues the Court had left open—the extent to which the First Amendment might play a role in decisions about press coverage of trials, the question of whether defendants' objection to press coverage was relevant, and Justice Frankfurter's question of whether any other limitations might be imposed on "the poisoners" themselves—remained open for the Supreme Court to decide.

Gannett Co., Inc. v. DePasquale—Attendance at Pretrial Proceedings

In almost all of the Supreme Court cases to follow, the defendant in the criminal proceeding at issue objected to the presence of the press or public at the trial or related proceedings. Thus, the Court was finally forced to consider whether anyone other than the defendant enjoyed a right to public trial, either under the Sixth or First Amendments, and to consider the relevance of the fact that a defendant, and sometimes all of the parties to the criminal proceeding, wanted the proceedings closed. Usually, the argument for closure was that closure was the only fully effective way to prevent publicity that might compromise the defendant's prospect of receiving a fair trial. Sometimes the countervailing interests involved were not those of the defendant, but the defendant nevertheless favored or at least did not oppose closed proceedings.

In Gannett Co., Inc. v. DePasquale (1979) the Supreme Court considered the right of the press to attend a suppression hearing when the defendants, without opposition from the prosecutor, had asked that the proceeding be closed. The trial, in Seneca County, New York, was for the murder of a man who had disappeared while fishing. As the Court recounted, the press had been fully covering the victim's disappearance, the decision of the police to focus on two particular suspects (Greathouse and Jones) who had gone fishing with the victim on the same morning as his disappearance, and various other developments in the case. The press reported, for instance, that Greathouse had led the police to a gun that had belonged to the victim, and that the police had also found ammunition at a motel where Greathouse was believed to have been staying before his arrest. The theory of the case developed by the police and reported by the press was that Greathouse and Jones had taken the victim out in his boat, robbed him, and then shot him with his own gun.

The defendants filed pretrial motions to suppress physical evidence the police had obtained, including the gun, and statements they had made to the police, on the ground that this evidence had been unconstitutionally obtained. It was at the beginning of the hearing scheduled on this motion to suppress that the defense made the motion to close the proceeding, arguing that the unabated buildup of adverse publicity had already jeopardized the ability of the defendants to receive a fair trial. The judge granted the motion. A reporter employed by Gannett newspapers who was present in the courtroom to cover the hearing did not object to the closure order at that time.

The following day, the reporter wrote a letter to the trial judge asserting a right to cover the suppression hearing and to be given a transcript of what had occurred while she had been excluded from the courtroom. The trial judge responded on that same day that the hearing was already over and that he was reserving decision on whether to release the transcript of the hearing. The judge then held a hearing on the press motion to set aside his exclusionary order. He concluded that the press did have a constitutional right to attend the proceeding but that right was outweighed by the defendants' right to a fair trial. That decision was reversed on appeal, by the New York Appellate Division, and then reversed again by the New York Court of Appeals, which agreed with the trial judge's reasoning and result.

Shortly before the entry of judgment by the Appellate Division, the defendants entered a plea bargain and pleaded guilty. After that resolution of the criminal charges, the newspaper petitioners were offered the transcript of the suppression hearing. Both the New York Court of Appeals and the U.S. Supreme Court decided, however, not to treat the case as moot.[180]

Justice Potter Stewart, writing for five Justices (and for only four on some issues, as will be discussed), began by focusing on the prejudicial publicity cases, including *Sheppard* and *Irvin*, stressing the obligation the Court had placed upon trial judges to minimize the effects of prejudicial pretrial publicity. Next, the Court stressed the special risks of unfairness that could be posed by coverage of a hearing on a motion to suppress. The point of such hearings is to determine whether evidence should be withheld from the jury because it is unreliable or unconstitutionally obtained, he noted. Publicity could well disclose inflammatory inadmissible evidence to potential jurors. Furthermore, the Court noted, reciting what the Justices might have learned from their experiences with prejudicial publicity cases, it may be difficult to measure with any degree of certainty the effects of such publicity on the fairness of a trial. Information publicized during a trial, the Court noted, may be kept from the jurors by a variety of means (including sequestration, as in *Estes*). But such measures are not possible pretrial.[181]

Even before analyzing the constitutional rights involved, the Court hastened to note that the fact that it was upholding the trial judge's decision to close the pretrial hearing, in this case, did not mean that failure to close a pretrial hearing or to take other protective measures to minimize the impact of prejudicial publicity "will warrant the extreme remedy of reversal of a conviction." It is precisely because reversal is such an extreme remedy, said Justice Stewart, that "our criminal justice system permits, and even encourages, trial judges to be overcautious in ensuring that a defendant will receive a fair trial. . . . And because of the Constitution's pervasive concern for these due process rights, a trial judge may surely take protective measures even when they are not strictly and inescapably necessary." *Gannett* was a relatively easy case for the Court, first, because the Court was upholding the trial judge's exercise of discretion; second, because the procedural context meant that it was unnecessary to reverse any conviction to uphold a defendant's fair trial rights in this case; third, because the defendants themselves had made the choice to trade one of their constitutionally protected interests—in public attendance—for another—in a fair proceeding untainted by prejudicial publicity; and, fourth, because both the prosecutor and trial judge had agreed to the defendants' choice.

In his broad language and interpretation of the Sixth Amendment, Justice Stewart placed a heavy thumb on the scale on the side of even "overcautious" closure of proceedings rather than of open process. As to the question of whether the press had a constitutional right to attend the suppression hearing, as the trial judge and New York Court of Appeals had found, the Court first eliminated the Sixth

Amendment right to a public trial as a possible basis of such a claim of right. The Sixth Amendment guarantees the right to a public trial, among its other rights, "to a person charged with the commission of a criminal offense, and to him alone." The purpose of the right, as the Court had explained in *Oliver,* is to provide the defendant a safeguard against possible abuse of judicial power. So although the Court had also recognized that the right provides various "benefits" to the public, no one but the criminal defendant has a right under the Sixth Amendment to insist on a public proceeding. The public has an "interest" in public trial, just as it does in speedy trial, and in jury trial. But, the Court said, recognition of such "interests" is a far cry from the creation of a constitutional right on the part of the public. Members of the public certainly could not insist that a defendant have a jury trial or that the court deny a continuance when the parties to the litigation had agreed to a judge trial or to delaying the trial. The public interest, the Court said "is fully protected by the participants in the litigation," particularly because the prosecutor is a representative of the public.

Gannett does not decide what range of interests the Sixth Amendment should be deemed to protect. The case only required the Court to decide whether or not the public or press have standing to raise a Sixth Amendment claim, a question the Court very clearly answered in the negative. Members of the public may not "insist on" a public trial on the basis of the Sixth Amendment; the parties to the litigation will adequately represent their interests in open proceedings. It is less clear whether *Gannett* should be read as going beyond this standing decision to interpret the substance of the Sixth Amendment right as "belonging" to the defendant in the broader sense that the only functions it will be deemed to serve are those related to the defendant's own interests. After *Gannett*, it may still be the case that the defendant, if invoking his right to an open trial under the Sixth Amendment, may also "protect" the interests of the public by arguing that the Sixth Amendment serves a broader range of functions than merely those benefiting that defendant.[182] Defendants frequently raise Sixth Amendment claims in the context of appealing a conviction, and so the broader the interpretation of the Sixth Amendment's functions, the greater the defendant's chance of winning a reversal if all or part of a trial has been closed. Appellate courts are likely to be reluctant to reverse a defendant's conviction because some members of the public have not been afforded their opportunity to educate themselves about the criminal justice system. If the *Gannett* Court's decision made criminal defendants the exclusive representatives of the public's interests, those interests could safely be ignored by trial judges were it not for the Court's subsequent finding of a public right of access under the First Amendment.

The *Gannett* Court, however, also decided that the Sixth Amendment right is not under the exclusive control of criminal defendants. The Court announced that defendants will not have the power to choose whether a proceeding will be open or closed. The right to a public trial does not include the converse right to compel a private trial. The Court resolved this issue with a one-sentence reference to the case of Singer v. United States (1965), in which the Court had held that the

Sixth Amendment right to trial by jury does not give defendants the converse right to waive a jury and be tried by a judge. The court did not note that jury trial, unlike public trial, is explicitly guaranteed in Article III, whose provisions address the structure of government rather than the rights of a criminal defendant.

Resolving this issue was unnecessary in deciding the *Gannett* case because, as the Court went on to say, the question in this case was whether members of the public or press had a right to attend criminal proceedings. These claims could be asserted independently of the parties in the litigation even in a case, like this one, in which all of the parties to the proceeding—the defendants, the prosecutor, and the trial judge—had agreed to closure of the proceeding. The Court's intention seems to have been to limit its holding by declaring that the defendant has no unilateral veto on open proceedings, but concurring Justice Rehnquist read the opinion as providing that the parties can decide to close a proceeding. *Singer* held that it was constitutional for a federal rule to allow the prosecutor to veto a defendant's choice to waive a jury, but did not suggest that the trial judge could reject a joint decision by the defendant and prosecutor to have a non-jury trial. *Gannett* certainly leaves room for a trial judge to rule against a defense request for closure after hearing the prosecutor's dissenting view. But the Court does not say whether the trial judge may rule against such a defense request if the prosecutor has concurred. Can an appellate court reverse that decision— even in a case like this one, in which the trial judge agreed with the defendant and prosecutor—on concluding (as the dissenting Justices would have in *Gannett*) that the fear of negative impact on the jury was unfounded?

The brief sentence and reference to *Singer* also do not explain what standard a trial judge should apply if the defendant and prosecutor disagree. In such a case, must the trial judge assess independently whether the defendant's right to a fair trial would be compromised, as the trial judge did in this case? Should the judge weigh in the balance the public's interest in open proceedings, even if the prosecutor has not objected to closure on those grounds? If the standard is danger of harm to the defendant's fair trial rights, might a trial judge even be permitted to close a proceeding over the defendant's objection on the ground that closure is necessary to ensure a fair trial? Must the trial judge consider and employ alternative methods to avoid prejudice before resorting to closure?

It is not clear that the majority intended to go so far as to impose a per se rule that trial participants may agree on closure. Stewart did emphasize the real danger in this case that defendants might not have received a fair trial had potential jurors been exposed to evidence that was suppressed at trial. At the same time, Stewart's opinion went beyond the needs of the holding by announcing that defendants would have no right to compel closure in cases in which the prosecutor and trial judge do not agree with the defendant's apprehensions.

The fact that the Court had now ruled that there was no public right to attend proceedings under the Sixth Amendment, or at least that the public had no standing to assert such a right, would affect all such future decisions. The majority's approach to interpreting the scope of the Sixth Amendment right focused on the language and structure of the Sixth Amendment more than on history. The petitioner had argued that historically, at common law, both civil and criminal trials had been open. The majority rejected this argument, stating that most common law rules were neither made part of the Constitution nor rejected by it. In either event, the majority said, even at common law, the right the Sixth Amendment describes would not have covered pretrial proceedings. Experience in the states was described as following the same pattern.

The Court was, once again, less anxious to resolve the question of whether the First Amendment should be interpreted as conferring a right to attend judicial proceedings on the public and press. The Court assumed *arguendo* that there is such a right and found that the trial judge had given appropriate deference to any First Amendment right of access that might exist.

Stewart's opinion drew several concurrences that cast the scope of some aspects of the Court's holding in considerable doubt. The first concurring opinion, by Chief Justice Warren Burger, emphasized the importance of the fact that the hearing in question was a pretrial proceeding and not a trial, and therefore was not covered by the language of the Sixth Amendment. In his view, *Gannett*'s interpretation of the Sixth Amendment public trial right was purely dicta.

In a second concurrence, Justice Lewis Powell argued that the Court should have taken on the question it ducked, and should have ruled once and for all that there is, as he believed, a First Amendment right of public and press access to courtroom proceedings, albeit a limited one. The author of the third concurring opinion, William Rehnquist, agreed with Powell that the Court should have addressed the First Amendment issue but, unlike Powell, would have held that no First Amendment right of access to judicial proceedings exists. Rehnquist also, as described above, deplored the majority's mention of the danger that prejudicial publicity might harm the defendant, which he did not believe was relevant to the holding of the case. He asserted that because a majority of the Court had held that the Sixth Amendment right to a public trial belongs only to the defendant and not to the press or public, if there is no First Amendment public or press right to attend judicial proceedings, as he believed, then not only pretrial proceedings but criminal trials themselves could be closed on agreement of the parties.

Justice Powell's opinion took issue with Rehnquist's assertion that the *Gannett* decision afforded trial judges discretion to close proceedings whenever the parties concurred, observing that he, as the fifth vote in the majority, agreed with the four dissenters that the public and press do have a constitutional interest in open proceedings (although he disagreed with them about its source), and that therefore five Justices believed that there must be judicially enforceable limitations on when proceedings can be closed. Trial courts must balance the wishes and interests of the parties with the interests of the public. Rehnquist, in turn, disagreed with Powell's jurisprudential mathematics, asserting that it was not proper to add the four dissenters to Powell's different rationale to create an alternative majority rationale. If Powell's approach of adding and subtracting votes is followed, Chief Justice Burger's limiting concurrence similarly casts doubt on Rehnquist's assertion that

Gannett permits closure of trials as well as pretrial proceedings on agreement of the parties. Burger can also be counted as a necessary fifth vote for the majority, and his reliance on the fact that the suppression hearing was a pretrial proceeding would also circumscribe the Court's holding.

In light of these limiting concurring opinions, it is unclear how far the holding of *Gannett* actually goes in allowing closure of either pretrial or trial proceedings.

A dissenting opinion by Justice Harry Blackmun, joined by William Brennan, Byron White, and Thurgood Marshall, disagreed vigorously with the Stewart plurality about the scope of the Sixth Amendment public trial right. According to the dissenters, the Sixth Amendment should be read to create a presumption in favor of holding all criminal trials in public, regardless of the wishes of the parties to the litigation. Like the majority, the dissenters sidestepped the question of whether the First Amendment guarantees such a right, beginning instead with "that provision of the Constitution that speaks most directly to the question of access to judicial proceedings, namely, the public-trial provision of the Sixth Amendment." Calling Stewart's analysis of the language and structure of the Sixth Amendment "easy but wooden," the dissenters first offered a different view of the Sixth Amendment's overall structure and of previous cases interpreting other Sixth Amendment rights. Stewart had ridiculed the idea that other Sixth Amendment rights belonged to the public as well as the defendant by pointing out that the public could not force a defendant to have a jury trial if the parties to the litigation had agreed to the defendant's waiver of that right. The dissenters viewed cases like *Singer*, in which the Court held that the defendant does not have a unilateral right to waive a jury trial, as reflecting the public interest in that right. If there were no public interest in jury trials, there would be no reason for a defendant not to choose whether to be tried by a jury in the same way that the Sixth Amendment empowers the defendant to choose whether to be represented by counsel or to represent himself or herself.[183]

The Sixth Amendment's "literal terms" might refer only to the accused, the dissenters argued, but the Court's previous recognition of the public interest in fair criminal proceedings should inform interpretation of the scope of the right, especially when added to the lessons of history. The dissenters urged examination of "the common-law and colonial antecedents of the public-trial provision as well as the original understanding of the Sixth Amendment." They then appeared, however, to recognize that there is no way to discern the "original understanding of the Sixth Amendment," especially if the amendment's facially limiting language is not taken as conclusive. Stewart's opinion had drawn a sharp distinction between the "purpose" and the "uses" of public trials, disavowing the relevance of the latter in constitutional interpretation. By contrast, in the absence of any evidence about the intent of the framers, the dissenters found a basis for interpreting the Sixth Amendment in what commentators had said about the functions of public trials both before and after the Sixth Amendment was written.

The dissenters went on to quote extensively from previous Supreme Court cases, Blackstone, Hale, and numerous other sources to describe the variety of critical functions served by opening criminal proceedings to the public. The right to public trial, with its deep roots in English common law heritage as a concomitant to the right to jury trial, was described as a "feature" of the Anglo-American criminal justice system, rather than just a right of the accused. Trials in England were public long before criminal defendants were provided with other rights guaranteed by the Sixth Amendment, like the right to counsel or prior notice of the charges. Commentators like Hale and Blackstone had described the function of publicity at common law "in terms of the effectiveness of the trial process." Publicity, among other functions, was viewed as a critical check on judicial abuse. Jeremy Bentham, in describing the function of the public trial, described publicity as such an essential safeguard against judicial abuse that he believed that a defendant should not be permitted to defeat the public interest by waiving that right.

Disagreeing with the plurality's contention that the parties would adequately represent the public interest, Blackmun listed societal interests in open trial proceedings that exist separately from, and at times in opposition to, the interests of the defendant. First, publicity is a safeguard against perjured testimony, because if the public is aware of a witness's testimony, others can come forward to correct a false account. In some cases, the defendant might want a helpful but perjured account to remain unchallenged. Thus, the public interest in having a trial decided on the basis of true and complete evidence will not always be championed by the defendant (or even by the prosecutor). Second, publicity is thought to provide a safeguard against judicial bias, because the public can scrutinize the judge's behavior. But, Blackmun noted, a defendant might be the beneficiary of a judge's bias and might therefore prefer a secret trial to conceal the partiality of a corrupt, biased, or incompetent judge. Third, public trials also allow for scrutiny of the actions of other public servants: prosecutors and police. Especially in jurisdictions where judges, prosecutors, and other public officials are elected, the public has a strong interest in observing how they are performing their public duties. The prosecutor cannot be an adequate guardian of the public interest when the prosecutor might have his or her own self-interest in controlling what the public knows about a particular proceeding and his or her own performance in it.

Finally, public trials are essential to the appearance of justice. As the Third Circuit Court of Appeals, the only lower federal court to have held that the Sixth Amendment public trial right belongs, in part, to the public, had said: "Secret hearings—though they be scrupulously fair in reality—are suspect by nature. Public confidence cannot long be maintained where important judicial decisions are made behind closed doors and then announced in conclusive terms to the public, with the record supporting the court's decision sealed from public view" (quoting the Third Circuit Court of Appeals in United States v. Cianfrani, 1978). If the right to public trial is a structural provision necessary to maintaining the integrity of the criminal justice system and of citizen participation in government, then "a court may give effect to an accused's attempt to waive his public-trial right only in certain circumstances." And those circumstances are not delimited by the concurrence of the prosecutor or trial judge.

Blackmun acknowledged that the right to attend trials could not be absolute. Exceptions would have to be made for unruly spectators, who could of course be excluded. "Reasonable restrictions," like those the Court had imposed on electronic media in *Estes* and the press generally in *Sheppard*, might be warranted. And a trial court could restrict access in cases in which restrictions are "necessary in order to ensure that a defendant not be denied a fair trial as a result of prejudicial pretrial publicity." But all exceptions to the public's exercise of a constitutional right should be narrowly drawn. Thus a trial court, before closing a trial, must find that the defendant arguing for closure, first, has provided an adequate basis to support a finding that there is a substantial probability that irreparable damage to his or her fair-trial right will result from conducting the proceeding in public; second, that alternatives to closure will not adequately protect his or her right to a fair trial; and, third, that there is a substantial probability that closure will be effective in protecting against the perceived harm. Members of the public, on the other hand, should not be asked to bear any burden of demonstrating that their interest in the proceeding is respectable.

Unlike Justice Frankfurter, whose opinion in *Irvin* had described the problem of prejudicial pretrial publicity as pervasive and intractable, Blackmun declared that ordinarily, the public's right to attend proceedings and the defendant's right to a fair trial would be in harmony, because cases in which publicity compromises a trial's decorum are "relatively rare" (quoting Nebraska Press Association v. Stuart, 1976).

The other issue the dissenters had to confront was explaining why the Sixth Amendment, which refers to public "trial," should be interpreted as covering the pretrial hearing on a motion to suppress evidence. Here again, Blackmun started with a general account of history instead of the language of the amendment. While the majority had argued that English common law had not provided a right for the public to attend pretrial proceedings, Blackmun argued that no cases had ever held that the public could be excluded from pretrial proceedings. Suppression hearings were not known to English common law, and so whoever is assigned the burden of showing how history answered the question of who can attend such a proceeding would seem destined to fail. Instead of tracing the history of the suppression hearing, Blackmun provided a functional explanation for why the public should be permitted to attend suppression hearings. The suppression hearing "resembles and relates to the full trial in almost every particular," he declared. Evidence is presented through the live testimony of witnesses, determination of the issue will depend on the trier of fact's evaluation of the evidence, and credibility is crucial. The publicity that would make it possible for additional witnesses to add to or correct the existing testimony is just as necessary with respect to this proceeding. Pretrial suppression motions are often critical and even decisive in the prosecution of a criminal case. If the defendant prevails, the prosecutor may have to dismiss the case or offer the defendant a favorable deal. If the defendant loses, there may be little prospect of prevailing at trial, and so the defendant might decide to plead guilty. In either case, the hearing on the motion to suppress might be the "only judicial proceeding of substantial importance that takes place during a criminal proceeding," as happened in the case of Greathouse and Jones, who did plead guilty after the motion was decided. Blackmun went on to note that in the county where this proceeding took place, Seneca County, New York, during the year when this case occurred, not one felony prosecution had actually gone to trial. Thus, the public in this county would have had no opportunity to observe its criminal justice system in action if the right to attend criminal proceedings were confined to trials.

In addition to having the right to learn about the functioning of the court and prosecutor, Blackmun emphasized that the public also should have the opportunity to learn about the conduct of law enforcement agents, the central subject of motions to suppress evidence. Typically, suppression motions examine the propriety of the conduct of law enforcement officers in searches and seizures or in interrogations. Because such conduct does not generally take place in public, suppression hearings will usually present the only opportunity for the public to learn about and evaluate how those charged with enforcement of the law are using their powers.[184]

In light of the factors described, Blackmun concluded that pretrial suppression hearings are "the close equivalent of the trial on the merits for purposes of applying the public-trial provisions of the Sixth Amendment." Under his approach, not all pretrial proceedings would be presumptively open. A trial court would have to analyze whether the proceeding was the functional "close equivalent" of the trial on the merits. And not all proceedings, whether trial or pretrial, would actually be open, because the trial court would then have to go on to evaluate the risk to defendant's right to a fair trial and the effectiveness of alternative measures, under the weighted balancing test Blackmun advocated.

Under the majority's approach, the thumb remained on the other side of the scale, although the guidance given to trial courts about how to exercise what discretion they had was less clear.[185] But the First Amendment cases in the near future were about to eclipse much of *Gannett*'s discussion of the Sixth Amendment right to public trial and pave the way for the Court's reversal of *Gannett*'s actual holding a mere five years later.

Nixon v. Warner Communications, Inc.—The Watergate Tapes and Press Access

In Nixon v. Warner Communications, Inc. (1978), the Supreme Court ruled that the press had no right under either the First or Sixth Amendments to copy and broadcast the famed Watergate tapes. Most of the opinion is devoted to an analysis of the First Amendment claim. The Court held that although there is a common law right of access to judicial records, this right is not absolute and could be overcome by the objections of President Nixon, who was deemed to have standing to challenge the broadcasting of the tapes.

As to the Sixth Amendment, the Supreme Court assumed *arguendo* that the press had standing to raise a Sixth Amendment claim on behalf of the criminal defendants in the underlying case, despite the fact that the Court had previously held in *Estes* that there is no such standing (albeit in a case in which the defendants had already registered their decision not to invoke their right to a public trial). There is no suggestion anywhere in the Court's opinion that the Watergate defendants themselves wished the tapes to be distributed publicly and, in fact, the trial judge had expressed concern that release of the tapes might prejudice the defendants' pending appeals. Thus, the Court unnecessarily reached the Sixth Amendment claim in a case in which the perspective of the defendant was missing. On the merits, the Court's treatment of the claim was casual. The Court found that "the requirement of a public trial is satisfied by the opportunity of members of the public and the press to attend the trial and to report what they have observed." The press has no special rights, said the Court, and there is no right to broadcast either tapes played in evidence or the testimony of live witnesses. This off-handed holding prevented later criminal defendants who did wish to broadcast or videotape their own trials from doing so. The Court easily could have held that any Sixth Amendment right, had they found one to exist *arguendo*, would have been overcome by the same presidential interests that defeated the First Amendment claim, and left the question of the scope of the Sixth Amendment for a case in which the criminal defendant's own interests in open proceedings could be more fully considered.

Richmond Newspapers, Inc. v. Virginia—Enter the First Amendment

Many of the issues the Court had struggled with in *Gannett* were revisited just one year later, in Richmond Newspapers, Inc. v. Virginia (1980). The Court's divisions about the meaning of the Sixth Amendment public trial right were superseded by a discussion, at last, of the extent of a First Amendment right of the public and press to attend criminal trials. But the confusion left by *Gannett* was not wholly clarified, in part because there was no majority opinion in this new case.

As had been the case in *Gannett*, a criminal defendant made a motion for closure, the prosecutor did not object, members of the press in attendance did not immediately object, and the trial judge, without having examined the possibility of employing other means to protect defendant's right to a fair trial, granted the motion and adhered to that ruling after hearing arguments from the press. Unlike *Gannett*, however, the proceeding involved in this case was the trial itself.

Defendant Stevenson had been convicted of second-degree murder in 1975, but his conviction was reversed on appeal when the Virginia Supreme Court held that a blood-stained shirt allegedly belonging to Stevenson had been improperly admitted into evidence. A second and third trial each ended in a mistrial. It was rumored that the second mistrial might have occurred because a juror had seen a news article, published the day after the first mistrial, discussing the bloodstained shirt that had not been admitted into evidence at the second trial, and had shared that information with other jurors. As Stevenson's fourth trial was about to begin, defense counsel asked that the trial be closed "because I don't want any information being shuffled back and forth when we have a recess to what—who testified to what." The trial judge asked whether the prosecutor objected and, when there was no objection, the judge invoked a Virginia statute leaving such decisions to the discretion of the court and ordered the courtroom to be kept clear.[186] Although this trial took place before the *Gannett* decision was handed down, the trial court's actions were consistent with the majority's opinion in that case, at least as interpreted by Justice Rehnquist, because both parties had agreed to closure. Seven other members of the Court, however, now disagreed with that result.[187]

The lone dissenter, Justice Rehnquist, true to his concurring opinion in *Gannett*, thought that the parties should have been able to close the proceeding in question because they all had concurred, and that neither the Sixth nor First Amendment provided any basis for second-guessing the trial court's closure ruling. He was alone in believing that, after *Gannett,* the trial participants should be allowed to decide to close a trial.

There was no one majority opinion but many concurrences. Justice Stewart—who, as author of the *Gannett* plurality opinion, had enthusiastically supported closure of the pretrial suppression hearing and had suggested in dicta that closure of trials might also be within the discretion of the parties—voted against closure here. He said that, whatever might be the result with respect to pretrial hearings, the First Amendment (not considered by a majority of the Court in *Gannett*) afforded the press and public the right to attend *trials*, whether criminal or civil.

Justice Blackmun—who had argued futilely in his *Gannett* dissent that the Sixth Amendment provides a right for the public and press to attend trials—advocated that position again here, but he also agreed that the First Amendment provides a discrete constitutional basis for the right to attend trials even over a defendant's objection. He welcomed what he described as the Court's return to history and observed complacently that commentary on the majority opinion in *Gannett* had been generally unfavorable.

Thus, seven members of the Court agreed that a First Amendment right to attend trials exists as a possible counter to a defendant's interest in a closed trial. Chief Justice Burger's plurality opinion, joined by Justices White and Stevens, began, as had *Gannett*, by declining to find the case moot, although the trial in question had ended long before the decision. Burger then recounted the increasingly familiar story of the deep historical roots of open trials, from common law to the colonies. Seemingly answering Earl Warren's skepticism about whether the public could remain decorous in notorious cases, Burger reported that in the mid-1600s, when the Virginia Assembly worried that the decorum of the courts was threatened by the "clamorous unmannerlyness of the people," their response was not to close proceedings, but to prescribe rules for the conduct of trial attendees.

Burger's account embraced both the majority and dissenting opinions in *Gannett*: "As we have shown, and as was shown in both the Court's opinion and the dissent in *Gannett*, the historical evidence demonstrates conclusively that at the time when our organic laws were adopted, criminal trials both here and in

England had long been presumptively open." He then continued with an inclusive account of the functions served by public trial, adding to the lists in both *Gannett* opinions a general tribute to the nexus between openness and fairness or the perception of fairness, and the novel contention that public trials had significant "therapeutic" value for the community, providing an outlet for the community's concern, hostility, and emotion, and satisfying the urge to punish. Burger also related the right for representatives to attend trial to the representative nature of the jury: "when the ancient 'town meeting' form of trial became too cumbersome, 12 members of the community were delegated to act as its surrogates, but the community did not surrender its right to observe the conduct of trials. The people retained a 'right of visitation' which enabled them to satisfy themselves that justice was in fact being done." Burger spoke more tolerantly than Warren had of the public attending trials for their entertainment value, reasoning that public inclusion, in whatever form and for whatever motivation, can serve the function of educating the public and promoting confidence in the legal system.

Virginia had argued that, this history notwithstanding, the Constitution does not mention any right for the public to attend trials beyond the limited Sixth Amendment right of the accused. As the Court's opinion in *Gannett* had said, some parts of the common law were included in the Constitution, while others were not. Focusing solely on the language of the Constitution, the Court might have concluded that the Sixth Amendment's specification that the public has a right to attend criminal trials, a right the Court had just announced did not belong to the public but only to the accused, was intended to be exclusive of any other public right to attend trials. Instead, the Court found a right to attend trials in the First Amendment and the penumbra of the Bill of Rights. "The right of access to places traditionally open to the public, as criminal trials have long been, may be seen as assured by the amalgam of the First Amendment guarantees of speech and press; and their affinity to the right of assembly is not without relevance." The Court even invoked the Ninth Amendment in pointing out that, in previous cases, the enumeration of some rights in the Bill of Rights had not been taken as precluding the existence of unenumerated rights.[188]

Having concluded the task of finding a presumptive public right to attend criminal trials, the Court did not need to spend much time on the question of whether the trial court in this case had acted in dereliction of that right. *Gannett* had already established, as the Court noted, that a defendant does not have the right to close a trial at will. The trial judge here had not made any findings to support closure and had not considered whether any alternative solution would have ensured a fair trial without excluding the public. Among the possible alternatives the Court mentioned were excluding witnesses from the courtroom during the trial or sequestering the jury. "Absent an overriding interest articulated in findings, the trial of a criminal case must be open to the public."

Justice Burger went on to delineate the limits of his plurality's holding. First, the trial judge may impose reasonable time, place, and manner restrictions on members of the public and press. Second, if there is insufficient space for all the members of the public who wish to attend, preference may be given to representatives of the media. This is because, although members of the press have no rights superior to the right of the public, they may serve as representatives of the public. Finally, and most significantly, Burger noted that whether or not the right to attend trials also applies to civil proceedings was not a question raised in this case, which involved a criminal trial. "[B]ut," he hinted, "we note that historically both civil and criminal trials have been presumptively open."

A heavy thumb had been placed on the other side of the scale.

The concurring opinions stressed the common ground that most of the Justices now shared, although individual Justices did not resist snide remarks about their pitched battle in *Gannett*. The sharp disagreement in *Gannett* about the scope of the Sixth Amendment right had now been substantially mooted by the new agreement on the alternate source in the First Amendment and its penumbra. But there were still many questions open about the scope of the newly declared right, including whether the plurality opinion's approach would hold. Blackmun, while agreeing about the existence of the First Amendment right, declared the plurality's penumbral approach "troublesome." He also described the plurality's standard for analyzing when the right of access could be denied as "uncertain," noting the difference between Chief Justice Burger's declaration that an "overriding interest" was required to close a trial, Potter Stewart's declaration that "reasonable limits" could be imposed, and Lewis Powell's proposal in *Gannett*. Added to these varied models was the framework Blackmun himself had provided in his *Gannett* opinion and the distinctive approach offered by William Brennan's *Richmond Newspapers* concurrence.

Brennan's framework was provided in an opinion, joined by Thurgood Marshall, concurring only in the judgment of the Court. In his analysis, Brennan did not diverge markedly from the sources Burger had used in deriving the First Amendment right. He supported the argument for finding unenumerated rights beyond the language of the Bill of Rights: "That the Sixth Amendment explicitly establishes a public trial right does not impliedly foreclose the derivation of such a right from other provisions of the Constitution. The Constitution was not framed as a work of carpentry, in which all joins must fit snugly without overlapping." Brennan believed that the First Amendment should sometimes be interpreted as providing a right of access to government-controlled information because of that amendment's "structural role" in "securing and fostering our republican system of self-government." He compared his derivation of the right of access to trials not to the penumbral right of privacy cases declaring personal liberties like reproductive rights, but to cases inferring a right of suffrage and right of association, because those rights are "preservative of other basic civil and political rights" (quoting Reynolds v. Sims, 1964).

Because "the stretch of this protection is theoretically endless," Brennan offered a method for analyzing when the First Amendment should confer a right to gather information. "An assertion of the prerogative to gather information must accordingly be assayed by considering the information sought and the opposing interests invaded." In balancing these interests, Brennan provided two principles for courts to use, which laid the groundwork for the Court's approach in later cases. Arguments for a right of access to information have special force, first, when backed by a tradition of public access and, second, when such access has a measurable value in furthering the goals of the trial process itself. Using much of the same history Burger had used in his plurality opinion, history also familiar from the opinions in *Gannett*, Brennan retold the story of the Anglo-American tradition of open trials. His account focused on the value of public trials in educating the public, providing a public check on abuse of official power (quoting Sheppard v. Maxwell, 1966), and acting as a safeguard against the use of the courts as instruments of persecution or for "suppression of political and religious heresies" (quoting In re Oliver, 1948). The latter point provided a link to other core First Amendment values. Brennan then discussed the function of public trials, again focusing more on the role of the trial process as a feature of our governing system of justice than as a matter of individual right. To the extent that the trial process serves broad political interests beyond the interest in a fair and accurate adjudication of a defendant's guilt, trial access is of structural significance. One function of trials, with their hedge of procedural protection, is to demonstrate that our system of law is fair to all. Furthermore, because the judiciary is a coordinate branch of government, a trial, as the forum for judicial fact-finding and the initial forum for legal decision making, is a "genuine governmental proceeding." Finally, Brennan argued that public attendance at trial is an indispensable part of the trial process because it does further the public purposes of the judicial proceedings themselves. Here, he again relied on arguments familiar from discussion of the scope of the Sixth Amendment public trial right, like Blackstone's assertion that open courtrooms are conducive to truthful testimony.

In Brennan's account, as in Burger's, a constitutional right to open trials could now spring from either the First or Sixth Amendment, but the geography of these rights was not yet mapped.

Chandler v. Florida—Cameras in the Courtroom Revisited

During the next term, Chief Justice Burger again wrote an opinion for a superficially unanimous Court, lifting the *Estes* ban on television cameras at criminal trials. The only source of disagreement among the Justices was whether *Estes* had been successfully distinguished or effectively overruled. All of the Justices now on the Court agreed that the time had come to allow the states to experiment with televising trials. Considering that the only three Justices still on the Court who had taken part in *Estes* had been in dissent in that case, this about-face was not surprising.

In 1977–78, the Florida Supreme Court had permitted a one-year pilot program in which the electronic media were permitted to cover all Florida judicial proceedings, even without consent of the parties, subject to detailed standards regarding technology and the conduct of the press. By 1979, when the Florida court evaluated the success of its program, five other states had adopted rules regarding electronic coverage of trials, and ten other states, like Florida, were experimenting with electronic coverage. By November 1980, when the Supreme Court heard argument in *Chandler*, twenty states were allowing coverage of trial and appellate courts, three permitted coverage of only trial courts, six permitted coverage of only appellate courts, and twelve other states were studying the issue.

After its evaluation of the pilot program, the Florida Supreme Court promulgated revised guidelines and permitted electronic coverage of judicial proceedings subject to those guidelines. Appellant Chandler, on trial for burglarizing a well-known Miami Beach restaurant, was one of the first to have his felony trial broadcast pursuant to the new guidelines, over his objection.[189] The trial judge denied a defense motion to sequester the jury, but did instruct the jurors not to watch or read anything about the case, and urged them to avoid local news and watch only national news during the trial. A television camera filmed the voir dire (at which the prospective jurors asserted that they would not be biased by the television coverage) and then recorded one afternoon of the trial when the state presented its star witness. The cameras were not present during the defense case and returned to cover closing arguments. About three minutes of the state's case were actually broadcast.

Appellants challenged their convictions on the ground that Florida had denied them due process under *Estes*, which had declared televising trials to be a per se constitutional violation. They did not point to any specific prejudice traceable to the coverage, but relied on the conclusion of the opinion of the Court in *Estes* that, because of the inherent nature of television coverage, prejudice would be presumed. Chief Justice Burger concluded that *Estes* had not established a per se rule at all, interpreting Justice Harlan's fifth-vote concurring opinion, objecting to "what was done in this case," as limiting the reach of the majority opinion.

Thus somewhat disingenuously considering the question as one of first impression, Burger declared, like the dissenters in *Estes*, that a speculative risk of prejudice did not justify an absolute ban on broadcast coverage. Defendants would have to establish that the media coverage, in whatever form, compromised their right to a fair trial, whether because of the potential impact of the publicized information on the jurors' ability to judge them fairly, or because of the impact of the cameras themselves on the trial participants.

Estes had promised that, if circumstances changed, the Court might reevaluate its deep skepticism of cameras in the courtroom. According to Burger, much had changed in the intervening fifteen years. First, some of the physical factors, like cumbersome equipment, cables, distracting lighting, and numerous personnel, that made television coverage seem so intrusive in 1965 had been ameliorated by more sophisticated technology. Second, the experience of numerous states in their experimental programs was encouraging. Many states had experimented with particular safeguards against disruption and prejudice built into their programs and regarded these safeguards as effective. The Court noted that empirical studies undertaken to prove or disprove the speculations of the *Estes* Court were not conclusive on such issues as the psychological impact of broadcast coverage on trial participants. However, reversing the direction of the *Estes* Court, Burger thought it significant that "at present no one has been able to present empirical data sufficient to establish that the mere presence of the broadcast media inherently has an adverse effect on that process."

An amicus brief submitted by members of the defense bar argued that televising particular defendants, as Chief Justice Warren's *Estes* opinion had maintained, was an unfair form of punishment in and of itself, because defendants would be selected for such treatment according to factors having little or nothing to do with their blameworthiness. Here, too, the Court reversed the inclination of the *Estes* plurality and announced that whether or not there was merit to that argument "must also await the continuing experimentation." *Estes* had disfavored cameras in the courtroom unless it were to be shown at some future date that cameras could be prevented from affecting the fairness of the proceeding; *Chandler* allowed cameras in the absence of proof that the cameras did demonstrable harm in a particular case.

As to this particular case, appellants were found not to have made a sufficient showing to justify reversal of their convictions. "To demonstrate prejudice in a specific case a defendant must show something more than juror awareness that the trial is such as to attract the attention of broadcasters." Whether *Estes* was said to be overruled or limited, prejudice would no longer be presumed whenever television cameras were present.

Motivating the Court's relaxation of its previous constitutional ban was a renewed attention to federalism. The Court quoted Justice Louis Brandeis's famous opinion (New State Ice Co. v. Liebmann, 1932) (Brandeis, J., dissenting) lauding the ability of the states to serve as laboratories for experimentation with new procedures. The fact that so many states were now experimenting with broadcasting, when at the time of *Estes* almost no state was willing to allow cameras into its courtrooms, encouraged the Court to leave the matter to the states, with the Court playing a backup role if any of the state experiments compromised a defendant's right to a fair trial. "It is not necessary either to ignore or to discount the potential danger to the fairness of a trial in a particular case to conclude that Florida may permit the electronic media to cover trials in its state courts. Dangers lurk. . . ." Chief Justice Burger expressed confidence that the states would remain alert to any problems and opined that there would be time enough to remedy unfairness if it actually occurred in a particular case. In the absence of such a showing in this case, the Court described itself as neither endorsing nor invalidating Florida's program.[190]

One point on which the majority did continue to agree with *Estes* was that the media have no First Amendment right to broadcast judicial proceedings. So even after *Richmond Newspapers* had found a First Amendment right of access to judicial proceedings, the manner of access was not considered to be of constitutional import. Nevertheless, the general public right of access declared in *Richmond Newspapers* was magnified by the new possibility of televising trials. Even if the recently declared First Amendment right of access did not play any explicit role in the *Chandler* opinion, the trend of the Court's decision, expanding the ability of the public to observe criminal trials, was consistent with the impetus that had led to recognition of the First Amendment right—public participation in and comment on criminal trials was more to be welcomed than feared.

Globe Newspaper Co. v. Superior Court—Closure to Protect Victim's Privacy?

During the next term, another case, Globe Newspaper Co. v. Superior Court for the County of Norfolk (1982), required the Supreme Court to amplify its holding in *Richmond Newspapers* by considering what countervailing interests might justify closure of part of a trial in the face of a newspaper's invocation of the First Amendment right of access the press and public now enjoyed.

A Massachusetts statute required trial judges to exclude the press and public in all cases during the testimony of a minor victim in a sex-offense trial. Representatives of the Globe Newspaper Company challenged this mandatory closure policy in a rape trial, raising claims under both the First and Sixth Amendments. The defense counsel also objected to closure, and the Commonwealth's attorney "on behalf of the victims" waived any right to exclude the press.[191] Nevertheless, in light of the state statute, the trial judge excluded the Globe reporters and the public during the complainants' testimony. While the newspaper's appeal was pending, the defendant was acquitted.[192] The Massachusetts Supreme Judicial Court had ruled that defendant's Sixth Amendment right was personal and could not be invoked by the press. The Supreme Court announced that it did not rule out the possibility of considering a Sixth Amendment claim raised by the acquitted defendant. There was no need to consider Globe's Sixth Amendment argument because the newspaper won its First Amendment claim.

Justice Brennan, writing the opinion of the Court, took the occasion to root the interpretation of the First Amendment he had propounded in his *Richmond Newspapers* concurrence in a majority opinion. The press and public have a First Amendment right to attend criminal trials in particular, he explained, because, first, criminal trials have historically been open and, second, the right of access to criminal trials plays a significant role in the functioning of the judicial process and the government as a whole. Brennan's two guiding principles, tradition and function, were now part of the case law. Although it was not until *Globe* that Brennan mustered a majority in support of his approach, this two-part test is usually referred to as the *Richmond Newspaper* test rather than the *Globe* test.

Brennan then went on to discuss in greater detail than he had in *Richmond Newspapers*, and now speaking for a majority, how the constitutionality of limits on this First Amendment right should be evaluated. He invoked a classic First Amendment standard. "Where, as in the present case, the State attempts to deny the right of access in order to inhibit the disclosure of sensitive information, it must be shown that the denial is necessitated by a compelling governmental interest, and is narrowly tailored to serve that interest." The interests the state asserted to justify the closure rule were twofold: (1) protecting minor victims of sex crimes from further trauma and embarrassment, and (2) encouraging minor victims to come forward and testify truthfully and credibly. The Court agreed that the first interest, protection of the victims, was indeed compelling. But this interest did not justify a blanket mandatory closure rule. A trial court can and should determine on a case-by-case basis whether closure is necessary to protect the welfare of a minor victim. Among the factors to be weighed, the Court said, are the victim's age, psychological maturity and understanding, the nature of the crime, the desires of the victim, and the interests of the victim's parents and relatives. If the trial court had been permitted to exercise discretion in this case, the Court said, closure might not have been deemed necessary. It should be noted that the victims had no objection to the presence of the press, although they did express a desire to get the press to promise not to publish their names or personally identifiable information.

The Court was more skeptical about the second interest asserted (encouraging victims to come forward), describing the proposition that victims would be more likely to come forward if trials were closed during their testimony as lacking empirical support, speculative, and "open to serious question as a matter of logic and common sense." The press would be able to publicize the substance of the victim's testimony on the basis of transcripts, even if reporters were physically excluded from the courtroom during the testimony, so secrecy might not be maintained in any event. And Brennan noted that the Court's own opinions had previously endorsed the idea that open court proceedings might improve the quality and credibility of testimony (quoting Gannett Co., Inc. v. DePasquale, 1979). Thus, this case was a good example of applying each of the two prongs of the Court's new test, because the state's asserted justifications for closure failed in two different ways—one because alternate means were available to serve a concededly compelling state interest, and the other because the state's theory was not demonstrably true and therefore could not be regarded as compelling.

Globe Newspaper followed the approach the Court had recently followed in *Chandler* of requiring case-by-case examination of limitations on open trials, rather than the blanket rule-oriented approach of *Estes*. And the Court once again was following the lead of the majority of states. While a number of states allowed closure of sex-offense trials during a victim's testimony in the trial judge's discretion, only Massachusetts had a mandatory closure statute applicable to all such cases. Because closure in a particular case might not be unconstitutional, if an appropriate showing were made, trial judges again would gain discretion to decide how open trials would be.

Justice Sandra Day O'Connor (a recent appointee who had not been on the Court when *Richmond Newspapers* was decided) wrote a separate opinion "concurring in the judgment." While she did not disagree with the majority that the First Amendment precluded a mandatory closure rule in criminal trials, she cautioned that the Court's ruling should not carry any implications outside the context of criminal trials. Her caution about the potential breadth of the majority's analysis of the First Amendment right seemed more directed to the Burger and Brennan opinions in *Richmond Newspapers*, which had suggested that the First Amendment might also supply a heavy presumption that trials must be open even in civil cases. Justice O'Connor evidently had not yet made up her mind how broadly she would rationalize the First Amendment right of access, and she had no need to do so in this case.

Chief Justice Burger, who had written the now superseded opinion of the Court in *Richmond Newspapers*, wrote a dissent, joined by Justice Rehnquist, in which he disagreed with the expansive interpretation the Court was now giving that case. Because, he recounted, there is a long history of exclusion of the public from trials involving sexual assaults, especially of minors, it cannot be said that there is an unbroken tradition of open proceedings in these cases, and thus closure of the courtroom during such proceedings cannot violate the First Amendment. Chief Justice Burger worried that it would be difficult to find a limiting principle to the majority's opinion. "The same reasoning might require a hearing before a trial judge could hold a bench conference or any *in camera* proceeding." Furthermore, Burger worried, putting together this decision with the decision in *Chandler*, it appeared that in half of the states, public courtroom testimony might also be televised, adding to the pain of a young victim.

Of course, trial judges would continue to have the discretion to close the courtroom during a victim's testimony in an appropriate case, because the Court had found the interest in protecting minor victims testifying in sexual offense trials to be potentially compelling. And trial judges would, presumably, also have discretion to exclude television cameras during the testimony of young victims. But Chief Justice Burger, while proclaiming his faith that most trial judges would exercise their discretion soundly, thought that victims and their families should be entitled to "assurance" of such protection. In other words, Chief Justice Burger believed that it was time for a court-imposed rule, rather than a case-by-case analysis, and seemed to sympathize with Justice Stewart's earlier invitation to trial judges to be "overcautious" in closing proceedings to serve particular interests. Justice Brennan had been right in surmising that his approach to the First Amendment, first propounded as an alternative to Burger's sketchier rationale in *Richmond Newspapers*, gave more weight to the First Amendment side of the balance.

Press-Enterprise I and II, Waller v. Georgia, and El Vocero de Puerto Rico—When Is a Pretrial Proceeding Part of a Trial?

During the next decade, the Court faced an issue left open by its decision that the public has, at the least, a First Amendment right to attend criminal trials: When do pretrial proceedings in a criminal case count as part of that "trial?" In each of these cases, the press had argued its right to attend a proceeding that at least one of the parties, usually the defendant, wished to close. *Gannett* had decided that defendants have no unilateral right to close proceedings, a conclusion that was relevant in these cases, in which defendants' desire for closure did not prevail. *Gannett* had also held that the public and press have no right under the Sixth Amendment to attend a pretrial hearing on a defendant's motion to suppress, and had treated the decision of the parties to the litigation as critical (at least where the parties were in agreement). But *Gannett* was decided before recognition of the First Amendment right of the public and press to attend trials, a new right demanding a new analysis.

By the time the Court had finished considering the issues raised in this series of cases, the public had a presumptive right to attend not only trials, but also voir dire examinations, preliminary hearings, and even pretrial motions to suppress evidence in criminal cases.

The first proceeding the Court now confronted was the voir dire examination of prospective jurors (Press-Enterprise Co. v. Superior Court of Calif., Riverside County, 1984 [*Press-Enterprise I*]). Albert Brown's California state court trial for the capital rape and murder of a teenage girl not surprisingly attracted considerable attention from the media and the public. The Press-Enterprise Company asked the court to open the voir dire examination, but the state objected, arguing that jurors might not answer voir dire questions candidly if the press were present and that defendant's right to a fair trial might thereby be jeopardized. The trial judge agreed and permitted the press to attend the "general" but not the "individual" questioning of the prospective jurors. In practice, this meant that all but three days of a six-week voir dire was closed to the public. After the voir dire had ended, the newspaper moved for release of the complete transcript of the voir dire proceedings. Both defense counsel and the prosecutor argued that release would violate the jurors' right to privacy, because the jurors had answered questions under an implied promise of confidentiality. The trial judge denied the newspaper's motion, finding that while most of the jurors' answers were "of little moment," a few had discussed personal problems in sensitive areas and were entitled to their privacy. The trial court also denied a renewed motion for release of the voir dire transcript after the defendant had been convicted and sentenced to death. As in *Gannett*, the parties all agreed to closure of the voir dire. But *Gannett* was distinguishable because a different constitutional right was being asserted and also because the petitioner argued that, unlike the pretrial suppression hearing considered in *Gannett*, voir dire was the beginning of the "trial" itself.

Chief Justice Burger, writing for a majority of the Court, returned to the approach of his own opinions in *Richmond Newspapers* and *Globe Newspapers*, and began with history. The question was whether "at the time when our organic laws were adopted," voir dire proceedings had been open (quoting Richmond Newspapers, Inc. v. Virginia, 1980). He concluded that "since the development of trial by jury, the process of selection of jurors has presumptively been a public process with exceptions only for good cause shown." Because, as the Court had previously described, trial by jury had initiated with trials by "moots," or town meetings, the public aspect was "almost a necessary incident of jury trials, since the presence of a jury . . . already insured the presence of a large part of the community."[193] He traced the development of the jury as it became a representative body and as the ideal of the impartial juror emerged, observing that since the sixteenth century the accused had generally enjoyed the right to challenge jurors "in open court at the outset of the trial." Burger patched together his story from the remarks of various commentators and noted, as he had in *Richmond Newspapers*, the sketchiness of his historical support: "[I]t is not surprising that there is little in the way of contemporary record of the openness of those early tribunals."

Remarking that "[f]or present purposes, how we allocate the 'right' to openness as between the accused and the public, or whether we view it as a component inherent in the system benefiting both, is not crucial," Burger avoided deciding whether to accept Brennan's *Globe Newspaper* revision of his own First Amendment theories as set out in *Richmond Newspapers*. He did, however, reiterate his view that public trials have "what is sometimes described as community therapeutic value" (quoting Richmond Newspapers, Inc. v. Virginia, 1980). Because, whatever the source, the public had a right to attend this traditionally open proceeding, the presumption of openness, Burger said, "may be overcome only by an overriding interest based on findings that closure is essential to preserve higher values and is narrowly tailored to serve that interest. The interest is to be articulated along with findings specific enough that a reviewing court can determine whether the closure order was properly entered." This statement of the standard to be applied, while not using the same language that Justice Brennan's opinion in *Globe Newspapers* had used to evaluate a closure order, was consistent with its direction.

Applying this standard, Burger found that the trial judge had failed on several counts. The interests asserted in favor of closure of the voir dire were, first, the defendant's interest in a fair trial and, second, the prospective jurors' privacy interests. As to the former, Burger chided the trial judge for not having made specific findings as to how the defendant's fair trial rights might have been affected. Hence, Burger said, it was not possible to conclude that closure was warranted. As to the jurors' privacy interests, the trial judge had failed to consider alternatives to closure as a means of protecting those interests. But juror privacy was recognized as a compelling interest that could, in an appropriate case, lead to a limited closure of proceedings, if "interrogation touches on deeply personal matters that a person has legitimate reasons for keeping out of the public domain." Burger also acknowledged that such deeply personal matters might well have arisen with respect to examination in this case, an alleged rape of a teenage girl. A prospective juror, he noted, might want to privately inform the judge that she had been raped and decided not to seek prosecution to spare herself embarrassment and emotional trauma. "The privacy interests of such a prospective juror must be balanced against the historic values we have discussed and the need for openness of the process." Here, Burger had specific instructions for how trial judges are to handle such a conflict: "To preserve fairness and at the same time protect legitimate privacy, a trial judge must at all times maintain control of the process of jury selection and should inform the array of prospective jurors, once the general nature of sensitive questions is made known to them, that those individuals believing public questioning will prove damaging because of embarrassment, may properly request an opportunity to present the problem to the judge *in camera* but with counsel present and on the record." At that point, Burger said, the trial judge would have sufficient information to decide how to exercise discretion: a very limited closure might be justified if disclosure would infringe a significant privacy interest, perhaps allowing the juror to answer questions privately and then making a transcript publicly available, or even sealing a part of the transcript of the examination of a particular juror to protect that juror from embarrassment. In an extreme case, the judge might decide to excuse the individual from service on the jury.

The thrust of the discussion of this alternative method was, as the Court had dictated previously, that closure, even where justified by a competing compelling interest, must be tailored as narrowly as possible. The Court once again resisted generalized rules authorizing closure, demanding case-by-case analysis to ensure that no closure was broader than its justification.

Justice Blackmun wrote a separate concurring opinion, attempting to simplify the lives of trial judges by noting that the Court had not actually decided that jurors have a "right to privacy" that could excuse them from being required to answer voir dire questions at all. He noted that the Supreme Court was assuming *arguendo* that jurors have privacy rights only because the trial court had not employed appropriate alternatives to safeguard such rights in any event.

Justice Stevens, in another concurring opinion, spelled out what Chief Justice Burger's opinion had declined to:

> The constitutional protection for the right of access that the Court upholds today is found in the First Amendment rather than the public trial provision of the Sixth. If the defendant had advanced a claim that his Sixth Amendment right to a public trial was violated by the closure of the voir dire, it would be important to determine whether the selection of the jury was a part of the 'trial' within the meaning of that Amendment. But the distinction between trials and other official proceedings is not necessarily dispositive, or even important, in evaluating First Amendment issues. *(footnotes omitted)*

Thurgood Marshall also wrote a concurring opinion, stressing that the constitutional rights of the public and press to access to all aspects of criminal trials "are not diminished in cases where 'deeply personal matters' are likely to be elicited in voir dire proceedings. . . . Indeed, the policies underlying those rights . . . are most severely jeopardized when courts conceal from the public sensitive information that bears upon the ability of jurors impartially to weigh the evidence presented to them." Like Justices Stevens and Blackmun, Marshall agreed with Burger's result, but feared that some of his language might be taken as overly restrictive of a First Amendment right that most of the Court now believed was broader than Burger himself might yet believe. All members of the Court agreed that the balance between public trial access and individual rights of privacy had not been struck properly at this proceeding, but there still appeared to be disagreement, at least on the part of Chief Justice Burger, about the weight of the privacy interests on the other side of the balance.

The next case, Waller v. Georgia (1984), decided just a few months later, involved another pretrial suppression hearing. In this case, unlike *Gannett*, it was the prosecutor who wished to close the hearing, over the defendant's objection. The evidence presented at the suppression hearing included court-authorized wiretaps that had been conducted by Georgia police over a sixth-month period. The wiretaps had disclosed a large lottery operation involving gambling on the volume of stocks and bonds traded on the New York Stock Exchange. As a result of the wiretaps, and of evidence seized pursuant to search warrants, petitioner Waller and thirty-five others were charged with violating the Georgia Racketeer Influenced and Corrupt Organizations Act. The petitioner and thirteen codefendants moved to suppress the wiretap evidence against them on the theory that the authorizing warrants were invalid.

The trial court held a hearing on the prosecutor's motion to close the suppression hearing, at which the prosecutor invoked a state statute providing that any "publication" of information obtained under a wiretap warrant that was not "necessary and essential" would be considered an unlawful invasion of privacy and would cause the information to become inadmissible as evidence. The prosecutor explained that the wiretap evidence would "involve" some individuals who had been indicted but were not yet on trial, and that disclosure might taint potential evidence against those individuals. The prosecution also argued that disclosure could jeopardize the reasonable expectation of privacy of people other than the defendants, some of whom had not even been indicted. The trial judge, agreeing that potential evidence might be tainted, closed the hearing to anyone other than witnesses, court personnel, the parties, and their lawyers. The hearing lasted for seven days; tapes of the disputed wiretaps were played for less than two and a half hours of that time.

Because the defense objected to the closure, issue was joined under the Sixth Amendment—the public trial right belonging to criminal defendants. For the first time since the *Oliver* case, the Court was considering a defendant who wished to claim the right to an open proceeding rather than try to veto it. As in *Oliver*, the Court easily found in favor of the defense claim. The decision was unanimous. Justice Lewis Powell, writing the opinion for the Court, broke Waller's claim down into three questions: First, does the accused's Sixth Amendment right to a public trial extend to a suppression hearing conducted prior to the presentation of evidence to the jury? Second, if so, was that right violated here? Third, if so, what is the appropriate remedy?

As to the first question, Powell noted that the Court had not recently considered the extent of the Sixth Amendment public trial right and had never considered the extent to which that right, as opposed to the First Amendment right of public access, extends beyond the actual proof at trial. He then went on to invoke the First Amendment cases as "relevant precedents." *Press-Enterprise I*, in which the public was found to have a presumptive right to attend voir dire, was cited as establishing that the First Amendment right extended beyond the testimony at trial. He also conscripted *Gannett* as a favorable precedent. Although the *Gannett*

Court had not reached the question of whether the Sixth Amendment right extends to a pretrial suppression hearing (because the petitioner was a newspaper and did not share that right), "a majority of the Justices concluded that the public had a qualified right to attend such hearings." Powell's "majority" was derived by adding his own concurring opinion in *Gannett*, which would have recognized a First Amendment right of the press to attend judicial proceedings, including pretrial suppression hearings, and Justice Blackmun's four-Justice dissent, which would have recognized a Sixth Amendment right for the press as well as the accused to attend pretrial suppression hearings. Powell was not troubled by the contrast between the limiting language of the Sixth Amendment, referring only to "trial," and the open-ended First Amendment penumbral right. He was more interested in the functions of the rights involved than in the wording of the amendments. "As noted, the analysis in these cases has proceeded largely under the First Amendment. Nevertheless, there can be little doubt that the explicit Sixth Amendment right of the accused is no less protective of a public trial than the implicit First Amendment right of the press and public. The central aim of a criminal proceeding must be to try the accused fairly, and '[our] cases have uniformly recognized the public-trial guarantee as one created for the benefit of the defendant' " (quoting Gannett Co., Inc. v. DePasquale, 1979).

Continuing to focus on the function of an open hearing, Powell quoted some earlier cases' remarks on the benefits of an open proceeding to the defendant—presence of the public may ensure that the proceeding is fair, additional witnesses may come forward, and judicial abuse can be constrained. These aims and interests are "no less pressing in a hearing to suppress wrongfully seized evidence." Powell referred to his and Justice Blackmun's opinions in *Gannett*, which had argued that a suppression hearing can be as important as the trial itself and, in fact, can sometimes provide the only judicial hearing if a case is dismissed (when the motion succeeds) or plea bargained (when the motion fails). Next, Powell declared that the suppression hearing "resembles" a bench trial, where witnesses are sworn and testify, counsel argues, and the outcome may depend on findings of fact. As had been argued in the *Gannett* dissent, the public also has an interest in police and prosecutor misconduct, and thus would be interested in exposing suppression hearings to "the salutary effects of public scrutiny." Powell seemed to acknowledge in a footnote that he was not relying only on benefits to the defendant in his account of the value of the public trial: "To the extent there is an independent public interest in the Sixth Amendment public-trial guarantee [see Gannett Co., Inc. v. DePasquale, 1979; Globe Newspaper Co. v. Superior Court for the County of Norfolk, 1982], it applies with full force to suppression hearings." Although Powell used both First and Sixth Amendment rationales and cases in concluding that the Sixth Amendment right does cover suppression hearings, he did not go so far as to merge the rights by permitting defendants to share the public's First Amendment access right. Waller had raised a First Amendment claim on his own behalf, but Powell announced that, in light of the Court's result, there was no need to reach that claim.

The First Amendment cases also played a role in answering the Court's second question, whether Waller's Sixth Amendment right had been violated by the closure of the hearing. Powell quoted the First Amendment test from *Press-Enterprise I* as providing the applicable rules for the petitioner's Sixth Amendment challenge as well: "The presumption of openness may be overcome only by an overriding interest based on findings that closure is essential to preserve higher values and is narrowly tailored to serve that interest. The interest is to be articulated along with findings specific enough that a reviewing court can determine whether the closure order was properly entered."[194] The source of Waller's public attendance claims scarcely matters if the test is the same under either the First or the Sixth Amendment, and if the specific "trial" language of the Sixth Amendment is not considered limiting. There was no reason for Waller to be disappointed that Powell had not decided his claim to share the First Amendment right, because only the Sixth Amendment would afford him the remedy he sought after the fact: the possibility of a new trial.

Once it was clear that the *Press-Enterprise I* test would be applied, the result was easy. The Court was respectful of the significance of the interest the state had proffered—protecting the privacy of people not parties to the litigation—commenting that "[u]nder certain circumstances, these interests may well justify closing portions of a suppression hearing to the public." However, the state had not been specific about whose privacy was at stake, how that privacy might be infringed, what portions of the tapes might pose a threat to that privacy, and what portion of the evidence at the hearing would consist of the tapes. And the trial judge had erred by entering findings that were "broad and general" as opposed to specific, by not justifying closure of the entire hearing, and by not considering alternatives to immediate closure. As a result, the Court ruled, the closure was far more extensive than necessary. It was no more permissible to close a seven-day hearing because of two and a half hours of questionable evidence than it had been to close a six-week voir dire to insulate a few suspect questions.

On the third question (what remedy was appropriate) the Solicitor General, arguing on behalf of the U.S. *amicus curiae*, maintained that the petitioner, who had been convicted of some of the charges against him and acquitted on others, should be entitled only to a new suppression hearing and not to a new trial. Justice Powell noted that the parties did not question the "consistent view of the lower federal courts that the defendant should not be required to prove specific prejudice in order to obtain relief for a violation of the public-trial guarantee." But the Court agreed that the appropriate remedy for the violation in this case was to hold a new, open suppression hearing. If the same evidence was found admissible at the new hearing, a new trial would be a "windfall" for the defendant. Waller would receive a new trial only if the new hearing resulted in the suppression of material evidence admitted at the first trial. But before that hearing was held, the state courts would have to review, in light of current and possibly changed circumstances, what portion, if any, of the new suppression hearing could properly be closed. As in the *Press-Enterprise I* case, the Court had not ruled that the proceeding in question must be wholly open. The holdings focused on the process used by the trial court to decide a motion for closure, and only chided the trial judges for not making sufficiently specific findings, for being too willing to close an unnecessarily large portion of a proceeding, and for not being creative enough in generating alternatives to closure.

The last two cases the Supreme Court decided on opening trial proceedings (Press-Enterprise Co. v. Superior Court of Calif. for the County of Riverside, 1986 [*Press-Enterprise II*] and El Vocero de Puerto Rico v. Puerto Rico, 1993) extended the reasoning of *Press-Enterprise I* and *Waller* to First Amendment press claims to attend preliminary hearings. Continuing the consistent trend of the post-*Gannett* cases, the Court ruled in favor of open proceedings in both cases.

In the first of these cases, defendant Robert Diaz, a nurse, attracted press attention when he was charged with killing twelve of his patients by administering massive doses of lidocaine to them. California allows prosecutors to decide whether to use a grand jury (composed of sixteen to twenty-three citizens) or a preliminary hearing before a magistrate to determine whether charges are based on probable cause. The preliminary hearing takes place after the commencement of formal proceedings, but it might result in dismissal of the case or reduction of the charges before trial. An old California statute had provided that defendants could decide whether to have preliminary hearings closed. When that statute was challenged on First Amendment grounds in 1982, the California courts held that it was not unconstitutional to give the defendant an unqualified right to close preliminary hearings, distinguishing the Supreme Court's recent decision in *Richmond Newspapers* (1980) on the ground that preliminary hearings are not trials (San Jose Mercury-News v. Municipal Court, 1982). After that decision, however, the California legislature passed a new statute to eliminate the defendant's veto and allow greater public access to preliminary hearings. The new California statue, in effect at the time of Diaz's trial, provided that such proceedings were to be open to the public unless the defendant could establish to the court's satisfaction that exclusion of the public was "necessary in order to protect a defendant's right to a fair and impartial trial." The California courts then interpreted this new statute as requiring defendants to show a "reasonable likelihood" that allowing the public to attend the preliminary hearing would jeopardize his fair trial right.

The Supreme Court decided that even this statutory accommodation of First Amendment interests went too far in allowing defendants control over judicial proceedings. Chief Justice Burger, who had written the majority opinion in *Richmond Newspapers*, held that Diaz had not shown that closure was "essential" to serve his right to a fair trial and narrowly tailored to serve that interest. The burden on defendants who want to close their hearings should have been, the Court said, to show a "substantial probability" of prejudice to his rights, a more demanding showing than the state court's requirement of showing a "reasonable likelihood." The state court had also failed, Burger noted, to determine whether alternative measures, as discussed in the earlier cases, might have protected the defendant's interests and still allowed public access to the proceeding. Once again, a heavy thumb had been placed on the scale, favoring open proceedings. Defendants could not choose to have a hearing closed, despite their fears of prejudice, and had to bear a heavy burden of persuading a judge that they would suffer unfairness caused by publicity.

The Court also disagreed with the state court's conclusion that preliminary hearings are not covered by the First Amendment right of access declared in *Richmond Newspapers. Press-Enterprise I*, which had been decided after the state court had made its decision in this case, provided standards to apply in deciding whether the public had a presumptive right to attend pretrial proceedings (like the voir dire in that case): (1) whether there was a tradition of accessibility to the type of proceeding in question, and (2) whether public access to the proceeding plays a particularly significant role in the actual functioning of the process.

On the first question, the Court said that there had been a tradition of accessibility to preliminary hearings of the type conducted in California. Most state courts considering the issue had decided that the tradition of accessibility to trials should cover preliminary hearings as well. This tradition was far from being as clear or unbroken as the tradition of public jury selection the Court had described in *Press-Enterprise I*. The New York Field Code of Criminal Procedure, published in 1850, had allowed preliminary hearings to be closed on motion of the defendant. California was not the only state to follow the Field Code's model by allowing defendants to make this decision.[195] In *Press-Enterprise I*, the Court had noted that jury selection had been public since the inception of the jury trial. As Justice Stevens' dissent pointed out, the majority was unable to argue here that preliminary hearings had a comparable history of openness, because at common law such pretrial proceedings were not open to the public. Burger's only example of a public probable cause hearing was the hearing held during the treason trial of Aaron Burr, in 1807, which, he noted, had to be held in the Hall of the House of Delegates in Virginia because the courtroom was too small to accommodate all the interested spectators. Some state courts had ruled that even if a particular pretrial proceeding does not have a historical counterpart, the traditional right of access should still apply, given the significance of pretrial proceedings to the criminal trial. Burger noted that preliminary hearings, unlike the grand jury proceedings for which they substituted in some jurisdictions, were not subject to the tradition of grand jury secrecy.

The Court's argument about tradition here, as the dissenters noted, is even thinner than the parallel argument in *Press-Enterprise I*. History is not as directly or solidly supportive. The state courts and legislatures were split on whether open proceedings should be required, although California was in a minority. In addition, there are counterarguments to which the majority did not respond. In dissent, Justices Stevens and Rehnquist argued that some of the same interests that justify grand jury secrecy might also justify affording a defendant a veto over public preliminary hearings. Grand jury proceedings, in which grand jurors are deciding whether there is sufficient evidence to warrant charging an individual with a crime, are secret in part so that a defendant whom the grand jury decides not to charge will not be exposed to public humiliation. California allows prosecutors to choose to have a judge, rather than grand jurors, serve this screening function; the Supreme Court had found this choice constitutionally permissible (Hurtado v. California, 1884). The Court's standard for closure allows a defendant who will be going to trial to have a proceeding closed if the fairness of the trial may be affected. But a defendant against whom unwarranted or oppressive charges have been brought may not be going to trial if the screening of the grand jury or preliminary hearing is working well. This defendant may avoid public humiliation if it is a grand jury that makes the decision not to allow the proceeding to continue, but not if it is a judge.

The Court might have responded that the public has a right to know if the criminal justice system is being used oppressively, and so the accused must suffer public scrutiny even if charges were unwarranted. But in a grand jury system, the privacy of the accused could have been protected. What distinguishes the grand jury is that there is already representative public participation in the decision to prosecute—the sixteen to twenty-three grand jurors. While the Court has offhandedly distinguished secret grand jury proceedings, in *Press-Enterprise II* and in *Oliver*, only on the basis of the tradition of secrecy, the fact that the grand jury inherently provides an opportunity for citizens, albeit a preselected group, to observe the criminal justice system in action, lessens the need for other public participation. Conversely, if a serious prosecution is initiated without the public participation the grand jury system allows, the need for the public to observe the proceeding is increased.

This distinction between grand jury proceedings and preliminary hearings could also have explained the Court's conclusion that preliminary hearings as they are used in California meet the second of the *Press-Enterprise I* criteria: the essential function served by public access. Instead, the Court explained that preliminary hearings in California are sufficiently "like trials" to render public access essential to the proper functioning of the state's criminal justice system. The Court described the features of the preliminary hearing—including the right of the accused to personally appear, to be represented by counsel, to cross-examine hostile witnesses, to present exculpatory evidence, and to exclude illegally obtained evidence. The applicability of these rights, most of which derive from the Sixth Amendment, also distinguishes the preliminary hearing from a grand jury proceeding, in which the accused has no right to appear, to counsel, to cross-examine, to present evidence, or to exclude illegally obtained evidence. But instead of contrasting the grand jury, the Court continued to compare the preliminary hearing to a trial. The hearing resembles a trial, as described above, and may, in some cases, provide the only opportunity for the public to observe the operation of the criminal justice system. If the public shared the Sixth Amendment right to public trial (as the dissenters in *Gannett* had argued), the Court would have had the opportunity to consider whether the Sixth Amendment right to attend a public "trial" should apply in all proceedings in which other Sixth Amendment rights, like the right to counsel, apply. The right to counsel, for example, applies at "critical stages" of a criminal proceeding, including preliminary hearings (see Coleman v. Alabama, 1970). Furthermore, the Court noted, jurors are not yet involved in the preliminary hearing. Jury selection, considered the beginning of the trial itself (see Crist v. Betz, 1978), would follow the preliminary hearing unless charges were dropped. In this case, Diaz waived his right to a jury, so no jurors were ever involved. Because jurors can provide a safeguard against corrupt or overzealous prosecutors, the Court said, it is all the more important to allow members of the public to observe criminal proceedings when jurors are absent. As in his earlier opinions, Burger identified the role of the community as being to assure fairness to the defendant, to assure themselves that the system is operating fairly, and to experience the "community therapeutic value" of open proceedings.

The two dissenters, a surprising pairing of Justices Stevens and Rehnquist, noted one feature of preliminary hearings that the majority had not discussed: they are essentially as one-sided as grand jury proceedings, generally consisting of only the prosecution's case. In this case, the preliminary hearing took eight weeks, and the transcript of the proceeding was 4,239 pages. As is typical at preliminary hearings, the defendant had called no witnesses on his own behalf. (Defendants are usually disinclined to give the prosecution a preview of their defense at trial.) The parties had agreed to seal the transcript, as well as close the hearing itself, for fear that release of this one-sided account of the case might undermine the likelihood that Diaz would receive a fair trial from impartial jurors. After Diaz had decided to waive his right to a jury, thereby eliminating the risk of juror prejudice, the trial court ordered the preliminary hearing transcript unsealed.

The most recent public trial case, El Vocero de Puerto Rico v. Puerto Rico (1993), confirmed that even in a jurisdiction with different traditions, a preliminary hearing similar to the California proceeding considered in *Press-Enterprise II* must be presumptively open. The "tradition" prong of the *Richmond Newspapers/Press-Enterprise I* test looks to nationwide traditions and not to the unique traditions of a place like Puerto Rico. Once again, the Court required trial judges to assess reasons for closure on a case-by-case basis.

STATE OF THE LAW TODAY

The Supreme Court's public trial cases have tipped the scale heavily in favor of open proceedings, although mostly under the aegis of the First Amendment. The Court has ruled that every aspect of a criminal prosecution it has considered, including preliminary hearings and voir dire, is presumptively open, and that anyone, whether a criminal defendant or a witness, has a heavy burden of showing that a compelling interest overrides the presumptive right of publicity. Under both the First and Sixth Amendments, the Court has also imposed a heavy burden on trial judges, who must hold hearings, make careful findings, and carefully consider alternatives to closure before issuing a closure order. Thus, as in the prejudicial pretrial publicity cases, the issues involved in closure decisions have progressed from legal to factual.

Although the Court has consistently favored keeping criminal proceedings as open as possible, the fact remains that only two of the Supreme Court cases described above were interpretations of the Sixth Amendment. In *Waller*, the Supreme Court applied the same demanding standard for evaluating the need for closure in a Sixth Amendment claim as it had in First Amendment claims.[196] Defendants who want their trials to remain open, or who wish to have their convictions reversed because all or part of their trial was closed, will benefit from this weighted standard. But it is less clear that other open questions about the Sixth Amendment are answered by *Waller*.

The Scope of the Public "Trial"

Waller did decide that a pretrial proceeding, a suppression hearing, was functionally similar enough to a trial to be covered by the Sixth Amendment guarantee. In reaching that conclusion, the Court used the same version of the *Richmond Newspapers* test it had used in *Press-Enterprise I* to decide whether a particular proceeding is presumptively open to the public under the First Amendment—asking, first, whether the proceeding is traditionally one that would have been open and, second, whether public involvement would promote the functions of the proceeding. Like the First Amendment cases, especially *Press-Enterprise II*, *Waller* focused more on the functions publicity might serve rather than a strict analysis of the traditions regarding attendance at a proceeding that had not existed at common law. Justice Powell remarked that the Sixth Amendment should be no less protective of a defendant's interests than the First Amendment is of the public's.

In deciding what proceedings are covered by the Sixth Amendment guarantee of a public "trial," most courts quote the *Waller* dictum and then simply apply the First Amendment tests and precedents. It may be taking Justice Powell's remark too literally to assume that First Amendment and Sixth Amendment interpretations and results will remain in lockstep on all issues. Several Supreme Court Justices, including Chief Justice Burger in *Gannett* and Justice Stevens in *Press-Enterprise I*, have noted that the Sixth Amendment does provide a textual limitation of the defendant's right— to a public "trial"—that does not exist for First Amendment claims. Various Justices have also believed that the range of interests protected by the two rights differ. If the Sixth Amendment includes only the defendant's instrumental interests and not the interests of the public, a question *Waller* treated as open, a functional analysis of the role of publicity under the Sixth Amendment would be likely to diverge from a parallel analysis under the First. Therefore, some independent Sixth Amendment analysis is necessary with respect to the threshold question of whether or not the Sixth Amendment right attaches to various parts of a criminal proceeding other than the trial itself.

So far, the lower federal and state courts considering whether a particular proceeding should be subject to the heavy presumption of openness have concentrated on the part of the *Richmond Newspapers/Press-Enterprise I* test asking what function will be served by allowing public access to a particular proceeding. The tradition prong of the test has not played as significant a role in judicial analysis. Although many courts recite some simplified public trial history, usually gleaned from a Supreme Court opinion, their decisions usually perceive that history is not a particularly helpful guide, except at the most general level. Criminal adjudication has changed substantially in many respects since the era of the Anglo-Saxons and even since the late-eighteenth century. Most criminal cases today are resolved through plea bargaining. In asking whether the public has a right to observe plea proceedings, is it relevant to ask whether the public attended pleas during earlier centuries when the role of plea bargaining was entirely different? Under the Federal Sentencing Guidelines, judges make sentencing decisions heavily based on findings of fact.[197] Should the public's right to attend such consequential proceedings be controlled by whether the public was invited to attend the ministerial imposition of mandatory sentences at common law?

Because the lower courts generally have not found history a useful guide on the issues raised in this section, their decisions turn on how broadly they define the purposes of the public trial guarantee, an issue that is not often brought to the surface in the opinions described below. No matter how broadly or narrowly the range of interests is defined, *Waller* suggests that the public can virtually always play a useful role. If the public's presence will be more damaging than helpful to some overriding interest, as in the grand jury context, a proceeding may be closed. Generally speaking, if a defendant invokes the Sixth Amendment right to a public trial, showing that he fears the public less than the government, all phases of the criminal prosecution should be presumptively open and the government or moving party should bear a heavy burden of showing that any closure is justified.

Except in unusual cases, there is no reason not to exercise a presumption in favor of allowing defendants to choose open proceedings. Defendants are not permitted to opt unilaterally to close proceedings because of the countervailing First Amendment right of the public. But in the unusual case in which a defendant sides with the public in wanting a proceeding to be as open as possible, their combined First and Sixth Amendment interests should be difficult to overcome.

Although it is uncommon for a court to rule against a defendant's claim for an open trial, this has happened in the loaded context of televising proceedings. One federal court of appeals in Florida, the state that in *Chandler* established the possibility of televising trials, ruled against the combined publicity demands of the public and a prominent defendant. Alcee Hastings, an African-American federal judge, believed that criminal charges had been brought against him as part of a plot to remove him from the bench. Anticipating the request of press intervenors, he asked that his trial be televised so that as many members of the public as possible would understand his point of view and support his return to the bench.[198] The court of appeals brushed off his Sixth Amendment claim on the ground that representative members of the public were invited to watch his trial in the courtroom and that the Sixth Amendment required no more. The Supreme Court has not yet interpreted the Sixth Amendment as requiring more; however, in cases in which defendants affirmatively want to enable the broadest public possible to observe their trials, there is usually no good reason not to comply.

This section will analyze the state and lower federal court opinions discussing the scope of the right to a public trial. First, which proceedings have courts found to be presumptively open to the public? Cases have considered pretrial hearings on motions to suppress evidence; voir dire; preliminary hearings; other pretrial hearings, including bail, disqualification, and competency hearings; plea proceedings; miscellaneous trial proceedings; post-trial proceedings, including sentencing; and juvenile proceedings. Second, how have courts analyzed partial closures of a covered proceeding? Trial judges have excluded some members of the public from criminal trials by deciding to hold trials in small, inaccessible, or intimidating venues; by locking courtroom doors during particular phases of a trial (most notably during the charge to the jury); or by deciding to exclude particular people, often a defendant's family or friends, during all or part of a proceeding. Third, what have the courts considered to be adequate justification for excluding some or all of the public from portions of a trial? Among the interests the state and federal governments have asserted as overriding the right to public trial are protection of witnesses from physical harm or intimidation, protection of the secrecy or integrity of ongoing government investigations, grand jury secrecy, protection of victims (especially minor victims of sex offenses), juror privacy, and various privileges, all of which can be genuine overriding interests depending on the circumstances of the case. Some courts have also ordered exclusions based on their own assessment of the defendant's interests or their own concerns about decorum and decency. These justifications are often more tenuous. Fourth, what procedural decisions have the courts made imposing or easing limitations on how public trial claims can be raised? Cases have discussed the timing of a defendant raising a complaint about a total or partial closure of the courtroom, that is, whether an interlocutory appeal will lie, what rules govern the preservation of such a claim, and what burden a defendant must bear to prevail in a public trial claim on appeal or in a habeas corpus proceeding.

"Trials"

The Maine Supreme Court posited that the scope of the term "public trial" as used in the Sixth Amendment must include at least proceedings for impaneling the jury, opening statements of counsel, presentation of evidence, arguments of counsel, instructions to the jury, and return of the verdict.[199] Under this appropriate minimum definition, the public presumptively has a right to attend all parts of a criminal proceeding taking place in the presence of the jury. This definition has become a baseline and there have been few disputes in the lower courts about whether the First or Sixth Amendment right of access applies to proceedings in which the jury is present.

Whether the public should have access to trial proceedings held outside the hearing of the jury, whether they occur before or during the course of the trial, is a question that has frequently been raised under the First Amendment and sometimes under the Sixth Amendment. The holding in *Waller* that the Sixth Amendment does apply to a suppression hearing, a proceeding held outside the presence of the jury, shows that the definition of "trial" for purposes of the Sixth Amendment is clearly broader than the Maine court's basic list. Under most lists of the functions of a public trial, all phases of a criminal prosecution that take place in court, even in the absence of the jury, should be presumptively open to the public at a defendant's request.

Pretrial Proceedings

Suppression Hearings

Because *Waller* is the Supreme Court's only Sixth Amendment case on scope questions, its analysis should apply to all other questions about which proceedings are covered by the Sixth as opposed to the First Amendment.

The functions the Court considered in *Waller,* in the course of concluding that suppression hearings must presumptively be open, focused on how the defendant's interests might be served—the resemblance of the hearing to a trial, the importance of the hearing, the need for public presence to ensure that prosecutor and judge act responsibly, and the possible impact on the quality of the testimony—would clearly be relevant in any other case interpreting whether or not a particular proceeding is covered by the Sixth Amendment. The Supreme Court was more circumspect about whether the public's interests, which provide a key rationale in the First Amendment cases, should also be counted in the Sixth Amendment analysis. "To the extent that there is an independent public interest in thc Sixth Amendment public-trial guarantee," said the Court, that interest would apply with full force in suppression hearings. The public has a strong interest in allegations of police misconduct, as exemplified in *Waller*, in which the defendant alleged that the police had conducted general searches and wholesale seizures in more than 150 homes and eavesdropped on 800 hours of telephone conversations without meaningful judicial supervision. The Court's reserve on this factor, viewed as relevant only "to the extent that" the public interest should be considered, is significant because it poses a possible limitation on how First Amendment cases will bear on Sixth Amendment analysis—the interests cognizable in these cases may or may not include public interests.

Waller also provided that the remedy for a violation of the right to a public trial at a discrete proceeding may not be a new trial. The remedy the Court offered in *Waller* was a new suppression hearing, because that was the proceeding that was improperly closed. Whether or not a new trial was required would depend, the Court said, on whether or not the new suppression hearing resulted in the suppression of material evidence admitted at the first trial, or some other material change in the positions of the parties.

Voir Dire

In its First Amendment case law, the Supreme Court has also found a public right of access to other specific phases of a criminal prosecution. *Press-Enterprise*

I held that voir dire must be presumptively open to the public, subject to limited exceptions that might be appropriate to preserve some aspects of jurors' privacy. In reaching this decision, the Court applied the *Richmond Newspapers* two-part test. With respect to the first criterion, tradition, the Court concluded that ever since the development of trial by jury, the process of selecting jurors has been presumptively open. On the second *Richmond Newspapers* criterion, the function to be served by allowing public access to voir dire proceedings, the Court described, briefly, how allowing attendance at trials promotes fair proceedings as well as public confidence in the fairness of proceedings. The Court also noted that, under the First Amendment, it was not necessary to parse the benefits to the defendant and the benefits to the public, which suggests that under the Sixth Amendment, such parsing might indeed be necessary and so the analysis might be different.

Lower courts that have examined the question of whether there is also a right for the public to attend voir dire under the Sixth Amendment have concluded that the Sixth Amendment is broad enough to encompass this right, although usually without much independent analysis. Courts generally cite *Press-Enterprise I* and *Waller* as establishing that there is a right to a public voir dire, without recognizing that the First Amendment and Sixth Amendment analyses may diverge,[200] an approach the *Waller* dicta may have encouraged.[201]

The conclusion that voir dire should be regarded as part of the Sixth Amendment's public "trial" is quite defensible on fuller analysis. Voir dire resembles a trial in some respects—lawyers must sometimes argue to the judge about whether there is a basis to challenge a juror for cause, and the judge renders a ruling after hearing adversarial arguments. Publicity might enhance accuracy of the basis on which jurors are selected by encouraging jurors to answer questions truthfully. Public scrutiny may also lead the prosecutor and judge to act responsibly. Jury selection is undoubtedly an important phase of a criminal proceeding from the point of view of the defendant. Many attorneys regard a case as won or lost during jury selection. Notorious cases like the trial of O.J. Simpson and of the police officers charged with using excessive force in arresting Rodney King have focused the attention of the public on the importance of the composition of juries. Although there is considerable public interest in who will serve on a jury or in how a judge is ruling on peremptory challenges, these public interests, as distinct from a defendant's interests, may or may not be relevant to the Sixth Amendment analysis, in light of *Waller.*

The Court's finding in *Press-Enterprise I* that voir dire has traditionally been open to the public, although this is not a necessary finding under *Waller*, could also be taken as relevant in a Sixth Amendment analysis. Evidence of the common law at the time of the drafting of the Sixth Amendment would certainly add weight to a defendant's argument for holding voir dire in public.

A number of defendants have invoked their Sixth Amendment right in objecting to the partial or total closure of jury selection proceedings and have succeeded in winning a new trial. Some trial judges have excluded spectators, including the defendant's family members, from attending voir dire because their small courtroom is filled by the large number of people in the jury pool. Appellate judges have been skeptical of these actions if the trial judge has not held careful hearings about the extent of the problem and possible alternatives. Appellate courts have taken the right to public trial very seriously and ordered new trials to remedy the exclusion of family members and spectators during voir dire.[202] Among the alternatives suggested to temporary closure of the courtroom are limiting the size of the jury pool, letting spectators stand to observe the proceedings, requesting a larger courtroom, and, even if a temporary closure is required, inviting spectators into the courtroom as soon as prospective jurors have been excused and vacated seats.

Publicity's duplicitous nature can show itself during voir dire. Not all defendants will prefer to select a jury in public. Boxing promoter Don King, for example, was charged with wire fraud and successfully moved to limit press access to voir dire proceedings. He argued that he was so notorious that fear of publicity might inhibit the prospective jurors from giving candid responses to questions asked in public and that candid responses would be particularly important to his ability to receive a fair trial.[203] Although King did not, of course, have the right to choose to have a portion of his trial held in private, the trial court honored his request to close voir dire and not release transcripts of the questioning. This decision was upheld by the appellate court, on the basis that King's was indeed a unique case requiring such closure.

If the Sixth Amendment right to a public trial is violated during voir dire, the proper remedy must be a new trial. *Waller* required an appropriate remedy for exclusion of the public, without demanding any showing of prejudice. As an Illinois court said, "even though the violation came during the jury selection process, it is impossible to separate that part from the rest of the trial. The Sixth Amendment protects all of the trial component parts, and not simply the right publicly to present evidence and witnesses."[204]

Preliminary Hearings

Press-Enterprise II and *El Vocero* held that preliminary hearings are presumptively open under the First Amendment. Most lower courts to have confronted the question have held that preliminary hearings are also covered by the Sixth Amendment. The Supreme Court's historical conclusion about the tradition of open preliminary hearings in *Press-Enterprise II*, scant as its historical support might have been, has been taken by some courts as transferable. Several of the benefits the Court mentioned in *Press-Enterprise II* and *El Vocero* could indeed serve the defendant's interest in a fair trial. Because live witnesses testify at such a hearing, it is as plausible in this context, as in the context of a trial, that public scrutiny will lead to more truthful testimony or the emergence of additional witnesses. Preliminary hearings are important parts of a criminal proceeding. Defendants have been held to have a right to counsel, a parallel Sixth Amendment right, at preliminary hearings on the ground that this proceeding constitutes a critical stage of the criminal prosecution.[205]

If the Sixth Amendment public trial right does apply to preliminary hearings, the difficult question of remedy arises if a preliminary hearing is closed in violation of that right. The remedy afforded in *Press-Enterprise II* and *El Vocero* was opening the proceeding, because the First Amendment claim was raised in interlocutory appeals brought by newspapers. Criminal defendants' Sixth Amendment claims are usually raised on appeal from their conviction, when it is too late to cure the violation. In State ex rel. Stevens v. Circuit Court for Manitowoc County (1987), the Wisconsin Supreme Court, which had previously held that preliminary hearings could be closed, concluded that *Press-Enterprise II* and *Waller* reflected a changed attitude toward the value of open proceedings and, overruling its previous case law, held that defendants do have a Sixth Amendment right to open preliminary hearings. However, in a subsequent case (State v. Webb, 1991), the court ruled that although the defendant's family had been excluded from a preliminary examination of a victim of the sexual assault forming the basis for the prosecution, there was no violation of the Sixth Amendment given that nothing from the preliminary examination was used at trial or had any actual impact on the trial itself, which was fair and error-free.

As the dissent noted in *Webb*, *Waller* clearly provides that a violation of the Sixth Amendment right to a public trial is not subject to a harmless error analysis. *Waller* also provided that the proper remedy for the denial of the right to an open suppression hearing was a new suppression hearing, which would only lead to a retrial if the conduct of the trial would be affected by new results at the suppression hearing. The majority of the Wisconsin court simply seems to have misapplied this aspect of *Waller* in concluding that there was not only no need to hold a new trial, but no need to hold a new preliminary hearing.

Analysis of the remedy question presented in *Webb* requires a close analysis of the reasons why preliminary hearings should be open under the Sixth Amendment, something the Wisconsin court did not accomplish in either of these decisions. On the one hand, a preliminary hearing, resulting in a finding of probable cause to hold the defendant for trial, results in an interim ruling that is, in some respects, subsumed by the later finding at trial that the defendant's guilt has been proved beyond a reasonable doubt. Some of the factors the Court relied on in *Press-Enterprise II*—that the preliminary hearing might be the main event in a criminal prosecution if the defendant then pleads guilty, and that there are no jurors present to observe the prosecution—are mitigated by the fact that the defendant has subsequently had an open trial before a jury. On the other hand, the basis for applying the Sixth Amendment right to preliminary proceedings may not be only to guarantee that the trial itself will be fair. Some of the rationales discussed above—whether the defendant might benefit because witnesses at the hearing will testify more accurately, or because new witnesses might emerge—suggest that the preliminary hearing has independent value. And to the extent that the public interest in observing preliminary hearings is relevant to Sixth Amendment analysis, the question left open in *Waller*, that interest may be independent of the public's interest in what happens at trial. As in *Press-Enterprise II,* it could be said that public observation is essential to ensure that preliminary hearings are fair and that the public has confidence in the fairness of these proceedings. It is also possible that closure of a preliminary hearing could influence a witness's testimony in an invisible manner that would then carry over to the testimony at the trial itself.

While the court's harmless error finding in *Webb* might be viewed as insufficiently attentive to the range of values the right to an open preliminary hearing might serve, the case also raises the interesting possibility that there may not be any real remedy for improper closure of a preliminary hearing other than conducting both the hearing and the trial again. The discrete subject matter of a suppression hearing, as in *Waller*, can be isolated and relitigated. But holding a new open preliminary hearing might not yield any noticeable difference that would have affected the trial. The Supreme Court has explained that no showing of prejudice is necessary when the right to a public trial has been denied, precisely because it is so difficult to identify how the defendant has been prejudiced in an individual case. Whether that same analysis should apply if the violation takes place at a pretrial proceeding other than a suppression hearing is an open question, although not in Wisconsin.

As with criminal trials, defendants will not always wish their preliminary hearings to be open. Indeed, some lower court cases examining the First Amendment right of the public to attend a preliminary hearing have arisen when defendants requested that the proceeding be closed.[206] Defendants who want their preliminary hearings to be open should not encounter difficulty in establishing their right to a presumptively public proceeding. Whether these defendants win reversal of their convictions to remedy violations after the fact is the harder question.

Other Pretrial Proceedings

The Supreme Court has not considered whether there is a right of public access under either the Sixth or First Amendment to any other pretrial proceedings. There are relatively few lower court cases interpreting the scope of the Sixth Amendment with respect to other proceedings. The lower court cases regarding First Amendment access are also useful because, as with issues discussed above, they can function as a first draft of what the Sixth Amendment could be viewed as covering.

Perceiving the Supreme Court's preference for open proceedings and impressed with the list of functions open proceedings serve, the lower courts have held that the First Amendment requires most pretrial judicial proceedings in criminal cases to be at least presumptively open. In some cases, because the pretrial proceeding being considered on appeal was in fact closed, it is not apparent what kind of pretrial proceeding was involved. In United States v. Cojab (1993), for example, the Second Circuit reviewed a District Court's decision to close "a pretrial hearing" in a drug-ring murder trial. The court generalized that "it is now established that a qualified right of access applies not only to public trials, but also to pretrial hearings, such as the one before us in the instant case" (citing the Second Circuit Court of Appeals in United States v. Haller, 1988). Although citing the Sixth Amendment, the court went on to employ a First Amendment analysis, never revealing whether the defendant favored closure or was asserting his Sixth Amendment rights.

As the Third Circuit generalized in its classic, frequently cited opinion in United States v. Cianfrani (1978), which anticipated *Waller* in holding a right to open suppression hearings, "our law strongly favors the presumption that all adjudicative proceedings are open to the public." Some courts have effectively modified the *Richmond Newspapers* two-part test by finding a right of access to all important parts of a criminal proceeding, regardless of tradition, based on the importance of transparency in the criminal justice system. The Alabama Supreme Court, for example, while acknowledging that certain pretrial hearings have not traditionally been open to the public, described pretrial hearings as "often critical, sometimes dispositive, to the outcome of a criminal prosecution," and urged courts to use a functional analysis "on the importance of the hearings to the case" even with respect to hearings with no tradition of openness.[207] And the Fifth Circuit in Rovinsky v. McKaskle (1984) generalized that in analyzing a Sixth Amendment claim, the right does not depend on whether the inquiry of the hearing is factual or doctrinal, substantive or procedural, but rather on the relationship of the issue raised at the hearing to (1) the merits of the charge, (2) the outcome of the prosecution, and (3) the integrity of the administration of justice. "The right to a public trial is not limited to issues that arise after a jury is sworn or times when the jury is present. It extends at least to those pretrial hearings that are an integral part of the trial, such as jury selection and motions to suppress evidence." The *Rovinsky* factors are a useful addition to the *Press-Enterprise I* test in evaluating Sixth Amendment claims, an area in which the Supreme Court has provided little guidance.

Courts have reviewed closure of such specific pretrial proceedings as a hearing on a change of venue motion, finding that the First Amendment presumption of openness should apply.[208]

Lower courts have also concluded that the public has a First Amendment right to attend bail or detention hearings. Bail hearings have not traditionally been open to the public. As the Fifth Circuit noted in United States v. Chagra (1983),[209] bail proceedings have historically been informal and have sometimes been held in open court at the defendant's first court appearance, but they have also been held in closed settings. Nevertheless, both the Fifth and Ninth Circuits decided that, under the second prong of the *Richmond Newspapers* test, the importance of public attendance at bail hearings is so great that such proceedings should be presumptively open. Such proceedings, the *Chagra* court noted, entail decisions that attract significant public interest, partly because of the public's concern about recidivism if an accused is released, and thus invite legitimate and public scrutiny.

The First Circuit, in In re Globe Newspaper Co. (1984), reached the same conclusion, stressing the importance of the bail hearing decision. The court noted that the decision to release a defendant who then absconds can effectively terminate a criminal proceeding, while a decision to detain a defendant takes away the liberty of someone who has not yet been convicted. "In either case, the bail decision is one of major importance to the administration of justice, and openness will help to assure the public that the decision is properly reached." The presumption in favor of open bail hearings may be overcome by specific findings of necessity in a particular case.[210] In the post–September 11 case In re Release of Sealed Transcripts in the Matter of Mohammed El-Atriss (2003), a New Jersey judge was so impressed with the government's claim that national security could be jeopardized by divulgence of evidence the government wished to introduce on the question of whether the defendant, charged with forging documents, should be released on bail, that she closed the proceeding not only to the public but, controversially, even to the defendant and his attorney.

Whether the same analysis would apply to a Sixth Amendment claim is an open question, and may remain open because it seems unlikely that a defendant would want to press a claim of right to an open bail proceeding. Defendant El-Atriss objected to his own exclusion, but when the judge later decided to unseal the bail hearing transcripts after he pleaded guilty to document forgery, he protested the disclosure, contending that the government's argument to the court that he was involved in terrorism, a charge never proved, could ruin his reputation.[211] In the cases described above, the public's interest in the proceeding was likely to be adverse to the defendant's. In all likelihood, the public would ordinarily favor a defendant being detained pending trial, particularly in notorious cases, or prosecutions of crimes of violence. And the public's presence might well encourage the judge to decide against release.

The usual considerations favoring public presence—preventing perjury, surfacing additional witnesses, and encouraging careful decision making—would argue in favor of opening release hearings. Some have also maintained that the release decision has an impact on the outcome of the trial itself, with those defendants detained pending trial more likely to be convicted.[212] Conversely, the release decision does not bear a strong resemblance to a trial and could be viewed as addressing an issue collateral to the defendant's guilt or innocence and thus outside the purview of the Sixth Amendment's concerns. Suppression hearings and voir dire can be viewed as "integral parts" of a trial, as the Fifth Circuit has said in Rovinsky v. McKaskle (1984), while bail hearings, even more than preliminary hearings, might not be viewed in this light. Thus, it might take a more expansive view of the purposes of the Sixth Amendment than the Supreme Court has endorsed thus far to hold that the Sixth Amendment right applies to release hearings.

Disqualification and Conflicts Hearings

When motions are made to disqualify a judge, a prosecutor, or a defense attorney (because of an alleged conflict of interest), courts have found the hearings on such motions also to be presumptively open under the First Amendment. In one case, the president of the Teamsters Union, Jackie Presser, moved to disqualify the judge assigned to his case because of previous conflicts between the judge, the defendant, and the defense attorneys. The prosecution then requested an inquiry into possible defense attorney conflicts of interest. Both sides requested that hearings on these motions be held *in camera* and that the supporting briefs be sealed. The Sixth Circuit, in Applications of National Broadcasting (1987), found a First Amendment right of access to both proceedings and vacated the District Court's closure order. The court concluded that both types of proceedings had traditionally been held in open court and that the public had a substantial interest in both decisions. "When a judge's impartiality is questioned, it strengthens the judicial process for the public to be informed of how the issue is approached and decided." These decisions, while not "like a trial," are like voir dire, the beginning of a trial, in that they decide who the key participants in the trial will be. They also generate factual and legal decisions that may affect all subsequent proceedings in the case, including the trial. And such hearings clearly can involve matters of great public interest because they entail an allegation by at least one party that the judge, prosecutor, or attorney has a conflict or would behave unethically to continue on the case. The integrity of the trial is very much at issue.

When defendants have challenged the holding of such hearings in a judge's chambers rather than open court, however, courts have found no violation of the Sixth Amendment. In State v. Mecier (1984), the Vermont Supreme Court held that a conference held in chambers to hear a defendant's motion to disqualify the prosecutor in addition to a defendant's motion to dismiss was not covered by the guarantee of a public "trial" because the conference did not include taking testimony from witnesses, but merely offers of proof from counsel. The Vermont court had previously declared that trials should be held in open court, with hearings in chambers the exception, but ruled that this case was within that exception. Although this case was decided after *Waller*, it was decided before *Press-Enterprise II* applied the First Amendment right of access to preliminary hearings, and so the court's description of when proceedings other than trials were to be held in open court has become somewhat outdated. Similarly, in Hayes v. United States (1961), the Eighth Circuit easily disposed of a claim that the defendant had been denied his right to a public trial when the judge held a hearing regarding whether or not Hayes would be permitted to represent himself in chambers rather than in open court. In this early case, before either *Waller* or *Press-Enterprise II*, the court announced that the conference was not part of the trial but merely a preliminary proceeding.[213] In light of more recent developments in the law, the defendant's argument would have to be analyzed more fully today.

Competency Hearings

A number of state courts have concluded that the same reasoning that requires open trials also mandates open competency proceedings. In these pretrial hearings to determine whether a defendant is competent to stand trial, the court must determine, usually on the basis of expert testimony and possibly the testimony of the defendant and other witnesses, whether the defendant has sufficient ability to consult with his or her lawyer with a reasonable degree of rational understanding and whether the defendant has a rational as well as factual understanding of the proceedings against him or her.[214] Courts applying the Supreme Court's current First Amendment standards conclude that the competency hearing is a critical stage of a criminal prosecution, requiring decisions by the court that "attract significant public interest and invite legitimate and healthy public scrutiny."[215] Even before the Supreme Court decided *Richmond Newspapers* and *Press-Enterprise*

I, the New York Court of Appeals had reached the same conclusion based on New York state law, in Westchester Rockland Newspapers, Inc. v. Leggett (1979).

Sixth Amendment claims respecting exclusion of thc public from competency hearings might seem unlikely. A finding of incompetency to stand trial is not always welcome and public scrutiny of a defendant's mental state might also be unwelcome. If a defendant were to raise a Sixth Amendment claim, here too analysis should resemble that in *Waller*. Defendants might receive the often touted benefits of more accurate testimony and discovery of additional witnesses. A defendant might believe that a prosecution, or even a competency hearing being held against his or her will, is oppressive and wish to invite the public's attention to an unwelcome tactic. If a defendant is found incompetent, trial will be obviated or at least deferred, so the competency hearing might be the only opportunity for a defendant who wishes the public to understand the nature of a prosecution to receive full public attention.

Change of Venue Hearings

The court of appeals in Charlotte Observer v. Bakker (1989) held that the public has a presumptive right to attend a hearing on a motion for change of venue. As described above, there should be a right of public access under the First Amendment wherever there is great public interest in a judicial proceeding, as there certainly would have been in the change of venue in the Rodney King case. Analysis under the Sixth Amendment, considering the three *Rovinsky* factors (evaluating the relationship of the proceeding to the merits of the case, the outcome, and the integrity of the administration of justice) might come out the same way. If a defendant wants the public to attend the venue hearing, it is likely that there will be considerable public interest and little legitimate reason for exclusion.

Plea Hearings

Courts have held, under a First Amendment analysis, that there is a right of public access to plea hearings and plea agreements.[216] Plea hearings, according to these courts, have traditionally been open to the public. Functionally, access, as in the case of criminal trials, serves to allow public scrutiny of the conduct of courts and prosecutors. The prosecutor or judge may be taking advantage of the defendant, the prosecutor may have bribed the defendant with a lenient sentence to avoid exposure of misconduct on the part of the prosecutor or government agents, the prosecutor or judge may have colluded with a defendant regarded as sympathetic, or the prosecutor or judge may have been bribed or influenced by a powerful defendant. In addition, plea hearings are even more likely than suppression hearings, as found in *Waller*, to be the main event in a criminal prosecution. The taking of a plea is the most common form of adjudication in criminal litigation,[217] with over 90 percent of criminal convictions in most jurisdictions resting on guilty pleas rather than trials.[218]

It seems likely that the same conclusion respecting this critical adjudicative procedure would be reached under the Sixth Amendment. Accepting a plea in secret would be the antithesis of the Sixth Amendment's preference for open trials. The *Rovinsky* test would easily be satisfied.

Proceedings during Trial

As described above, the Sixth Amendment right to a public trial universally applies to proceedings for empaneling the jury, opening statements of counsel, presentation of evidence, arguments of counsel to the jury, instructions to the jury, and return of the verdict. Virtually all proceedings held in the presence of the jury are understood to be presumptively open, even including questions the jury asks the judge after deliberations have begun. The Illinois Supreme Court, in People v. Childs (1994), considered ex parte communications between a deliberating jury and the judge to violate a defendant's right to a public trial, as well as his coordinate Sixth Amendment right to be present and have the assistance of counsel at all critical stages of the prosecution, reversing the conviction of the defendant whose trial was involved.[219]

A rare exception to the general rule that the public is invited to hear everything heard by the jury was a special proceeding the trial judge held in the case of United States v. Ivester (2003) to speak with jurors about whether or not they shared concerns about their security that one juror had raised with the judge in chambers. The appellate court ruled that the exclusion of the public from the mid-trial questioning of jurors on this subject did not violate the Sixth Amendment because it was just "administrative" and unrelated to the trial itself.

Most courts agree with the Ninth Circuit, which said in United States v. Ivester (2003) that the right to a public trial does not extend to "every moment" of a trial. The Fifth Circuit in United States v. Norris (1986) drew a distinction between discussions of counsel and the judge on technical legal issues or routine administrative problems, on the one hand, and proceedings in which the public has a significant role to play, on the other. Unsurprisingly, the courts have not always had an easy time distinguishing which proceedings fall into which category.

Although *Globe Newspaper* said that there is no First Amendment right for the public to observe the contents of sidebar proceedings held out of hearing of the jury—see also Richmond Newspapers, Inc. v. Virginia (1980) (Brennan, J., concurring)—the Sixth Amendment public trial right may be violated if a judge holds specific proceedings outside the hearing of the jury and the public.

Whether or not the jury is present for the proceeding is not dispositive, because some proceedings that do not involve a jury, like a suppression hearing, are covered by the public trial guarantee. This is one context in which decisions can depend on the breadth of a court's view of the functions of the public trial. If the public is regarded as a jury of the whole and its chief purpose is to provide a check to ensure that its representatives on the petit jury are acting properly, then there is little need for the public to be present at any proceeding not held before the jury. If, on the other hand, the public is expected to provide a check on all of the trial participants, then it is even more important for the public to hear conversations that take place outside the jury's hearing, because the jury itself cannot fulfill that function. There is often good reason for the judge and attorneys to hold sidebar discussions outside the presence of the jury, because they are often discussing evidence that might not be presented at the trial, or information that might prejudice a jury. However, a judge or prosecutor could also use a sidebar conference improperly to browbeat a defendant, or the parties could collude to prevent the jury from hearing evidence that should be admissible. In such a case, the public could provide a check on potential abuse that the jury cannot.

The Fifth Circuit's opinion in United States v. Norris (1986) provides a good example of a functional analysis of whether the public trial right should apply. The defendant in that case had objected to the closure of a bench conference about a particular piece of evidence—a chart. The court did not believe anything that happened at this hearing could hinder the objectives fostered by the right to public trial because no facts were being found, the issues did not bear on the guilt or innocence of the defendant, and such colloquies do not ordinarily pose any threat of judicial, prosecutorial, or public abuse. The court contrasted the role the public can play in observing a suppression hearing.

Applying the same analysis in another case, the Fifth Circuit in United States v. Edwards (2002) held that the right to public trial did apply to a hearing on the subject of whether or not to empanel an anonymous jury. Because of the nature of the charges at issue, the trial judge decided to withhold some information about the jurors from the defendant and defense counsel. The reviewing court considered the functions of the public trial right, contrasting the suppression hearing considered in *Waller*, where there is a vital public role in discouraging perjury and ensuring that the government conducts itself responsibly, with routine legal arguments about administrative matters for which there is no vital role for the public. The court believed that the public had a role to play in the hearing on the degree of anonymity of the jury, even if this decision was unlikely to affect the outcome of the trial. Because the defendant was challenging the prosecution's assertions that he posed a threat to the integrity of the jury, the public could serve the same watchdog function as the public attending a suppression hearing. The court therefore applied the *Waller* factors, but concluded that the trial court's closure had been appropriate and carefully tailored.[220]

The Fifth Circuit's opinion in this case, following on the same court's rejection in the *Rovinsky* case of formalistic distinctions, provides a good reminder that only if there is an overriding reason to keep the subject matter of a sidebar conference confidential should the public be excluded over a defendant's objection. Trial judges do not always explore whether there is actually a good reason to exclude the public from a bench or sidebar conference and sometimes simply assume that any proceeding can be closed if it can be characterized as administrative, or if it occurs outside the presence of the jury. The Eleventh Circuit Court of Appeals in United States v. Valenti (1993), for example, held that trial judges have traditional authority to conduct closed bench conferences within their discretion and may satisfy the need for public disclosure by releasing transcripts after the conference.

The idea of a broad right of public access to all proceedings, including a presumptive right to hear colloquies between counsel and the judge, runs up against practical considerations as well as a sense of tradition. If the public has a right to "attend" sidebar conferences, often conducted in whispers at the front of a courtroom, this might mean that the jury would be required to leave the room during every sidebar, a practice which would lengthen the trial and inconvenience the jurors. The conference would also have to be made audible to the spectators.

In some cases, courts have believed that it is necessary to make this effort. A California court, for example, ruled that it is a violation of the right to a public trial for a judge to hear and decide on peremptory challenges to prospective jurors in chambers (People v. Harris, 1992). However, when a trial judge decided to hear peremptory challenges and arguments about whether some of those challenges were impermissibly based on race in a sidebar proceeding, the same California appellate court held that this decision did not deny defendant's public trial right because the judge then announced the rulings on the peremptory challenges in open court (People v. Williams, 1994).

Post-Trial Proceedings

Sentencing proceedings have been held to be presumptively open under the First Amendment. The Fourth Circuit in In re Washington Post (1986) regarded sentencing as part of, in fact the culmination of, the trial. Sentencing proceedings, as far as history reveals, have traditionally been open.[221] Public access certainly serves the important function of ensuring that neither the prosecutor nor the judge will engage in arbitrary or wrongful conduct. Other courts have agreed that there is no reason to treat sentencing proceedings differently from trials or pretrial proceedings.[222] Even a motion for a downward departure under the Federal Sentencing Guidelines has been held to require an open proceeding. "Few things would cause the public to be more suspicious of our system of criminal justice than to have secret proceedings that lead to special sentencing treatment for select criminal defendants."[223]

These same arguments could render the sentencing proceeding part of a public trial within the meaning of the Sixth Amendment. This holding would be less dramatic than holding that some of the earlier proceedings discussed above are covered by the Sixth Amendment, because it is clear that the appropriate remedy for any violation would be a limited one. If a defendant's sentencing proceeding was improperly closed, under the theory of *Waller,* that defendant would be entitled only to a new sentencing proceeding and not to a new trial. Like the suppression hearing in *Waller,* sentencing is a discrete procedure; unlike the suppression hearing, revisiting a sentencing proceeding does not create any possibility that a retrial will be necessary because any error at sentencing, by definition, occurs after conviction.

Other proceedings occurring after a trial might call the integrity of the trial into question. Post-trial claims of juror misconduct, for example, have often been conducted *in camera.* The Third Circuit in United States v. Simone (1994)[224] held that the First Amendment right of access does attach to inquiries into juror misbehavior. The court found that there was no real tradition of holding such inquiries in private, unlike grand jury proceedings, and so "experience" proved a limited guide. Instead, the court focused on the functions to be served by opening such inquiries to public scrutiny and found no reason to treat these proceedings any differently from any other aspect of a criminal trial. Public scrutiny here too could serve to discourage perjury, encourage careful decision making, and ensure the integrity of the process. The same reasoning was applied to a motion to set aside a guilty verdict by the New York Appellate Division Fourth Department in Gannett Co. v. Mark (1976).

Post-conviction proceedings should be presumptively open, according to the Ninth Circuit in CBS, Inc. v. United States Dist. Ct. (1985).

The greater the distance between a post-trial proceeding and the trial itself, the greater the likelihood that courts will disagree as to whether proceedings should be presumptively open. Probation revocation proceedings, for example, were found to be covered by the First Amendment in Montana ex rel. Great Falls Tribune Co. v. Montana Eighth Judicial District (1989).[225] The Mississippi court in Williams v. State (1982), however, found probation revocation proceedings to be in the nature of an administrative summary proceeding, growing out of a privilege the court had granted by suspending the defendant's sentence and placing him on probation, and therefore not subject to the First Amendment right of access. A release hearing in a controversial challenge to prison overcrowding was also been held to be presumptively open by the Eleventh Circuit Court of Appeals in Newman v. Graddick (1983).

Juvenile Proceedings

On the theory that juvenile proceedings are traditionally confidential, noncriminal proceedings, most courts have not recognized any right of public access to juvenile proceedings. The Sixth Amendment right to jury trial "in all criminal prosecutions" does not apply in juvenile proceedings, and the Supreme Court has held that the Due Process Clause does not guarantee juveniles a right to a jury trial (see McKeiver v. Pennsylvania, 1970). Despite the Supreme Court's ruling in *McKeiver*, in State in Interest of Dino (1978), the Louisiana Supreme Court concluded that the right to a public trial is of fundamental importance in any adversary proceeding that may lead to confinement and therefore should apply in juvenile proceedings. This decision was derived from the Supreme Court's decision in In re Gault (1967), which guarantees juveniles the essential elements of due process before they may be incarcerated. The Louisiana court agreed that juveniles do not have a right to jury trial, but nevertheless held that the right to a public trial plays a critical role in guaranteeing the fairness of proceedings. The court reached this conclusion after reviewing the functions and historical role played by the right to public trial. In the absence of a jury, there is actually a greater need for the public to play a role in monitoring the operations of the juvenile courts and the fairness of a particular juvenile proceeding.[226]

Outside Louisiana, claims for press or public access to juvenile proceedings based on the First Amendment have been generally unsuccessful, given the tradition of confidentiality of these proceedings.[227] Some commentators, emphasizing the second prong of the *Richmond Newspapers* test (function) argue that given the evolving function of juvenile proceedings, which has moved away from rehabilitation and toward simple punishment, their similarity to criminal adjudications, and the strong public interest in the workings of the juvenile justice system, there should be a First Amendment–based right of presumptive public access to juvenile proceedings.[228] The ABA has endorsed this position.[229] In about nine states, state law provides that juvenile records and proceedings are presumptively open in cases that involve offenses that would be felonies if committed by adults.[230] In many states, although juvenile proceedings are presumptively closed, some public or press access may be allowed.[231] Even if courts were to recognize a right of public access to juvenile proceedings based on state statutes, state constitutional provisions, or the First Amendment, the subjects of these proceedings would not be likely to benefit in any direct way. Juveniles who want their proceedings to be closed might find their wishes trumped by the First Amendment. Juveniles who object to the court closing their proceedings will not have the remedy provided by the Sixth Amendment—reversal of their conviction—unless their state courts decide, like the Louisiana Supreme Court, that public trial is an aspect of due process.

Reviewing all of these cases on the scope of the right of public access confirms that, as Justice Burger predicted, the *Richmond Newspapers* two-part test, especially as modified by judges who focus primarily on the function prong, will encompass virtually any proceeding that is part of a criminal prosecution. Whether the Supreme Court will interpret the Sixth Amendment more narrowly remains to be seen.

Partial Closures and *De Minimis* Violations

In *Waller*, the Supreme Court held that prejudice need not be shown to establish a violation of the Sixth Amendment right to a public trial. The lower courts have held, however, that some incursions on the right of the public to attend criminal trials, whether intended or de facto, may be deemed *de minimis* and will not be considered infringements of the defendant's Sixth Amendment right. A court may impose "reasonable and neutral" time, place, and manner restrictions on the right of public access to judicial proceedings without violating the First Amendment.[232] The Supreme Court has not announced whether the same standard applies to determine when a temporary or limited restriction on public attendance constitutes a presumptive violation of the Sixth Amendment. The Court did say, in Waller v. Georgia (1984), that the Sixth Amendment is no less protective of a public trial than the implicit First Amendment right, but it has not considered whether the Sixth Amendment might, in some respects, be more demanding. Whether or not trial judges should be afforded the same degree of discretion when their closure decisions are challenged by a defendant under the Sixth Amendment is a subject of some disagreement among the lower courts.[233] It could be argued that although a defendant has no absolute right to close a proceeding, a defendant who wishes his trial proceedings to be open should usually be entitled to make that judgment. The defendant's and the public's interests coalesce, and the defendant is effectively choosing the right to publicity over a potential claim of unfairness; thus, the standard for closing even part of a trial over the defendant's objection should be higher than a reasonableness standard.

Many appellate courts have allowed trial judges considerable leeway in controlling courtroom decorum by declaring some restrictions too trivial to amount to a presumptive Sixth Amendment violation, and therefore not even demanding that the state show the closure to have served an overriding interest or that there were no less restrictive alternatives. Courtrooms are not always big enough to accommodate all the spectators who might like to attend a trial; courts have ruled that individual people may be excluded, without rigorous appellate scrutiny, as long as the proceeding is accessible to "the public" generally. Trials, or portions of trials, are sometimes held in a location other than a courtroom, making it more difficult for spectators to attend; courts have held this practice permissible, as long as the proceedings are still sufficiently accessible to some. Judges may decide to close the courtroom door and not allow any additional spectators to enter or to leave during a critical phase of a trial, usually summations or the court's charge to the jury; some appellate courts have sympathized with the trial judge's desire to instruct the jurors without interruptions or distractions, as long as some members of the public were able to observe this phase of the trial. Not surprisingly, courts have differed on how to draw the line between the *de minimis* and the constitutional violation in these and other examples of partial closure.

In addition, a number of federal Courts of Appeals have put a gloss on the Waller v. Georgia test, applying a more lenient test to partial closures that are more than *de minimis*: if the impact of a partial closure does not reach the level of a total closure, the state need show only a "substantial" rather than "compelling" reason for the closure.[234] Other jurisdictions have disagreed with this lowered standard of review, insisting that if a closure is more than *de minimis*, it must be scrutinized under the four-part *Waller* test.[235] Of course, under *Waller*, even if a closure is legitimate, it must not be any greater in scope than necessary to serve the purpose.[236]

The lower courts' approaches are very much dependent on their views of the functions of the right of public trial, although most opinions do not expressly recognize this. If, as Earl Warren argued, the members of the public attending a trial are representative and the real point of the guarantee is to prevent secret trials, then trial judges may be granted leeway to exclude some of the people who wish to attend a trial as long as others remain. If, on the other hand, the trial is viewed as the public's trial and members of the public have their own right to attend in order to educate themselves and observe for themselves what their elected and appointed representatives are doing, then any individual's exclusion is significant and must be scrupulously justified.[237] This same choice becomes critical in the context of the cameras in the courtroom debate, for which these cases provide some interesting precedent.

The fact that these questions arise in the context of criminal appeals or collateral challenges to criminal convictions clearly has an effect on the courts. The Supreme Court case law discussed above should have impressed on trial judges the importance of ensuring that criminal proceedings are as open as possible. But while favoring an open proceeding is usually the right answer when that proceeding has not yet taken place, appellate courts viewing closure decisions in hindsight are frequently not sufficiently impressed with the right to public trial to be willing to reverse convictions for violations less extensive than those the Supreme Court has considered.

Size and Location of Courtroom

The fact that a courtroom cannot hold all members of the public who want to attend a trial has generally been held not to violate the Sixth Amendment right, as long as some significant number of spectators and representatives of the press are able to be present.[238] Even if a judge has decided to conduct the trial in a relatively small courtroom instead of a larger courtroom that could have been available, courts have held that there is no violation as long as "the public," through its representatives, has not been excluded.[239] It is possible to disagree with this conclusion if one believes that the right to public trial is more than an instrumental right for defendants. Max Radin, for example, argues that if it is possible to hold a trial in a courtroom large enough to accommodate all members of the public who wish to attend, perhaps there should be some obligation for the court to try to do so.[240]

Some courts also evidently believe that the right to public trial means only that judges should not intentionally exclude the public. One Iowa court, for example, thought it was relevant whether the trial judge, in designating an alternative place for trial even though it contained very limited space for spectators, had done so specifically to exclude the public. In this case, the presiding judge decided to hold trial proceedings in a room in the basement of the local post office after a fire marshal declared the courthouse to be unsafe. The defendant argued that the lack of physical capacity and decorum deprived him of his right to a public trial. The test, said the Iowa Supreme Court in State v. Jones (1979), is not the size of the courtroom or whether everyone who wishes to be present can be seated, but whether or not "the general public" has freedom of access to the courtroom. This, said the court, was not in intent or effect a "star chamber proceeding." While evaluating the extent to which the public was excluded may be relevant in deciding whether or not a violation has taken place, the judge's purpose in selecting an inaccessible venue for proceedings probably should not be considered relevant. The evils of a secret proceeding, as described above, can take place regardless of a judge's intent in closing the courtroom doors.

Other courts have also rejected defendants' claims that they were denied the right to a public trial when their trials were held in alternate venues such as a church hall[241] or a law library,[242] even over the objection of the parties, so long as some portion of "the public" and press had not been excluded.

By way of contrast, defendants have been found to have been denied their right to a public trial when their trials were held in a venue not accessible to the public.

In a Virginia Supreme Court case, Jones v. Peyton (1967), for example, the petitioner was tried in a judge's chambers, where only the trial judge, the clerk of the court, the Commonwealth's attorney, the prosecuting witness, two police officers, counsel for the petitioner, and counsel for the codefendant were present. The petitioner's mother and sister and some of his codefendant's relatives were seated in the courtroom when the petitioner and the codefendant passed through the courtroom into the judge's chambers. The petitioner's relatives did not see him, nor did he see them seated there. Shortly thereafter, while seated in the courtroom, the petitioner's sister, who was prepared to testify on his behalf, saw the prosecuting witness leave the judge's chambers. She inquired of a court attache when the petitioner's trial would be held and was told that he had already been tried and was on his way to the penitentiary. The Virginia court noted that the mere fact that the petitioner was tried in the judge's chambers and not in open court did not in itself constitute a denial of a public trial, but that here, although the judge did not order the public excluded, members of the public, including the petitioner's relatives, did not have free access to the trial.

The next year, a federal court in Virginia held that a defendant was not denied his right to a public trial when his trial was held in a judge's chambers, with the door open, because of inadequate heating facilities in the courtroom, when there was no proof other than the defendant's unsupported assertion that any members of the public had actually been excluded from this *in camera* trial (Via v. Peyton, 1968). The difference in the result in this case may, in part, be attributed to a procedural difference: in this federal case, the petitioner bore a greater burden of proof because he was petitioning the federal court for a writ of habeas corpus. In a Fourth Circuit Court of Appeals case, another habeas corpus petitioner successfully challenged the taking of testimony at his judge trial in a capital case (he had waived a jury trial) in the bedroom of a bedridden complainant in her private home (Lewis v. Peyton, 1965). The court had not entered any official order concerning the venue of the trial, and neighbors were told to leave the tiny bedroom to make space for the court officials. This was considered an exclusion of the public, even under the more demanding standards of a habeas corpus proceeding.

Questions regarding accessibility often arise with respect to trials or related proceedings held within a prison. The defendant in an Ohio Supreme Court case (State v. Lane, 1979), for example, was a prisoner charged with an attempt to escape from his penitentiary. Although his trial was begun at the courthouse, during jury selection the court granted the state's attorney's motion, over the objection of defendant, to transfer the trial to a room in the Administration Building of the penitentiary, in the interest of security and convenience. The Ohio Supreme Court ruled that the defendant had been denied his right to a fair trial because of the prison venue (inmates subpoenaed to testify for the defense refused to do so out of fear of retaliation by the prison administrator) and also his right to a public trial. The court explained that most members of the public would be inhibited from attending a trial held within the prison. "In addition to the initial fear of entering a maximum security correctional facility, there were extensive physical and electronic admittance procedures which resulted in temporary confiscation of personal belongings, extensive waiting periods, partial strip searches, and additional security clearances at various junctures which were offensive to the public and to the officers of the court. Notwithstanding the above impediments, a sign on the pseudo-courtroom door which stated, 'No One Is To Enter Here At Any Hours,' would definitely dissuade the spectator from entering." The trial judge's efforts within the courtroom itself to make the trial seem like the usual public trial were found to have been inadequate to alleviate this constitutional error.[243] The Massachusetts Supreme Court in Foley v. Commonwealth (1999) found that it did not violate the public trial right to hold arraignments in a correctional facility where, in contrast, the facility "looks like a courtroom" and spectators were not subjected to any greater security measures than they would have been in a courthouse.

The petitioner in a Central California District Court case, King v. Fitzharris (1970), on the other hand, was not successful in challenging the holding of his preliminary hearing in the prison ward of a hospital. Even assuming that the public trial requirement of the Sixth Amendment applied to state preliminary hearings, an issue not yet decided at that time, the court held that the petitioner was not denied his right to a public hearing because his physical condition required the hearing to be conducted in the hospital, in light of the fact that he was confined to a traction bed.

Temporarily Locked Courtroom Doors

A number of public trial challenges have arisen when trial judges have decided to lock the doors of their courtrooms temporarily, frequently to avoid interruption of the court's charge to the jury. Such an order typically denies access to those who arrive after the beginning of the charge and prohibits those who have decided to stay in the courtroom from leaving during its delivery. The theory of these judges is that the jury charge is a crucial part of the trial and so jurors should not be distracted from listening carefully to all of the judge's instructions. Most appellate courts have been tolerant of such decisions, ruling that as long as those within the courtroom can still observe this phase of the trial, the trial is sufficiently public.[244]

The New York Court of Appeals in People v. Colon (1988), engaged in a fuller analysis than most other courts of a defendant's challenge to this practice. The defendant, who had objected to the doors being locked during the jury instructions, argued that there is nothing unique about this phase of a trial that justifies special restrictions. He contended that if jurors were to become distracted during the court's charge, it would actually be easier for the judge to repeat an instruction without losing anything than it would be to have a witness repeat testimony, in which case the witness's demeanor or delivery might change in a significant manner on repetition. Few appellate courts have tolerated the closing of a courtroom during testimony and Colon argued that the result should be the same with respect to the jury charge. Colon also argued that there is a less restrictive alternative to locking the doors: simply posting a sign urging unobtrusive entry and exit, which can be enforced by a court officer.

The New York court held that the defendant's points, which would have been relevant in weighing whether or not an infringement upon the right to public trial was justified, were irrelevant because what had occurred was not substantial enough to amount to a "closure" of the trial and thus did not constitute an infringement of the right. Thus, the *Waller* test was not applied, even in the diluted form some courts have applied to partial closures (demanding only a "substantial" state interest). During the course of its opinion, the court announced that any "reasonable" time, place, or manner restrictions imposed by the trial court should be upheld, thus applying accepted First Amendment standards to the defendant's Sixth Amendment claim. The court was also impressed by the fact that the trial judge had not intended the action of locking the doors to exclude members of the public.

Not all courts have agreed that courtroom doors may be locked during jury instructions in a routine case. The Iowa Supreme Court in State v. Lawrence (1969), held that this practice was reversible error, although in this case the bailiff had evidently misunderstood the judge's order, during a recess, that no one be permitted to enter or leave the courtroom during jury instructions and prevented all members of the public and press from entering the courtroom. The court found this closure, unintended by the judge, to violate the Constitution, despite showing some interest in the question of whether the trial judge's motivations were relevant to the inquiry. Years before the Sixth Amendment right was incorporated, a Michigan court in a frequently cited case (People v Micalizzi, 1923) found it to be a reversible error to lock the courtroom doors during jury instructions. In that case, a court officer rather than the trial judge had decided to lock the doors during the charge, announcing to the spectators in the courtroom that anyone who wished to leave should do so before the doors were locked. Some members of the public and even one of the defendant's attorneys were prevented from being present during the charge, although, the appellate court noted, there were vacant seats in the courtroom. The *Micalizzi* court did not particularly rely on these facts, however, appearing to conclude that it was a violation to have this part of the trial conducted behind locked doors.

When an Arizona trial court issued an administrative order that denied access to court proceedings to any person who had not entered the courthouse by 3:00 P.M., the Arizona Supreme Court had an opportunity to demonstrate the distinction between First Amendment and Sixth Amendment analysis. The appellate court held that the criminal defendant had not been denied his Sixth Amendment right to a public trial because his trial had not been "closed" to the point of implicating the Sixth Amendment. The court stressed the fact that the order had been publicized in advance so that members of the public had adequate notice, that the order was only in effect during four days of defendant's ten-week trial, and that members of "the public" were able to attend the trial. Nonetheless, the court found the order, which routinely limited access to trials, to violate the First Amendment (Ridenour v. Schwartz, 1994). Another court ruled that a judge's routine practice of locking doors after the commencement of each session of trial proceedings and not unlocking the doors until recess, was error under the Sixth Amendment.[245] The Fourth

Circuit Court of Appeals, however, in Bell v. Evatt (1995), found that the Sixth Amendment was "not implicated" by a trial court placing limits on when spectators could enter and leave the courtroom. Some members of the public were in the courtroom, and the petitioner had presented no evidence, in this habeas corpus proceeding, that any member of the public who wished to attend was prevented from doing so. More recently, the Second Circuit, also in a habeas corpus proceeding, agreed that preventing jury distraction could be considered an overriding interest and that locking the courtroom doors during the testimony of an important witness, except during breaks, did not violate the Sixth Amendment (Williams v. Artuz, 2001).

Courts have been far less tolerant of any closure of a courtroom during the taking of testimony if the closure has not been carefully and explicitly justified by some compelling need, and have been less likely to find such closures *de minimis*.[246] Even a brief, inadvertent closure of a courtroom during the taking of testimony has been found not to be too trivial to warrant reversal of a defendant's conviction on Sixth Amendment grounds in cases in which the closure had not been justified under the standards of *Waller*. The Second Circuit Court of Appeals, in Gonzalez v. Quinones (2000), dealt with a trial judge's creative effort to eliminate the need for an unnecessary closure hearing with respect to the testimony of two undercover officers by posting a guard outside the courtroom to determine whether anyone other than defendants' lawyers and families was going to seek entry, in which case a closure hearing would be necessary. In carrying out the judge's instructions, the guard inadvertently locked the door, effectively denying access to members of the public when no hearing had yet been held to determine whether such exclusion was justified.

There are exceptions to appellate disapproval of temporary courtroom closures during testimony. One Alabama court ruled that it was within the judge's discretion to close a courtroom for an hour or two to prevent the trial from being disrupted by a commotion outside, without even determining whether testimony was being taken during that period or whether alternative measures would have sufficed to preserve decorum (Davidson v. State, 1991). Other courts have also ruled that a brief and inadvertent closing of a courtroom, depending on the circumstances, might be too "trivial" to give rise to a constitutional violation.[247]

The Maryland Court of Appeals ruled that a deputy sheriff's closure of a courtroom to prevent overcrowding for one morning of a defendant's trial, which included voir dire, was not *de minimis* (Watters v. State, 1992). This appellate court also properly rejected the state's argument that it mattered that it was a deputy sheriff and not the trial judge who had effected the closure. The Virginia court in Spencer v. Commonwealth (1990), on the other hand, thought it significant, in denying the defendant's appeal, that the trial judge had not been aware of a deputy sheriff's telling an attorney not connected with the case that the courtroom was closed, had not given the order, and had not heard about the closure while the hearing was in progress. The right to a public trial is not impaired, the court opined, where there is no record of purposeful exclusion of the general public by order of the court. The result in this case may have been appropriate as only one person was excluded and members of the public and press were present at the trial, but, as the Maryland court understood, it should not matter who has effected a closure if it is not *de minimis* and not carefully justified.

Exclusion of Some People

As described above, the Supreme Court has never overruled its holding in Gannett Co. Inc. v. DePasquale (1979) that the Sixth Amendment public trial right is not a right belonging to the public, or at least not a right that the members of the public have standing to assert. The right of the public to attend judicial proceedings is subsumed under the First Amendment; the Sixth Amendment right, at least so far, belongs solely to the criminal defendant. Thus, individuals who wish to attend a criminal trial but who are unable to do so, either because there is insufficient space in the courtroom, or because the judge has ordered them excluded, are told that they have no claim under the Sixth Amendment. Long before the Sixth Amendment was applied to the states, case law upheld restrictions on attendance because of the limited seating capacity of the courtroom[248] or a desire to prevent overcrowding and disruptive conditions.[249] Trial judges do not, however, have total discretion to decide when a courtroom is too overcrowded[250] or what constitutes "decorum."[251] The New York Court of Appeals reversed a defendant's conviction after finding that the trial judge had been concerned not so much with the decorum of the trial, but with protecting the morality of the would-be spectators.[252]

Some appellate courts in older cases had agreed with Earl Warren that it is not only possible but desirable for trial judges to exclude members of the public who come to a sensational trial to gawk rather than to perform their civic duty. The Massachusetts Supreme Judicial Court in Commonwealth v. Blondin (1949), for example, which was decided before the incorporation of the Sixth Amendment public trial right, allowed an *in camera* trial in a sex offense case involving a minor, where it did not appear that all of the public or press were excluded, on the ground that the court may distinguish between spectators who have a respectable interest in the proceedings and those who have a prurient interest in attending sensational trials.[253] Because a majority of the Supreme Court has not shared Warren's disdain for sensationalism to the extent of authorizing inspection of the public's reasons for attending trials, the motivations of the spectators in attending a trial should not matter any more than the motivation of a judge in excluding spectators. The constitutional test asks only objective questions. Is a sufficient number of members of the public able to attend a trial if they wish to do so? Is a court's exclusion order justified by circumstances as opposed to good or suspect intentions?

Even under the First Amendment, the right to attend proceedings has not been considered an individual right, but a right of the public collectively. If a sufficient number of public representatives has access to a proceeding, therefore, most courts hold that the right has not been violated by exclusion of some number of individuals. A defendant's Sixth Amendment right will also be deemed violated if trial proceedings are not open to a sufficient number of members of the public and press, but not merely because some individual members of the public and press are unable to attend.[254]

Courts have also held that excluding particular people may be considered a Sixth Amendment violation, depending on who the people are, their relationships with the defendant, and the reasons for exclusion. Some courts have taken very seriously the Supreme Court's dictum in In re Oliver (1948) that a defendant is at least entitled to have his "friends, relatives and counsel" present, no matter what crime is charged against him or her. The Massachusetts Supreme Court in Commonwealth v. Marshall (1969), for example, quoting *Oliver*, held that a defendant was denied his right to a public trial when his mother, sister, brother, and friend were excluded during his sex crimes trial. Some courts have seen the presence of a defendant's friends and family during the trial as serving a purpose distinct from the attendance of members of the general public. As a Texas Appellate Court noted: "The presence of an accused's friends in the courtroom lends moral support to the accused and helps insure honest proceedings. If an accused is denied the presence of his friends, he is denied a public trial, unless the trial court can articulate on the record some compelling reason for excluding them" (Addy v. State, 1993).[255]

Trial judges have excluded defendants' friends and relatives from all or portions of a trial on a variety of theories, often to spare victims in sex offense cases embarrassment when they testify. The courts have not treated targeted exclusions of a defendant's supporters from an entire proceeding as *de minimis*. Some courts have found that exclusion of a limited number of people for a limited period of time, as described above, is insufficient to trigger heightened scrutiny under the Sixth Amendment, even if those excluded include a defendant's family or friends. In State v. Rusin (1989), for example, the Vermont Supreme Court upheld a defendant's conviction despite the exclusion of his wife and neighbor during the testimony of a child victim, reasoning that other members of the public were permitted to attend the defendant's trial, and the defendant showed no reason why he "needed" his wife and neighbor present. This analysis was based not on the idea that there had been no infringement of the defendant's right to public trial, but on the theory put forward by some federal Courts of Appeals as described above—that is, where a closure is only partial, the trial judge need not have had a compelling reason supporting the closure but only a "substantial" one. Other jurisdictions apply the *Waller* test and require that any exclusion of a defendant's family members be justified by a compelling need and be no broader in scope than necessary.[256] One case reversed a defendant's conviction because of the exclusion of his mother and several cousins during the testimony of an undercover officer, without any inquiry into whether their exclusion was necessary.[257]

However heavy the burden of justification, courts generally agree that the court's reason for excluding particular people must be based on evidence and not on speculation or uncorroborated fears. In Guzman v. Scully (1996), for example the Second Circuit Court of Appeals reversed the state court conviction of a habeas corpus petitioner because four women, allegedly friends and family of defendant, had been excluded from the courtroom during cross-examination of a prosecution witness. The trial court had relied on unsubstantiated statements by the prosecutor that the witness was intimidated by the four women, rather than conducting an inquiry of the witness on whose behalf the closure request was made. Similarly, when judges barred defendants' family members during jury selection for fear they would "contaminate" the jury by making prejudicial remarks, those defendants' convictions were reversed in cases in which the trial judges had not made adequate findings that the proceedings would be adversely affected.[258]

In a Ninth Circuit Court of Appeals case (United States v. Sherlock, 1989), on the other hand, no violation was found when a defendant's family members had been observed making faces and giggling during the testimony of a minor victim who had demonstrated apprehension about testifying in front of them. More dramatically, a New York trial court was found not to have acted unconstitutionally in excluding members of a defendant's family who had caused a mistrial at his first trial by rioting and creating pandemonium in the courtroom (Cosentino v. Kelly, 1996).

Conversely, allowing a defendant's friends and relatives to stay while excluding other members of the public and press may nevertheless violate the Sixth Amendment. The New York Court of Appeals, discussing a state statutory provision governing the right to public trial before incorporation of the Sixth Amendment, found the right not satisfied simply by allowing relatives and friends of a defendant's choosing to be present. "A trial open only to such a limited class of persons may not be regarded as public, particularly if no representative of the press is permitted to attend. A defendant may not have any relatives or friends available or willing to attend the trial, and, even if he has, such a handful is not by any means sufficiently representative of the public to provide the protection to an accused and the 'contemporaneous review in the forum of public opinion' that a public trial is designed to assure and afford" (People v. Jelke, 1954). Because the press is not considered to have any greater right to attend trials than other members of the public, allowing members of the press to attend a trial while excluding members of the general public is also insufficient to satisfy the public trial right.[259]

Although prejudice is not required to establish a violation, courts appear to be more inclined to find a violation of the public trial right when there is some reason to believe that the exclusion of particular spectators might have affected the fairness of the trial. In the aforementioned Texas case Addy v. State (1993), for example, six of a defendant's friends were excluded from the courtroom when the prosecutor peremptorily declared them to be potential witnesses, over the defendant's objection and protestations that these friends had no relevant knowledge. The appellate court reversed the conviction without requiring a showing of prejudice, but after remarking on the fact that the jurors had seen these spectators removed from the courtroom and were not given any instruction on that issue.

Grounds for Exceptions

If all or part of a proceeding within the scope of the public trial has been closed in a fashion considered to be more than *de minimis*, or if a trial court is considering closing all or part of a proceedings, then the *Waller* test requires the court to decide whether the presumption of openness is overcome by an "overriding interest based on findings that closure is essential to preserve higher values and is narrowly tailored to serve that interest." This test is broken down into four parts: (1) the party seeking closure must advance an overriding interest that is likely to be prejudiced, (2) closure must be no broader than necessary to protect that interest, (3) the trial court must consider reasonable alternatives to closing the proceeding, and (4) the trial court must make findings adequate to support closure.[260]

Which interests are sufficiently "overriding" to justify closure of courtrooms has been a matter of some debate in the lower courts. The Supreme Court has already found that various secrecy and privacy interests may be considered overriding, if they are shown to be real dangers, subject to the remaining *Waller* factors. Thus, if it is established that closure is truly necessary to protect a witness from harm, or to preserve a juror's privacy on a sensitive issue, the *Waller* test can be satisfied as long as alternative measures would not suffice to prevent the harm and the closure is narrowly tailored.

Protection from Harm or Intimidation

One potential overriding interest is the need to protect witnesses from harm, or from intimidation so severe that they would be unable to testify truthfully. The Eighth Circuit Court of Appeals in United States v. Farmer (1994), for example, permitted partial closure of a trial when the victim had good reason to fear the defendant (who had admitted assaulting him) as well as the defendant's family.[261] It is not enough for a witness simply to express fear, however.[262] The trial court in another case had held a hearing to decide whether to honor a witness's request for closure, but the appellate court found that there was no objective reason, like evidence of threats, to credit the witness's claimed fear that he was in danger, and that the trial court's findings were too general. If an uncorroborated expression of fear was a sufficient basis for closing the courtroom during the testimony of this important government witness, said the court, then any witness could close any courtroom at will. Careful factual findings are needed in each case, the Second Circuit observed, so it is impossible to generalize about when closure will be allowed.

Many courts are especially sympathetic to requests for protection by government witnesses and informants, but this sympathy does not always translate into courtroom closures. If a witness or party truly needs protection, said Judge Dolliver of the Washington Supreme Court in Seattle Times Co. v. Ishikawa (1982), "this must be accomplished by appropriate police action and not by closure of the court."

Undercover Officers and Informants

Many lower court cases allow closure during the testimony of undercover agents, both to protect their safety and to protect their identities so that they can continue to work undercover.[263] The latter justification only applies if the court determines that the undercover agent is still actively engaged in undercover work in the community and would be endangered or that there is a risk of undermining the integrity of an ongoing investigation.[264]

The order of exclusion must, of course, be carefully tailored to be no broader than necessary. Thus, the New York Court of Appeals reversed a conviction in People v. Gutierez (1995), in which the defendant's wife and children were excluded during the testimony of an undercover officer. Although the court held a proper hearing and credited the officer's testimony that he feared for his life if his identity were revealed, the record reflected no reason to be concerned that the defendant's family could be a source of danger or disclosure. In Sevencan v. Herbert (2002), on the other hand, the court found that the trial judge did not err in issuing a closure order during an undercover agent's testimony and had properly refused to exempt the defendant's wife because the prosecution had shown that she was likely to encounter the informant in the future. The use of physical screens to conceal a witness may be a viable alternative to closure of the courtroom.[265] A transcript of the testimony may also be made available to the public after the hearing or trial to minimize the consequences of closure.[266] And the Ninth Circuit recently approved the use of live audio transmission into another room to protect the identity of a confidential informant, after an appropriate hearing (United States v. Leos-Hermosillo, 2000).

In the context of evaluating whether or not a trial court had an adequate basis for closing the courtroom during the testimony of an undercover officer, a panel of the Second Circuit, in Ayala v. Speckard (1996), discussed how alternatives to closure should be handled, suggesting that the trial court may have an obligation to consider alternatives *sua sponte*, even if no alternatives are suggested by the party objecting to closure. The debate sparked over the question of who must suggest alternatives and whether measures like disguising the officer or using screens are too prejudicial to a defendant's fair trial rights was not resolved, even in the Second Circuit itself.[267] The Second Circuit also described the burden involved in justifying closure as a substantial one, given the confluence of First and Sixth Amendment rights favoring opening proceedings. Whether an interest is "overriding" depends on the degree of closure sought. To close the defendant's trial during the testimony of the undercover officer, the state was required to show that an "extremely serious interest" in the officer's continued effectiveness would be "seriously prejudiced" by testimony in open court.[268]

The state's interest in preserving the secrecy of an ongoing law enforcement investigation, even in contexts other than the familiar one of undercover agents or informants testifying, may also be considered overriding if the state can bear the same demanding burden of justification.[269] The Third Circuit Court of Appeals upheld the exclusion of everyone but testifying witnesses and counsel during testimony about the contents of the Federal Aviation Administration Anti-Air Hijack profile in order to preserve the utility of the profile, although this was in a case in which the search the defendant was challenging did not depend upon the profile (United States v. Slocum, 1972).

Grand Jury Secrecy

Traditional grand jury proceedings are not subject to the right to public trial, as the Supreme Court recognized in In re Oliver (1948). Preservation of the secrecy of grand jury proceedings, like ongoing criminal investigations, is another of the "higher values" that may, in appropriate circumstances and subject to adequately protective procedures, justify closure of a part of a trial in which grand jury proceedings will be exposed.[270] In Levine v. United States (1960), a defendant challenged the trial court's exclusion of the public from his contempt trial for refusal to answer questions before the grand jury. The Supreme Court did not decide whether this exclusion was proper to maintain grand jury secrecy, ruling instead that the defendant had defaulted on his public trial claim by not having raised it at a time when the court could correct its course.

Minor Victims and Witnesses

Globe Newspaper established that the protection of a minor witness in a rape trial might be a compelling interest. State statutes providing for mandatory closure of courtrooms where minor victims of sexual offenses were testifying were not uncommon. *Globe,* of course, ruled that a mandatory closure rule was unconstitutional and required trial courts to carefully examine the risk to the victim/witness in each case, considering circumstances such as age, psychological maturity and understanding, the nature of the crime, the victim's wishes, and the interests of parents and relatives. Courts must bear in mind that the injury must be "incremental," that is, attributable solely to the presence of the public and press, because the victim may suffer some of the same harm from testifying even in a closed court. Applying these standards, lower courts have most often found that preventing psychological damage to a minor victim would justify a closure order, provided that the exclusion is narrowly tailored and based on specific findings.[271] Some courts have continued to be so sympathetic to minor victims that they find the scales to tip heavily in their direction.[272]

It seems that, with respect to minor victims, the only real difference between mandatory closure statutes and the Supreme Court's *Globe* test is that the courts must take care to go through the proper process by holding a hearing and finding facts[273] and not to close proceedings for too long or to too many people. The Illinois courts, for instance, have provided that it may be proper to exclude the public while a minor victim testifies if representatives of the press are permitted to stay.[274] Appellate courts do not tend to find that trial judges have erred in concluding that child victims should be protected while testifying and frequently find that the prosecution has met the heavy burden of justifying a temporary closure.

Another court, as a less restrictive alternative to excluding members of the defendant's family, required the family members to sit behind a screen during a minor victim's testimony.[275] Another alternative courts have employed is to set up a television monitor outside the courtroom so that spectators who are excluded by a temporary closure order may still see and hear the testimony of a sensitive witness or victim.[276]

Protecting adult complaining witnesses who testify in sexual offense cases may be deemed to serve an overriding interest, subject to the same procedural requirements,[277] including specific findings about the nature and degree of any psychological or emotional impact testifying in court might have on the witness.[278]

Juror Privacy

The Supreme Court in *Press-Enterprise I,* although holding that there is a presumptive First Amendment right of access to voir dire proceedings, also recognized that the privacy of prospective jurors might, in an appropriate case, constitute an overriding interest that might justify holding some aspects of a voir dire proceeding *in camera. Press-Enterprise I* also set out the procedure to be followed: the juror must affirmatively ask to express privacy concerns *in camera*, and the judge must then determine whether the privacy interest raised outweighs the public interest in access. The Supreme Court explained that a juror's interest in keeping certain matters private becomes compelling "when interrogation touches on deeply personal matters that [a] person has legitimate reasons for keeping out of the public domain." Because, as discussed above, the reasoning of *Press-Enterprise I* should also lead to the conclusion that defendants have a right under the Sixth Amendment to open jury selection, the same inquiry and procedure should be applicable if it is the defendant rather than the press or public who objects to closure.

The lower courts have understood *Press-Enterprise I* to disfavor closure of voir dire, even when sensitive information might be involved. The District of Columbia Court of Appeals, for example, reversed a trial court's decision to close voir dire proceedings because the questionnaire submitted to prospective jurors called for highly personal information. The trial court allowed the jurors to decide whether to answer questions *in camera* or in the open courtroom. The appellate court noted that the trial judge had not followed the *Press-Enterprise I* requirements of determining whether each juror's request for a private session is "legitimate" and had not considered alternatives, like holding voir dire in open court and then speaking with individual concerned jurors in private.[279] Other courts have agreed that *Press-Enterprise I* requires trial judges to consider each juror's situation individually and not to issue preemptive rulings when jurors have not requested *in camera* hearings.[280]

Those cases were decided under the First Amendment, but the same analysis would apply under the Sixth Amendment if a defendant objected to a closure. Not many Sixth Amendment challenges to closed voir dire proceedings arise, partly because defendants often favor closed voir dire proceedings. The courts appear to have been more likely to permit closure of voir dire in cases in which defendants believe their right to a fair trial will be undermined if voir dire is held in public. In United States v. Peters (1985), for example, a defendant in a drug prosecution had asked the trial court to exclude reporters during voir dire on the ground that jurors, who were being individually questioned about their impartiality, might be exposed to the answers of other jurors reported in the press. The Seventh Circuit Court of Appeals held that the need to protect the defendant's right to fair trial could override the First Amendment access right, but that the trial court had not followed the *Press-Enterprise I* requirements of making specific findings, considering alternative solutions, and narrowly tailoring its relief. Defendants are often especially anxious to avoid publication of the questions and answers on voir dire in a notorious and controversial case—like the prosecution of members of the Nazi party and Ku Klux Klan for the murder of civil rights workers[281] or the prosecution of notorious boxing promoter Don King,[282] during which closure of voir dire was upheld on the ground that in the glare of publicity prospective jurors might be disinclined to give candid and truthful answers to questions and that the defendant might thus be denied a fair trial. In situations in which trial courts have allowed voir dire proceedings to remain open over defendants' objection, on the other hand, appellate courts have not been quick to conclude that defendants were in fact denied their right to a fair trial.[283] When the trial court declined to close voir dire, defendant King argued, unsuccessfully, that he had been forced to limit questions to the venire about their knowledge of prior publicity for fear of generating additional adverse publicity and thus was denied a fair trial.

Convictions have been reversed for total closure of voir dire.[284] Defendants who raise a Sixth Amendment challenge to a trial court's decision to shield an individual juror's privacy, on the other hand, are unlikely to prevail on appeal if the judge has made the requisite findings.[285]

Several courts have also held, as described above, that ancillary hearings involving jurors or prospective jurors are not within the scope of the right to a public trial. The Massachusetts Supreme Judicial Court in Commonwealth v. Gordon (1996) held that a defendant had not been denied any constitutional right when the trial court provided jurors a hearing *in camera* on the issue of whether jury service would be an undue hardship, on the ground that the right to public trial during voir dire applies only to questioning about juror qualifications and not to such administrative decisions as whether to excuse a juror for undue hardship or inconvenience. More dramatically, a California Appellate court in People v. Feagin (1995) held that the defendant's Sixth Amendment right was not denied when the court questioned jurors *in camera* before deciding to excuse three jurors for misconduct. The jury foreperson had sent a note to the judge after several days of deliberation alleging that one juror was not following the jury instructions. The juror in question, in turn, accused the other jurors of having assumed the defendant's guilt and acting on the basis of racial prejudice. The defense did not object to the private questioning of the jurors about these issues until after the judge had already questioned several jurors, and the court then proceeded with private questioning, *in camera* in the presence of counsel, despite the defense objection. After the *in camera* questioning, the attorneys presented their arguments on the juror misconduct motion in open court. The appellate court upheld the juror exclusion as well as the *in camera* questioning, ruling that any public trial claim had been waived because, by the time the defense objected, there was already adequate basis to exclude the juror. Even if not waived, the court found that the right to public trial did not apply to this questioning because the public is not entitled to observe conferences relating to legal matters as opposed to matters submitted to the trier of fact. The court said that this case was covered by the rule that defendants are not entitled to be present, or to have the public present, at proceedings that do not have any bearing on their ability to defend themselves. Alternatively, the court held that the trial judge was entitled to question the jurors in private because of the sensitive nature of the information sought. Finally, the court found that this was only a partial closure of the proceedings, and that partial closures are not per se prejudicial.

Privileges

Protection of attorney-client privilege is another privacy interest that may justify closure in an appropriate case.[286] Other claims of privilege might also be raised and evaluated on a case-by-case basis.

Courtroom Decorum

The need to maintain order during trial proceedings may sometimes be a sufficient reason to exclude some or all of the public from all or part of a trial. In a Second Circuit Court of Appeals case (Orlando v. Fay, 1965), for example, a closure order was upheld where the trial court conducted a hearing and determined that a significant number of the defendant's sympathizers in the courtroom were threatening and intimidating witnesses and threatened to disrupt the trial.[287]

Most courts have thought that preservation of the dignity of judicial proceedings is an important enough value to justify properly limited closure orders.[288] Courts have allowed spectators to be ejected for misconduct as mild as shaking their heads during a witness's testimony.[289]

Some of these cases err on the side of allowing the trial judge too much control. Picturing the rowdy Anglo-Saxon trial audiences might help judges to remember that the very point of the Sixth Amendment right is to declare that the trial belongs to the people and not just to the court. If the public is actually interfering with the conduct of the trial, the court should be permitted to maintain the integrity of the proceedings and ensure that the trial will be able to be completed. However, if the trial judge's idea of decorum is that spectators must not shake their heads or that spectators must be protected against testimony the judge finds offensive, these interests, far from being overriding, should be recognized as the antithesis of the public trial guarantee.

In any event, the trial court must articulate the findings on which it is basing a closure order and must not issue an order that sweeps more broadly than necessary to address the court's documented concerns. The Third Circuit Court of Appeals in United States v. Kobli (1949), for example, believed that it would have been proper for the trial judge to close the courtroom to protect young girls from hearing salacious anticipated testimony, but ruled that the court's closure order, which cleared the courtroom, was too broad, because it did not limit itself to the threatened young girls.[290]

Cases and summaries of the law written before the Court's decision in *Waller* sometimes describe the right to public trial as being "subject to the inherent power of the court to limit attendance as the conditions and circumstances reasonably required for the preservation of order and decorum in the courtroom, and to reasonably protect the rights of parties and witnesses."[291] The more demanding *Waller* test, of course, supersedes this milder "reasonableness" test.

Defendant's Right to a Fair Trial

There are occasions on which, as described above, the public nature of a trial can compromise the right to a fair trial. Disruptive spectators can compromise the fairness of proceedings or prevent their completion. Publicity about proceedings at preliminary stages of a trial may prejudice jurors or intimidate witnesses from coming forward. However, in a Sixth Amendment challenge, the defendant, by definition, opposes the court's closure decision because otherwise there would be no Sixth Amendment claim. In this respect, the Sixth Amendment is unlike the First Amendment, where the press often seeks entry to proceedings a defendant wishes to close. There are many First Amendment cases evaluating whether the defendant's desire to exclude the press in order to maximize the prospect of a fair trial is indeed compelling under the circumstances of the case (see *Press-Enterprise I*, 1984; *Press-Enterprise II*, 1986), but these cases are not apposite in a Sixth Amendment challenge.

The fact that a defendant desires rather than fears the public's presence should be controlling, except in the extreme case in which a defendant demonstrably does not want a fair trial but an aborted trial. Trial judges should not patronize defendants by protecting them against dangers they prefer to risk. This does not mean the trial judge cannot exercise control over the public's participation or act to minimize the potential for distortion of the trial.

As the Second Circuit observed, the right to a public trial "has always been interpreted as being subject to the trial judge's power to keep order in the courtroom. Were this not so a public trial might mean no trial at all at the option of the defendant and his sympathizers."[292] But if the defendant's supporters are not interfering with the conduct of the trial, the defendant should be permitted to invite public attendance, whatever his or her motivations in doing so.

Procedures for Raising and Litigating Claims

The Right and the Remedy

The cases described above raised closure issues in the context of a criminal appeal or collateral attack, where claims were raised under the Sixth Amendment and the requested remedy was reversal of the defendant's criminal conviction, as in Waller v. Georgia (1984). First Amendment access claims may be raised in civil proceedings, or as collateral matters in criminal proceedings in which the press has intervened, as in all of the Supreme Court cases naming a media party (e.g., *Gannett, Richmond Newspapers, Press-Enterprise I, Press-Enterprise II*). It is not always possible to know from the title of a proceeding whether a First or Sixth Amendment claim is being raised. In United States v. Hastings (1983), for example, the court of appeals heard an interlocutory appeal in a criminal case raising both a Sixth Amendment claim by the defendant and a First Amendment claim by the press. The court considered interlocutory appeals (appeals taken before trial concludes) a proper means of raising such claims (citing Cohen v. Beneficial Industrial Loan Corp., 1949). Ordinarily, appeals in criminal cases are considered premature if no conclusion has been reached, on the theory that if a defendant is acquitted, there will be no need for an appellate court to decide whether he or she has had a fair trial. The First Amendment claim, of course, cannot be postponed, because the issue is whether the press may cover the trial, and so this collateral issue may be decided on appeal before or even during a trial. It is therefore interesting that the court in *Hastings*, in the rare case in which a defendant was asserting a Sixth Amendment right to open his trial to the press and public, allowed the defendant to raise this claim on an interlocutory appeal. By way of contrast, the Seventh Circuit in United States v. Kerley (1985) allowed a defendant whose request to videotape his own trial had been denied to take an interlocutory appeal only on the ground that he had also raised a First Amendment claim. If a defendant is denied the Sixth Amendment right, the court said, holding a new trial will be an effective remedy for that violation. The First Amendment claim, on the other hand, concerns the right to broadcast a particular trial and so cannot await resolution when the trial has ended. Nevertheless, having allowed the interlocutory appeal, the court also ruled on the defendant's Sixth Amendment claim.

The New York Court of Appeals, in Oliver v. Postel (1972), had held that First Amendment access claims become moot after trial, although Sixth Amendment claims do not. In *Chandler* (1981), the Supreme Court disagreed, holding that even a First Amendment claim of right of access was not moot after the trial ended and the defendant was acquitted.

Most lower courts have held that a defendant waives the Sixth Amendment public trial right by not raising a timely objection. The Illinois Appellate Court case of People v. Lawrence (1994) is typical. The public address system was inadvertently shut off during the prosecution's rebuttal argument, and the appellate court ruled that the defendant was required to have objected at the time so that the court would have had the opportunity to remedy the problem by asking the prosecutor to repeat the unheard portion of his argument for the benefit of the spectators.[293] If defense counsel objects to a closure on the basis of the public's First Amendment right of access, that objection might not be sufficient to raise a Sixth Amendment claim.[294] The Second Circuit ruled that a defendant could not raise a claim on the basis of the exclusion of his infant child from the courtroom when no objection was made at the time and no prejudice was shown to have resulted. This dual ruling suggests the possibility that in a case in which prejudice was shown, the failure to object might not be dispositive. However, as the Supreme Court recognized in *Waller*, it is uniquely difficult to identify the sort of prejudice that exclusion of spectators might cause, because the right to public trial is more than just a means of ensuring a fair trial. Other courts have held that defendants need not object to an exclusion if the objection would have been futile.[295]

Under usual constitutional waiver principles, waiver of Sixth Amendment rights must be knowing and voluntary. The classic case cited for this principle is Johnson v. Zerbst (1938), in which the Supreme Court held that the right to counsel is only waived if the defendant intentionally relinquishes or abandons a known right or privilege. The Supreme Court and criminal procedure laws have required explicit waivers of not only the Sixth Amendment right to counsel, but also of the Sixth Amendment right to trial by jury.[296] If the right to public trial, argued one author, is considered essential to a fair trial, express waiver of this right should also be required, so that the trial court can ensure that any waiver is knowing and intelligent.[297] The Seventh Circuit Court of Appeals agreed in Walton v. Briley (2004) and issued a writ of habeas corpus ordering that a defendant was entitled to a new trial, where two-thirds of the trial had taken place after the courthouse was locked, despite the fact that his counsel had not objected. Another court found that case law does not answer the open question of whether defense counsel can waive the right to public trial or whether this is a personal right that the defendant himself or herself must decide to waive.[298]

Waller v. Georgia (1984) clearly established that an automatic reversal rule applies to public trial violations. Harmless error analysis thus should not be applicable, and the cases described above in which courts found certain exclusions not to constitute Sixth Amendment violations in the absence of any discernible impact on the fairness of the trial are tantamount to harmless error findings. The harm done by a significant exclusion is the exclusion itself.

Nevertheless, the existence of prejudice can become a factor when an appellate court decides whether or not to consider a public trial claim brought by a defendant who did not register an objection to the closure at trial. Under procedural rules, courts may still consider a claim not raised if it is "plain error." Plain error analysis entails considering whether or not the outcome of the trial might have been different but for the alleged error. An Ohio Appellate Court in State v. Rector (2003) provided an example of plain error analysis, finding that the outcome of the trial would not have been affected by closure of the courtroom during the victim's testimony, but leaving room for a finding that exclusion of the public could be plain error if it occurred throughout the trial.

Another question exposing fundamental questions about the nature of the public trial right is whether a violation can be cured by releasing transcripts of a proceeding to the public after the fact. One California court, in People v. Harris (1992), found that after-the-fact access to a transcript of portions of a voir dire proceeding—peremptory challenges that had been closed to the public—was insufficient. The court noted that the after-the-fact record was "cold" and that, although the proceedings were transcribed verbatim by a court reporter, certain details an observer in the courtroom could have noted were omitted from the transcript, such as the identity of the challenger. A majority of the Third Circuit panel in United States v. Simone (1994) agreed with the California court's result, and with Justice Brennan's suggestion in his concurring opinion in *Richmond Newspapers* (1980) that the release of transcripts after an improper exclusion (in that case from post-trial proceedings) was not the equivalent of access to the proceeding itself and could not cure the violation. This opinion drew a dissent from Judge Garth, who argued that timely provision of a transcript can indeed satisfy the right to public trial.

Not only may a defendant raise a Sixth Amendment claim on appeal, assuming it has been properly preserved, but such claims may also be raised in habeas corpus petitions, collaterally attacking a criminal conviction.[299] If a violation of the public trial right is established and a defendant's conviction is reversed, the appropriate remedy, if the violation took place during the trial itself, will be a new trial.

Cameras in the Courtroom

Whether or not there should be a presumptive right to broadcast trials under the Sixth Amendment is a question the Supreme Court has never analyzed. In both *Estes* and *Chandler*, the only cases in which the Supreme Court considered televising trials, the defendants had opposed the presence of cameras, believing that their own interests in receiving a fair trial would be harmed. The Court has never confronted a defendant who desired this highly public form of trial. Because most defendants have agreed with Estes and Chandler in fearing camera coverage, most of the discussions of the pros and cons of cameras in the courtroom, both in cases and in commentary, take as their background the First Amendment right of public and press access to judicial proceedings. The chief question asked about defendant's rights is generally whether defendants should be afforded a veto over this manner of publicity.

Other defendants might disagree about whether cameras are necessarily harmful to their interests. Chandler, who objected to camera coverage, was nonetheless acquitted. Defendants who believe that they will enjoy community support may also believe that they have only to gain from extensive coverage. At least one commentator thought that television coverage helped O.J. Simpson win an acquittal.[300] The question of whether there should be a presumptive right to camera coverage in a case in which the defendant claims that right under the Sixth Amendment requires independent analysis. Much of the First Amendment discussion in cases and commentary, examining whether the danger to defendant's rights can be contained, is inapposite if the defendant prefers to seek the benefits of a highly public trial even at some risk to the fairness of the trial.

One unusual defendant who did demand that his federal criminal trial be televised was Alcee Hastings, the African-American federal judge described previously who claimed that he was being railroaded by politically motivated criminal charges brought against him, aimed at removing him from the bench. He argued that, despite a federal rule's ban on broadcasting federal criminal trials, he had a right under the Sixth Amendment to a trial as public as the limits of technology permitted and that without television coverage the public's understanding of his trial would be incomplete. Hastings believed that he would benefit if as many members of the public as possible could observe the nature of the prosecution, because he wanted to clear his reputation so that he could return to the bench.

Having spent many pages of its opinion carefully analyzing and then rejecting the claim of intervening media that they had a First Amendment right to televise the trial, the Eleventh Circuit Court of Appeals quickly disposed of Hastings's Sixth Amendment claim with a citation to Nixon v. Warner Comm. Inc. (1978), the case in which the Supreme Court ruled that the press had no right to copy and broadcast the famed Watergate tapes: "[t]he requirement of a public trial is satisfied by the opportunity of members of the public and the press to attend the trial and to report what they have observed." The *Hastings* court recognized that *Nixon* was distinguishable, both because Hastings was challenging an absolute ban as opposed to a decision tailored to the facts of the Watergate case and, more significantly, because Hastings, unlike most defendants, affirmatively wanted as public a trial as possible and had anticipated the press request with his own discrete constitutional claim.

Other courts have followed *Hastings* in finding that federal defendants are barred by Rule 53 from having their trials broadcast and by *Nixon* from arguing that the Rule is unconstitutional.[301] This analysis was applied to the defendant in the Seventh Circuit Court of Appeals case United States v. Kerley (1985), who was charged with resisting the draft and who wanted to videotape his trial.

Decades before *Hastings,* an Oklahoma Appellate Court in Cody v. State (1961) had just as easily rejected a request to broadcast a trial. Cody, a defendant in a rape trial, claimed that the complainant was a psychopathic personality. He believed that the press was likely to convey a sympathetic picture of her to the public and that the jurors in his case would therefore fear adverse public reaction if they voted to acquit him. He asked that the trial be broadcast because he believed that if the public were able to actually see the complainant testify, they would be able to discern that she was fabricating the charge against him and the jurors would therefore feel more comfortable voting to acquit him. Under Oklahoma law, trial judges had, even at that time, discretion to permit broadcasting (see Oklahoma Appellate Court in Lyles v. State, 1958). The trial court denied Cody's request, however. Affirming that decision, the appellate court said, like the Supreme Court in *Nixon*, "[t]he right to a public trial as guaranteed by our constitution is to prevent secret trials and Star Chamber proceedings, away from the view of the public. This guarantee is fulfilled when, as in the instant case, the proceeding is conducted at a place where any member of the general public can attend, subject to the rules of the trial court as promulgated by the presiding judge in reference to the conduct of visitors in the courtroom." Without discussing the functions Cody asserted a public trial might serve in his case, the court went on to say "[a] cursory examination of the fact summation made at the outset of this opinion will clearly reveal that no public good could be achieved by transmitting into private homes or by displaying to our youth the sordid and perverted details in this case. In many instances the foulest conceivable language was used."

Most commentators and courts, divided on the issue of whether the First Amendment should be interpreted as encompassing a presumptive right to televise trials, scarcely mention the Sixth Amendment. Much of the discussion about cameras in the courtroom in cases, commentary, and pilot project reports focuses on civil trials or civil and criminal appeals, which are generally regarded as a less loaded context because there is no criminal defendant with countervailing fair trial rights.

Like the majority in *Estes,* those who favor a blanket ban on cameras in criminal trials generally stress the incalculable risk to a criminal defendant's right to a fair trial. These critics are generally unwilling, unlike the Court in *Chandler*, to try to contain those risks by more limited means than an outright prohibition of cameras, either because they do not believe that containment is possible or because they do not believe that electronic coverage will actually generate any significant additional benefits.[302] The cost benefit analysis leading to this conclusion usually assigns a significant amount of weight to the defendant's fair trial rights on one side of the scale, and minimizes the benefits of more universal rather than representative public knowledge of criminal proceedings on the other. One frequent source of disagreement is who should bear the burden of proof on this issue. If studies do not conclusively show that cameras adversely affect the participants in a trial, does that mean that cameras should be allowed, or should cameras be banned until and unless studies show that there is no adverse affect? A third variable that carries weight with some commentators and judges is the value of allowing the court to control the public's image of the criminal justice system.

Judge Dolores Sloviter of the Third Circuit Court of Appeals wrote an article responding to Steven Brill (the founder of Court TV) that exemplifies this kind of cost benefit analysis. Judge Sloviter agreed with the *Hastings* court that the right to public trial is satisfied as long as some members of the public and the press are allowed to attend the trial and to report what they have observed.[303] She traced the traditional Blackstonian reasons why public trial is said to enhance the right to a fair trial—that witnesses will be more likely to testify truthfully, that additional witnesses might come forward, and that public scrutiny can deter prosecutorial or judicial overreaching—and concluded that televising a trial would not be likely to add much to enhance these benefits beyond what print media already offer. On the other side of the balance, she quoted Earl Warren's concurring opinion in *Estes* deploring as "evil" the unique psychological impact of television cameras on trial participants, said to stem from their awareness that they are being televised. She argued, again like the majority in *Estes*, that proponents of cameras in the courtroom cannot prove that the posturing of counsel and witnesses, which presumably accompanies televised trials, will not lead to an unacceptable distortion of the trial process. Under this cost benefit analysis, if the risks to a defendant's fair trial are magnified by televising the trial and there is only a marginal advantage to be gained by doing so, the answer seems clear.

The equation changes, of course, if the right to public trial is viewed as serving additional functions. Judge Sloviter recognized one additional function of public trials included in Blackstone's and the Supreme Court's usual lists: assuring the public that proceedings are being conducted fairly. Here, too, she believed that the advantage of broadcasting proceedings would be marginal, especially because most courtroom footage, as found in a 1994 Federal Judicial Center study, is used to illustrate news reports rather than to tell the whole story of the trial.[304]

Judge Sloviter's list of purposes of a public trial ended there, as she quoted Warren's concurring statement in *Estes* that the purpose of a trial is not to educate (Estes v. Texas, 1965). Part of the reason Judge Sloviter doubted that televised trials would educate or inform the public or reassure the public that justice is being done was that, unlike the events in the courtroom itself, what a television audience sees is not within the control of the court. She referred to the "patent inability of courts to require that televising be uncut, fair, and comprehensive." Echoing Warren's contempt for those members of the public who watch trials out of curiosity or thrill-seeking rather than republican virtue, she found "no reason to assume that the televised proceedings will not be primarily of the sensational, notorious, or shocking portions of a trial that may fail to give the public the well-balanced look into litigation that is really necessary to understand how the judicial system operates." How deeply her views correspond with Earl Warren's is shown by her decision to give Warren the last word in her article: "The right of the communications media to comment on court proceedings does not bring with it the right to inject themselves into the fabric of the trial process to alter the purpose of that process."

Those who argue for a broader view of First Amendment requirements may disagree with one of Sloviter's minor premises—they might portray the risk to a defendant's fair trial rights as manageable, or her psychological assumptions about whether witnesses will become less truthful as unproven. More fundamentally, the proponents of televising trials usually embrace Justice Brennan's republican view of the First Amendment rather than the contrary view of Justice Warren who, after all, had concurred with the opinion the Supreme Court reversed in *Chandler*.[305] Brennan's list of the functions to be served by a public trial, under the First or Sixth Amendment, is considerably more expansive than Blackstone's or Sloviter's. If the purpose of access to judicial proceedings is to inform and empower observers, the more who observe a trial first hand, the better. Brennan, unlike Warren and Sloviter, does not assume that the base instincts of the public will prevail in the marketplace of ideas or that there is no purpose to a public trial if those who attend do so for what might be characterized as ignoble reasons. Brennan, as described previously, does not assume that describing a trial as a theatrical event is pejorative. [306]

If the Sixth Amendment public trial right does serve goals of the public as well as of the defendant, Brennan's optimistically republican vision of the First

Amendment, with its informed and engaged citizens, can translate in Sixth Amendment terms into a public that is truly a jury of the whole. The role the trial-watching public can be expected to play, in Brennan's view, is as positive as the role jurors are expected to play. Warren's skepticism about whether the public will watch trials only for thrills, leading to his inclination to limit the number of spectators to reduce the anticipated damage, parallels the skepticism about jurors that has led the Supreme Court over time to curb the jury's powers and prerogatives.[307] The possibility feared by Warren, that the public might make its own uses of the opportunity to observe trials, parallels judicial fear of the jury's ability to nullify the law.

Although there are no cases attempting a full functional analysis of how the Sixth Amendment should be interpreted in a case in which a defendant seeks the broadest possible audience, there are some useful precedents in cases considering whether exclusions of certain spectators from a courtroom is a violation of the defendant's right. Some courts have taken the position that the Sixth Amendment public trial right, like the right to jury trial, is essentially representative. On this theory, attendance at trials may be limited, because there are not enough seats in the courtroom for all who wish to attend or because particular individuals have been excluded, without violating the Sixth Amendment, as long as some members of the public are able to observe the trial. Other courts have taken the position that each exclusion of a member of the public from the courtroom must be justified.[308] Some commentators have even argued that the courts err in not requiring trial judges to make an effort to find a courtroom large enough to accommodate those who wish to attend a trial.[309]

If the "public" at a trial is to be merely representative, then Earl Warren's theory that it is a sufficient check for those in attendance to be able to report what they have observed will prevail. If the public has its own discrete interest under the Sixth Amendment in observing proceedings, however, then even if the size of the traditional courtroom might, of necessity, have required representation by some limited number of members of the public or press, the broadcast media may provide an opportunity to more fully serve that function and to more fully realize the right. As described in the discussion of the history of the public trial right, the Anglo-Saxon and Norman putative ancestors of the right to a public trial, like the moots, apparently took place out of doors before the entire community. In colonial America, "court day" was a shared experience for the entire community. Trials moved indoors into courtrooms with limited seating in communities that are too large to fit into one courtroom. The fact that courtrooms do not have the capacity to accommodate the entire community forced the courts to move to a more representative model. Television restores the possibility of recapturing the model of full community attendance and participation in the criminal justice system, if that is considered to be one of the Sixth Amendment's ideals.

In a Sixth Amendment case, it is a given that the defendant prefers a highly public trial and therefore has chosen to risk whatever incalculable harm a televised trial might pose to the fairness of that trial rather than risk the harm of limiting public attendance to those who can fit into the courtroom or read one-dimensional print coverage. In the absence of demonstrable prejudice to the fairness of his or her trial, a defendant has no right to decide to exclude the public from the courtroom because the public has an independent right of access under the First Amendment. The defendant's wish to open a proceeding may also be overborne in a First Amendment case—if the proceeding at issue does not pass the Court's First Amendment test or if the prosecution objects. But the Sixth Amendment context is different. To the extent that the Sixth Amendment public trial right belongs to the defendant, why not let the defendant choose the greater form of publicity?

In situations in which the defendant's and the public's wishes coincide, there should be a presumptive right of access to fuller publicity, and challenges to open proceedings by people other than the defendant—whether the prosecution, witnesses, or jurors—should be subjected to strict scrutiny. Unlike the First Amendment context, where time place and manner restrictions do not need to meet strict scrutiny (see Globe Newspaper Co. v. Superior Court for the County of Norfolk, 1982), strict scrutiny should apply to any limitations on the openness of a defendant's trial imposed over a defendant's objection. If the government has a sound argument that particular testimony should not be made available to some or all members of the public, or if a juror or witness has a compelling interest that cannot be served in any other way, then a proceeding may be closed or cameras excluded to the extent necessary. But if the press wishes to broadcast a proceeding, the defendant agrees, and no other person can show any compelling reason not to televise all or some part of the proceedings, the Sixth Amendment should require the court to accede.

This leaves open the question of whether the state may raise its own interest in a fair and decorous trial as a potential compelling interest justifying closure, even if the defendant disagrees or is willing to waive that right. The *Hastings* court explained, in its analysis of the First Amendment claim for electronic coverage made by the press and joined by the defendant, that the court has an independent interest in preserving order and decorum and its own institutional interest in providing a fair trial. To the extent that "decorum" describes the court's desire to close all or part of a proceeding in which a defendant's supporters or members of the public or press are subverting the trial, the need to complete the proceedings in an orderly fashion can indeed be a compelling interest. However, the concept of decorum, as the cases described above showed, has sometimes proven too much. Trial judges have used their concerns for decorum to protect the public's morality by excluding the public from prostitution cases. A concern for "decorum" might also cover a judge's desire to make a good impression on the public, deserved or not. At some level, a court's interest in its own image is exactly what the Sixth Amendment public trial right can and should expose. A desire to allow trial judges to manipulate their own public images or the images of the courts generally is not a good reason to maintain an absolute ban on cameras. The Sixth Amendment public trial right should not be reduced to a tool for convincing the public that justice is being done, if it is not. The ideal of the Sixth Amendment right is to allow the public to gather information about the courts and make independent decisions about the quality of justice. In a republican reading of the Bill of Rights, the government should listen to the public and not just instruct them.[310]

Because the Supreme Court has not recognized either a First or Sixth Amendment presumptive right of access for electronic media, debates about cameras in the courtroom in most jurisdictions have taken place among policymakers rather than among courts. In 1981, shortly after the *Chandler* decision, the ABA followed the Supreme Court's trajectory by replacing its canon banning cameras with a new canon permitting cameras in the courtroom under controlled conditions. Canon 3A(7) of the 1981 Code of Judicial Conduct was then superseded in 1991 by Standard 8-3.8 of the *ABA Standards for Criminal Justice, Fair Trial and Free Press*, which echoes *Chandler* in its reliance on procedure, guidelines, and case-by-case evaluation to curb potential problems.

Virtually all of the states have followed the ABA recommendation by prescribing rules allowing broadcasting pursuant to guidelines, sometimes only allowing broadcasting of appellate arguments, and sometimes allowing broadcasting only as part of an experimental or pilot program, although in some states the invitation to cameras has remained more theoretical than real.[311] Conversely, the federal courts have remained resistant to electronic coverage. Federal Rule of Criminal Procedure 53 explicitly prohibits cameras in federal proceedings.[312] The Judicial Conference adopted its own prohibition against "broadcasting, televising, recording, or taking photographs in the courtroom and areas immediately adjacent thereto" in criminal or civil proceedings.[313] The Judicial Conference did authorize a pilot program, conducted from 1991 to 1994, to study televising civil proceedings in six federal district courts and two courts of appeals. Those conducting and evaluating the study recommended authorization of nationwide use of cameras in civil proceedings, finding that it did not disrupt court proceedings, affect participants in the proceedings, or interfere with the administration of justice. Despite this recommendation, the Judicial Conference adhered to its ban.[314] Federal appellate courts were authorized to continue to experiment with camera coverage, and several courts of appeals have chosen to do so. The Supreme Court, notably, has not.

Not all federal judges have been content with these prohibitions. Judge Pierre Leval, District Judge in the highly notorious libel case Westmoreland v. CBS (1984), thought that it was very much in the interest of the federal judiciary to televise the proceedings, optimistically believing that the public esteem for the federal courts would grow if the public were more familiar with the court's work. Regretfully recognizing that existing Judicial Conference and court rules prohibited him from allowing the trial to be televised, he declared that he thought that cameras in federal court are "inevitable."[315] Meanwhile, some accommodations have been made to allow large numbers of interested people to observe trials. In the trial of Timothy McVeigh for the Oklahoma City bombing, for example, the venue of the trial was moved to Denver to minimize the possibilities of disruption or unfairness (United States v. McVeigh, 1996). Because many of the victims and others affected by the bombing were unable to travel so far to attend the trial, Congress enacted a statute authorizing closed circuit televising of trials to crime victims in cases in which the trial is moved more than 350 miles to a different state.[316] Under this statute, the court must screen those who wish to watch the closed circuit proceedings. "[T]he court shall order closed circuit television of the proceeding . . . for viewing by such persons as the court determines have a compelling interest in doing so and are otherwise unable to do so by reason of the inconvenience and expense caused by the change of venue." In the same case, the District Judge wrote an opinion distinguishing proper use of electronic sound equipment to preserve a record of court proceedings, which Congress permits, and extended access to such recordings, which amounts to unauthorized broadcasting of proceedings.[317] In the absence of any declared constitutional right, Congress and the courts reserve the power to decide what public will attend a trial and who is empowered to record proceedings, separating worthy and unworthy motivations.

New York has remained one of only nine states to continue banning cameras in the trial courtroom. Like the federal Judicial Conference, New York authorized an experimental program; a commission evaluated the experiment favorably and recommended authorization of camera coverage, but that recommendation was rejected.[318] Like the federal judges, some New York state trial court judges have disapproved, and even held the state statutory ban unconstitutional. When the four New York City police officers charged with shooting the unarmed Amadou Diallo in the Bronx won a change of venue to Albany County, the trial judge allowed the proceedings to be broadcast, although to do so, he had to hold the New York statutory ban unconstitutional on the basis of the First Amendment (see People v. Boss, 2000). The judge expressed dismay that the legislature maintained its increasingly anachronistic total ban on cameras and, as in the Oklahoma City case, wished to allow the public access to a trial of great public interest, which many of the individuals most concerned, because of the change of venue, were unable to attend. The defendants in that case opposed television coverage, although solely on the basis that it was banned by statute, so the court did not have occasion to decide whether the Sixth Amendment also would have been violated by the statute. Several other cases followed the lead of the *Boss* case, the most significant of which is a New York County Court in People v. Santiago (2000). The *Boss* trial court granted the motion of media intervenors to televise a capital murder trial even over the defendant's objection, holding the New York statutory ban violative of the First Amendment as well as the New York State Constitution. Justice Bristol's opinion in that case does a thorough job of canvassing the history of cameras in the federal courts and providing a general road map for First Amendment challenges to bans on camera coverage. At defendant Santiago's behest, an appellate court then reversed Bristol's order.

Several years later, Court TV brought a suit seeking a declaratory judgment that the New York statutory ban violated both the state and federal constitutions, but lost in the New York Supreme Court. Justice Shirley Kornreich noted that no state or federal case had applied strict scrutiny to restrictions on audio-visual coverage of trials and described the decision about cameras as one to be made by the legislature rather than the courts (Courtroom Television Network LLC v. State of New York, 2003).[319] As in most other cases regarding cameras in the courtroom, the claim was analyzed under the First Amendment. Thus, Justice Kornreich's reluctance to invalidate the statutory ban was based, in large measure, on the fact that she believed that the record New York had compiled during its experiments contained sufficient evidence of negative impact on the fairness of trials for a legislature to have been able to rationally decide not to take that risk. There was testimony on the record, for example, that some witnesses had been deterred from testifying because of their concern about being filmed and others had been negatively affected at trial. New York courts have not had occasion to consider a Sixth Amendment claim from a defendant requesting that his or her trial be broadcast.

Televising the trial of O.J. Simpson for the murder of his wife was a pivotal experience for California as well as the rest of the country. California, which had allowed extensive television coverage at the trial court's discretion, imposed new limitations on television coverage—prohibiting media coverage of jury selection, of individual jurors or spectators, and conversations and conferences that take place outside the hearing of the jury[320]—and new limitations on the discretion of trial judges to decide when to allow cameras. California judges must now consider a list of eighteen factors, including privacy rights of participants, the importance of public access, and the interest in maintaining public confidence in the judicial system, and the dignity of the courtroom, before allowing film or electronic coverage.[321] That infamous trial, watched by 70 million Americans, also led to a slew of commentary on the pros and cons of televising trials.[322]

It remains to be seen whether Judge Leval was clairvoyant in declaring the arrival of cameras in federal courtrooms as inevitable, but the trend has been moving steadily in that direction. Because legislatures and courts have been edging into fuller camera coverage as a matter of policy, and because so few defendants have demanded camera coverage as an aspect of their Sixth Amendment public trial right, the courts may never have to decide whether there is such a presumptive right.

National Security, Public Trials, and Military Commissions

National Security and Public Trials

In the criminal prosecution of Zacarias Moussaoui (United States v. Moussaoui, 2002), alleged by the government to be the intended twentieth September 11 hijacker, the federal district judge confirmed that the public was welcome to attend the trial and pretrial proceedings, although she denied Court TV's motion to broadcast the proceedings.[323] Had Moussaoui not pled guilty, the government could have sought to close the courtroom at any point during his trial if particular testimony or documentary evidence was alleged to pose a risk to national security, and the judge would then have examined the government's contentions. Neither the Sixth Amendment nor the First Amendment would bar excluding the public from a portion of a terrorism trial, if the district court were persuaded that there was an actual risk, appropriate specific findings were made, and the order was sufficiently narrowly tailored. Under *Waller* and *Richmond Newspapers,* the government must bear the burden of persuading the judge to restrict access to the courtroom or to documents. Mere invocation of national security concerns would not be sufficient. The government's experience prosecuting this terrorism suspect in federal court under the Constitution's criminal procedure rules, including the rights of the Sixth

Amendment, was seen by many as a test case for bringing such prosecutions in civilian court instead of an alternative forum.

Military Commissions

Shortly after September 11, 2001, President George W. Bush signed an executive order authorizing the creation of military tribunals to try suspected terrorists who are not U.S. citizens.[324] These tribunals were designed to operate differently from criminal trials in a number of respects, one of which was that proceedings before the military tribunals could be closed without the rigorous justification required by the First or Sixth Amendments.[325] Even before any such proceedings had taken place, this and other discrepancies in procedure were widely criticized.[326] Department of Defense regulations promulgated under this order empowered the presiding officer to close all or portions of military commission proceedings to protect classified information or national security.[327] Whether the presiding officer should be required to apply the stringent *Waller/Richmond Newspapers* test in making such a determination has been the subject of considerable discussion, although no such closure has yet occurred.

Commentators have argued that the First Amendment, under the *Richmond Newspapers* experience and logic test, should apply even if trials of alleged terrorists take place before a military commission rather than a civilian court.[328] The *Richmond Newspapers* test is sufficiently open-textured to support such a result. The Committee on Communications and Media Law of the Association of the Bar of the City of New York, tracing the history of trials of terrorists and enemy combatants throughout American history, concluded that there is a long tradition of inviting the public to attend trials of terrorists, with the chief deviation being a World War II proceeding that has been the subject of heavy criticism. The trial of the British soldiers charged with participation in the Boston Massacre, for example, was open to the public, even including jury selection;[329] the Manila trial of General Yamashita for World War II war crimes committed by the soldiers under his command, although criticized in other respects, was open to representatives of the press.[330] Conversely, military tribunals held during the Civil War to try confederate soldiers, spies, and even civilians who criticized President Lincoln or the war were held in secret. Lincoln suspended the writ of habeas corpus to avoid judicial review of the decisions in these proceedings, but in 1866 the Supreme Court reviewed a military tribunal proceeding and ruled, in *Ex parte* Milligan (1866), that it was unconstitutional to use military tribunals to try civilians in areas in which the civilian courts were open and functioning. The Court remarked that martial law "destroys every guarantee of the Constitution," including in its list of constitutional rights violated by subjecting civilians to martial law the Sixth Amendment "right to a speedy and public trial by an impartial jury."[331]

The most recent Supreme Court case considering the constitutionality of military commission procedures upheld a proceeding that was held in secret and whose procedures departed from the norm of a criminal trial in a number of significant respects. In *Ex parte* Quirin (1942), the Supreme Court considered the question of whether the trial before a military commission of eight alleged Nazi saboteurs violated the Sixth Amendment right to be tried in a civil court before a jury, and held that it did not. The defendants, one of whom was evidently an American citizen, invoked the safeguards of the Fifth and Sixth Amendments, including the right to trial by jury. Had the Sixth Amendment jury trial right applied, the right to public trial would have followed. The Court did not discuss the closed nature of the proceedings, which the defendants had raised in connection with their claim that the secrecy of the proceedings would make it difficult to challenge their validity. *Quirin* was decided before the First Amendment was found to include an independent public right of access to judicial proceedings, so the press played no role in the case.

The question in *Quirin*, as it would be in connection with trials of alleged terrorists before military tribunals, was the president's authority to create a procedure that wholly supplants the Sixth Amendment because it is not considered a criminal prosecution but an aspect of the war powers. The language of the Sixth Amendment guarantees a public trial to an "accused" in all "criminal prosecutions." The Bush administration has taken the position that if a suspected terrorist is not formally charged with a crime, that person is *ipso facto* not entitled to any of the rights guaranteed by the Sixth Amendment. This was the justification for holding Jose Padilla, a U.S. citizen, in custody for several years without permitting him to see a lawyer. He had not been "accused" in a "criminal prosecution." The Supreme Court, confronted with the question of whether the administration may avoid the restraints of the Sixth Amendment by simply categorizing an individual as an "unlawful enemy combatant," ducked the issue on the ground that Padilla's habeas corpus petition had not been brought in the correct venue.[332] In another case, Hamdi v. Rumsfeld (2004), the Court held that a U.S. citizen detained as an "unlawful enemy combatant" nevertheless had a right to due process protections, although the form that due process should take would be derived by weighing the government's interests in the balance.

The Court in *Quirin* ruled that the accused had no right to a jury trial on the ground that, at the time of the framing of the Constitution, such proceedings would not have been tried to a jury. This holding might serve to eliminate a Sixth Amendment public trial claim as well, although the history of whether a proceeding is open to the public does not correspond fully with the history of whether jurors or military personnel decided a case. A number of commentators have argued that *Quirin* is distinguishable from the military commissions the Bush order contemplates in a number of respects. Some of these arguments are legal: World War II was a declared war; the saboteurs were concededly enemy soldiers charged with war crimes. Other questions about the continuing viability of the *Quirin* ruling are historical: Goldsmith and Sunstein argue that there has been a trend since World War II toward greater criminal procedure protection.[333] When *Quirin* was decided, the provisions of the Sixth Amendment had not yet been applied to the states, so even a criminal defendant in Louisiana would have had no right to trial by jury. The right of the public to attend trials is now covered by the overlapping First Amendment right of access. Others argue that *Quirin* was simply wrong. David Glazier points out that most accounts of *Quirin* in the literature overlook the fact that in 1945, when a second group of Nazi saboteurs was tried before a military commission, President Roosevelt issued a new directive modifying some of the controversial provisions of the earlier order challenged in *Quirin.*[334]

One central question is whether process at a military commission is required, by the Constitution, relevant statutes, or logic and policy, to conform to procedures used in courts-martial. Commentators have expressed different opinions on this question. Glazier interprets the applicable statute as being somewhat ambiguous on this question, but he argues that the better view is that practice in the military commissions should follow the practice at courts-martial.[335] The ABA disagrees, maintaining that the relevant statutes do not require that court-martial procedures be used.[336] The Court of Military Appeals has held that a right to a public trial, commensurate with the Sixth Amendment right, does apply to courts-martial (Brown v. United States, 1956); that the public has the right to attend courts-martial under the First Amendment (United States v. Hershey, 1985); and that the presiding officer must strictly scrutinize any claim that national security requires excluding the public (United States v. Grunden, 1977).

The Bush administration has held some proceedings against alleged enemy combatants in Guantanamo to determine their status. The administration's argument that Guantanamo is not within the jurisdiction of any American court or subject to American constitutional law was rejected by the Supreme Court in Rasul v. Bush (2004). The constitutionality of the procedures being employed in the Guantanamo hearings has been challenged in other respects, but proceedings so far have been open to some members of the press and public. Of course, because travel to Guantanamo is completely under the control of the government, not every member of the public or press who wishes to is able to attend the hearings. The government has selected a representative sample of press and watchdog organizations. As this book goes to press, the Supreme Court had not yet decided whether the procedures to be applied in military commission proceedings are constitutional. Hamdan v. Rumsfield (05-184). Even if the Sixth Amendment does not apply to these noncriminal prosecutions, members of the press and public may claim a right to attend on the basis of the First Amendment or of international law.[337]

Issues concerning secret proceedings also arose when the Bush administration decided to exclude the public and press from deportation hearings of "special interest" detainees. The Third Circuit and Sixth Circuit Courts of Appeals reached contradictory conclusions about whether this categorical exclusion violated the First Amendment.[338]

Any future terrorism trials, whether conducted in the courts or in military tribunals, will undoubtedly spark a renewed public debate about the meaning and scope of the right to public trial.

Notes

1. Plato, *The Last Days of Socrates,* trans. Hugh Tradennick (New York: Penguin, 1987), 43–44; I. F. Stone, *The Trial of Socrates* (Boston: Little, Brown, 1988), 223, 225. ("Basic to a free city was the right to speak back to the state, to criticize its actions in the assembly, the courts, the theater, or conversation.")

2. Aeschylus, in *The Eumenides* (458 B.C.E.), trans. Robert Fagles (New York: Penguin, 1977), lines 572–767, recounts the myth of the creation of the courts by Athena, portraying the first trial—of Orestes for the murder of his mother. The trial takes place in the highly public location of the Craig of Ares, with ten citizens chosen by Athena to be the judges, various gods, and a chorus of Furies participating, and the theater audience.

3. See S. C. Todd, *The Shape of Athenian Law* (New York: Clarendon Press, 1993), 4.

4. Sir Thomas Smith, *De Republica Anglorum, A Discourse on the Commonwealth of England,* 1st ed. (1583; Cambridge, The University Press, 1906), 70; see also Sir James Fitzjames Stephen, *A History of the Criminal Law of England* (London: Macmillan & Co., 1883), 43–48 (on Roman law).

5. Luke 23:14, New English Bible. In John's account, the Jews of the assembly who, functioning as a sort of grand jury, decided to bring Jesus before Pilate, would not enter Pilate's praetorium for fear of ritual defilement so Pilate spoke to them outside, questioned Jesus inside, and then went back out to the crowd to announce his verdict. John 18:28–33. Matthew and Mark describe the assembly, but do not describe the setting of the questioning of Jesus by Pilate.

6. Matthew 27:1–26; Mark 15:1–15.

7. Frederic W. Maitland and Francis C. Montague, *A Sketch of English Legal History* (New York: G.P. Putnam's Sons, 1915), 46; see also Frederick Pollock and Frederic W. Maitland, *The History of English Law Before the Time of Edward I* (Cambridge: Cambridge University Press, 1980), 140–42; Albert Lieck, *Justice and Police in England* (Toronto: Butterworth & Co., 1929), 21 (crediting the Normans with introducing the trial by jury, and the concept of the "King's Peace" whereby the Crown began to exert more comprehensive control over criminal cases as a means of securing order and power).

8. See Sir Matthew Hale, I *The History of the Common Law of England* (Chicago: University of Chicago Press, 1971), 219.

9. Sir John Hawles, *The English-Mans Right: A Dialogue Between a Barrister at Law and a Jury-Man* (London: Printed for Richard Janeway, 1680), 3–4.

10. See also William Blackstone, III *Commentaries on the Laws of England in Four Volumes* (London: Cavendish 2001), *349. Blackstone based much of his account on Hale's; see II Hale, *The History of the Common Law of England,* 134-35 n. A.

11. I Hale, *The History of the Common Law of England,* 219; see Pollock and Maitland, *The History of English Law Before the Time of Edward I,* 142.

12. Hawles, *The English-Man's Right: A Dialogue Between a Barrister at Law and a Jury-Man,* 5.

13. Hawles, *The English-Man's Right: A Dialogue Between a Barrister at Law and a Jury-Man,* 143. See also III Blackstone at *350 ("the truth seems to be, that this tribunal was universally established among all the northern nations").

14. "The several methods of trial and conviction of offenders established by the laws of England, were formerly more numerous than at present," according to Blackstone. IV Blackstone, Commentaries, *342.

15. Pollock and Maitland, *The History of English Law Before the Time of Edward I,* 40.

16. Sir Frederick Pollock, *The Expansion of the Common Law* (Boston: Little, Brown, 1904), 140.

17. Plucknett contends that Saxon communal courts cannot truly be said to be the harbingers of the modern jury because they did not find facts. Theodore F. T. Plucknett, *A Concise History of the Common Law,* 5th ed. (Boston: Little, Brown, 1956), 108.

18. Pollock, *The Expansion of the Common Law,* 28 (describing the communal courts as late as the twelfth century as being "rather like a disorderly public meeting than a court of justice").

19. Pollock and Maitland, *The History of English Law Before the Time of Edward I,* 37.

20. Pollock and Maitland, *The History of English Law Before the Time of Edward I,* 37–38; see also Pollock, *The Expansion of the Common Law,* 139–40 (both the local and county courts were "open-air meetings of the freemen who were bound to attend them"). See also Smith, *De Republica Anglorum, A Discourse on the Commonwealth of England,* 96 (judges tried criminal cases "in some open or common place").

21. Pollock and Maitland, *The History of English Law Before the Time of Edward I,* 38.

22. Pollock and Maitland, *The History of English Law Before the Time of Edward I,* 38.

23. IV Blackstone, Commentaries, *342–46.

24. IV Blackstone, Commentaries, *344.

25. Plucknett, *A Concise History of the Common Law*; David Bodenhamer, *Fair Trial: Rights of the Accused in American History* (New York: Oxford University Press, 1992), 11–12.

26. Plucknett, *A Concise History of the Common Law,* 108.

27. Pollock and Maitland, *The History of English Law Before the Time of Edward I,* 141.

28. Room for debate about when trial by jury began is created by the variety of functions served by petit and grand juries. Pre-Norman English ancestors of juries, for example, did not have investigatory powers. Hale, *The History of the Common Law of England,* 219.

29. Pollock and Maitland, *The History of English Law before the Time of Edward I,* 67; Edward Jenks, *The Book of English Law* (Athens: Ohio University Press, 1967), 13.

30. Pollock and Maitland, *The History of English Law Before the Time of Edward I,* 143.

31. 1 See Plucknett, *A Concise History of the Common Law,* 88–91; Pollock, *The Expansion of the Common Law,* 140.

32. Pollock and Maitland, *The History of English Law Before the Time of Edward I,* 143.

33. Pollock and Maitland, *The History of English Law Before the Time of Edward I,* 153.

34. III Blackstone, Commentaries at *350.

35. Plucknett, *A Concise History of the Common Law,* 111.

36. Leonard Levy, *The Palladium of Justice* (Chicago: I.R. Dee, 1999), 9.

37. Maitland and Montague, *A Sketch of English Legal History,* 53 n. 1.

38. Pollock and Maitland, *The History of English Law before the Time of Edward I,* 146–47.

39. Pollock and Maitland, *The History of English Law before the Time of Edward I,* 157.

40. Pollock and Maitland, *The History of English Law before the Time of Edward I,* 157–58.

41. Pollock, *The Expansion of the Common Law,* 39.

42. Pollock and Maitland, *The History of English Law before the Time of Edward I,* 151.

43. Levy, *The Palladium of Justice,* 9; Leonard Levy, *Origins of the Bill of Rights* (New Haven: Yale University Press, 1999), 210–14 (promoting importance of truth; seeking to replace trial by ordeal and by battle).

44. See Levy, *Origins of the Bill of Rights,* 45.

45. Pollock, *The Expansion of the Common Law,* 40. As Stephen astutely observed, it is not surprising that official accounts do not stress the need for procedural protections. "The whole policy of the Parliamentary party, was to represent their proceedings as justified by law, and that of their opponents as being illegal and oppressive. That the law itself might be oppressive was an admission which they could never afford to make." Sir Fitzjames Stephen, II *A History of the Criminal Law of England,* 359 (London: Macmillan, 1883).

46. Levy, *The Palladium of Justice,* 15–17.

47. I Hale, *The History of the Common Law of England,* 264–66.

48. This view has been traced to Ferdinando Pulton, who published a treatise on "Triall by the Countrie" in 1623, in which he asserted that the jury system was derived from chapter 39 of Magna Carta, a view Lord Coke, in his influential commentary on Magna Carta, then endorsed. See Levy, *The Palladium of Justice,* 55.

49. Sir William Searle Holdsworth, IX *A History of English Law* (Boston: Little, Brown, 1932); Lieck, *Justice and Police in England,* 26; see also Levy, *Origins of the Bill of Rights,* 212.

50. Pollock, *The Expansion of the Common Law,* 28.

51. Pollock, *The Expansion of the Common Law,* 30.

52. Lieck, *Justice and Police in England,* 23–24.

53. II Hale, *The History of the Common Law of England,* 135–36 n. B. See also Maitland and Montague, *A Sketch of English Legal History,* 56 (jurors are called not in order that they may hear, but in order that they may give, evidence).

54. Maitland and Montague, *A Sketch of English Legal History,* 64. ("Only by slow degrees did the judges insist that the jurors ought to listen to evidence given by witnesses in open court, and rely upon the evidence that was there given.")

55. Bodenhamer, *Fair Trial: Rights of the Accused in American History,* 12.

56. Levy, *The Palladium of Justice,* 42.

57. Sir John Fortescue, "In Praise of the Laws of England" in *On the Laws and Governance of England,* ed. Shelley Lockwood (Cambridge: Cambridge Univ. Press, 1997) 36–38, 73–74.

58. Fortescue, "In Praise of the Laws of England" in *On the Laws and Governance of England,* 98.

59. Fortescue, "In Praise of the Laws of England" in *On the Laws and Governance of England,* 98.

60. Sir Edward Coke, *Institutes of the Laws of England* (London: E. & R. Brooke, 1797), 48–49.

61. Coke, II *Institutes of the Laws of England,* 103.

62. Smith, *De Republica Anglorum, A Discourse on the Commonwealth of England,* 79, 101. These procedures may seem "strange to all nations that does use the civill Lawe of the Romane Empererours, that for life and death there is nothing put in writing but the endictement onely. All the rest is doone openlie in the presence of the Judges, the Justices, the enquest, the prisoner, and so manie as will or can come so neare as to heare it, and all depositions and witnesses given aloude, that all men may here from the mouth of the depositors and witnesses what is saide."

63. IV Blackstone, Commentaries, *379.

64. Smith, *De Republica Anglorum, A Discourse on the Commonwealth of England,* 349.

65. See Jenks, *The Book of English Law,* 350.

66. IV Blackstone, Commentaries, *4.

67. IV Blackstone, Commentaries, *372.

68. Pollock, *The Expansion of the Common Law,* 31–32.

69. I Stephen, *A History of the Criminal Law of England,* 170–79.

70. I Stephen, *A History of the Criminal Law of England,* 178–79. See also Maitland and Montague, *A Sketch of English Legal History,* 128–34; Lieck, *Justice and Police in England,* 28–29.

71. II Stephen, *A History of the Criminal Law of England,* 337–57; Sir Frederick Pollock, *The Genius of the Common Law* (New York: Columbia University Press, 1912), 66.

72. See Jenks, *The Book of English Law,* 74 ("the notorious Star Chamber is the most conspicuous" divergence from public trials); Bodenhamer, *Fair Trial: Rights of the Accused in American History,* 13; Pollock and Maitland, *The History of English Law Before the Time of Edward I,* 116–28 (on the Star Chamber generally).

73. Levy, *The Palladium of Justice,* 45; see also V Holdsworth, *A History of English Law,* 195 (although other rights integral to a fair trial, like calling witnesses and preparing one's defense, were denied in the Star Chamber, "the trials were at least public"); Pollock, *The Genius of the Common Law,* 83–86; G. R. Elton, *The Tudor Constitution* (Cambridge: Cambridge University Press, 1982), 171.

74. Max Radin, "The Right to a Public Trial," 6 *Temple L.Q.* (1932), 381, 386–87. Radin also notes that the landmark opinion in Entick v. Carrington (1762), which described the Star Chamber as the epitome of judicial impropriety, did not complain about secret proceedings. Ronald Goldfarb interprets the omission of complaints about lack of public trial as evidence that public trial was not really viewed as a right. Ronald L. Goldfarb, *TV or Not TV: Television, Justice, and the Courts* (New York: New York University Press, 1998), 42.

75. II Stephen, *A History of the Criminal Law of England,* 358.

76. See also I Holdsworth, *A History of English Law,* 336; Jenks, *The Book of English Law,* 72.

77. II Stephen, *A History of the Criminal Law of England,* 358.

78. Jenks, *The Book of English Law,* 73–74.

79. IV Blackstone, Commentaries, *281.

80. G. R. Elton, *The Tudor Constitution* (Cambridge: Cambridge University Press, 1982), 82 (noting that Henry also used the attainder law of 1459 to dispose of political enemies who would have successfully defended themselves at trial).

81. John Bellamy, *The Tudor Law of Treason* (London: Routledge & K. Paul, 1979), 133–38.

82. Bellamy, *The Tudor Law of Treason,* 134.

83. Bellamy, *The Tudor Law of Treason,* 137.

84. *The Trial of Lieutenant-Colonel John Lilbourne*, 4 How. St. Tr. 1269, 1273 (1649).

85. Id. at 1274.

86. Id. at 1273.

87. Id. at 1273–74.

88. Id.

89. Id. at 1280

90. 11 How. St. Tr. 455, 460 (1685).

91. Pollock, *The Expansion of the Common Law,* 97.

92. Pollock, *The Expansion of the Common Law,* 32.

93. See John Henry Wigmore, VI *Evidence in Trials at Common Law* (Boston: Little, Brown & Co., 1976), section 1835 at 443–52.

94. For a description of the public punishments during part of the Colonial Era, see Bradley Chapin, *Criminal Justice in Colonial America: 1606-1660* (Athens: University of Georgia Press, 1983), 50–52.

95. Bodenhamer, *Fair Trial: Rights of the Accused in American History,* 10.

96. Bernard Schwartz, *The Bill of Rights: A Documentary History* (New York: Chelsea House Publishers, 1971), 148.

97. See Schwartz, *The Bill of Rights: A Documentary History,* 50.

98. Levy, *Origins of the Bill of Rights,* 219.

99. Joseph Story, II *Commentaries on the Constitution of the United States: With a Preliminary Review of the Constitutional History of the Colonies & States Before the Adoption of the Constitution* (Boston: Hilliard, Gray, 1833), 571 (The rights guaranteed in the Sixth Amendment "follow out of the established course of the common law in all trials for crimes. The trial is always public. . . . ").

100. Bodenhamer, *Fair Trial: Rights of the Accused in American History,* 15.

101. Schwartz, *The Bill of Rights: A Documentary History* 73 (twelfth right, protecting the freedom of speech and right to petition, gives people the opportunity to "come to any publique Court, Councel, or Towne meeting, and either by speech or writeing to move for any lawfull, seasonable, and materiall question"); Schwartz, *The Bill of Rights: A Documentary History,* 74 (eighteenth right, providing for a defendant's release, refers to "open Court"); Schwartz, *The Bill of Rights: A Documentary History,* 76 ("Everie man shall have libertie to record in the publique Rolles of any Court any Testimony given upon oath in the same Court, or before two Assistants, or any deede or evidence legally confirmed there to remaine in perpetuam rei memoriam, that is for perpetuall memorial or evidence upon occasion."). See also Schwartz, *The Bill of Rights: A Documentary History,* 108 (noting the Fundamental Constitutions of Carolina, drafted by John Locke in 1669, also refer to "open court" in its Article 70).

102. Schwartz, *The Bill of Rights: A Documentary History,* 129.

103. William Penn, "Frame of Government V," in Schwartz, *The Bill of Rights: A Documentary History,* 131. The entire text of V reads "That all courts shall be open, and justice shall neither be sold, denied nor delayed." "Open" might refer to the availability of the courts and so does not necessarily refer to attendance of the public, but Penn's other writings are consistent with a positive view of the value of public trial.

104. Bodenhamer, *Fair Trial: Rights of the Accused in American History,* 28.

105. William Penn, "The People's Ancient and Just Liberties Asserted," in Schwartz, *The Bill of Rights: A Documentary History,* 146.

106. Levy, *Origins of the Bill of Rights,* 185; Schwartz, *The Bill of Rights: A Documentary History,* 53, 67–68.

107. Bodenhamer, *Fair Trial: Rights of the Accused in American History,* 16–18, 40–41.

108. Levy, *Origins of the Bill of Rights,* 229–30. Rhode Island provided by statute for refusal to accept paper money, for example, to be an action triable without a jury.

109. Bodenhamer, *Fair Trial: Rights of the Accused in American History,* 20–24 (also noting that an alternate explanation for jury trials being uncommon is that populations in some colonies were sparse).

110. Samuel Adams, *The Rights of the Colonists and a List of Infringements and Violations of Rights* (1772), cited in Schwartz, *The Bill of Rights: A Documentary History,* 209–10. See Schwartz, *The Bill of Rights: A Documentary History,* 215–18 (describing these Acts and the Continental Congress's Declaration and Resolves objecting to them; this grievance became a centerpiece of the Declaration of Independence).

111. Schwartz, *The Bill of Rights: A Documentary History,* 265.

112. Article IX, see Schwartz, *The Bill of Rights: A Documentary History,* 287.

113. Schwartz, *The Bill of Rights: A Documentary History,* 371–72.

114. Schwartz, *The Bill of Rights: A Documentary History,* 223.

115. Committee on Communications and Media Law of the Association of the Bar of the City of New York, "The Press and the Public's First Amendment Right of Access to Terrorism on Trial: A Position Paper," 22 *Cardozo Arts & Ent. L.J.* (2005): 767, 777, citing Hiller B. Zobel, *The Boston Massacre* (New York: Norton, 1970), 248.

116. "The Press and the Public's First Amendment Right of Access to Terrorism on Trial," 794–95, citing Rhys Isaac, *The Transformation of Virginia, 1740–1790* (Chapel Hill: University of North Carolina Press, 1982), 90, and A.G. Roeber, *Faithful Magistrates and Republican Lawyers* (Chapel Hill: University of North Carolina Press, 1981), 74.

117. U.S. Const., art. III, §2, ¶3.

118. Federalist no. 83, Jacob Ernest Cooke, ed., *The Federalist* (Middletown, CT: Wesleyan University Press, 1961), 562.

119. V Herbert J. Storing and Murray Dry, eds., *The Complete Anti-Federalist* ("A Maryland Farmer") (Chicago: University of Chicago Press, 1981), 36, 38.

120. Schwartz, *The Bill of Rights: A Documentary History,* 435–36.

121. Schwartz, *The Bill of Rights: A Documentary History,* 912.

122. Schwartz, *The Bill of Rights: A Documentary History,* 628, 658, 1167 (interpreting this proposal as including a right to a public trial).

123. See James J. Tomkovicz, *The Right to the Assistance of Counsel* (Westport, CT: Greenwood, 2002), 14–20, for background on the formulation of the Bill of Rights.

124. See Schwartz, *The Bill of Rights: A Documentary History,* 466–74 (Richard Henry Lee); 486 (Elbridge Gerry); 508 ("Brutus"); 580 (Alexander Hamilton). See also II Herbert J. Storing, ed., *The Complete Anti-Federalist* (Chicago: University of Chicago Press, 1981), 245–50, 315–21 (the "Federal Farmer," who refers to and praises the significance of the right to a public trial); V *The Complete Anti-Federalist* ("A Maryland Farmer"), 37–40.

125. Levy, *Origins of the Bill of Rights,* 230.

126. Schwartz, *The Bill of Rights: A Documentary History,* 1027.

127. See Francis Howard Heller, *The Sixth Amendment to the United States Constitution: A Study in Constitutional Development* (Lawrence: University of Kansas Press, 1951) for a fuller description of these events.

128. I *Annals of Congress,* 756.

129. See Schwartz, *The Bill of Rights: A Documentary History,* 1114, 1123, 1160, 1162, 1163, 1165 (mentioning, without discussing, these rights).

130. II Story, *Commentaries on the Constitution of the United States,* 571.

131. See Tomkovicz, *The Right to the Assistance of Counsel,* 2–15 (describing the traditional English common law position prohibiting the assistance of counsel; challenges to that position in England and the colonies; and the inclusion of right to counsel, a distinct change from the common law, in the Sixth Amendment). See Tomkovicz, *The Right to the Assistance of Counsel,* 4 (accused also had no right to compulsory process at common law).

132. This was the suggestion of my colleague Jason Mazzone, who has argued that the right to jury trial embodied in Article III is in large measure a public right and therefore should be less subject to waiver by a criminal defendant than the additional rights in the Sixth Amendment, like the right to counsel and to confrontation, which are more fully rights of the accused. See Jason Mazzone, "The Waiver Paradox," 97 *Nw. U.L. Rev.* (2003): 801, 850–55.

133. See Nelson Lasson, *The History and Development of the Fourth Amendment to the United States Constitution* (Baltimore: Johns Hopkins Press, 1937).

134. IV Blackstone, Commentaries, *4; see also Levy, *The Palladium of Justice,* 42 (on English judges abjuring torture).

135. Smith, *De Republica Anglorum, A Discourse on the Commonwealth of England,* 101.

136. Sir John Hawles, *The English-Man's Right: A Dialogue Between a Barrister at Law and a Jury-Man,* 7, 17–22 (London: Printed for Richard Janeway, 1680). See also Smith, *De Republica Anglorum, A Discourse on the Commonwealth of England,* 7, 30–31.

137. IV Blackstone, Commentaries, *372–73.

138. IV Blackstone, Commentaries, *349 (jury trials are more important in a criminal case in which "more is to be apprehended from the violence and partiality of judges, appointed by the crown, in suits between the king and the subject").

139. Fortescue, "In Praise of the Laws of England" in *On the Laws and Governance of England,* 36–38, 73–74; see also Plucknett, *A Concise History of the Common Law,* 130 n. 1.

140. Hale, *The History of the Common Law of England,* 145–46, 156. III Blackstone, Commentaries, *287–93. ("This open examination of witnesses *viva voce*, in the presence of all mankind, is much more conducive to clearing up of truth.")

141. 11 How. St. Tr. 455, 460 (1685).

142. Hale, *The History of the Common Law of England,* 147–48.

143. See Susan N. Herman, "Why the Court Loves *Batson*: Representation Reinforcement, Colorblindness, and the Jury," 67 *Tulane L. Rev.* (1993): 1807 (observing that juries are a better protector of liberty than of equality, having been responsible for what are now believed to have been miscarriages of justice in a number of cases involving racial minorities as defendants).

144. IV Blackstone, Commentaries, *5.

145. Jeremy Bentham, *Treatise on Judicial Evidence* (London: J.W. Paget, 1825), 67.

146. Bentham, *Treatise on Judicial Evidence,* 70–71.

147. Bentham, *Treatise on Judicial Evidence,* 71.

148. Bentham, *Treatise on Judicial Evidence,* 78.

149. Bentham, *Treatise on Judicial Evidence,* 77; see also Jenks, *The Book of English Law,* 73–74. ("[T]he enormous force of public opinion is brought to bear on the proceedings in court." "[M]uch of the effectiveness of English public opinion, whether expressed by word of mouth or in the Press, may be said to be due to [the right to a public trial.]")

150. Jeremy Bentham, *The Rationale of Judicial Evidence,* ed. J. Stuart Mill (London: Hunt & Clarke, 1827), 597.

151. II Story, *Commentaries on the Constitution of the United States,* §§1779–80.

152. II Story, *Commentaries on the Constitution of the United States,* §1791.

153. John Henry Wigmore, VI *A Kaleidoscope of Justice* (Washington, DC: Washington Law Book Co., 1941), 435–37.

154. Cited in VI Wigmore, *A Kaleidoscope of Justice,* 448.

155. See Estes v. Texas (1965) at 570.

156. Justice Ginsburg was quoted by Australian Chief Justice Gleeson, who said that he agreed with the observation she had made during a recent visit. Ian Henderson, "Chief Justice Says Only a Sick Society Would Televise Courts," *Australian*, June 25, 2001, at 4.

157. William J. Brennan, Jr., "The Criminal Prosecution: Sporting Event or Quest for Truth?" 68 *Wash. U.L.Q.* (1990): 1, 17; see Craig M. Bradley and Joseph L. Hoffman, "Public Perception, Justice, and the 'Search for Truth' in Criminal Cases," 69 *S. Cal. L. Rev.* (1996): 1267, 1273, n. 13 (describing criminal trials as "a form of civic theater").

158. Todd, *The Shape of Athenian Law,* 9 (citing Ober, Strauss, and Hall).

159. Todd, *The Shape of Athenian Law,* 161 (citing Osborne).

160. Todd, *The Shape of Athenian Law,* 77.

161. Benjamin B. Ferencz, "International Criminal Courts: The Legacy of Nuremberg," 10 *Pace Int'l L. Rev*. (1998): 203, 210.

162. See John Schultz, *The Chicago Conspiracy Trial,* rev. ed. (New York: Da Capo Press, 1993); for a transcript of the proceedings, see Mark L. Levine, George C. McNamee, and Daniel Greenberg, *Tales of Hoffman* (New York: Bantam Books: 1970).

163. Thurman Arnold, *The Symbols of Government* (New Haven: Yale Univ. Press, 1935).

164. See Barbara A. Babcock, "Fair Play: Evidence Favorable to an Accused and Effective Assistance of Counsel," 34 *Stan. L. Rev.* (982): 1133, 1140 (describing cathartic function of criminal trials).

165. See Radin, "The Right to a Public Trial" (the historical foundations of public trial are "mythical").

166. The Court had previously interpreted the right to counsel—see Powell v. Alabama (1932), Betts v. Brady (1942)—and had reversed state proceedings as denials of due process—see Moore v. Dempsey (1923). The public trial claim posed issues of first impression.

167. Footnotes have been omitted from the quote. The term "criminal trial" does not include military commissions, which have been held in secret as recently as 1942, see discussion infra.

168. In re Oliver (1948) (citing Radin, "The Right to a Public Trial").

169. Justice Rutledge discussed the issue of incorporation in a separate opinion. In re Oliver (1948) (Rutledge, J., concurring).

170. See Estes v. Texas (1965) at 71.

171. See Estes v. Texas (1965) at n. 3 (on the number of states sequestering jurors).

172. Rule 53 of the Federal Rules of Criminal Procedure barred broadcasting of federal trials. The section on the issue of cameras in the courtroom, infra, will discuss the history of the ban on cameras after the opinion in *Estes*.

173. Estes v. Texas (1965), citing Gerhard O.W. Mueller, "Problems Posed by Publicity to Crime and Criminal Proceedings," 110 *U. Pa. L. Rev.* (1961): 1, 6; and Wigmore, *A Kaleidoscope of Justice,* 487 ("The people thought holding court one of the greatest

performances in the range of their experience. . . . The country folks would crowd in for ten miles to hear those 'great lawyers' plead; and it was a secondary matter with the client whether he won or lost his case, so the 'pleading' was loud and long.").

174. Harlan argued here, as he did in many other opinions, that forbidding the innovation of televised trials "would impinge upon one of the valuable attributes of our federalism by preventing the States from pursuing a novel course of procedural experimentation."

175. In the television series and film *The Fugitive,* the Dr. Sheppard–based protagonist was innocent of the crime.

176. The measures suggested included limiting the number of reporters, requiring the reporters to remain outside the bar, and regulating the reporters' conduct.

177. Subsequent cases discussed more stringent measures a trial judge could take to prevent prejudicial pretrial publicity. Gentile v. State Bar of Nevada (1991) (rule prohibiting lawyers from making extrajudicial statements to the press under circumstances which she or he "knows or reasonably should know . . . will have a substantial likelihood of materially prejudicing an adjudicative proceeding" is constitutional); Nebraska Press Ass'n v. Stuart (1976) (discussing the constitutionality of gag orders on press).

178. Yount, a high school teacher, had been convicted in 1966 for murdering one of his students, but the conviction was reversed on appeal and he was retried. He claimed that the prejudicial publicity surrounding the retrial had denied him a fair trial, but the Supreme Court disagreed, finding that the passage of time had "softened" the community's reactions.

179. Mu'Min was a Vietnamese immigrant who had been serving a sentence for murder when he was convicted of another murder committed while he was released from prison as part of a work program. The circumstances of the case generated considerable hostile publicity, and defense counsel asked the trial judge to question prospective jurors individually about the publicity and its possible impact on them. The Supreme Court upheld the trial judge's decision to pose questions to the whole group, and then to panels of four, rather than individually.

The assumption that voir dire can be effective as a remedy for prejudicial pretrial publicity in any event has been questioned. See Christina A. Studebaker and Steven D. Penrod, "Pretrial Publicity: The Media, the Law and Common Sense," 3 *Psychology, Pub. Policy & L.* (1997): 428.

180. Although the Supreme Court generally finds cases to be moot once the parties can no longer benefit from a ruling in their favor, there is an exception for cases that are capable of repetition yet evading review.

181. The Court did not discuss whether or not such pretrial publicity could be cured through voir dire, as in *Yount* and *Mu'Min*, but could well have believed that this alternative is not fully effective.

182. In another area involving the public's participation in judicial proceedings, the Supreme Court has explicitly allowed criminal defendants or other litigants to raise challenges to biased jury selection based on the equal protection rights of the prospective jurors. Batson v. Kentucky (1986); Powers v. Ohio (1991).

183. The Court held in Faretta v. California (1975) that a defendant has the right to choose whether to exercise the Sixth Amendment right to counsel or represent himself or herself.

184. Akhil Amar argues that before the exclusionary rule was created as a remedy for illegal searches and seizures, the public was deeply involved in judging the conduct of government investigators because the chief remedy for misconduct was a civil jury trial for damages. Amar, *The Constitution and Criminal Procedure,* 21–22, 29, 40–42. Because the exclusionary rule transfers decision making on such issues from juries to judges, the

public's only role, in what used to be the decision of their representatives, will be to observe how judges are wielding this power.

185. The consensus of commentators was that *Gannett* was unclear. See the articles cited in the first two footnotes of Justice Blackmun's opinion.

186. Defense counsel had won another important motion that resolved the case.

187. It could be said that eight members of the Court subscribed to that result because Lewis Powell, who recused himself in this case, had already declared in his concurring opinion in *Gannett* that he believed the First Amendment created a right of access to criminal trials.

188. Among the rights mentioned by the Court were the right of association (NAACP v. Alabama, 1958), the right of privacy (Griswold v. Connecticut, 1965), the presumption of innocence (Estelle v. Williams, 1976), the standard of proof beyond a reasonable doubt (In re Winship, 1970), and the right to interstate travel (Shapiro v. Thompson, 1969).

189. Another fact that piqued public interest in Chandler's trial was that one of the state's key witnesses was an amateur radio operator who accidentally overheard Chandler and his codefendant talking over their police walkie-talkies during the burglary and had recorded that conversation.

190. Justice Stevens recused himself and so the decision was made by an eight-member Court.

191. The attorney for the Commonwealth explained that, because the defendant was asserting his right to public trial, the trial judge could consider that right to outweigh the "otherwise legitimate statutory interests, particularly where the Commonwealth [acts] on behalf of the victims in the sense that they were consulted fully by the prosecutor in this case."

192. Again, the Court did not find the case to be moot even though the defendant had been acquitted.

193. Quoting Radin, "The Right to a Public Trial," 388.

194. Quoting *Press-Enterprise I* (1984), and aligning this statement of principle with similar statements in *Globe Newspaper*, Justice Burger's opinion in *Richmond Newspapers*, and his own and Justice Blackmun's separate opinions in *Gannett.*

195. The opinion lists half a dozen additional states that had closure statutes based on the Field Code, but whose courts had found a right of access to preliminary hearings nevertheless.

196. See, e.g., the Fifth Circuit Court of Appeals in Rovinsky v. McKaskle (1984). ("Because the public's first amendment right and the defendant's sixth amendment right serve common interests, however, the legal principles appropriate for enforcing one are usually applicable to the other.")

197. Susan N. Herman, "The Tail that Wagged the Dog: Bifurcated Fact-finding Under the Federal Sentencing Guidelines and the Limits of Due Process," 66 *S. Cal. L. Rev.* (1992): 289.

198. See the Eleventh Circuit Court of Appeals in United States v. Hastings (1983).

199. The Maine Supreme Court in State v. Pullen (1970).

200. See, e.g., an Illinois Appellate Court in People v. Taylor (1993); the Maryland Supreme Court in Watters v. State (1992); the Massachusetts Supreme Judicial Court in Commonwealth v. Gordon (1996). Even before *Press Enterprise I* and *Waller,* lower courts found this an easy question. The Colorado Supreme Court in Anderson v. People (1971), for example, announced that it was "undisputed" that the right to public trial extended to voir dire, citing Third Circuit case law from 1949, see United States v. Kobli (1949).

201. This conclusion was reached, for example, by the Rhode Island Supreme Court in State v. Torres (2004).

202. For some examples, see the Rhode Island Supreme Court decision in State v. Torres (2004) and the Washington Supreme Court decision in In re Personal Restraint of Orange (2004).

203. The Second Circuit Court of Appeals in United States v. King (1998).

204. An Illinois Appellate Court in People v. Taylor (1993).

205. See Coleman v. Alabama (1970); Massiah v. United States (1964).

206. See, e.g., the Eastern Washington District Court in United States v. Hegge (1986).

207. The Alaska Supreme Court in Ex parte Consolidated Publishing Co. (1992).

208. The Fourth Circuit Court of Appeals in In re Charlotte Observer (1989).

209. See also the Ninth Circuit Court of Appeals in Seattle Times Co. v. United States Dist. Ct. (1988).

210. See, e.g., the Eastern New York District Court in United States v. Gotti (1990), where the court ruled that a bail hearing could be closed under the standards of *Press-Enterprise II.*

211. This was reported by the Reporters Committee for Freedom of the Press at www.rcfp.org/news/2003/0613inrere.html. For a fuller account of the case, see Robert Schwaneberg, "Six Months in Jail on a False Assumption," *Star-Ledger,* October 20, 2003, available at http://www.nj.com/specialprojects/index.ssf?/specialprojects/court/court2.html.

212. The plaintiffs in the case of Bellamy v. Judges and Justices (1973), a challenge to the New York bail system, had conducted a study with the Columbia University Bureau of Applied Research purporting to show that those incarcerated pretrial were more likely to be convicted. The court rejected the study's interpretation of the correlation between pretrial detention and conviction, believing it likely that those who were likely to be convicted were also likely to be denied bail.

213. In another case raising the issue of exclusion of the public from a hearing in chambers on a possible conflict of interest, the Second Circuit held that the defendant had waived the claim by failing to object. See United States v. Re (1967).

214. See Dusky v. United States (1960); 18 U.S.C. §4241(a).

215. See a Louisiana Appellate Court in State v. Eaton (1986); a Florida Appellate Court in Miami Herald Publishing Co. v. Chappell (1981); the Utah Supreme Court in Society of Prof'l Journalists v. Bullock (1987); the Vermont Supreme Court in State v. Koch (1999).

216. See the Second Circuit Court of Appeals in United States v. Haller (1988); the Fourth Circuit Court of Appeals in In re Washington Post (1986).

217. See Brady v. United States (1970).

218. *Criminal Justice Statistics Online,* 31st ed., Table 5.46.2002: Statistics for Felony Convictions in State Courts (http://www.albany.edu/sourcebook/pdf/t5462002.pdf, last accessed March 23, 2006).

219. However, the court did allow the state the opportunity to establish that the communication had been harmless error, an incorrect procedure according to *Waller* if the Sixth Amendment public trial right had indeed been violated.

220. The same court had held in an earlier opinion that the closure of voir dire in the trial of the same defendant did not violate the First Amendment, United States v. Brown (2001).

221. See Kate Stith and Jose A. Cabranes, *Fear of Judging* (Chicago: University of Chicago Press, 1998).

222. See the Ninth Circuit Court of Appeals in CBS Inc. v. United States Dist. Ct. (1985); the South Carolina District Court in United States v. Byrd (1993); a Florida Appellate Court in Palm Beach Newspapers, Inc. v. Cook (1983); a Florida Appellate Court in Miami Herald Publishing Co. v. Florida (1978).

223. The Northern Texas District Court in United States v. Raybould (2000).

224. See also the Massachusetts Supreme Judicial Court in Globe Newspaper Co. v. Massachusetts (1990) (post-verdict questioning of jurors); the Minnesota Supreme Court in Mankato Free Press v. Dempsey (1998).

225. The court concluded that, in this case, the probationer's privacy rights outweighed the public right of access.

226. See also a New York Family Court in In re Chase (1982).

227. See e.g., the Vermont Supreme Court in In re J.S. (1981); see also Kathleen M. Laubenstein, "Media Access to Juvenile Justice: Should Freedom of the Press Be Limited to Promote Rehabilitation of Youthful Offenders," 68 *Temp. L. Rev.* (1995): 1897 (arguing that juvenile proceedings should continue to be presumptively closed).

228. See Edward J. McLaughlin and Lucia Beadel Whisenand, "Jury Trial, Public Trial and Free Press in Juvenile Proceedings: An Analysis and Comparison of the IJA/ABA, Task Force and NAC Standards," 46 *Brook. L. Rev* (1979): 1; James F. Brelsford and Rachel A. Silvers, "Juvenile Courts: Part I, The Battle for Access," 12 *Comm. Law* (1994): 7; Joshua M. Dalton, "At the Crossroads of *Richmond* and *Gault*: Addressing Media Access to Juvenile Delinquency Proceedings Through a Functional Analysis," 28 *Seton Hall L. Rev.* (1998): 1155, 1229; Gilbert Geis, "Publicity and Juvenile Court Proceedings," 30 *Rocky Mtn. L. Rev.* (1958): 101.

229. American Bar Association, Institute of Judicial Administration, *Juvenile Justice Standards*, Summer 2.4 (1990).

230. See Reporter's Committee for Freedom of the Press, "Access to Juvenile Courts: A Reporter's Guide to Proceedings and Documents in the 50 States and D.C." (Spring 1999), http://www.rcfp.org/juvcts/index.html.

231. See Laubenstein, "Media Access to Juvenile Justice: Should Freedom of the Press Be Limited to Promote Rehabilitation of Youthful Offenders," 1908–13 (describing state and federal legislation limiting access to juvenile proceedings).

232. See the Massachusetts Supreme Judicial Court in Globe Newspaper Co. v. Massachusetts (1990).

233. See the New York Court of Appeals in People v. Colon (1988) ("reasonable" time place or manner restrictions should be upheld).

234. See, e.g., the Second Circuit Court of Appeals in Woods v. Kuhlmann (1992); the Tenth Circuit Court of Appeals in Nieto v. Sullivan (1989); the Ninth Circuit Court of Appeals in United States v. Sherlock (1989); the Second Circuit Court of Appeals in Jones v. Henderson (1987); the Eleventh Circuit Court of Appeals in Douglas v. Wainwright (1984).

235. See, e.g., the Illinois Appellate Court in People v. Taylor (1993).

236. See the Third Circuit Court of Appeals in United States v. Cianfrani (1978); the Seventh Circuit Court of Appeals in United States ex rel. Latimore v. Sielaff (1977).

237. In Mallott v. State (1980), the Alaska Supreme Court explicitly adopted Justice Brennan's position that the right to public trial belongs to the public, not just the accused.

238. See the Kentucky Supreme Court in Tinsley v. Commonwealth (1973).

239. See the Rhode Island Supreme Court in State v. Lerner (1973) (in which the court focused on whether the defendant was denied a "fair trial" because of the exclusion of

some members of the public, instead of confining itself to the question of whether the public was actually excluded).

240. Radin, "The Right to a Public Trial," 391–92.

241. The Second Circuit Court of Appeals in Knapp v. Leonardo (1995).

242. The Arkansas Supreme Court in Morris v. State (1990).

243. See also the West Virginia Supreme Court in State ex rel. Varney v. Ellis (1965) (finding a trial in a jailer's office to violate West Virginia state constitution); the Southern New York District Court in Lasky v. Quinlan (1976) (permitting the trial of an inmate to be transferred to a Bankruptcy Court located near the prison, to alleviate security concerns while preserving the dignity and accessibility of the trial by holding the trial in an actual courthouse).

244. See the Pennsylvania Supreme Court in Commonwealth v. Hartman (1994); the Connecticut Supreme Court in State v. Herring (1989) (door locked and "Do Not Enter" sign posted during jury charge); the Alaska Appellate Court in Renfroe v. State (1973); a Michigan Appellate Court in People v. Bails (1987) (stressing the fact that defendant had not objected, and so the trial court did not have the opportunity to adopt alternative measures to prevent the jury from being distracted by the heavy flow of traffic on the court's sentencing day.

245. The Vermont Supreme Court in State v. Robillard (1986) (the court then went on to find the error to have been harmless).

246. See, e.g., the Connecticut Supreme Court in State v. Sheppard (1980).

247. See the Second Circuit Court of Appeals in Peterson v. Williams (1996) (courtroom was inadvertently closed for twenty minutes during defendant's testimony, which was repeated during summation; the court stressed that the circumstances were unique, and distinguished its triviality analysis from a harmless error analysis; although the court found no violation, this was a habeas corpus proceeding, in which the burden on the petition is more difficult to meet); see also the Tenth Circuit Court of Appeals in United States v. Al-Smadi (1994) (courthouse door was closed at 4:30 P.M., at the end of the business day, while the defendant's trial extended until 4:50 P.M. and the defense attorney's wife and child were prevented from entering during that period of time; court stressed that the closing was inadvertent, not noticed by the trial participants, and not likely to recur); the Fourth Circuit Court of Appeals in Snyder v. Coiner (1975) (bailiff briefly refused to allow people to enter or leave courtroom during counsel's summation, until judge instructed otherwise).

248. The Kentucky Supreme Court in Tate v. Commonwealth (1935).

249. The Georgia Supreme Court in Myers v. State (1895) (court has "police power" to control conditions in the courtroom).

250. See the Eighth Circuit Court of Appeals in Davis v. United States (1917) (defendant's conviction was reversed when the courtroom in a notorious trial was ordered cleared of everyone but counsel, defendants' relatives, the press and a few other selected people, although there were enough seats for one hundred spectators and only about twenty-five were actually present).

251. See the New York Court of Appeals in People v. Jelke (1954), a frequently cited case, considering a trial judge's decision to exclude members of the public from a prostitution trial.

252. See Radin, "The Right to a Public Trial," 391–92, arguing even in 1932 that trial judges should not be allowed to exclude the public to protect their own sensibilities or for the convenience of policing the courtroom.

253. See also the Minnesota Supreme Court in State v. Schmit (1966) (protecting public from obscenity).

254. See the Kentucky Supreme Court in Tinsley v. Commonwealth (1973) (Constitution does not require that all who wish to attend a trial be admitted—courtroom was relatively small with security procedures); the Mississippi Supreme Court in Young v. State (1977) (exclusion of one individual from courtroom does not violate right—trial judge ordered an individual spectator who resembled the defendant, possibly his brother, to be excluded from the courtroom so as not to "confuse" an in-court identification of the defendant).

255. The Second Circuit Court of Appeals held in Vidal v. Williams (1994) that a heightened standard of scrutiny must apply to the exclusion of the defendant's family, in light of the dicta in *Oliver*, but later, when habeas corpus standards of review changed, backed off of this rigorous standard, at least in the context of habeas corpus review, see the Second Circuit Court of Appeals in Sevencan v. Herbert (2002); Yung v. Walker (2002).

256. See, e.g., a New York Appellate Court in People v. Green (1995).

257. See also an Illinois Appellate Court in People v. Taylor (1993) (using overriding interest test of *Waller* to evaluate exclusion of defendant's siblings from voir dire rather than the substantial interest test).

258. An Illinois Appellate Court in People v. Willis (1995); People v. Taylor (1993).

259. The North Dakota Supreme Court in State v. Klem (1989).

260. Waller v. Georgia (1984); the Second Circuit Court of Appeals in Guzman v. Scully (1996).

261. See also the Fifth Circuit Court of Appeals in Rovinsky v. McKaskle (1984); the Ninth Circuit Court of Appeals in United States v. Hernandez (1979).

262. See, e.g., the Southern District of New York Court in Ip v. Henderson (1989), in which an appellate court held the defendant's right to public trial to have been violated by closure of the courtroom during the testimony of the defendant's accomplice, who asserted that he feared retaliation.

263. The Fifth Circuit Court of Appeals in United States v. De Los Santos (1987) (closing suppression hearing was proper to avoid endangering or disclosing identity of informant); the Second Circuit Court of Appeals in Brown v. Kuhlmann (1998) (even if closure was error, habeas corpus petition should be denied).

264. The New York Court of Appeals in People v. Martinez (1993); a New York Appellate Court in People v. Rodriguez (1994).

265. See a Missouri Appellate Court in State v. Suarez (1993).

266. The Second Circuit Court of Appeals in Bobb v. Senkowski (1999).

267. See the Second Circuit Court of Appeals in Ayala v. Speckard (1997); see also the New York Court of Appeals in People v. Ayala (1997) (state court taking a different approach to the question of whether closure was proper).

268. The Second Circuit Court of Appeals in Ayala v. Speckard (1997).

269. The Eleventh Circuit Court of Appeals in In re Tribune Co. (Sierra) (1986); the Second Circuit Court of Appeals in In re Herald (Klepfer) (1984).

270. The Second Circuit Court of Appeals in United States v. Haller (1988).

271. See, e.g., the Eleventh Circuit Court of Appeals in Judd v. Haley (2001); the Ninth Circuit Court of Appeals in Geise v. United States (1958); a Michigan Appellate Court in In re Closure of Preliminary Examination (1993); the Minnesota Supreme Court in State v. Fageroos (1995).

272. See, e.g., a Florida Appellate Court in Clements v. Florida (1999) (upholding state mandatory closure statute on the ground that only the "idly curious" were excluded); an Illinois Appellate Court in People v. Benson (1993) (court upheld a statute providing that "In a prosecution for a criminal [sexual] offense . . . where the alleged victim of the offense is a minor under 18 years of age, the court may exclude from the proceedings while the victim is testifying, all persons, who, in the opinion of the court, do not have a direct interest in the case, except the media," Ill. Rev. Stat. 1991, ch. 38, par. 115–11, holding that the Sixth Amendment right to public trial was not implicated by this statute and that the *Waller* criteria did not even apply). Compare the New Hampshire Supreme Court in State v. Weber (1993) (state statute imposing burden on defendant to show good cause why courtroom should not be closed during a minor victim's testimony held unconstitutional).

273. See Virginia Supreme Court in Cumbee v. Commonwealth (1979) (reversing conviction when judge excluded spectators in incest trial in view of "the type of case"); see also a Military Appellate Court in United States v. Hershey (1985).

274. See the Illinois Supreme Court in People v. Holveck (1990); see also Gilbert Geis, "Publicity and Juvenile Court Proceedings," 30 *Rocky Mt. L. Rev.* (1958): 101.

275. The Iowa Supreme Court in State v. Schultzen (1994).

276. Lena v. State (2005).

277. See the Seventh Circuit Court of Appeals in United States ex rel. Latimore v. Sielaff (1977).

278. The New York Court of Appeals in People v. Clemons (1991).

279. The D.C. Court of Appeals in Cable News Network, Inc. v. United States (1987).

280. See the Fifth Circuit Court of Appeals in In re Dallas Morning News (1990), in which the court also suggested that a trial judge may close voir dire for the limited purpose of explaining to jurors their option of requesting private questioning and allowing jurors to make such requests in that closed session. See also the Fourth Circuit Court of Appeals in In re Landmark Communications, Inc. (1999) (trial court had good reason to fear for safety of jurors in multidefendant case, but it was required to give notice and make findings before closing voir dire).

281. See the Fourth Circuit Court of Appeals in In re Greensboro News Co. (1984) (closure of voir dire upheld).

282. See the Second Circuit Court of Appeals in United States v. King (1998).

283. See a New York Appellate Court in People v. Knapp (1985), in which a defendant objected to the presence of the press during voir dire in his highly publicized case.

284. See the Maryland Supreme Court in Watters v. State (1992) (reversing a defendant's conviction for deputy sheriff's closure of courtroom during voir dire in the defendant's murder trial, even without showing of prejudice, in the absence of specific findings); an Illinois Appellate Court in People v. Willis (1995) (reversing a defendant's conviction when trial judge excluded the defendant's family from the voir dire "to avoid contamination" without making any specific findings); an Illinois Appellate Court in People v. Taylor (1993).

285. See a Massachusetts Appellate Court in Massachusetts v. Jaynes (2002) (defendant was not denied right to public trial when the trial court excluded the public from portions of the voir dire of individual jurors involving sensitive personal issues, including history of sexual abuse and attitudes toward gays and people of other races, when the trial judge carefully followed the procedure of inviting jurors to request a private session if they were concerned about their privacy and agreeing to hold a private session only on finding that the particular juror's concern was legitimate).

286. See an Alabama Appellate Court in Ex parte Birmingham News (1993).

287. See also Cosentino v. Kelly (1996) (defendant's supporters had rioted and caused a mistrial at the first trial); the Utah Supreme Court in State v. Harding (1981) (public may be excluded from reading of the verdict where the judge has reason to fear violent reactions). Compare the New York Court of Appeals in Oliver v. Postel (1972) (court may not exclude spectators unless necessary to meet serious and imminent threat to the integrity of the trial).

288. The Seventh Circuit in United States ex rel. Latimore v. Sielaff (1977), for example, minimizes the importance of the "gaze of the curious."

289. See an Alabama Appellate Court in Williams v. State (1975).

290. See also a New York Appellate Court in People v. Haley (1993) (upholding exclusion of a defendant's eleven-year-old daughter during opening statements, after the court held a detailed hearing about the nature of prosecutor's anticipated remarks, in order to avoid prejudicing the fact-finders and to avoid exposing the child to obscenities attributed to her father).

291. See Annotation, *Exclusion of Public During Criminal Trail*, 48 A.L.R.2d 1436, 1448.

292. The Second Circuit Court of Appeals in United States ex rel. Orlando v. Fay (1965).

293. See also a New York Appellate Court in People v. Lopez (1992) (defense did not preserve issue of trial court's exclusion of the defendant's mother and sister, both of whom had testified on the defendant's behalf, during summation); the Utah Supreme Court in State v. Butterfield (1989); compare Levine v. United States (1960).

294. See a California Appellate Court in People v. Harris (1992).

295. See the Fifth Circuit Court of Appeals in Rovinsky v. McKaskle (1984).

296. See Fed. R. Cr. P. 23(a) (requiring written waiver of jury trial right).

297. "Note: The Right to a Public Trial in Criminal Cases," 41 *N.Y.U.L. Rev.* (1966): 1138, 1148.

298. Daughtry v. Greiner (2002).

299. See, e.g., Rovinsky v. McKaskle (1984).

300. See Dolores K. Sloviter, "If Courts Are Open, Must Cameras Follow?" 26 *Hofstra L. Rev.* (1998): 873 n. 1.

301. See the Sixth Circuit Court of Appeals in Conway v. United States (1988); the Fifth Circuit Court of Appeals in United States v. Edwards (2002). State courts have also followed *Nixon*, see the Indiana Supreme Court in Van Orden v. State (1984).

302. See Taffi Smith, "The Distortion of Criminal Trials Through Televised Proceedings," 21 *Law & Psych. Rev.* (1997): 257 (risks that televising trials will prejudice public opinion, influence jurors, and cater to sensationalism outweigh potential benefits); Christo Lassiter, "TV or Not TV—That Is the Question," 86 *J. Crim. L. & Criminology* (1996): 928, 1001 (arguing that print media are effective, as well as less intrusive and disruptive than electronic media, at satisfying the public's need for information about trials).

303. Sloviter, "If Courts Are Open, Must Cameras Follow?" 873, 886, citing Nixon v. Warner Communications, Inc. (1978).

304. Sloviter, "If Courts Are Open, Must Cameras Follow?" 887, citing Federal Judicial Center, *Electronic Media Coverage of Federal Civil Proceedings: An Evaluation of the Pilot Program in Six District Courts and Two Courts of Appeals* (Washington, DC: Federal Judicial Center, 1994), 7.

305. See Steven Brill, "Courtroom Cameras," 72 *Notre Dame L. Rev.* (1997): 1181; Kelli L. Sager and Karen N. Frederiksen, "Televising the Judicial Branch: In Furtherance of the Public's First Amendment Rights," 69 *S. Cal. L. Rev.* (1996): 1519 (although critical of the O.J. Simpson trial coverage).

306. "[T]he theater metaphor is legitimate, I think, because criminal trials are and are intended to be richly symbolic and educational—that is part of their function in a society governed by the rule of law. . . ." Brennan, "The Criminal Prosecution: Sporting Event or Quest for Truth," 1, 17; Bradley and Hoffman, "Public Perception, Justice, and the 'Search for Truth' in Criminal Cases," 1267, 1273, and n.13 (describing criminal trials as "a form of civic theater"); see also Peter Arenella, "The Perils of TV Legal Punditry," *U. Chi. Legal F.* (1998): 25, 42 (on the legitimacy of using trials for their entertainment or catharsis value).

307. See Jeffrey Abramson, *We, the Jury: The Jury System and the Ideal of Democracy* (New York: Basic Books, 1994).

308. See "Note: The Right to Public Trial in Criminal Cases," 41 *N.Y.U.L. Rev.* (1966): 1138. The *Hastings* court treated a ban on electronic coverage as merely a permissible time, place, and manner restriction subject to a less demanding standard of review than the strict scrutiny afforded actions infringing on First Amendment rights.

309. Radin, "The Right to a Public Trial," 391–92.

310. See Bradley and Hoffman, "Public Perception, Justice, and the 'Search for Truth' in Criminal Cases," 1271–81.

311. See Levine, 2002 Supplement Sec. 4-3 at 34; National Center for State Courts, *Summary of TV Cameras in the State Courts* (1998). For a current source of the rules in each state, see http://www.rtnda.org/foi/scc.shtml.

312. "[T]aking of photographs in the court room during the progress of judicial proceedings or radio broadcasting of judicial proceedings from the court room shall not be permitted by the court." This rule, adopted in 1946, does not explicitly mention television cameras, but it is interpreted as including all electronic media, see the Eleventh Circuit Court of Appeals in United States v. Hastings (1983).

313. *Code of Judicial Conduct for United States Courts*, Canon 3A(7) (1972).

314. See Federal Judicial Center, *Electronic Media Coverage of Federal Proceedings* 43 (1994).

315. See also the Second Circuit Court of Appeals in Westmoreland v. CBS (1984) (Winter, J., concurring).

316. 42 U.S.C. 10608(a) (1996).

317. See the Colorado District Court in United States v. McVeigh (1996).

318. See N.Y. State Comm. to Review Audio-Visual Coverage of Court Proceedings, *An Open Courtroom: Cameras in New York Courts* (1997).

319. See Tom Perrotta, "New York Law Banning Cameras in State Courts Found Constitutional," *N.Y.L.J.* (July 16, 2003): 1.

320. Cal. R. Ct. 980(e)(6).

321. Cal. R. Ct. 980(e)(3).

322. See Laurie L. Levenson, "Media Madness or Civics 101?" 26 *U.W. L.A.L. Rev.* (1995): 57, 58 n. 5 (arguing that televising the preliminary hearing and the prospective televising of the trial would add to the public's understanding of the criminal justice system); Peter Arenella, "O.J. Lessons," 69 *S. Cal. L. Rev.* (1996): 1233, 1252–58 (arguing that many high-profile trials should not be televised because of the risks involved); Bradley and Hoffman, "Public Perception, Justice, and the 'Search for Truth' in Criminal Cases," 1267 (search for truth is not the only purpose of a criminal trial; the public reaction to the Simpson trial was a "wake-up call" that should lead to a renewed effort to include the viewpoint of the public in a dialogue about how trials are to be conducted).

323. The Eastern District of Virginia in United States v. Moussaoui (2002), 184–85.

324. *Detention, Treatment, and Trial of Certain Non-Citizens in the War against Terrorism*, 66 Fed. Reg. 57, 833 (Nov. 13, 2001).

325. *Military Order: Detention, Treatment, and Trial of Certain Non-Citizens in the War Against Terrorism*, 66 Fed. Reg. 57833, 57835 §4 (c)(4)(B) (Nov. 13, 2001), 3 C.F.R. 918 (2002).

326. See, e.g., Neal K. Katyal and Laurence H. Tribe, "Waging War, Deciding Guilt: Trying the Military Tribunals," 111 *Yale L.J.* (2002): 1259, 1260 (criticizing the order for providing "authorization for the tribunals to operate in secret, without any publicity to check their abuses and with no threshold requirement of a showing that such secrecy is needed"); ABA Task Force on Terrorism and the Law "Report and Recommendations on Military Commissions," January 4, 2002 (urging that proceedings be open to the press and public, except for specific and compelling reasons, and that proceedings validly closed be open to trial observers with appropriate security clearance); Reporters Committee for Freedom of the Press, *Homefront Confidential: How the War on Terrorism Affects Access to Information and the Public's Right to Know,* 6th ed. (http://www.rcfp.org/homefront-confidential/Homefront_Confidential_6th.pdf, last accessed March 23, 2006), 31–33.

327. Department of Defense Military Commission Order No. 1 (March 21, 2002) Section 4A(5), which provides that closure be consistent with another section, 6B(3), permitting closure to protect classified or classifiable information, trial participants, or "intelligence and law enforcement sources, methods, or activities; and other national security interests."

328. See Committee on Communications and Media Law of the Association of the Bar of the City of New York, "The Press and the Public's First Amendment Right of Access to Terrorism on Trial: A Position Paper," 22 *Cardozo Arts & Ent. L.J.* (2005): 767; Paul Haridakis, "The War on Terrorism: Military Tribunals and the First Amendment," 9 *Communic. L. & Policy* (2004): 317.

329. The Press and the Public's First Amendment Right of Access to Terrorism on Trial, 773–78.

330. The Press and the Public's First Amendment Right of Access to Terrorism on Trial, 789–90.

331. Ex parte Milligan (1866), 2, 124–25.

332. Rumsfeld v. Padilla (2004). Padilla was subsequently charged with a criminal offense.

333. Jack L. Goldsmith and Cass R. Sunstein, "Military Tribunals and Legal Culture: What a Difference Sixty Years Makes," 19 *Const. Commentary* (2002): 261.

334. David Glazier, "Kangaroo Court or Competent Tribunal? Judging the 21st Century Military Commission," 89 *Va. L. Rev.* (2003): 2005, 2059–61. Not all the controversial features of the *Quirin* military commission were modified—the standard for admissibility of evidence and the allowance of conviction and sentencing by a two-thirds instead of a unanimous vote remained. Id. at 2060.

335. Glazier, "Kangaroo Court or Competent Tribunal?" 2013–23.

336. "Report and Recommendations on Military Commissions," n. 28.

337. Glazier, "Kangaroo Court or Competent Tribunal?" 2019 n. 353.

338. North Jersey Media Group v. Ashcroft (2002) (constitutional); Detroit Free Press v. Ashcroft (2002) (unconstitutional).

Bibliographic Essay

ENGLISH SOURCES

Many of the usual sources of information about early English law, like Henry de Bracton's *On the Laws and Customs of England,* trans. Samuel E. Thorne (Cambridge: Harvard Univ. Press, 1968), have little or nothing to say about the right to public trial.

One of the earliest extant discussions of English criminal procedure, "In Praise of the Laws of England," was written by Sir John Fortescue, an influential fifteenth-century political theorist who was appointed Chief Justice of the King's Bench in 1442 and presented King Edward IV with this book in 1471. Fortescue champions English procedure and takes particular pride in the institution of trial by jury, including its public nature, id. at 51, 74–75. He maintains that the superior English legal customs remained intact since the early days of the Britons and were not changed either by the Romans (because "the customs of the English are not only good but the best") or the Norman Conquest, id. at 26–27. *On the Laws and Governance of England,* ed. Shelley Lockwood (Cambridge: Cambridge Univ. Press, 1997), xxiv–xxv, contains Fortescue's dialogue. An introduction describes Fortescue's work as aspirational—an account of how the English criminal justice system *should* work as opposed to how it actually did. Fortescue did not invoke sources, so it is impossible to judge to what extent his account is based on actual incidents and to what extent it is simply a manifestation of his desire to establish the superiority of the English over the French. Reliable or not, Fortescue's work influenced Sir Thomas Smith and later commentators including Blackstone.

Sir Thomas Smith, Queen Elizabeth I's secretary of state and ambassador to France, as well as a member of the Privy Council, wrote a highly regarded treatise on English law between 1562 and 1566 called *De Republica Anglorum, A Discourse on the Commonwealth of England,* 1st ed. (London, 1583; reprint, New York: Harper & Row, 1972). F. W. Maitland, in a preface to the Harper & Row edition, says that "no one would think of writing about the England of Elizabeth's day without paying heed to what was written about that matter by

[Smith]," id. at vii. In his treatise, Smith discusses the development of both civil and criminal proceedings, including some references to the value of public trials, id. at 79 and 101.

Sir Edward Coke, in his 1628 classic *Institutes of the Laws of England* (London: E. & R. Brooke, 1797), is one of the principle sources on seventeenth-century English law, although his writings are fragmentary. He wrote about Magna Carta, and has been blamed for having adopted and perpetuated Ferdinando Pulton's mischaracterization of Magna Carta's mention of jury trials as having created, then and there, a full-blown right to jury trial. His *Institutes*, while a popular source for the framers of the Constitution, do not mention publicity of trials, although they do comment on the importance of speedy trials.

Sir John Hawles, as Solicitor General, commented on Lilburne's 1649 treason trial (see 11 How. St. Tr. 455, 1685) in one of the earliest and most articulate tributes to the significance of the public trial. He also wrote *The English-Man's Right: A Dialogue Between a Barrister at Law and a Jury-Man* (London: Printed for Richard Janeway, 1680), a paean to the jury, which discusses the historical roots of trial by jury. William Walwin, in 1651, wrote a book with similar themes and messages, *Juries Justified* (New York: Garland Publishing, 1978), in which he also contends that juries are necessary to prevent oppression and arbitrary punishment.

Sir Matthew Hale lived from 1609 to 1676. His book, *The History of the Common Law of England* (Chicago: University of Chicago Press, 1971) was published posthumously in 1713. In volume I of his book, he also describes the development of the jury trial, from "long before" the Norman conquest, through Magna Carta, and the trial by ordeal, and describes favorably the English system of giving evidence in open court, id. at 218–21, 264–67, 345. Hale was one of Blackstone's principal authorities.

William Blackstone's *Commentaries on the Laws of England in Four Volumes* (London: Cavendish, 2001), originally published in 1783, have played an unparalleled role in analysis of the common law origins of American constitutional rights. In volume IV of his commentaries, about "Public Wrongs," Blackstone discusses the history of the criminal trial and the role of the jury and lavishly praises public trials, describing the open examination of witnesses as conducive to uncovering truth.

Sir Fitzjames Stephen, in his book *A History of the Criminal Law of England* (London: Macmillan, 1883), covers, in volume I, Roman criminal procedure and its influence on English criminal procedure, id. at 43–50, and criminal proceedings in the Privy Council and Star Chamber. Volume II discusses later Star Chamber proceedings, and the introduction of canon law into England, id. at 440 et seq.

Sir Frederick Pollock's works, with and without coauthors, provide extensive coverage of common law history from a later vantage point. Pollock's *The Expansion of the Common Law* (London: Stevens & Sons, 1904), in the eponymous chapter one, discusses the rise of the public jury trial, from the twelfth century, and discusses the impact of canon law. The third chapter ("The Sword of Justice") discusses the Star Chamber, described as a departure from the common law, and fixes the sixteenth century as the date from which public trials were "essential," although it was possible during that era to hold secret proceedings, id. at 98. *The History of English Law Before the Time of Edward I* (Cambridge: Cambridge University Press, 1980), a two-volume work Pollock coauthored with Frederic W. Maitland in 1898, provides greater detail about Anglo-Saxon law and covers some of the same territory, particularly regarding the twelfth century, as Pollock's subsequent individual work.

Maitland later wrote, with Francis C. Montague, *A Sketch of English Legal History* (New York: G.P. Putnam's Sons, 1915). The chapter "Legal Reforms of Henry II," covering the period from 1066 to 1216, provides an account not very different from those written by or with Pollock, although some interesting additional detail is supplied. Maitland and Montague challenge the English myth that the right to jury trial was native to England. Albert Lieck, in his *Justice and Police in England* (Toronto: Butterworth & Co., 1929), discusses the modes of trial from the Saxon period (fifth to sixth century) to the early twentieth century, but he does not explicitly discuss the public nature of trials.

Theodore F. T. Plucknett, author of *A Concise History of the Common Law* (London: Butterworth, 1956), provides one of the most comprehensive accounts of the rise of the jury, harmonizing previous accounts, including some not listed above. Plucknett agrees with the Pollock and Maitland view that juries did not exist in anything close enough to current form before the Norman Conquest, and that attempts to trace juries back to the "supposed golden age of Anglo-Saxon institutions" are expressions of a romanticization of juries that began in the seventeenth century when juries began to act counter to the interests of government. He makes few comments on the public trial right.

Edward Jenks, in chapter seven of *The Book of English Law* (Athens: Ohio University Press, 1967), discusses "General Principles of English Justice," including the public trial as one outstanding feature of English trials. Jenks also wrote *A Short History of English Law* (London: Methuen & Co., 1938), which covered some of the same ground.

Jeremy Bentham, writing his *Treatise on Judicial Evidence* (London: J.W. Paget, 1825) after the Sixth Amendment was added to the Constitution, spends two chapters on the publicity of proceedings. The first of these, chapter ten, discusses rationales for public trials.

SOURCES ON AMERICAN CONSTITUTIONAL HISTORY

The classic sources on American constitutional history provide no evidence of any discussion of the right to public trial around the time the Sixth Amendment was drafted and ratified.

Alexander Hamilton in Federalist Paper No. 83 (reprint, Middletown, CT: Wesleyan University Press, 1961) endorsed public jury trials as "a safeguard to liberty" and "the very palladium of liberty," but he does not discuss what he thought the public nature of a trial contributed.

Bernard Schwartz, in *The Bill of Rights: A Documentary History* (New York: Chelsea House Publishers, 1971), includes documents from the Constitutional Convention, including the debate over whether a Bill of Rights was necessary. The descriptions of the ratification debates include no discussion at all of the right to public trial. Schwartz also provides copies of colonial charters, which often included a right to trial in open court, with commentary, and then copies of state constitutions, most of which contain similar provisions.

Jonathan Elliot's *Debates in the Several State Conventions on the Adoption of the Federal Constitution as Recommended by the General Convention at Philadelphia in 1787,* 2d ed. (Philadelphia: J.B. Lippincott, 1891; reprint, Buffalo, NY: Hein & Co., 1996) is a valuable source of information about debates surrounding the Constitution, but it shows no evidence of any discussion, no less debate, about the right to public trial.

Joseph Story's *Commentaries on the Constitution of the United States* (Boston: Hillard, Gray, 1833), 71, has disappointingly little to say of the right to public trial. Story discusses the value of the jury trial and then simply announces that "[t]he trial is always public."

AMERICAN POST-CONSTITUTIONAL SOURCES

Thomas M. Cooley, in *A Treatise on the Constitutional Limitations Which Rest Upon the Legislative Powers of the States of the American Union* (Boston: Little Brown & Co., 1927), 647, described his contemporary courts as believing that a trial was sufficiently public as long as it was not held in secret.

One of the first law review articles written on the subject of the Sixth Amendment right to public trial and still one of the most interesting is Max Radin's frequently cited "The Right to a Public Trial," 6 *Temple L.Q.* (1932): 381, which debunked the notions that the right to public trial represented either an important ancient privilege or a reaction to the supposed secrecy of the Star Chamber, and described the introduction of public trial into English law as more or less accidental. Radin expresses a marked skepticism about whether an unqualified right to public trial would indeed serve any of the functions ascribed to it.

Wigmore's *Evidence in Trials at Common Law* (Boston: Little Brown, 1940), 435–53, follows Bentham's account closely in identifying and discussing the functions of the public trial, including improving the quality of testimony, averting abuses, and educating the public.

Francis H. Heller's book, *The Sixth Amendment to the Constitution of the United States: A Study in Constitutional Development* (Lawrence: University of Kansas Press, 1951), covers Sixth Amendment rights generally. In a chapter on the right to trial by jury, Heller discusses the common law origins of that right, tracing the developments from ordeals to the modern trial, and then moves on to summarize the American colonial experience with jury trials and the constitutional convention. Heller spends only about three pages commenting on the right to public trial (in which he anticipates the debate between Brennan and Warren about the scope and nature of the right) and on the current status of the law's interpretation of the two fellow Sixth Amendment rights to speedy and to public trial.

Ronald Goldfarb, in an article written decades before his 1998 book on the debate over televising trials, "Public Information, Criminal Trials and the Cause Celebre," 36 *N.Y.U.L. Rev.* (1961): 810, endorses Radin's view that the right to public trial was an accidental feature of English law, treated with reverence because it was believed to be ancient. He argues, more pointedly than Radin had, that the right should be deemed to belong to the defendant alone rather than to the public at large.

The student author of the note, "Legal History: Origins of the Public Trial," 35 *Ind. L.J.* (1960): 251, 251–56, presents a very different picture of the functions of the right from that of Radin or Goldfarb. Canvassing familiar English history regarding the origins of the jury trial and public trial, this author concludes that the form of public jury trial that served the purposes of the Crown as well as the interests of those being tried cannot really be said to have been viewed as a "right" at all. Another student note, "The Right to a Public Trial in Criminal Cases," 41 *N.Y.U.L. Rev.* (1966): 1138, favors a more generous definition of the Sixth Amendment right than most earlier American commentators on such other issues as waiver (defendants should not be considered to have defaulted if they did not object to a courtroom closure, unless their waiver was knowing and intelligent) and prejudice (defendants should not be required to show prejudice as a result of a violation of their public trial right).

David J. Bodenhamer's book, *Fair Trial: Rights of the Accused in American History* (New York: Oxford University Press, 1992), focuses on the development of the concept of a defendant's fair trial rights in state constitutions, courts, and legislatures. Bodenhamer's chapter on the colonial background of trial rights, id. at 10–29, is one of the richest treatments of this issue. Bodenhamer is particularly interested in correcting anachronistic assumptions about the colonists' and framers' views of what we now conceptualize as individual "rights."

Another historian of the Bill of Rights, Leonard W. Levy, has written extensively about the history of the right to trial by jury. See *The Palladium of Justice* (Chicago: I.R. Dee, 1999), which traces the development and functions of the jury trial in England, but without providing sources. In *Origins of the Bill of Rights* (New Haven: Yale University Press, 1999), Levy describes the colonists as utilizing public jury trials before other procedures later embodied in the Sixth Amendment, the right to counsel and right to confront witnesses.

Akhil Reed Amar, in his reconstructive march through the Bill of Rights, reached the Sixth Amendment in 1996. In his article, "Sixth Amendment First Principles," 84 *Geo. L.J.* (1996): 641, 677–81, later incorporated in his book, *The Constitution and Criminal Procedure* (New Haven: Yale Univ. Press, 1997), 116–19, he argues that the function of the right to public trial, like other Sixth Amendment provisions, is to protect innocent defendants by making the truth of their innocence visible both to a jury and the public, and not to provide the guilty with any procedural protection. Amar's endorsement of the republican function of a public trial coincides with Brennan's view, but he does not provide any historical basis for choosing this vision as a correct constitutional interpretation over the view that the Sixth Amendment right, unlike the First Amendment right of access, should belong to the accused, whether guilty or innocent.

On the whole, the general subject of the right to public trial has not received much critical attention. In their book, *In Our Defense: the Bill of Rights in Action* (New York: Morrow, 1991), intended to enhance public understanding of the Constitution, Ellen Alderman and Caroline Kennedy devote more than sixty pages to the Sixth Amendment, discussing the right to an impartial jury, right to counsel, right to confrontation, and right to compulsory process, but they do not mention the right to speedy or public trial. Alfredo Garcia, whose book *The Sixth Amendment in Modern American Jurisprudence: A Critical Perspective* (Westport, CT: Greenwood, 1992) is devoted to an analysis of Sixth Amendment rights, does not include the right to public trial at all. Several discrete issues about how public trials should be, however, have garnered considerable attention.

Cameras in the Courtroom

There is a vast body of literature on the pros and cons of allowing television cameras into the courtroom, frequently framed as a struggle between the right to a fair trial and a free press. Many of the books and articles on this subject discuss these questions as a matter of policy. Those authors who address whether or not the Constitution might require opening courtrooms to cameras usually limit themselves to discussing the First Amendment as the source of that potential right, and the Sixth Amendment as the source of the defendant's conflicting fair trial rights. Discussions of the meaning of the Sixth Amendment public trial right are rare. Discussions of how the balance of interests would be affected if a defendant were, like Alcee Hastings, to invoke his or her sixth amendment public trial right in requesting television coverage are virtually nonexistent.

One useful, recent source, Ronald L. Goldfarb's *TV or Not TV: Television, Justice, and the Courts* (New York: Twentieth Century Fund, N.Y.U. Press, 1998), discusses the development of the right of access to courtrooms under both the First and Sixth Amendments. Goldfarb provides information about the status of the right to broadcast coverage in each state and in federal court at the end of the twentieth century, reports on the results of studies of the pros and cons of television coverage of trials, and recounts the history of Court TV. Goldfarb's conclusion is that the current trend toward fuller television coverage is appropriate, for reasons discussed in the text above. The authors of another recent book, Marjorie Cohn and David Dow, *Cameras in the Courtroom: Television and the Pursuit of Justice* (Jefferson, NC: McFarland, 1998), a criminal defense attorney and a journalist, respectively, reacted to the O.J. Simpson trial. Cohn and Dow seek to provide a balanced account of the history of the camera in the courtroom, analysis of the arguments pro and con, a description of the status of broadcasting proceedings in various states and in the federal courts, and an analysis of options for minimizing disruption and prejudice. Joseph Jaconelli, *Open Justice: A Critique of the Public Trial* (Oxford: Oxford University Press, 2002), 304, concludes that "the values that are served by open justice are not secured in the highest possible measure by the greatest degree of publicity."

For other recent discussions favoring televising of trials and a broad concept of the "public" trial, see Steven Brill, "Courtroom Cameras," 72 *Notre Dame L. Rev.* (1997): 1181; Kelli L. Sager and Karen N. Frederiksen, "Televising the Judicial Branch: In Furtherance of the Public's First Amendment Rights," 69 *S. Cal. L. Rev.* (1996): 1519; and Craig M. Bradley and Joseph L. Hoffman, "Public Perception, Justice, and the 'Search for Truth' in Criminal Cases," 69 *S. Cal. L. Rev.* (1996): 1267 (on the role the public should play in monitoring the criminal justice system). David Harris makes the interesting point that the public will see criminal trials on television whether or not there are cameras in real courtrooms but, without coverage of actual trials, their perceptions of the criminal justice system will depend on what stories television producers choose to portray in fictional courtrooms. See David A. Harris, "The Appearance of Justice: Court TV, Conventional Television, and Public Understanding of the Criminal Justice System," 35 *Ariz. L. Rev.* (1993): 785. Another author discussing proposals for expanded access to information about judicial proceedings is Diane L. Zimmerman in "Overcoming Future Shock: *Estes* Revisited, or a Modest Proposal for the Constitutional Protection of the News-Gathering Process," *Duke L.J.* (1980): 641. Daniel Stepniak, in "A Comparative Analysis of First Amendment Rights and the Televising of Court Proceedings," 40 *Idaho L. Rev.* (2004): 315, compares the approaches of the United States and England, Canada, New Zealand, and Australia, concluding that the experiences of these countries shows that courts, not just the media, should champion the televising of their proceedings.

For more skeptical evaluations of the value of extensive publicity and the impact of cameras on the courtroom itself, see Dolores Sloviter, "If Courts Are Open, Must Cameras Follow?" 26 *Hofstra L. Rev.* (1998): 873 (discussed above); Peter Arenella, "Televising High Profile Trials: Are We Better Off Pulling the Plug?" 37 *Santa Clara L. Rev.* (1997): 879 (cameras filter trial proceedings and do not convey an accurate picture to the television audience, given that most audience members will only see snippets of coverage); and Christo Lassiter, "The Appearance of Justice: TV or Not TV—That Is the Question," 86 *J. Crim. L. & Criminology* (1996): 928, 1001 (television is not superior to print media, which adequately meet the public's need for information, and causes a "feedback loop" distorting the trial itself). Lassiter's article is a good example of commentary sharing Earl Warren's skepticism about public motivations in observing trials and their unwholesome influences on the trial itself.

The many reports written by ABA committees, the Federal Judicial Center, and numerous state commissions reporting on the wisdom of televising trials, on experiments with cameras, and on the effectiveness of guidelines and regulations are also a valuable source of arguments and information. See, for example, *ABA Standards for Criminal Justice: Fair Trial and Free Press* (1992); *Federal*

Judicial Center, Electronic Media Coverage of Federal Proceedings (1994); *The Committee on Audio-Visual Coverage of Court Proceedings, N.Y.* (1995). On the history of the ban on cameras in the United States, see Richard B. Kielbowicz, "The Story Behind the Ban on Courtroom Cameras," 63 *Judicature* (1979): 14.

Some worthwhile earlier sources include two prominent judges writing in the ABA Journal. Supreme Court Justice William O. Douglas, "The Public Trial and the Free Press," 46 *A.B.A.J.* (1960): 840, anticipated many of the arguments against cameras made by Earl Warren in his *Estes* opinion. His contemporary, J. Skelly Wright, who sat on the United States Court of Appeals for the District of Columbia Circuit, took the opposing Brennan point of view in his article, "A Judge's View: The News Media and Criminal Justice," 50 *A.B.A.J.* (1964): 1125.

Jerome Frank, in his classic book, *Courts on Trial: Myth and Reality in American Justice* (Princeton: Princeton Univ. Press, 1949), 2–3, argues that the public should have the right to know what its public servants, including judges, are doing and that courts should not be permitted to gain public esteem through public ignorance. Frank's legal realist argument that "the cult of the robe" may need some debunking and that the courts should belong to the public, rather than only to the judges and lawyers, has continued to reverberate, gaining endorsement by Ronald Goldfarb in his book and David Harris in his article.

The Web site of the Radio-Television News Directors Association offers updated information about the current rules governing cameras in the courtrooms in each state. See http://www.rtnda.org/foi/scc.shtml.

National Security, Antiterrorism, and Open Proceedings

Since the events of September 11, 2001, the question of when and whether proceedings involving suspected or alleged terrorists may be partially or wholly closed has generated a great deal of writing. As described in the text, deportation proceedings of "special interest" detainees actually were closed to the public. Challenges to this practice by media and other plaintiffs, on the basis of the First Amendment right of access, resulted in split decisions by two federal courts of appeals. Commentators overwhelmingly favored the Sixth Circuit decision, which ruled that the routine closure of such proceedings is unconstitutional. See, for example, J. Andrew Walkup, "Comment: Please Take Back Your Huddled Masses: A Look at the First Amendment Right to Access Deportation Hearings After September 11, 2001," 22 *St. Louis U. Pub. L. Rev.* (2003): 593; and Dale L. Edwards, "If It Walks, Talks and Squawks Like a Trial, Should It Be Covered Like One? The Right of the Press to Cover INS Deportation Hearings," 10 *Communic. Law & Policy No. 2* (2005): 217 (arguing that deportation proceedings are structurally similar to courts-martial, which have historically been open) and 219–20 nn. 10 and 15 (listing other articles discussing whether there is a First Amendment right of access to deportation proceedings). These discussions focus on the First Amendment right of access to judicial proceedings because deportation hearings are not part of a "criminal prosecution," so the Sixth Amendment does not apply.

President Bush's order establishing military commissions to try noncitizens in terrorism cases also occasioned a tremendous of amount of commentary, even before any such proceeding had been held. One of the most interesting treatments of whether there is a public right of access to such proceedings is The Committee on Communications and Media Law of the Association of the Bar of the City of New York, "The Press and the Public's First Amendment Right of Access to Terrorism on Trial: A Position Paper," 22 *Cardozo Arts & Ent. L.J.* (2005): 767, which provides an expansive account of the history of American proceedings against suspected terrorists and enemy combatants from the Boston Massacre on. This article supplements the history provided in many other sources on the history of military commissions, usually limited to discussion of Civil War and World War II precedents, and focuses directly on whether such proceedings have been or should be open to the public. The principal article on military commission procedure that focuses on the defendant's point of view, although it does not focus on the particular issue of public access, is David Glazier's "Note: Kangaroo Court or Competent Tribunal?: Judging the 21st Century Military Commission," 89 *Va. L. Rev.* (2003): 2005, which argues that the procedures in military commissions have historically conformed to the procedures of courts-martial, except for the deviation of the proceeding considered in the *Quirin* case, and that relevant statutory law should be interpreted as requiring them to do so. Other commentators have argued that military commissions should be open to the public under the *Richmond Newspapers* and *Press-Enterprise I* test, see, for example, Paul Haridakis, "The War on Terrorism: Military Tribunals and the First Amendment," 9 *Communic. Law & Policy* (2004): 317, 327–28 (discussing the First Amendment cases and describing Court of Military Appeals law providing for open proceedings in courts-martial on the basis of a Sixth Amendment right to public proceedings, even before the First Amendment was found to provide a public right of access). Other authors, including the ABA Task Force on Terrorism and the Law in their "Report and Recommendations on Military Commissions" (January 4, 2002) and Louis Fisher in his book *Nazi Saboteurs on Trial: A Military Tribunal and American Law* (Lawrence: Univ. of Kansas Press, 2003) provide a fuller account of the arguments surrounding the use of military commissions and the relevance of the World War II precedents to the 2001 Executive Order. See also Neal K. Katyal and Laurence H. Tribe, "Waging War, Deciding Guilt: Trying the Military Tribunals," 111 *Yale L.J.* (2002): 1259, 1260 (criticizing the order for providing "authorization for the tribunals to operate in secret, without any publicity to check their abuses and with no threshold requirement of a showing that such secrecy is needed"); Reporters Committee for Freedom of the Press, *Homefront Confidential: How the War on Terrorism Affects Access to Information and the Public's Right to Know,* 6th ed. (http://www.rcfp.org/homefrontconfidential/Homefront_Confidential_6th.pdf, last accessed March 23, 2006), 31–33; and Jack L. Goldsmith and Cass R. Sunstein, "Military Tribunals and Legal Culture: What a Difference Sixty Years Makes," 19 *Const. Commentary* (2002): 261, 271–73.

Treatises

There is no comprehensive treatise on the Sixth Amendment right to public trial. C. Thomas Dienes, Lee Levine, and Robert C. Lind, *Newsgathering and the Law,* 2d ed. (Charlottesville, VA.: Matthew Bender, 1999, with supplement) is a useful treatise covering case law elaborating on the First Amendment right of the public and press to attend criminal proceedings. Wayne R. LaFave, Jerold H. Israel, and Nancy J. King, *Criminal Procedure,* 4th ed. (St. Paul, MN: West, 2004), section 24.1, 1103–5, provides only a very brief account of Sixth Amendment public trial case law; section 23.1, id. at 1069–1101, offers a fuller discussion of the prejudicial publicity cases, the First Amendment right of access, and permissible measures to avoid prejudice to a defendant, including closure of proceedings.

Table of Cases

United States Supreme Court

Batson v. Kentucky, 476 U.S. 79 (1986)
Betts v. Brady, 316 U.S. 455 (1942)
Brady v. United States, 397 U.S. 742 (1970)
Chambers v. Florida, 309 U.S. 227 (1940)
Chandler v. Florida, 449 U.S. 560 (1981)
Cohen v. Beneficial Industrial Loan Corp., 337 U.S. 541 (1949)
Coleman v. Alabama, 399 U.S. 1 (1970)
Crist v. Betz, 437 U.S. 28 (1978)
Duncan v. Louisiana, 391 U.S. 145 (1968)
Dusky v. United States, 362 U.S. 402 (1960)
El Vocero de Puerto Rico v. Puerto Rico, 508 U.S. 147 (1993)
Estelle v. Williams, 425 U.S. 501 (1976)
Estes v. Texas, 381 U.S. 532 (1965)
Ex parte Milligan, 71 U.S. 2 (1866)
Ex parte Quirin, 317 U.S. 1 (1942)
Faretta v. California, 422 U.S. 806 (1975)
Gannett Co., Inc. v. DePasquale, 443 U.S. 368 (1979)
Gentile v. State Bar of Nevada, 501 U.S. 1030 (1991)
Globe Newspaper Co. v. Superior Court for the County of Norfolk, 457 U.S. 596 (1982)
Griswold v. Connecticut, 381 U.S. 479 (1965)
Hamden v. Rumsfeld (05-184)
Hamdi v. Rumsfeld, 542 U.S. 507 (2004)
Houchins v. KQED, Inc., 438 U.S. 1 (1978)
Hurtado v. California, 110 U.S. 516 (1884)
In re Gault, 387 U.S. 1 (1967)
In re Oliver, 333 U.S. 257 (1948)
In re Winship, 397 U.S. 358 (1970)
Irvin v. Dowd, 366 U.S. 717 (1961)
Johnson v. Zerbst, 304 U.S. 458 (1938)
Levine v. United States, 362 U.S. 610 (1960)
Marshall v. United States, 360 U.S. 310 (1959)

Massiah v. United States, 377 U.S. 201 (1964)
McKeiver v. Pennsylvania, 403 U.S. 528 (1971)
Miller-El v. Cockrell, 537 U.S. 322 (2003)
Miranda v. Arizona, 384 U.S. 436 (1966)
Moore v. Dempsey, 261 U.S. 86 (1923)
Mu'Min v. Virginia, 500 U.S. 415 (1991)
Murphy v. Florida, 421 U.S. 794 (1975)
NAACP v. Alabama, 357 U.S. 449 (1958)
Nebraska Press Ass'n v. Stuart, 427 U.S. 539 (1976)
New State Ice Co. v. Liebmann, 285 U.S. 262 (1932)
Nixon v. Warner Communications, Inc., 435 U.S. 589 (1978)
Patton v. Yount, 467 U.S. 1025 (1984)
Powell v. Alabama, 287 U.S. 45 (1932)
Powers v. Ohio, 499 U.S. 400 (1991)
Press-Enterprise Co. v. Superior Court of Calif., Riverside County, 464 U.S. 501 (1984) [Press-Enterprise I]
Press-Enterprise Co. v. Superior Court of Calif. for the County of Riverside, 478 U.S. 1(1986) [Press-Enterprise II]
Rasul v. Bush, 542 U.S. 466 (2004)
Reynolds v. Sims, 377 U.S. 533 (1964)
Richmond Newspapers, Inc. v. Virginia, 448 U.S. 555 (1980)
Rumsfeld v. Padilla, 542 U.S. 426 (2004)
Shapiro v. Thompson, 394 U.S. 618 (1969)
Sheppard v. Maxwell, 384 U.S. 333 (1966)
Singer v. United States, 380 U.S. 24 (1965)
Waller v. Georgia, 467 U.S. 39 (1984)
Williams v. Florida, 399 U.S. 78 (1970)

United States Courts of Appeal
Applications of National Broadcasting Co., 828 F.2d 340 (6th Cir. 1987)
Ayala v. Speckard, 102 F.2d 649 (2d Cir. 1996), rev'd, Ayala v. Speckard, 131 F.3d 62 (2d Cir. 1997) (en banc), cert. denied, 524 U.S. 958 (1998)
Bell v. Evatt, 72 F.3d 421 (4th Cir. 1995), cert. denied, 518 U.S. 1009 (1996)
Bobb v. Senkowski, 196 F.3d 350 (2d Cir. 1999)
Brown v. Kuhlmann, 142 F.3d 529 (2d Cir. 1998)
Cable News Network, Inc. v. United States, 824 F.2d 1046 (D.C. Cir.), cert. denied, 484 U.S. 914 (1987)
CBS, Inc. v. United States Dist. Ct., 765 F.2d 823 (9th Cir. 1985)
Charlotte Observer v. Bakker, 882 F.2d 850 (4th Cir. 1989)
Conway v. United States, 852 F.2d 187 (6th Cir.), cert. denied, 488 U.S. 943 (1988)
Cosentino v. Kelly, 102 F.3d 71 (2d Cir. 1996), cert. denied, 520 U.S. 1229 (1997)
Daughtry v. Greiner, No. 01-2466, 2002 U.S. App. LEXIS 25867 (2d Cir., Dec. 16, 2002), cert. denied sub nom. Daughtry v. Senkowski, 538 U.S. 1041 (2003)
Davis v. United States, 247 F. 394 (8th Cir. 1917)
Detroit Free Press v. Ashcroft, 303 F.3d 681 (6th Cir. 2002)
Douglas v. Wainwright, 739 F.2d 531 (11th Cir. 1984)
Geise v. United States, 262 F.2d 151 (9th Cir. 1958), cert. denied, 361 U.S. 842 (1959)
Gonzalez v. Quinones, 211 F.3d 735 (2d Cir. 2000)

Guzman v. Scully, 80 F.3d 772 (2d Cir. 1996)
Hayes v. United States, 296 F.2d 657 (8th Cir. 1961), cert. denied, 369 U.S. 867 (1962)
In re Charlotte Observer, 882 F.2d 850 (4th Cir. 1989)
In re Dallas Morning News, 916 F.2d 205 (5th Cir. 1990)
In re Globe Newspaper, 729 F.2d 47 (1st Cir. 1984)
In re Greensboro News Co., 727 F.2d 1320 (4th Cir.), cert. denied, 469 U.S. 829 (1984)
In re Herald (Klepfer), 734 F.2d 93 (2d Cir. 1984)
In re Landmark Communications, Inc., No. 99-2387, 1999 U.S. App. LEXIS 38810 (4th Cir., Nov. 3, 1999)
In re Tribune Co. (Sierra), 784 F.2d 1518 (11th Cir. 1986)
In re Washington Post, 807 F.2d 383 (4th Cir. 1986)
Jones v. Henderson, 809 F.2d 946 (2d Cir. 1987)
Judd v. Haley, 250 F.3d 1308 (11th Cir. 2001)
Knapp v. Leonardo, 46 F.3d 170 (2d Cir.), cert. denied, 515 U.S. 1136 (1995)
Lewis v. Peyton, 352 F.2d 791 (4th Cir. 1965)
Newman v. Graddick, 696 F.2d 796 (11th Cir. 1983)
Nieto v. Sullivan, 879 F.2d 743 (10th Cir. 1989)
North Jersey Media Group v. Ashcroft, 308 F.3d 198 (3d Cir. 2002)
Orlando v. Fay, 350 F.2d 967 (2d Cir. 1965)
Peterson v. Williams, 85 F.3d 39 (2d Cir. 1996)
Rovinsky v. McKaskle, 722 F.2d 197 (5th Cir. 1984), reh. en banc denied (1984)
Seattle Times Co. v. United States Dist. Ct., 845 F.2d 1513 (9th Cir. 1988)
Sevencan v. Herbert, 316 F.3d 76 (2d Cir. 2002)
Snyder v. Coiner, 510 F.2d 224 (4th Cir. 1975)
United States v. Al-Smadi, 15 F.3d 153 (10th Cir. 1994)
United States v. Brown, 22 C.M.R. 41 (1956)
United States v. Brown, 250 F.3d 907 (5th Cir. 2001)
United States v. Chagra, 701 F.2d 354 (5th Cir. 1983)
United States v. Cianfrani, 573 F.2d 835 (3d Cir. 1978)
United States v. Cojab, 996 F.2d 1404 (2d Cir. 1993)
United States v. De Los Santos, 810 F.2d 1326 (5th Cir.), cert. denied, 484 U.S. 978 (1987)
United States v. Edwards, 303 F.3d 606 (5th Cir. 2002)
United States v. Farmer, 32 F.3d 369 (8th Cir. 1994)
United States v. Grunden, 2 M.J. 116 (C.M.A. 1977)
United States v. Haller, 837 F.2d 84 (2d Cir. 1988)
United States v. Hastings, 695 F.2d 1278 (11th Cir.), cert. denied sub nom. Post-Newsweek Stations, Florida, 461 U.S. 931 (1983)
United States v. Hernandez, 608 F.2d 741 (9th Cir. 1979)
United States v. Hershey, 20 M.J. 433 (C.M.A. 1985), cert. denied, 474 U.S. 1062 (1986)
United States v. Ivester, 316 F.3d 955 (9th Cir. 2003)
United States v. Kerley, 753 F.2d 617 (7th Cir. 1985)
United States v. King, 140 F.3d 76 (2d Cir. 1998)
United States v. Kobli, 172 F.2d 919 (3d Cir. 1949)
United States v. Leos-Hermosillo, No. 98-50546 2000 U.S. App. LEXIS 5012 (9th Cir., Mar. 22, 2000)
United States v. Norris, 780 F.2d 1207 (5th Cir. 1986)
United States v. Peters, 754 F.2d 753 (7th Cir. 1985)
United States v. Re, 372 F.2d 641 (2d Cir.), cert. denied, 388 U.S. 912 (1967)

United States v. Sherlock, 962 F.2d 1349 (9th Cir. 1989), cert. denied, 506 U.S. 958 (1992)
United States v. Sherlock, 865 F.2d 1069, 1076 (9th Cir. 1989)
United States v. Simone, 14 F.3d 833 (3d Cir. 1994)
United States v. Slocum, 464 F.2d 1180 (3d Cir. 1972)
United States v. Valenti, 987 F.2d 708 (11th Cir. 1993)
United States *ex rel.* Latimore v. Sielaff, 561 F.2d 691 (7th Cir. 1977), cert. denied, 434 U.S. 1076 (1978)
United States *ex rel.* Orlando v. Fay, 350 F.2d 967 (2d Cir. 1965)
Vidal v. Williams, 31 F.3d 67 (2d Cir. 1994)
Walton v. Briley, 361 F.3d 431 (7th Cir. 2004)
Westmoreland v. CBS, 752 F.2d 16 (2d Cir. 1984), cert. denied, 472 U.S. 1017 (1985)
Williams v. Artuz, 237 F.3d 147 (2d Cir.), cert. denied, 534 U.S. 924 (2001)
Woods v. Kuhlmann, 977 F.2d 74 (2d Cir. 1992)
Yung v. Walker, 296 F.3d 129 (2d Cir. 2002)

United States District Courts
Ip v. Henderson, 710 F. Supp. 915 (S.D.N.Y.), aff'd, 888 F.2d 1376 (2d Cir. 1989)
King v. Fitzharris, 311 F. Supp. 400 (C.D. Cal. 1970)
Lasky v. Quinlan, 406 F. Supp. 265 (S.D.N.Y. 1976)
United States v. Byrd, 812 F. Supp. 76 (D.S.C. 1993)
United States v. Gotti, 753 F. Supp. 443 (E.D.N.Y. 1990)
United States v. Hegge, 631 F. Supp. 512 (E.D. Wash. 1986)
United States v. McVeigh, 931 F. Supp. 753 (D. Colo. 1996)
United States v. Moussaoui, 205 F.R.D.183, 184-85 (E.D. Va. 2002)
United States v. Raybould, 130 F. Supp. 2d 829 (N.D. Tex. 2000)
Via v. Peyton, 284 F. Supp. 961 (W.D. Va. 1968)
Westmoreland v. CBS, 596 F. Supp. 1166, 1167-69 (S.D.N.Y.), aff'd, 752 F.2d 16 (2d Cir. 1984), cert. denied, 472 U.S. 1017 (1985)

State High Courts
Anderson v. People, 176 Colo. 224, 490 P.2d 47 (1971), cert. denied, 405 U.S. 1042 (1972)
Commonwealth v. Blondin, 324 Mass. 564, 87 N.E.2d 455 (1949), cert. denied, 339 U.S. 984 (1950)
Commonwealth v. Gordon, 422 Mass. 816, 666 N.E.2d 122 (1996)
Commonwealth v. Hartman, 536 Pa. 211, 638 A.2d 968 (1994)
Commonwealth v. Marshall, 356 Mass. 432, 253 N.E.2d 333 (1969)
Commonwealth v. Martin, 417 Mass. 187, 629 N.E.2d 297 (1994)
Cumbee v. Commonwealth, 219 Va. 1132, 254 S.E.2d 112 (1979)
Ex parte Consolidated Publishing Co., 601 So. 2d 423 (Ala.), cert. denied, 506 U.S. 1024 (1992)
Foley v. Commonwealth, 429 Mass. 496, 709 N.E.2d 794 (1999)
Globe Newspaper Co. v. Massachusetts, 407 Mass. 879, 556 N.E.2d 356 (1990)
Great Falls Tribune Co. v. Montana Eighth Judicial District Court, 238 Mont. 310, 777 P.2d 345 (1989)
In re J.S., 140 Vt. 458, 438 A.2d 1125 (1981)
In re Personal Restraint of Orange, 152 Wn. 795, 100 P.3d 291 (2004)
Jones v. Peyton, 208 Va. 378, 158 S.E.2d 179 (1967)
Mallott v. State, 608 P.2d 737 (Alaska 1980)

Mankato Free Press v. Dempsey, 581 N.W.2d 311 (Minn. 1998)
Morris v. State, 302 Ark. 532, 792 S.W.2d 288 (1990)
Myers v. State, 97 Ga. 76, 25 S.E. 252 (1895)
New Jersey v. Hauptmann, 115 N.J.L. 412, 180 A. 809, cert. denied, 296 U.S. 649 (1935)
Oliver v. Postel, 30 N.Y.2d 171, 282 N.E.2d 306 (1972)
People v. Ayala, 90 N.Y.2d 490, 685 N.E.2d 492 (1997), cert. denied, 522 U.S. 1002 (1997)
People v. Childs, 159 Ill.2d 217, 636 N.E.2d 534 (1994)
People v. Clemons, 78 N.Y.2d 48, 574 N.E.2d 1039 (1991)
People v. Colon, 71 N.Y.2d 410, 521 N.E.2d 1075, cert. denied, 487 U.S. 1239 (1988)
People v. Gutierez, 86 N.Y.2d 817, 657 N.E.2d 491 (1995)
People v. Holveck, 141 Ill. 2d 84, 565 N.E.2d 919 (1990)
People v. Jelke, 308 N.Y. 56, 123 N.E.2d 769 (1954)
People v. Martinez, 82 N.Y.2d 436, 624 N.E.2d 1027 (1993)
People v. Micalizzi, 223 Mich. 580, 194 N.W.2d 540 (1923)
Ridenour v. Schwartz, 179 Ariz. 1, 875 P.2d 1306 (1994)
San Jose Mercury-News v. Municipal Court, 30 Cal.3d 498, 638 P. 2d 655 (1982)
Seattle Times Co. v. Ishikawa, 97 Wash.2d 30, 640 P.2d 716 (1982)
Society of Prof'l Journalists v. Bullock, 743 P.2d 1166 (Utah 1987)
Spencer v. Commonwealth, 240 Va. 78, 393 S.E.2d 609, cert. denied, 498 U.S. (1990)
State v. Butterfield, 784 P.2d 153 (Utah 1989), aff'd, 817 P.2d 333 (Utah Ct. App. 1991), cert. denied, 826 P.2d 651 (Utah 1991)
State v. Fageroos, 531 N.W.2d 199 (Minn. 1995)
State v. Harding, 635 P.2d 33 (Utah 1981)
State v. Herring, 210 Conn. 78, 554 A.2d 686, cert. denied, 492 U.S. 912 (1989), 511 U.S. 1059 (1994)
State v. Klem, 438 N.W.2d 798 (N.D. 1989)
State v. Koch, 169 Vt. 109, 730 A.2d 577 (1999)
State v. Lane, 60 Ohio St.2d 112, 397 N.W.2d 1338 (1979)
State v. Lawrence, 167 N.W.2d 912 (Iowa 1969)
State v. Lerner, 112 R.I. 62, 308 A.2d 324 (1973)
State v. Mecier, 145 Vt. 173, 488 A.2d 737 (1984)
State v. Pullen, 266 A.2d 222 (Me. 1970)
State v. Robillard, 146 Vt. 623, 508 A.2d 709 (1986)
State v. Rusin, 153 Vt. 36, 568 A.2d 403 (1989)
State v. Schmit, 273 Minn. 78, 139 N.W.2d 800 (1966)
State v. Schultzen, 522 N.W.2d 833 (Iowa 1994)
State v. Sheppard, 182 Conn. 412, 438 A.2d 125 (1980)
State v. Sheppard, 165 Ohio St. 293, 135 N.E.2d 293 (1956)
State v. Webb, 161 Wis. 2d 600, 468 N.W.2d 694 (1991)
State v. Weber, 137 N.H. 193, 624 A.2d 967 (1993)
State *ex rel.* Stevens v. Circuit Court for Manitowoc County, 141 Wis. 2d 239, 414 N.W.2d 832 (1987)
State *ex rel.* Varney v. Ellis, 149 W. Va. 522, 142 S.E.2d 63 (1965)
State in Interest of Dino, 359 So.2d 586 (La.), cert. denied, 439 U.S. 1047 (1978)
State of Iowa v. Jones, 281 N.W.2d 13 (Iowa 1979)
Tate v. Commonwealth, 258 Ky. 685, 80 S.W.2d 817 (1935)
Tinsley v. Commonwealth, 495 S.W.2d 776 (Ky.), cert. denied, 414 U.S. 1077 (1973)
United Press Ass'ns v. Valente, 308 N.Y. 71, 123 N.E.2d 777 (1954).

Van Orden v. State, 469 N.E.2d 1153 (Ind. 1984), cert. denied, 471 U.S. 1104 (1985)
Watters v. State, 328 Md. 38, 612 A.2d 1288 (1992), cert. denied, 507 U.S. 1024 (1993)
Westchester Rockland Newspapers, Inc. v. Leggett, 48 N.Y.2d 430, 399 N.E.2d 518 (1979)
Williams v. State, 409 So.2d 1331 (Miss. 1982)
Young v. State, 352 So.2d 815 (Miss. 1977)

State Appellate Courts

Addy v. State, 849 S.W.2d 425, 429 (Tex. Crim. App. 1993).
Clements v. State, 742 So.2d 338, 342 (Fla. Dist. Ct. App. 1999)
Cody v. State, 361 P.2d 307 (Okla. Crim. App. 1961).
Courtroom Television Network LLC v. State of New York, 769 N.Y.S.2d 70 (N.Y. Sup. Ct. 2003)
Davidson v. State, 591 So.2d 901 (Ala. Crim App. 1991)
Ex parte Birmingham News, 624 So.2d 1117, 1130 (Ala. Crim. App. 1993)
Gannett Co. v. Mark, 54 A.D.2d 818, 387 N.Y.S.2d 336 (N.Y. App. Div. 1976).
In re Closure of Preliminary Examination, 200 Mich. App. 566, 505 N.W.2d 24, (Mich. Ct. App. 1993)
In re Chase, 112 Misc. 2d 436, 446 N.Y.S.2d 1000 (N.Y. Fam. Ct. 1982)
Lena v. State, 901 So.2d 227 (Fla. App. 3d Dist. 2005)
Lyles v. State, 330 P.2d 734 (Okla. Crim. App. 1958)
Massachusetts v. Jaynes, 55 Mass. App. Ct. 301, 770 N.E.2d 483 (Mass. App. Ct. 2002)
Miami Herald Publishing Co. v. Chappell, 403 So.2d 1342 (Fla. Dist. Ct. App. 1981)
Miami Herald Publishing Co. v. Florida, 363 So.2d 603 (Fla. Dist. Ct. App. 1978)
Palm Beach Newspapers, Inc. v. Cook, 434 So.2d 355 (Fla. Dist. Ct. App. 1983)
People v. Bails, 163 Mich. App. 209, 413 N.W.2d 709 (Mich. Ct. App. 1987)
People v. Benson, 251 Ill. App. 3d 144, 621 N.E.2d 981 (Ill. App. Ct. 1993), app. denied, 154 Ill.2d 562, 631 N.W.2d 711 (Ill. 1994)
People v. Boss, 182 Misc. 2d 700, 701 N.Y.S.2d 891 (N.Y. Sup. Ct. 2000)
People v. Feagin, 34 Cal. App. 4th 1427, 40 Cal. Rptr. 2d 918 (Cal. Ct. App. 1995)
People v. Green, 221 A.D.2d 363, 633 N.Y.S.2d 521 (N.Y. App. Div. 1995)
People v. Haley, 195 A.D.2d 873, 600 N.Y.S.2d 842 (N.Y. App. Div. 1993), app. denied, 82 N.Y.2d 896, 610 N.Y.S.2d 163 (N.Y. 1993)
People v. Harris, 10 Cal. App. 4th 672, 12 Cal. Rptr. 2d 758 (Cal. Ct. App. 1992)
People v. Knapp, 113 A.D.2d 154, 495 N.Y.S.2d 985 (N.Y. App. Div. 1985), app. denied, 67 N.Y.2d 945, 494 N.E.2d 123 (N.Y.), cert. denied, 479 U.S. 844 (1986)
People v. Lawrence, 268 Ill. App. 3d 327, 644 N.E.2d 19 (Ill. App. Ct. 1994), app. denied, 161 Ill.2d 534, 649 N.E.2d 421 (Ill. 1995)
People v. Lopez, 185 A.D.2d 189, 585 N.Y.S.2d 764 (N.Y. App. Div.), app. denied, 80 N.Y.2d 975, 605 N.E.2d 880 (N.Y. 1992)
People v. Rodriguez, 209 A.D.2d 237, 618 N.Y.S.2d 335 (N.Y. App. Div. 1994).
People v. Santiago, 185 Misc. 2d 138, 712 N.Y.S.2d 244 (County Ct. 2000)
People v. Taylor, 244 Ill. App. 3d 460, 612 N.E.2d 543 (Ill. App. Ct.), app. denied, 152 Ill. 2d 577, 622 N.E.2d 1224 (Ill. 1993)
People v. Williams, 26 Cal. App. 4th Supp. 1, 31 Cal. Rptr. 2d 769 (Cal. App. Dep't Super. Ct. 1994).
People v. Willis, 274 Ill. App. 3d 551, 654 N.E.2d 571 (Ill. App. Ct. 1995)
Renfroe v. State, 49 Ala. App. 713, 275 So.2d 692 (Ala. Crim. App. 1973)
Santiago v. Bristol, 273 A.D.2d 813, 709 N.Y.S.2d 724 (N.Y. App. Div. 2000)

State v. Eaton, 483 So.2d 651 (La. Ct. App. 1986)
State v. Rector, No. 01 AP 758, 2003 WL 22331979 (Ohio Ct. App. 2003)
State v. Suarez, 867 S.W.2d 583 (Mo. Ct. App. 1993)
Williams v. State, 57 Ala. App. 158, 326 So.2d 686 (Ala. Crim. App. 1975), cert. denied, 295 Ala. 428, 326 So.2d 692 (Ala. 1976)

State Trial Courts

Bellamy v. Judges and Justices, 41 A.D.2d 196, 342 N.Y.S.2d 137 (1973)
In re Release of Sealed Transcripts in the Matter of Mohammed El-Atriss, L-917-03 (Passaic Cty. Ct., N.J. 2003)

English Cases

Entick v. Carrington, 19 State Trials, 1044-76 (1762)

PART II

The Right to a Speedy Trial

3

History: The Origins of the Right to a Speedy Trial

PREAMBLE

Like its Sixth Amendment companion right to public trial, the right to a speedy trial does not have a fully documented historical pedigree. There is little documentation of horror stories of prolonged proceedings at any point in colonial or in recent English history that the framers of the Constitution might have believed they were acting to change. There is virtually no legislative history explaining why the framers decided to articulate this right in the Sixth Amendment or what range of functions they wanted the right to serve. However, unlike the public trial, speedy trial had been the subject of two important English documents—Magna Carta and the Habeas Corpus Act of 1679—both of which identified lengthy pretrial detention as an evil needing remediation. While a traditional concern with the speed of proceedings can be traced to these enactments, there is little history to show how the English would have answered the central questions raised in applying the speedy trial guarantee: To what extent do individuals who are not incarcerated, or who are incarcerated because of another conviction, share the right to a speedy trial? What does "speedy" mean in terms of months and days? Is the guarantee relative, and if so, on what does the permissible amount of time depend? When does the speedy trial clock start ticking—when an investigation is begun, on arrest, or only on formal commencement of judicial proceedings? If a pending proceeding is continued or abated, is the clock tolled? How much control will a defendant have over whether to demand or waive a speedy trial? Does the reason for the delay matter? Does the public also have a cognizable interest in the speed of the proceedings? Other than release of a languishing pretrial detainee, what remedies are available for denial of the right? When is dismissal of a proceeding or reversal of a conviction an appropriate remedy?

This section will recount what is known of the pre-constitutional history of the speedy trial guarantee, the events surrounding its inclusion in the Sixth Amendment, the Supreme Court's struggles to interpret the scope of the right, and several twentieth-century developments that have preempted much of what might otherwise have been litigation about the meaning of the constitutional guarantee: the Interstate Agreement on Detainers and the advent of federal and state statutes and rules prescribing specific time limits and rules governing the timing of criminal prosecution.

ENGLISH HISTORY, TWELFTH TO EIGHTEENTH CENTURIES

The earliest evidence of an official attempt to promote prompt criminal trials dates from 1166—the Assize of Clarendon, during the time of Henry II. If a suspect was held in a remote county, the Assize required the sheriff having custody of that suspect to send word to the royal justices so that a prompt trial could be initiated.[1] One early document explained how this process worked: "And when a robber or murderer or thief or receiver of them has been arrested through the aforesaid oath, if the justices are not come speedily enough into the country where they have been taken, let the sheriffs send word to the nearest justice by some well-informed person that they have arrested such men, and the justices shall send back word to the sheriffs informing them where they desire the men to be brought before them; and let the sheriffs bring them before the justices."[2] Speedy prosecution was a problem during this era, because although criminal prosecutions, whether brought by private parties or by presentment, were essentially local and tried in the county courts, "appeals" of crimes like robbery and murder—prosecutions brought by private individuals—involved breaches of the king's peace and thus could be tried only by royal justices who traveled the country.[3] During the thirteenth century, an accused prosecuted by appeal could wait as much as four or even twenty years before the court of royal justices, called the eyre, was convened.[4]

Fifty years later, Magna Carta enshrined thirteenth-century ideals of fair procedure: "No freeman shall be taken, or imprisoned, or be disseised of his freehold, or liberties, or free customs, or be outlawed, or exiled, or any otherwise destroyed; nor will we not pass upon him, nor condemn him, but by lawful judgments of his peers, or by the law of the land. We will sell to no man, we will not deny or defer to any man either justice or right."[5]

Edward Coke, in his influential seventeenth-century treatise, interpreted this language as guaranteeing a remedy for unfair treatment and endorsing the principle that a right to speedy disposition was a significant component of justice. "And therefore, every subject of this realme, for injury done to him . . . be he outlawed, excommunicated, or any other without exception, may take his remedy by the course of law, and have justice, and right for the injury done to him, freely without sale, fully without any deniall, and speedily without delay."[6]

Special writs and commissions were issued, under which the jails were cleared several times a year.[7] By the end of the thirteenth century, justices armed with commissions of gaol delivery, or oyer and terminer, visited the country and, according to Coke, "have not suffered the prisoner to be long detained, but at their next coming have given the prisoner full and speedy justice, . . . without detaining him long in prison."[8] In Coke's interpretation, doing "justice and right, according to the rule of the law and custome of England," as the king's commissions instructed,[9] included the quality of speed.[10] Detainees could also use the writ of habeas corpus to challenge prolonged detention.[11]

Chapter 26 of Magna Carta provided another remedy, the writ *de odio et atia*, which gave prisoners the right to protest lengthy detentions before trial.[12] In 1278, the Statute of Gloucester, enacted under Edward I, repealed this writ, perhaps because it was thought to be unnecessary because the justices of oyer and terminer traveled to different counties frequently enough that cases were tried within a reasonable period of time.[13] Twelve years later, the writ was reinstated, giving "the prisoner full and speedy justice, by due trial, without detaining him long in prison."[14] Coke was critical of the Statute of Gloucester for repealing the writ *de odio et atia* provided by Magna Carta.[15] Coke again took the occasion to note that "the law of England is a law of mercie . . . for three causes: First, that the innocent shall not be worn and wasted by long imprisonment, but (as hereby, and by the statute of Magna Charta appeareth) speedily come to trial. . . ."[16]

Coke also gives examples of individuals—the Abbot of S. Albon and the Abbot of Crowland—being sanctioned for detaining prisoners for too long, or without proper authority.[17]

Coke himself seems to have revived interest in the right to speedy trial. There seems to have been little published discussion of the right or its abuse between the thirteenth and seventeenth centuries. But the idea that prolonged detention was an evil to be remedied under English law does seem to have been recognized during the thirteenth century, so it was not merely Coke's anachronistic invention. Henry de Bracton, in his definitive thirteenth-century treatise, described what happened to people accused of homicide or breach of the peace by appeal, a private prosecution. A person ordinarily was "arrested at once, thrust into prison, and kept there until [convicted] or delivered by judgment. . . ."[18] According to Bracton, such people had a limited remedy for prolonged detention: "[S]ince it is iniquitous that the innocent as well as the guilty be kept *in prison for a long time* . . . an inquest is ordinarily made as to whether such persons imprisoned for homicide were guilty of said death or not, that is whether they were appealed because of hate and spite."[19] If hate and spite were found to have motivated the prosecution, the prisoner was to be released, but otherwise, he would remain in prison "no matter how long that may be, until he can prove by inquest that he is innocent."[20] In cases other than homicide, the prisoner could protest his innocence and seek release through other writs.[21]

Sir John Fortescue, in his fifteenth-century dialogue between the exiled Prince Edward (son of Henry VI) and himself (the chancellor) titled "In Praise of the Laws of England," has the prince question Fortescue on delays in the king's court. Fortescue admits that there might be some delays, but maintains that "the laws of England do not permit frivolous and unfruitful delays."[22] Fortescue introduced the idea that speedy proceedings may also be disadvantageous if there is too much speed involved, pointing to some cases in which the accused was rushed to trial, condemned, and, after it was too late, found to be innocent.[23]

It may be that concern about speedy proceedings subsided after the thirteenth century as the private appeal, which had been especially slow because of the need to wait for the arrival of royal justices, became a less popular mode of proceeding.[24] It may also be that Coke, Chief Justice of the King's Bench, revived the subject of speedy trial in response to perceived seventeenth-century abuses involving lengthy imprisonment before indictment. Or Coke might have been acting in his partisan role as a leading parliamentary antagonist to the Stuart monarchy, raising specters of the potential evils of unconstrained royal power.[25] The seventeenth century was marked by struggles between royal prerogative and Parliament, culminating in Parliament's enactment of the Habeas Corpus Act of 1679,[26] described by Blackstone as "the bulwark of the British Constitution."[27] This act evidently was inspired by perceived abuses of process.[28] The Habeas Corpus Act required that prisoners indicted for treason or felony be tried at the next session or released on bail,

> unless it appears to the Judges and Justices upon Oath made, that the Witnesses for the King could not be produced the same Term, Sessions or General Gaol Delivery; 2) and if any Person or Persons committed as aforesaid, upon his Prayer or Petition in open Court the first Week of the Term or first Day of the Sessions, to be brought to his Trial, shall not be indicted and tried the second term, Sessions or General Gaol Delivery, after his Commitment, or upon his trial shall be acquitted, he shall be discharged from his imprisonment.

It is notable that the chief concern of the Act seems to have been prolonged incarceration without trial. The Act does not limit its remedy to those against whom formal proceedings have been instituted, and it does not provide for any remedy for an individual who has been convicted after prolonged detention. The Act does provide that an accused shall have the remedy of release if not tried within one term, and allows the king one and only one second chance if the reason for delay was that the witnesses could not be produced at the same term. A prisoner who remains untried during a second term, for whatever reason, is not only released but acquitted.

Blackstone, who waxed so eloquent about the right to public trial, had little to say about speedy trial, other than expressing general enthusiasm for the Habeas Corpus Act.[29] Sir Matthew Hale, one of Blackstone's principal sources, described the role of the Habeas Corpus Act as honored by the British during the seventeenth century.[30] The Act would have been known to the framers of the U.S. Constitution, who had their own concerns about peremptory royal action.

COLONIAL PRACTICES AND CHARTERS

Other than Blackstone, Coke was one of the commentators who would have been most familiar to the colonists, including the framers of the Sixth Amendment (see Klopfer v. North Carolina, 1967), so the framers of the Sixth Amendment were likely to have been familiar with the concerns he expressed about delay of process.[31]

Colonial justice was often harsh, but was doled out after speedy and public trials.[32] The codes of a number of colonies gave prominent attention to the rights of the accused, including the right to speedy proceedings, some seeking to emulate Magna Carta and others adding rights to the English model.[33] The Massachusetts Body of Liberties, adopted in 1641, is a good example of a progressive list of rights, many of which anticipated the protections later embodied in the Bill of Rights.[34] Among the fair trial rights specified in the second of ninety-three provisions was a right to speedy and equal justice: "Every person within this Jurisdiction, whether Inhabitant or forreiner shall enjoy the same justice and law, that is generall for the plantation, which we constitute and execute one towards another without partialitie or delay."[35]

Section 41 was more specific: "Everie man that is to Answere for any Criminall cause, whether he be in prison or under bayle, his cause shall be heard and determined at the next Court that hath proper Cognizance thereof, And may be done without prejudice of Justice.[36] The Pennsylvania Frame of Government of 1682 similarly described itself as including a "charter of liberties" and the "laws Agreed upon in England." Among the liberties it promised was that trials would take place in open court and that "justice be speedily administered" in English.[37] Other charters, like those of New York, Carolina, and West New Jersey, did not explicitly mention speedy trial; the charters of the remaining colonies did not enumerate rights at all.[38] Commentator David Bodenhamer discusses the reasons for the colonists' increased attention to the idea of rights of the accused, as well as the question of whether these guarantees were actually respected in practice. (He concludes that they were, for the most part).[39] The speedy trial language in these colonial charters bears a striking resemblance to Coke's descriptions of English law on this subject.

Commentator Francis Heller also draws a connection between the importance colonists attributed to speedy prosecutions and their antipathy, expressed in the Declaration of Independence, to the idea of "transportation"—being transported for trial to some other colony or even to Great Britain.[40] The revolutionary Samuel Adams wrote a vehement protest in 1772 decrying two Acts of Parliament authorizing the royal government to try colonists without juries and outside their vicinage.[41] While such prosecutions would have been terribly burdensome and prolonged, there is some question among historians as to how often, and even whether, such abuses actually took place, with some speculating that the authors of the Declaration were merely scoring rhetorical points.[42]

After independence, a number of states included the right to a speedy trial prominently in their state constitutions. The influential Virginia Declaration of Rights of 1776, drafted by George Mason, provided in Section 8 that "in all capital or criminal prosecutions, a man hath a right to demand the cause and nature of his accusation, to be confronted with the accusers and witnesses, to call for evidence in his favour, and to a speedy trial by an impartial jury of his vicinage, without whose unanimous consent he cannot be found guilty, nor can he be compelled to give evidence against himself; that no man be deprived of his liberty except by the law of the land, or the judgment of his peers."[43] This package of rights contains most of the ingredients of what would become the Sixth Amendment. The Pennsylvania Declaration of Rights of 1776 also granted the right to a "speedy public trial";[44] the Delaware Declaration of Rights of 1776 guaranteed a right "to a speedy trial by an impartial jury,"[45] as did the Maryland Declaration of Rights of 1776.[46] Vermont's Declaration of Rights of 1777 guaranteed "a speedy public trial, by an impartial jury of the country, . . ."[47] and this provision became part of Vermont's Constitution of 1792 after Vermont's admission to the Union. Kentucky[48] and Tennessee[49] followed suit on their admissions to the Union. Oddly, the 1980 Massachusetts Declaration of Rights omitted mention of the right to speedy and public trial, included in an early draft, although its "law of the land" provision, which uses the word "prompt," has been construed to guarantee all citizens the right to a speedy trial.[50]

Today, the constitutions of every state except Nevada, New York, and North Carolina include a speedy trial guarantee, usually in the exact language the Sixth Amendment uses.[51]

THE SIXTH AMENDMENT

The constitutional convention at which the delegates decided to amend the Constitution by adding a Bill of Rights was described in the section on the right to a public trial. James Madison, who drafted the proposals, did not leave records to reveal his thoughts or process in drafting. Madison relied, in part, on proposals submitted by the state conventions[52] and on provisions of the Virginia Declaration of Rights of 1776.[53] Four states asked for protection of the right to "the law of the land" or due process, speedy public trial, assembly and petition, and against excessive bail and fines and cruel and unusual punishments.[54] Of twenty-two amendments supported by four or more states, Madison incorporated fourteen in his recommendations to Congress, including the right to speedy trial.[55]

The amendment including language about speedy trial that Madison introduced on June 8, 1789, was almost identical to the language ultimately comprising the Sixth Amendment: "In all criminal prosecutions, the accused shall enjoy the right to a speedy and public trial, to be informed of the cause and nature of the accusation, to be confronted with his accusers, and the witnesses against him; to have a compulsory process for obtaining witnesses in his favor; and to have the assistance of counsel for his defence."[56] While the right to jury trial provision was added and descriptions of some of the other rights were slightly edited, the language of the speedy trial guarantee was not changed at all. The only recorded reference to speedy trial during the debates was an amendment moved by Representative Burke of South Carolina, who was concerned that overly speedy proceedings might disadvantage defendants. He moved to amend the speedy trial reference "in such a manner as to leave it in the power of the accused to put off the trial to the next session, provided he made it appear to the court that the evidence of the witnesses, for whom process was granted but not served, was material to his defence."[57] Other delegates commented that the amendment was unnecessary, as the courts had sufficient discretion to accommodate a defendant's needs, and the motion to amend failed, forty-one to nine.[58]

The mysteries surrounding the Sixth Amendment's mention of a right to public trial extend to the speedy trial reference as well. If trial by jury was ineluctably presumed to be speedy and public, as it was throughout English and colonial history and in the commentaries familiar to the framers, why did the framers find it necessary to add the speedy and public trial provision? Article III already required the federal government to provide "trial . . . by jury" for criminal offenses. That reference to jury trial presumably would have been understood to describe the English model of a speedy and public trial. Under canons of construction accepted at least since the time of Chief Justice John Marshall, no part of the Constitution should be interpreted in a manner that would leave it a mere redundancy. The framers might have viewed the Sixth Amendment rights as personal to the defendant, as opposed to the structural provision of Article III. If this is the case, then perhaps the Sixth Amendment should not be interpreted as conferring any speedy trial right on the public but as increasing a defendant's power to prevent or remedy a delay. But, as with the public trial right, it is difficult to be an originalist in identifying the historical functions of speedy trial. Not only did the framers say almost nothing about why they added this provision, the pre-constitutional commentators, while occasionally deploring lengthy incarceration before trial, did not show the enthusiasm for exploring and parsing the rationales and benefits of speedy trial that commentators on the public trial right had indulged. Therefore, there is even less basis than in the right to public trial area for understanding what the framers thought they were incorporating from common law or changing. Compounding the originalist's dilemma, the framers' opinions about the right to a speedy trial and its protections at common law are likely to have been derived from Coke, because Blackstone is uncharacteristically taciturn on this subject, and Coke's opinions about the nature of this right do not necessarily accurately reflect history.

4

The Right to a Speedy Trial: Analysis

DEVELOPMENT OF THE RIGHT

Until the middle of the twentieth century, the Supreme Court had heard only one speedy trial case. State courts interpreting their own constitutional and statutory provisions, and some lower federal courts anticipated many of the issues the Supreme Court would eventually address, although not always with the same results.[59]

The Supreme Court Cases

The Supreme Court had decided only three speedy trial cases before the Warren Court decided, in Klopfer v. North Carolina (1967), to apply the speedy trial guarantee to state criminal proceedings. Before *Klopfer*, the Court did not find a constitutional violation in any of the three federal cases it considered. In the decade after *Klopfer*, the Court decided three cases arising in state courts (Smith v. Hooey, 1969; Dickey v. Florida, 1970; Barker v. Wingo, 1972) and three cases arising in federal court (United States v. Marion, 1971; Strunk v. United States, 1973; Dillingham v. United States, 1975), finding constitutional violations in all but two. One of those two cases, *Barker,* created a template for deciding all future speedy trial cases. That template features a four-factor balancing test that has been criticized by some commentators as overly grudging to speedy trial claims and by some later Justices as including more factors than should actually be considered relevant. Another of these foundational cases, *Strunk*, has been criticized as overly willing to afford criminal defendants a dismissal of the charges pending against them after a finding of a speedy trial violation. Most of the Supreme Court cases decided during the 1960s (starting with *Klopfer*) and in the 1970s were decided unanimously.

As the composition of the Court shifted, speedy trial claims fared less well. United States v. Marion anticipated this trend in 1971, finding that the scope of the Sixth Amendment right was limited to addressing delays between a formal accusation and trial. Delay in instituting proceedings could only be challenged, *Marion* held, under the Due Process Clause. But the Due Process Clause set a forbiddingly high bar for criminal defendants. In *Marion* and subsequent cases, no Supreme Court litigant ever won a due process claim based on delay. The Court also considered the applicability of the Sixth Amendment right to two federal defendants who had been subjected to multiple proceedings over lengthy periods of time (United States v. MacDonald, 1978; United States v. Loud Hawk, 1986) and ruled against the defendants in each case after dividing up the years between the initial charge and eventual trial into periods that counted and periods that did not count toward the length of delay. Warren Court holdovers William Brennan and Thurgood Marshall dissented from a number of these rulings. The last Supreme Court decision of the 1980s, *Loud Hawk*, split the Court five to four, with Justice Marshall writing a dissent on behalf of a dwindling Warren Court presence.

Anyone noting this trend and predicting that constitutional speedy trial claims in the Supreme Court were destined for hostility and probable failure after the demise of the Warren Court would have been surprised by the only subsequent Supreme Court speedy trial case to date. This case, Doggett v. United States (1992), was another five to four decision in which the Court applied the Barker v. Wingo factors for its first time, in favor of a defendant's claim that he had been denied his right to a speedy trial. The Court reached this result even though the defendant had not been incarcerated pending trial, had not proved that he had been prejudiced in his ability to defend himself, and had not shown that the government had acted purposely to delay the proceedings against him or to try to gain any tactical advantage. The *Doggett* decision was criticized by some and hailed by others for reversing the antidefendant trend of the Court's prior decisions. This most recent Supreme Court speedy trial case also revealed a Court deeply split over the functions to be ascribed to the Sixth Amendment Speedy Trial Clause and that guarantee's relationship with the Due Process Clause.

Especially after *Doggett*, it is fair to say that the Court's decisions interpreting the Speedy Trial Clause have been ambivalent, sometimes expansively interpreting the function of the guarantee and sometimes appearing more grudging in finding violations. The Court's reluctance to find speedy trial violations on appeal may be attributed, in part, to the fact that the remedy the Court has found to be required to redress such violations (dismissal of the charges with prejudice) seems extreme, allowing a person convicted of committing a crime to be set free. The problem of remedy provides one theme in the Court's cases. Other themes include attempts to answer questions like whether the speedy trial guarantee applies to defendants who are incarcerated on another charge, when the speedy trial guarantee comes into play, whether a defendant waives his or her right to a speedy trial by not demanding a trial, whether a defendant must show prejudice in order to prevail, and whether the Sixth Amendment confers on society an independent interest in speedy trials that might require speedy trial in a case in which the defendant is not suffering and might even prefer to stall.

It is not surprising that the Supreme Court has not decided any constitutional speedy trial cases since 1992. One of the major problems with which the Court struggled—what to do about a defendant who claimed the right to a prompt trial in one jurisdiction while in the custody of another jurisdiction—was largely resolved by the 1970 adoption of the Interstate Agreement on Detainers, which provides procedures for interjurisdictional cooperation and remedies for prisoners who want to dispose of outstanding charges. In addition, constitutional speedy trial claims have now been largely superseded by the federal Speedy Trial Act of 1974 and its state counterparts, and related statutes and rules, which provide more specific timetables and rules governing how long a trial may be deferred.

Federal Speedy Trial Cases, 1905–66

In its first look at the Speedy Trial Clause of the Sixth Amendment (Beavers v. Haubert, 1905), the Supreme Court decided that the Clause was irrelevant to the dispute at hand.

Beavers had been indicted in the Eastern District of New York on July 16, 1903, and ordered removed from his home in the Southern District of New York on September 3, 1903. He was released on bail pending trial in the Eastern District during the next regular term. When he appeared in court in June 1904, the prosecutor declined to proceed with prosecution of the indictments, stating his intention to institute proceedings to remove Beavers to the District of Columbia for proceedings before a U.S. Commissioner. Beavers was arrested and brought a habeas corpus petition to challenge his removal to the District. Among other claims about the validity of the proceedings in the District of Columbia, Beavers contended that he was being denied his constitutional right to a speedy trial by jury on the indictments.

The Court agreed that everyone has a right to a speedy trial, but analyzed Beavers' case as involving not the speed of his prosecution, but its order and location. If a defendant is charged with more than one offense, the Court reasoned, he cannot be tried for all offenses simultaneously, and the speedy trial right cannot prevent a defendant from being arrested and tried on a new charge. Beavers had argued, according to the Court, that once his speedy trial right attached in the first proceeding "whatever be the demands of public justice they must wait." A more modern opinion probably would have stressed that Beavers had been awaiting trial on his original indictments for less than a year, had not been incarcerated, and had shown no reason to think his prosecution would be unfair because evidence had been lost. But the Court had not yet developed any list of questions to ask about whether a trial is being granted in an appropriately "speedy" fashion. Instead, the Court appeared to be balancing the right to a speedy trial against the "demands of public justice" in a manner that was not necessary to decide the case. The Court declared that the speedy trial right is not "absolute" and asked rhetorically whether the degree of a defendant's crimes may be considered in analyzing his constitutional claim. The speedy trial right was described as "necessarily relative."

This dismissive dicta, although not necessary to the decision of the case, set the tone for the Court's handful of speedy trial rulings over the next half century. Pollard v. United States (1957) involved a defendant who had pleaded guilty to a federal offense and, in a colloquy with the judge, was advised that he should join Alcoholics Anonymous and stay out of trouble or "you will be back here again." Later that day, after Pollard had left the court, a prosecutor inquired as to whether the judge was imposing a period of probation on Pollard. In Pollard's absence, the judge then formally entered an order suspending Pollard's sentence and placing him on probation for three years. Nearly two years later, Pollard was arrested for a probation violation and the judge entered a formal judgment sentencing him to two years imprisonment. Pollard complained that the sentence imposed upon him had been invalid due to his absence; the Court agreed and the government conceded on this point. He also claimed that the delayed sentence of incarceration, imposed two years after conviction, violated his speedy trial right. The Court assumed *arguendo* that the Sixth Amendment right would include a right to speedy sentencing as well as trial, but found that Pollard had not suffered a constitutional violation.

Citing *Beavers*, the Court explained that whether delay in completing a prosecution violates the Constitution "depends upon the circumstances." Among the circumstances the Court found relevant was the fact that the delay was not "purposeful or oppressive." The Court was also unreceptive to the remedy Pollard sought. "Error in the course of a prosecution resulting in conviction calls for the correction of the error, not the release of the accused." The Court also noted that Pollard had not made any motion to secure prompt sentencing, "often considered important in questions involving the Speedy Trial Clause" (citing Petition of Provoo, 1955).

The first Supreme Court voice speaking in favor of the importance of the right to speedy trial, along with its companion Sixth Amendment rights, was that of Chief Justice Earl Warren, who wrote a dissent joined by three other Justices who would become the nucleus of the Warren Court: Hugo Black, William Douglas, and William Brennan. The first sentence of the dissent, like the beginning of a Beethoven symphony, announced Warren's theme: "Our law, based upon centuries of tragic human experience, requires that before a man can be sent to a penitentiary, he is entitled to a speedy trial, to be present in court at every step of the proceedings, at all times to be represented by counsel, or to speak in his own behalf, and to be informed in open court of every action taken against him until he is lawfully sentenced." Warren noted that Pollard was impecunious and was not a dangerous criminal but an alcoholic. Warren did not go on to analyze whether Pollard's experience was unconstitutional, however, because he found a violation of Federal Rule of Criminal Procedure 32(a), which requires that, upon conviction, sentence be imposed without unreasonable delay. Noting that Pollard had already spent two years incarcerated while litigating his claim, Warren said that the Court could not "unring" the bell that so casually sent him prison but that the Court should declare that he was not committed to prison in accordance with accepted standards of criminal procedure.

The issue in the next case, Smith v. United States (1959), was whether Smith had the right to be prosecuted by indictment. Writing an opinion for a majority of the Court concluding that Smith did have that right on the facts of the case, Warren responded to the contention that the defendant might have benefited from the speed with which the prosecution could have proceeded if an indictment were not required. He noted that speed of prosecution is not always beneficial. "While justice should be administered with dispatch, the essential ingredient is orderly expedition and not mere speed." Smith had in fact suffered because of the undue speed with which his prosecution had been handled, but, noted Warren, "if arrest and incarceration are followed by inordinate delay prior to indictment, a defendant may, under appropriate circumstances, invoke the protection of the Sixth Amendment." This dictum anticipated an issue the Court would not actually reach until 1975—whether the Sixth Amendment right to speedy trial comes into play at the point of arrest (as the Court ultimately held) or, as is true of the Sixth Amendment right to counsel, only when formal judicial proceedings are commenced.

In United States v. Ewell (1966), the Court also found no constitutional speedy trial issue to be involved. In the course of discussing the facts of the case, the Court reiterated the principles set out in its earlier cases and added some new thoughts on the meaning of the Sixth Amendment speedy trial protection, including the Court's first explication of the functions of the guarantee. Ewell had been indicted on a drug offense, pleaded guilty, and was sentenced. About a year later, he filed a motion to vacate his conviction on the basis of a finding in an intervening case that an error that had occurred in his indictment was fatal. His motion was granted and he was promptly rearrested and reindicted on the same drug offense as well as an additional charge. The Supreme Court found that, although nineteen months had passed between the original arrests and the hearings on the later indictment, this did not constitute either double jeopardy or a denial of speedy trial rights. First, the Court pointed out that reprosecution following a reversal of a conviction on appeal was permissible and that, in one of the Supreme Court cases allowing reprosecution, seven years had passed before retrial. The implication seemed to be that the speedy trial ruling Ewell sought would effectively overrule the Court's double jeopardy decisions, because the process of appealing a conviction, getting a reversal, and being reprosecuted typically would be lengthy.

In reaching its speedy trial ruling, the Court noted that Ewell's prosecution was within the relevant statute of limitations, usually considered the "primary guarantee" against bringing overly stale criminal charges. Ewell would not have had a speedy trial claim, the Court observed, if there had been no earlier charges brought against him. So, like *Pollard*, this case involved the application of the speedy trial guarantee to a case involving multiple proceedings. Would the fact that there had been an earlier charge brought against Ewell start the speedy trial clock ticking?

Beginning a functional analysis, the Court announced that the speedy trial right "is an important safeguard to prevent undue and oppressive incarceration prior to trial, to minimize anxiety and concern accompanying public accusation and to limit the possibilities that long delay will impair the ability of an accused to defend himself." Nothing was cited in support of these propositions, which were destined to become a source of citation in future cases. However, the Court continued, following the *Beavers* tradition of balancing in speedy trial claims, overly speedy proceedings, as *Smith* had noted, might also harm a defendant's interests as well as the "ability of society to protect itself." And so, as *Beavers* said, the right of speedy trial is necessarily relative and "does not preclude the rights of public justice." The Court also repeated the statement from *Pollard* that whether delay is unconstitutional depends on the circumstances, including whether the delay was purposeful or oppressive. The Court found that the government's purpose was not oppressive in this case for two reasons: (1) because the new indictment followed on the vacating of Ewell's sentence and (2) because including the new charge, which carried a lesser sentence, provided Ewell with the opportunity to have the time he had already served credited against a new sentence. Justice Brennan, in a concurring opinion, had a different estimation of the government's purpose in adding the new charge, which he thought was to coerce a guilty plea. But Brennan agreed with the majority that Ewell had not shown that he was prejudiced by the delay and that this factor was critical.

Klopfer v. North Carolina—Speedy Trial Rights and the States

Klopfer v. North Carolina (1967) had all the hallmarks of a Warren Court landmark case. The case involved a Duke University professor of zoology who appears to have been a civil rights activist engaged in an attempt to desegregate a restaurant. Klopfer was indicted for the misdemeanor of criminal trespass on charges that he entered a restaurant on January 3, 1964, and "after being ordered to leave the said premises, willfully and unlawfully refused to do so." Klopfer was tried quite speedily, in March 1964, but the jury failed to reach a verdict and a mistrial was declared and the case was continued. In April 1965, the state's solicitor advised Klopfer that he intended to file for a *nolle prosequi* (declining to prosecute) "with leave" (meaning that the prosecution could be reinstated at some point in the future). Klopfer objected that his trespass charge was no longer sustainable in light of the Civil Rights Act of 1964 as construed by the Supreme Court. Instead of moving for the *nolle prosequi*, the solicitor successfully moved to have the case continued. When the calendar for the August 1965 session of the court did not list his case, Klopfer filed a motion asking that the case be concluded as soon as possible, contending that the pendency of the criminal charge interfered with his professional activities and his ability to travel freely. When, in response to Klopfer's motion, the trial judge inquired about the status of the case, the state's solicitor moved for a *nolle prosequi* with leave. This motion was granted, over Klopfer's objection, although no reason had been given to justify the state's desire to allow for future prosecution on this charge.

The North Carolina appellate court decision concluding that Klopfer had no right to object to the open-ended order was, according to Justice Warren's opinion, in disagreement with every other state to have considered whether a *nolle prosequi* indictment may be reinstated at a subsequent term. As in the public trial case, In re Oliver (1948), the Court had chosen an idiosyncratic state procedure to begin a serious look at the meaning of a Sixth Amendment guarantee. Chief Justice Warren thought that the states other than North Carolina that allowed a defendant to insist that the state choose between prompt prosecution and dismissal were clearly correct, and that the Sixth Amendment mandated that result. Klopfer was not relieved of the oppressiveness of a pending charge, Warren noted, just because the charge was suspended. The pendency of the indictment could still subject him to scorn, deprive him of employment, and force him to curtail his speech, associations, and "participation in unpopular causes."

The more substantial question was whether the Speedy Trial Clause should be applied to the states. The Court had held in earlier cases that other provisions of the Sixth Amendment—the right to counsel (Gideon v. Wainwright, 1963) and the right of confrontation (Pointer v. Texas, 1965)—were incorporated and applied to the states through the Fourteenth Amendment's Due Process Clause because they were "fundamental." Warren had no difficulty in concluding that the right to a speedy trial was just as fundamental as the other Sixth Amendment rights already incorporated. Warren traced the right back to the Assize of Clarendon, Magna Carta, and the writings of Edward Coke, and on through the state declarations of rights, concluding that "[t]he history of the right to a speedy trial and its reception in this country clearly establish that it is one of the most basic rights preserved by our Constitution."

The Court was unanimous as to the result in Klopfer's case.

Smith v. Hooey, Dickey v. Florida—Defining the Speedy Trial Rights of the Incarcerated

Once the speedy trial right had been applied to state proceedings, the number of constitutional speedy trial issues being litigated would inevitably increase exponentially, providing the Court with more opportunities to answer questions about the scope and application of the right. The next speedy trial case the Supreme Court heard raised the significant and common question of whether a prisoner of one jurisdiction is denied his or her right to a speedy trial if another jurisdiction lets an outstanding charge against the prisoner linger until after he or she is released. Having decided in *Klopfer* that an accused who was not incarcerated at all could still suffer a speedy trial violation, the Court confronted the question of the speedy trial rights of those who would remain incarcerated even if a trial on the new charge were held and culminated in an acquittal.

Smith was a federal prisoner when he was indicted in 1960 on a Texas state criminal charge. For the next six years, while he remained incarcerated, he persistently demanded a speedy trial on the Texas charge. In 1967, he filed a motion in Texas court asking that the charge be dismissed for lack of prosecution. The Texas courts held that, ordinarily, Smith would have been entitled to be brought to trial before such a long period of time had elapsed, but that a different rule applied because he was being held by another jurisdiction and thus it was not within the power of Texas to bring him to trial. Smith then filed a habeas corpus petition in federal court. In Smith v. Hooey (1969), ruling on that petition, the Supreme Court held that on Smith's demand, the Sixth Amendment required Texas to make a good faith effort to try him. The Court expressed confidence that the federal Bureau of Prisons would cooperate in producing the petitioner, a confidence inspired by the state's concession that they believed that the Bureau of Prisons would in fact produce Smith on demand, and the United States Solicitor General's affirmation in a Supreme Court memorandum that this expectation would be fulfilled.

What is most noteworthy about the Court's opinion is the conclusion that the speedy trial right still has a role to play even for those who will remain incarcerated, under another jurisdiction's conviction, regardless of the outcome of the pending proceeding. The Court quoted *Ewell*'s list of the three functions of the speedy trial guarantee and found that all three applied to Smith, despite his status as a prisoner. The first function, to prevent undue and oppressive incarceration before trial, was found to apply in a different manner than it would with respect to the usual pretrial detainee. First, a defendant already in prison will lose any opportunity to receive a sentence concurrent with the sentence he or she is serving, if the pending charge is deferred until after the prisoner has completed his or her sentence. Second, the duration of the prisoner's current imprisonment could be increased, and the conditions under which he or she is serving the sentence could be aggravated by the existence of a pending charge. Prisoners with detainers (requests by another jurisdiction to be notified when the prisoner is released so he or she may be turned over to that jurisdiction for prosecution) filed against them might, for example, be ineligible for a pardon or for certain rehabilitation programs. The second function, to minimize the anxiety and concern accompanying public accusation, also applies to a person already incarcerated, who may become depressed or be less open to rehabilitative efforts. The third function, to limit the possibilities that a long delay will impair the ability of the accused to defend himself, does not become irrelevant simply because the accused is incarcerated. In fact, the Court thought that the likelihood that the ability to defend oneself would be impaired was greater with respect to an incarcerated person, who may be unable to confer with potential witnesses or even to keep track of them.

The Court also noted that its holding, declining to absolve the state from affording a speedy trial just because the accused is detained in another jurisdiction, was consistent with its previous interpretation of another Sixth Amendment right, the right of confrontation. In Barber v. Page (1968), the Court had ruled that a state has an obligation to seek production of a witness a defendant wishes to confront and cross-examine, even if that witness is incarcerated in another jurisdiction. A state may not have control over the production of the prospective witness, any more than of its prospective defendant, but that does not absolve the state from at least seeking the other jurisdiction's cooperation.

The holding that Texas had a constitutional obligation to make a diligent, good-faith effort to try Smith was unanimous.

Dickey v. Florida (1970), concerned a prisoner in federal custody, like Smith, who had an outstanding criminal charge against him in Florida. Like Smith, he had made repeated unsuccessful attempts, over a period of seven years, to secure a prompt trial in Florida. Eventually, Dickey was tried in Florida, his motion to dismiss on the ground that he had been denied his right to a speedy trial was denied, and he was convicted. Dickey won his appeal in the Supreme Court because he was able to show not only that he had been available to Florida for more than seven years and that Florida had no tenable reason for not bringing him to trial earlier, but also that he had in fact been prejudiced by the delay. While he awaited trial, two witnesses died and another potential defense witness allegedly became unavailable. Possibly relevant police records were lost or destroyed.

The most interesting opinion in *Dickey* is the concurrence written by Justice William Brennan and joined by Justice Thurgood Marshall, laying out a road map for analysis of future speedy trial claims. Brennan understood the majority opinion to rest on the Due Process Clause, because the events described had occurred before the *Klopfer* case had been decided and Florida argued that its holding, applying the speedy trial right to the states, should not be applied retroactively. He therefore reasoned that the majority's potentially limiting comments in this case should not govern future Sixth Amendment claims that arose post-*Klopfer*. It is worth describing Brennan's analysis in some detail because commentators have used this concurring opinion as a benchmark against which to measure the Supreme Court's subsequent development of speedy trial doctrine.

According to Brennan, there are two kinds of issues to be addressed in interpreting the right to a speedy trial: (1) those concerning when during the criminal process the guarantee attaches, and (2) those concerning the criteria by which to judge the constitutionality of delays to which the right attaches. Brennan observed that both of these questions would have to be answered in light of the purposes of the Speedy Trial Clause. Recognizing that there was no record of the intent of the framers, he provided a list of purposes quite similar to the lists in the earlier cases of *Klopfer* and *Ewell*: primarily, sparing an accused the penalties and disabilities "incompatible with the presumption of innocence" that may result from delay in the criminal process. These included (1) preventing undue and oppressive incarceration, (2) minimizing anxiety and concern and other adverse consequences accompanying public accusations, (3) avoiding impairment of the ability to mount a defense, and (4) penalizing official abuse of the criminal process to prevent the government from persecuting, instead of prosecuting, a defendant.

In addition, consistent with his interpretation in the Public Trial Clause in Gannett Co., Inc. v. DePasquale (1979), Brennan declared that the Speedy Trial

Clause also protects societal interests, including the desire to restrain those convicted of crime in order to preserve the deterrent value of convictions, to obviate the possibility that a defendant awaiting trial might abscond or commit other criminal acts, and to avoid impairing the government's ability to prove its case. Brennan cited little support for these propositions.[60]

Brennan then canvassed the law of speedy trial as it had developed in the lower courts on the two issues he had identified. When the speedy trial right attaches was a question that had been answered only in part. Authorities agreed, he said, that delay between indictment and trial was subject to speedy trial analysis, as was delay between two separate indictments or trials on the same charge and, assumed *arguendo* (in *Pollard*) although not decided, between judgment and sentence. Authorities also agreed that the guarantee did not apply to delays before arrest or indictment. The major open question was whether the right attached between arrest and sentencing, or only upon indictment. His own answer was that it should apply upon arrest rather than only after formal proceedings had begun, because the functions he had described earlier would apply: defendants would suffer exposure to incarceration, anxiety, and an increasing risk of dissipation of evidence. He thought it plausible that pre-arrest delay, if it constituted a deliberate governmental abuse of the criminal process, might also constitute a denial of the right to a speedy trial because some, although not as many, potential harms to an accused were still present.

On the second issue, the criteria to be used in judging the constitutionality of delays to which the safeguard applies, Brennan incorporated the observations of the Supreme Court's earlier cases (*Beavers* and *Smith*) about the relativity of the definition of speed and the demands of public justice. The lower courts had clearly identified three factors Brennan endorsed for consideration in weighing whether a speedy trial violation had occurred: (1) the source of the delay, (2) the reasons for the delay, and (3) whether the delay prejudiced interests protected by the Speedy Trial Clause. Two other factors the lower courts had mentioned seemed to Brennan not to constitute independent considerations. Brennan thought the length of the delay, mentioned by some courts as a fourth factor, was relevant only insofar as it would affect the legitimacy of the reasons for delay and the likelihood that the defendant had been prejudiced. He thought a fifth factor some courts had listed, waiver by the accused, was relevant primarily to the source of the delay.

Brennan also objected to the "demand waiver" rule some courts had adopted (that an accused loses his or her right to speedy trial by silence or inaction), noting three problems with the premises underlying the view that defendants who do not actively request a prompt trial thereby waive that right. First, courts espousing this rule assumed that delay would generally benefit a defendant, as the prosecution's evidence would grow stale. Brennan noted that delay causes defendants to suffer other forms of harm, like anxiety or deterioration of potential evidence for the defense. Second, the Court had rejected the equation of silence with waiver with respect to other fundamental rights, including the

Sixth Amendment right to counsel. Finally, he argued that the demand waiver rule misallocated the burden of ensuring a speedy trial. If a defendant has not caused the delay of his prosecution, the responsibility for delay will generally lie with a government authority, whether law enforcement, prosecutor, or court personnel.

On the second relevant factor, reason for the delay, Brennan raised the question of what made a delay caused by the government "unreasonable." Included in the unreasonable category were certainly deliberate attempts to harm a defendant, and purposeful or oppressive delays. Brennan, like some lower court judges, thought that a negligent delay—an unintentional and unnecessary delay that might reasonably have been avoided—should also be included because defendants would suffer the same harms regardless of the government's motivation. In considering the reason for the delay, what Brennan believed would be relevant was the intrinsic importance of the reason for delay, measured against the length of the delay and its potential for causing prejudice to the interests protected.

Finally, Brennan noted the division of the lower courts on the issue of proof of prejudice, which some courts required. He proposed, without necessarily endorsing, a method of dealing with proof of prejudice by shifting burdens of proof. While prejudice may be an essential element of speedy trial violations, Brennan thought that the element of prejudice should be regarded as satisfied if a defendant had been incarcerated for a lengthy period of time, or if the government had delayed in bad faith. Failing that, Brennan noted the inherent difficulty of proving what evidence has been lost or why it would have been material, as defendants would have to demonstrate to establish that their ability to defend themselves had been impaired. "In a very real sense, the extent to which [the defendant] was prejudiced by the Government's delay is evidenced by the difficulty he encountered in establishing with particularity the elements of that prejudice" (quoting Ross v. United States, 1965). This problem could be dealt with by presuming prejudice after some period of delay, a period that would have to be fixed. Before that yet-to-be-determined point, Brennan suggested, the defendant could be required to bear the burden of showing that he or she was actually harmed; after that, prejudice would be presumed unless the government wished to argue that the speedy trial violation had been harmless error. He also noted that proof of prejudice was not required in determining whether other Sixth Amendment rights, including the rights to counsel, confrontation, public trial, impartial jury, notice of the charges, trial in the district where the crime was committed, and right to compulsory process.

Brennan concluded by remarking that his comments did not provide definitive answers but did show how many questions about the meaning of the Speedy Trial Clause remained to be answered. He expressed his hope that speedy trial would receive a "more hospitable" interpretation than it had yet been accorded. His challenge to the Supreme Court provided an agenda for the next several decades of cases.

Barker v. Wingo—The Court Chooses Criteria

Two years later, the Court took up the second of the questions Brennan had posed in his *Dickey* concurrence: what criteria apply to determining whether a speedy trial violation has occurred?

Willie Barker and codefendant Silas Manning were arrested for killing an elderly couple on July 20, 1958, and indicted in September of the same year. Barker's trial was set for October 21 of the same year, but the Commonwealth of Kentucky decided that it had a stronger case against Manning and needed Manning's testimony to convict Barker. Manning was unwilling to testify because he did not want to incriminate himself; the Commonwealth decided to try Manning first, so that he would be available to testify against Barker. (Manning's privilege against self-incrimination would no longer apply if he had already been convicted for the offense because he would not be "incriminating" himself; if he had been acquitted, the privilege would also be inapplicable because the Double Jeopardy Clause would ban his reprosecution for the same offense.) It took the Commonwealth an unexpectedly long time to obtain a conviction of Manning, however. His first trial ended in a hung jury; the second resulted in a conviction that was reversed on appeal; a third trial resulted in another conviction which was again reversed on appeal, but this time on a different ground; the fourth trial resulted in another hung jury. In a fifth trial, Manning was finally convicted of murdering one of the victims and, in a sixth trial, four-and-a-half years after the crime had been committed, of murdering the other victim.

Meanwhile, the Commonwealth obtained a series of sixteen continuances of Barker's trial and did not bring Barker to trial until October of 1963, more than five years after the crime had been committed. Barker spent ten months in jail before being released on bail. His counsel did not object to the first eleven continuances but, in February of 1962, did object to the twelfth by filing a motion to dismiss the indictment. After this motion was denied, Barker did not object to the further continuances until his trial was scheduled for March 1963. On the day of his trial, the Commonwealth moved for another continuance on the basis that the sheriff who was the chief investigating officer was ill. Barker objected. Trial was reset for June, at which time the sheriff was still unable to testify, and Barker objected to a further continuance. In October, on the day of the actual trial, Barker again moved to dismiss the indictment, arguing that his speedy trial right had been violated.

Justice Lewis Powell, in his first term on the Court, wrote a majority opinion which began by asserting that the right to speedy trial is "generically different" from any other constitutional right because society has its own interests in providing a speedy trial, which exist apart from and at times in opposition to the interests of the accused. He elaborated on the harm done to society by having charges remain untried, including the costs of incarceration of detainees and the risk that those not incarcerated will commit other crimes. He also elaborated on the idea, mentioned in earlier Supreme Court cases, that deprivation of the right may work to an accused's advantage. Finally, he noted that it is "impossible to determine with precision when the right has been denied," characterizing the right as "amorphous." So far, Powell's analysis would not show that speedy trial was unique among constitutional rights. As described above, the same observations apply to the Sixth Amendment right to a public trial. Society has its own interest in observing trials, that interest may not be consistent with the interests of a defendant who might wish to close a trial, and it has been difficult for the courts to draw lines between what counts as a "public trial" and what does not. Powell's fourth point, however, did distinguish the right to a speedy trial: "The amorphous quality of the right also leads to the unsatisfactorily severe remedy of dismissal of the indictment when the right has been deprived. This is indeed a serious consequence because it means that a defendant who may be guilty of a serious crime will go free, without having been tried. Such a remedy is more serious than an exclusionary rule or a reversal for a new trial, but it is the only possible remedy."[61]

Whether dismissal is indeed the only remedy has been a source of some debate,[62] but Powell's point that it is impossible to correct a speedy trial violation after it has occurred by holding a new trial—to "unring" the bell in Warren's expression—does distinguish speedy trial from most other procedural rights. Usually, if a constitutional right has been violated at trial, a new trial can be ordered in which the procedural error can be corrected. It is only in the case of a violation like speedy trial, or double jeopardy, that holding a new trial would compound rather than alleviate the error.[63] A number of commentators have concluded that the prospect of having to dismiss prosecutions tried in violation of the speedy trial right has left courts disinclined to find violations at all.[64] The fact that Powell began his opinion by pointing out this feature of the speedy trial right can be taken as a harbinger of the result in Barker's case—a finding that there was no speedy trial violation.

Also by way of preamble, having noted that the Court had decided very few speedy trial cases and none that set forth criteria for decision, Powell examined two "rigid approaches" the parties had proposed and rejected both. The first suggestion was for the Court to hold that the Constitution requires a defendant to be tried within a certain time frame. Powell characterized this approach as requiring the Court to engage in inappropriate legislative or rule-making activity. (The Court, however, did allow that courts in the exercise of their supervisory powers could set presumptive time periods in which cases must usually be brought.) The second proposal was that the Court adopt the demand-waiver rule. Powell reached the same conclusion about the desirability of this rule as Justice Brennan had in *Dickey*, noting that such a rule would be generally inconsistent with the Court's constitutional waiver rulings.

Instead, the Court adopted a balancing approach not, on its surface, very different from the balance Brennan had proposed in *Dickey*. The Court stated that it was identifying "some" of the factors to be balanced and then described four factors that subsequent courts have frequently taken as a comprehensive and talismanic list: (1) the length of delay, (2) the reason for the delay, (3) the defendant's assertion of his or her right, and (4) prejudice to the defendant, assessed in light of the three functions of the speedy trial guarantee (as previously articulated by Brennan and in the *Ewell* case). By way of explanation of the first factor, Powell described the length of delay as "to some extent a triggering mechanism." The length of delay that will provoke a constitutional inquiry will depend on the circumstances of a case, including the seriousness of the offense. "[T]he delay that can be tolerated for an ordinary street crime is considerably less than for a serious, complex conspiracy charge."

The second factor, "closely related to length of delay," is the reason the government assigns to justify the delay. Here also, Powell noted, different weights should be assigned to different reasons. A deliberate attempt to hamper the defense should weigh more heavily than a "more neutral" reason, such as negligence or overcrowded courts, although Powell, like Brennan, believed that the ultimate responsibility for all such circumstances must rest with the government rather than with the defendant. Thus, negligent delay would also be cognizable, even if it would count as less weighty. The third factor, defendant's responsibility to assert his or her right, was also described as closely related to the other factors. In rejecting the demand waiver rule, which would have required such an assertion as a precondition to a speedy trial claim, Powell had said that assertion of the right should be weighed as one factor in the balance. In his explication of the four factors, however, he elevated the importance of this factor: "The defendant's assertion of his speedy trial right . . . is entitled to strong evidentiary weight in determining whether the defendant is being deprived of the right. We emphasize that failure to assert the right will make it difficult for a defendant to prove that he was denied a speedy trial." The fourth factor, prejudice, could be shown, as Justice Brennan had suggested, by prejudice to any of the three interests the speedy trial right protects: preventing oppressive pretrial incarceration, minimizing anxiety, and limiting the possibility that the defense will be impaired. Of course, said Powell, the most serious is the last.

Powell then commented on the nature of the factors he had described: "We regard none of the four factors identified above as either a necessary or sufficient condition to the finding of a deprivation of the right of speedy trial. Rather, they are related factors and must be considered together with such other circumstances as may be relevant. In sum, these factors have no talismanic qualities; courts must still engage in a difficult and sensitive balancing process."

Powell then applied his new balancing test to Barker's circumstances. His conclusion that under this analysis Barker had not suffered a constitutional violation drew no dissent. Powell remarked that he considered Barker's case to be "close," largely because the length of the delay—five years between arrest and trial—was extraordinary and because, although seven months of the delay could be attributed to a "strong excuse" (the illness of the sheriff), four years was too long a time to try to render Manning an available witness by obtaining his conviction—the state's principal reason for the delay. However, balanced against these "deficiencies" was the fact that the prejudice suffered by Barker was "minimal." Powell noted that Barker had lived for more than four years under a cloud of suspicion and anxiety and that he had spent ten months in jail before being released on bail. "But there is no claim that any of Barker's witnesses died or otherwise became unavailable owing to the delay." And, "more important than the absence of serious prejudice, is the fact that Barker did not want a speedy trial." Powell reviewed the number of continuances to which defense counsel had not objected. Barker's objections only began as the trial date approached. In Powell's view, Barker had hoped to take advantage of the delay, in which he acquiesced, by having the charges against him dismissed and only asserted his speedy trial right as his trial approached: "he definitely did not want to be tried."

How close Powell's account of the balancing test is to Brennan's *Dickey* proposal may be gauged by comparing his approach to that suggested in Justice White's concurring opinion, joined by Brennan. The White-Brennan approach is sequential rather than a free-for-all balancing of interests. Any defendant is entitled to trial within a "reasonable" period of time; that right can be counterbalanced if the government shows that special circumstances exist that outweigh the defendant's presumptive right. Only at that point, White and Brennan maintained, should an inquiry into whether the defendant was actually prejudiced by the delay be necessary. In other words, White and Brennan deemphasized the significance of establishing prejudice in making out a speedy trial claim, arguing that it should not be an essential element of a speedy trial claim. However, White and Brennan agreed with the majority that Barker had "clearly acquiesced" in the major delays involved and so they agreed that Barker himself had not been denied his right to speedy trial.

A dissenting view from both the Court's conclusion and the analytical framework in Barker v. Wingo was registered by Professor H. Richard Uviller in his law review article, "*Barker v. Wingo*: Speedy Trial Gets a Fast Shuffle."[65] In his critique of the four-factor test, Uviller identified and anticipated many of the issues that have confused lower courts trying to follow Barker v. Wingo.

Beginning with the first factor, the length of delay, Uviller notes that, although Justice Powell's opinion foreswears any desire to formulate a speedy trial rule, his treatment of the length of delay as a triggering mechanism is inconsistent with the concept of a flexible, multifactor balancing test. A relatively short delay might nevertheless constitute a violation if it was malicious, unjustified, and substantially prejudiced the defendant. Conversely, a lengthy delay, in Uviller's view, should be treated as more than just a trigger and should weigh more heavily in the balance. Lower court cases, as will be seen, usually designate a specific period of time as prerequisite to a constitutional claim. Most cases then tend to forgive lengthy delays if the defendant has not made a strong showing with respect to the other factors, suggesting that Uviller was right in thinking that Justice Powell's opinion was, at the least, unclear on how this factor should be handled.

Powell used the term "presumptive prejudice" in describing a length of delay that would trigger a speedy trial claim, a locution Uviller interpreted as inadvertent, because *Barker* did not seem to envision shifting the burden on proof of prejudice to the government, as Brennan's *Dickey* opinion had proposed. Finally, Uviller objected to Powell's generalization that the length of the delay triggering a claim could vary depending on the nature of the crime involved, with lengthier delay being appropriate if the charge was especially serious or complex but intolerable in a case involving a routine street crime. Uviller thought that the prosecution has an obligation to bring any case to trial within a reasonable period of time after charges are instituted. He also thought that Powell's generalization probably was backward: in many complex cases, unlike violent street crimes, the prosecution will actually have ample time to prepare the case before deciding to institute charges. If a particular case presents unusual circumstances that delay prosecution, Uviller thought such circumstances should be properly considered as bearing on the reason for delay, not as minimizing the magnitude of the delay.

The second factor, reason for the delay, seemed to Uviller to be at the heart of the matter, along with length of the delay, but he again thought that Powell's generalizations were neither helpful nor apt. The Court had grouped potential reasons for delay into three categories: (1) prosecutorial delays intended to disadvantage the defendant, which weigh heavily against the state; (2) "neutral" reasons like negligence or court congestion; and (3) valid reasons, like the unavailability of a witness. Uviller thought the Court was stacking the deck against the defendant in this part of the analysis too. In the first category, he thought that if there was proof of malicious prosecutorial intent, it should not be necessary to consider any other factors, because the prosecution would be defying its obligation to try cases in a speedy manner.

With respect to the third category, the valid reasons, he thought the opinion might be read to suggest that a defendant's claim would be defeated if the government makes out a plausible claim of necessity (because the defendant evidently bears the burden of proof on this issue), while the real question should be whether the delay was overly long given the actual circumstances (an issue Justice Powell does not address). There seemed to Uviller to be a lack of parity between the Court's treatment of the first category of reasons, where a defendant who prevailed on this factor by showing that the government had acted intentionally would still need to make a persuasive case on some or all of the other factors before winning a constitutional claim, and the third category of reasons, where the defendant would immediately lose the whole game if the government prevailed on this factor.

The second category of reasons, the "neutral" reasons, seemed to Uviller to lump unlike situations together. If prosecutorial negligence means, as he thought it did, "avoidable delay occasioned by prosecutorial dereliction," then such negligence should, *ipso facto*, be considered a strike against the government rather than as neutral. This conclusion again reflects Uviller's view that the Sixth Amendment imposes on the government an affirmative obligation to bring an accused to trial and not just a negative prohibition on maliciously causing a lengthy delay. Uviller also noted that, with respect to the very real problem of court congestion, the Court had offered no advice at all.

The Court's treatment of the third factor, defendant's assertion of the right, seemed to Uviller to undermine the Court's rejection of the demand waiver rule. Again, there seemed to be a lack of parity: Powell specified that a defendant who had not asserted the right would be unlikely to prevail, evidently regardless of the strength of any showing made on the other factors, while a defendant who prevailed on this factor would still have to do battle with respect to the remaining factors. Uviller also commented on Powell's indignant conclusion that Barker did not want a speedy trial, noting that a misguided tactical decision to wait out the results of the codefendant's trial was not the equivalent of a constitutional waiver.

With respect to the fourth factor, prejudice, Uviller's analysis again focused on the asymmetry of the Court's approach: a defendant cannot win on a showing of prejudice by itself, but evidently could be defeated by failing to make a strong showing of prejudice, regardless of the other three factors. This was one area in which the Supreme Court subsequently agreed with Uviller's point, holding in later cases, as will be described, that proof of prejudice is not a *sine qua non* of constitutional speedy trial claims. Uviller noted that although the Court listed three types of prejudice cognizable under the speedy trial rubric, marking one of these factors—adverse impact on the defense—as the most important skewed analysis because this potential consequence is not highly correlated with the length of the delay. Evidence may be lost after eight months as well as after eight years. The anxiety an accused suffers, in Uviller's estimation, does grow as the charges remain unresolved and so, if the Court took that form of prejudice more seriously, defendants who have suffered especially long delays would have a greater prospect of succeeding in their speedy trial claims.

Finally, Uviller disagreed with Powell's generalization about the unique nature of the right to speedy trial. In Uviller's account, the right is no vaguer than legions of other constitutional guarantees, it is not the only right defendants might affirmatively wish to forego, society shares the defendant's interests with respect to other rights, and the appropriate remedy for violations of other rights can also immunize defendants from reprosecution (like the ban on double jeopardy, or the exclusionary rule if evidence excluded is critical to a prosecution). Discussing the application of the Court's test to Barker's own case, Uviller argued that instead of allowing this hard case to make bad law, the Court should have been willing to pay the price necessary to revive the constitutional right to a speedy trial. All in all, Uviller thought that Justice Brennan's opinion in *Dickey* remained a more promising foundation for constitutional speedy trial law than the Court's superseding opinion in Barker v. Wingo.

Moore v. Arizona—Without Prejudice

During the next term, in a *per curiam* opinion in Moore v. Arizona (1973), the Court confirmed its remark in Barker v. Wingo (1972) that no one of the four factors listed was an indispensable prerequisite to a finding of speedy trial violation. Moore had been tried three years after he was charged, and twenty-eight months after demanding a prompt trial. The period of unjustified delay was at least two years and, unlike Barker, Moore had demanded a speedy trial before that period and not only on the eve of trial. The Court held that even though Moore had not proved prejudice in the form of impairment of his ability to present a defense at trial, his speedy trial claim should not have been dismissed without a hearing.

Strunk v. United States—The Remedy of Dismissal

A year after *Barker*, the Court answered one question it had left open in Smith v. Hooey (1969): whether the Court would order dismissal as a remedy for a speedy trial violation. Strunk v. United States (1973), a federal case, involved another petitioner who, like the petitioners in *Smith* and *Dickey*, was incarcerated by a second jurisdiction while awaiting trial. Strunk was serving a one- to three-year sentence in a Nebraska State Penitentiary when he was tried on a federal indictment, after a delay of ten months. He moved to dismiss the federal charge on speedy trial grounds and when his motion was denied, he was tried, did not call witnesses or take the stand in his own defense, and was convicted.

The Court of Appeals ruled that Strunk had indeed been denied his right to a speedy trial because the government gave an explanation for the delay that the court thought was tenuous: that Strunk had stated that he intended to demand a speedy trial under Rule 20 of the Federal Rules of Criminal Procedure. Thus, the government claimed that a large part of the delay was attributable to Strunk as the prosecutors awaited his procedural move. The government also offered the lack of personnel in the U.S. Attorney's office as a justification. The appellate court, like Justices White and Brennan, thought that lack of resources was not a good justification for delay, and noted that Strunk had put the government on notice that he was preserving his speedy trial claim. Having found a violation, however, the appeals court heeded Barker v. Wingo's (1972) description of dismissal as "an unsatisfactorily severe remedy" and so, instead of reversing Strunk's conviction, the court ingeniously ordered that Strunk's five-year federal sentence be reduced by 259 days—an amount of time equal to the unnecessary delay.

The Supreme Court was not impressed with this creative remedy. In an opinion written for a unanimous Court by Chief Justice Burger, the Court explained that once a speedy trial violation has been found, the only proper remedy for a trial that occurred too late is dismissal. Such severe remedies are not unique in the application of constitutional standards, said the Court, and Barker v. Wingo had described dismissal as the only possible remedy following a finding that speedy trial rights had been violated. Burger's opinion did suggest that the government had missed a bet by not cross-appealing the finding that there had been a speedy trial violation, noting that on the record presented, it seemed clear that Strunk was responsible for a large part of the ten-month delay, and that if the reason for any additional delay was understaffing due to insufficient appropriations, such unintentional delays were not to weigh as heavily under the Barker v. Wingo calculus as intentional, calculated delay. The government and the lower courts were on notice both that the Court was serious about the remedy of dismissal and that the only way to avoid dismissal was to avoid a finding of a speedy trial violation.

Marion, Dillingham, Lovasco, and Gouveia—When Does the Right to Speedy Trial Attach? When Does the Due Process Clause Apply?

Another line of cases provided answers to some of the issues raised by Justice Brennan's first question: when during the criminal process does the right to speedy trial attach? In other words, what delays are cognizable as part of a speedy trial analysis—delays before or only after indictment, delays after or even before arrest, and/or delays in between multiple proceedings? In these cases, the Court circumscribed the scope of the Sixth Amendment speedy trial right and offered the Due Process Clause as a backup, albeit a demanding one.

The defendant in United States v. Marion (1971) claimed that he had been denied a speedy trial because three years had elapsed between the occurrence of the alleged criminal acts and the filing of an indictment. When the prosecution came to court, the district court granted Marion's motion to dismiss the indictment on speedy trial grounds and the government appealed that ruling, so no trial had yet taken place. Six members of the Supreme Court ruled that the district court had erred in finding in Marion's favor, because the Sixth Amendment right to a speedy trial did not attach until "the putative defendant in some way becomes an 'accused,'" the word used in the Sixth Amendment to describe the individual afforded speedy trial rights. Justice Byron White, writing for the Court, found nothing in the admittedly sparse history of the Sixth Amendment provision to suggest that the word "accused" meant anything other than "what it appears to say." The defendant had cited several British cases, including one predating the Bill of Rights, for the proposition that the speedy trial guarantee applied even to pre-indictment delay, but the Court was not persuaded that these cases established "a definite rule that the Founders sought to constitutionalize." The Court was more impressed with the argument of the government, which pointed out that the Habeas Corpus Act of 1679, which had become the model for many state speedy trial provisions, did not allude to delay before arrest. Most lower courts had reached the same conclusion, and most statutes governing time of trial also applied only after a person was accused of a crime. The Court found this conclusion logical because the evils associated with a long-delayed trial intensify once a defendant is arrested. Knowing of the impending prosecution, the accused will experience greater anxiety and be subject to scorn and disruption of his or her life. Such considerations, the Court pointed out, had been sufficient as underpinnings for decisions finding that defendants had been denied a speedy trial even if they had not been incarcerated, like Klopfer, and had no reason to believe their ability to defend themselves had been impaired.

The Court recognized that delay before prosecution could still create a risk of unfairness because memories might fade or evidence and witnesses be lost. But the Court quoted *Ewell*'s observation that statutes of limitations are the chief protection against that evil. And even if the Sixth Amendment did not apply, the Due Process Clause would require dismissal of an indictment if a pre-indictment delay were shown to have caused substantial prejudice to a defendant's right to a fair trial *and* if the delay was an intentional device to gain tactical advantage.

Because the thirty-eight month pre-indictment delay did not extend beyond the applicable statute of limitations and the defendant had not shown prejudice to the conduct of his defense or intentional government manipulation, the Court reversed the dismissal and cleared the way for Marion's trial. Although the Court recognized that there was indeed a possibility that Marion had been prejudiced by the lengthy delay, the Justices deemed a mere possibility of prejudice insufficient to base a defendant's claim. Marion was invited to return with a due process claim if events at his trial demonstrated actual prejudice.

Three Justices, William Douglas, William Brennan, and Thurgood Marshall, wrote a concurring opinion to agree with the result but not the reasoning of the majority. Following Justice Brennan's suggestion in *Dickey*, these Justices argued that the speedy trial guarantee should apply even at the pre-indictment stage of a proceeding. Justice Douglas's opinion interpreted the word "accused" in the Sixth Amendment to refer to the person who has standing to complain of prosecutorial delay, a category certainly including Marion. He answered the majority's references to history by noting, first, that the British cases, including those dismissed by the majority, considered delay connected with issuance of an information, regarding such delays as unjust. Second, he noted that common law prosecutions were quite different from contemporary prosecutions and encompassed a more complex variety of procedures. Prosecutions by private parties, which included the ordinary criminal case, were considered to have commenced with the filing of a lawsuit, not with a procedure requiring a defendant to show cause why he or she should not be imprisoned—in other words, the prosecution commenced and an individual was "accused" before a formal indictment. Douglas also argued that many of the purposes the Court had identified as served by the speedy trial guarantee, for the benefit of both the accused and society generally, applied equally if the pre-prosecution delay was pre-indictment. "The duty which the Sixth Amendment places on Government officials to proceed expeditiously with criminal prosecutions would have little meaning," Douglas observed, "if those officials could determine when that duty was to commence."

Despite their disagreement with the Court's formalistic approach to the question of when the speedy trial guarantee applied, the concurring Justices thought the record insufficient to determine whether there had been a speedy trial violation in Marion's case, "although a three-year delay . . . goes to the edge of a permissible delay," and so they agreed that the case should be remanded.

In Dillingham v. United States (1975), the government argued that under the principle of *Marion*, the Speedy Trial Clause should be considered to apply only after the commencement of formal judicial proceedings, like indictment or information, and not after an arrest. A brief *per curiam* opinion, with Chief Justice Burger dissenting (without opinion), thought the answer was obvious: *Marion* had explicitly mentioned that arrest caused an individual to become an "accused" and had explained that the evils a speedy trial is intended to counteract—including prolonged incarceration as well as anxiety—intensify upon arrest as much as indictment. The opinion did not mention whether Dillingham was incarcerated while awaiting his trial. Oddly, the Court's opinion in *Dillingham* did not even mention what could have been the centerpiece of the government's argument: that other provisions of the Sixth Amendment, like the right to counsel, do not apply upon arrest but only upon commencement of formal judicial proceedings (see Massiah v. United States, 1964; Kirby v. Illinois, 1972; Brewer v. Williams, 1977). This different treatment of the two Sixth Amendment provisions may be explained by what the Court has found to be their divergent functions. *Massiah* describes the purpose of the right to counsel as being only to aid a defendant during judicial proceedings. The Court has also found, in Miranda v. Arizona (1966), that there is a right for suspects to have counsel when another of their constitutional rights, the Fifth Amendment privilege against self-incrimination, is jeopardized by custodial interrogation regardless of whether judicial proceedings have commenced, but that right does not spring from the Sixth Amendment.

United States v. Lovasco (1977) gave the Court an opportunity to review a due process claim based on pre-indictment delay and to apply its generalizations in *Marion* to a developed set of facts. Lovasco was indicted for possessing stolen firearms and selling a firearm without a license, based on events occurring more than eighteen months before the indictment was filed. When he moved to dismiss the indictment, the district court held a hearing at which Lovasco persuaded the court that the delay was unnecessary, because the government had gathered "all the information" relating to the offense a month after the offense was committed and seventeen months before presenting the case to the grand jury. The government did not provide any affirmative explanation of the reason for the delay, although it had rebutted some of Lovasco's assertions about how complete the investigation was after one month. The trial court also ruled that Lovasco's ability to defend himself had been impaired because two material witnesses had died in the interim. On appeal, the government justified the delay by explaining that the investigation was being kept open to establish Lovasco's son's access to the stolen firearm. The appellate court, although accepting this explanation, found that Lovasco had been denied due process of law because the delay was unjustified, unnecessary, and unreasonable.

The Supreme Court, in an opinion by Thurgood Marshall, confirmed that the Sixth Amendment speedy trial right was irrelevant, because the delay had occurred before indictment or arrest and that the Due Process Clause has some "limited role" to play in preventing unfair pre-indictment delay because statutes of limitations do not fully define the extent of a defendant's rights. The Court also confirmed that the Due Process Clause sets a high bar for defendants. Under *Marion*, proof of prejudice to a defendant's ability to defend himself or herself at trial is a "necessary but not sufficient" element of a due process claim. The government has no responsibility to begin a formal prosecution at the earliest possible point, said the Court, and so the mere fact that a defendant has suffered prejudice from the government's delay does not in and of itself establish that the defendant has been denied any right. Proof of actual prejudice, the Court explained, makes a due process claim concrete and ripe for adjudication but does not make the claim "automatically valid." The second element required to establish a due process violation entails a review of the reasons for the delay. The Court of Appeals found the government's reason for the delay—to continue its investigation in the hope of discovering others who had participated in the firearm theft—too flimsy to support such a lengthy delay. The Supreme Court chided the lower court for being overly intrusive: "the Due Process Clause does not permit courts to abort criminal prosecutions simply because they disagree with a prosecutor's judgment as to when to seek an indictment."

Applying the two-pronged due process test to the facts at hand, the Court found that the government's reason for delay was not the sort of deliberate abuse the Due Process Clause checks. Investigative delay is fundamentally unlike delay undertaken "to gain tactical advantage over the accused," which is what the Court had condemned in its dicta in *Marion*. No one's interests would be served if prosecutors were required to indict too early during the course of an investigation, the Court explained. Prosecutors should be encouraged to determine that they can meet the "proof beyond a reasonable doubt" standard of trial before bringing charges against a defendant and unleashing potential incarceration, anxiety, and expense on the defendant. Society's interests would not be served by premature prosecution, nor would the interests of the courts, which would have to expend scarce resources on prosecutions that turned out to be insubstantial or incomplete. The Court also noted that the recent enactment of the Speedy Trial Act of 1974 provided an additional reason not to require the government to commence a prosecution as soon as it had probable cause to believe a suspect had committed a crime. Once a person is indicted, the statutory clock would begin and if the government could not progress from the probable cause necessary to arrest or indict a defendant to the proof beyond a reasonable doubt necessary to convict at trial within a very short period of time, the prosecution would be dismissed (even if the delay would not have offended the Sixth Amendment) and many guilty people would escape punishment.

The government had conceded in its brief that if, as *Marion* had suggested, the government had delayed the prosecution for "tactical" advantage and thereby prejudiced Lovasco's ability to defend himself, Lovasco would have been denied due process. Justice Marshall added to the definition of the due process standard: "A due process violation might also be made out upon a showing of prosecutorial delay incurred in reckless disregard of circumstances, known to the prosecution, suggesting that there existed an appreciable risk that delay would impair the ability to mount an effective defense." Having reiterated *Marion*'s explanation of the elements of a due process claim, elaborated on the legal standard, and applied that standard to the facts in *Lovasco*, the Court seemed inclined to declare its own job on this issue done.

In *Marion*, we conceded that we could not determine in the abstract the circumstances in which preaccusation delay would require dismissing prosecutions. . . . More than five years later, that statement remains true. Indeed, in the intervening years so few defendants have established that they were prejudiced by delay that neither this Court nor any lower court has had a sustained opportunity to consider the constitutional significance of various reasons for delay. We therefore leave to the lower courts, in the first instance, the task of applying the settled principles of due process that we have discussed to the particular circumstances of individual cases.[66]

Justice Stevens, in a solitary dissent, was critical of the Court for deciding the case on the basis of an inadequate record on the subject of the government's explanation for the delay, because the government had offered no explanation at the district court's hearing on the motion to dismiss. Deeming the case to be one in which the government had given no reason to explain an eighteen-month delay in a routine case in which the evidence against the defendant had been assembled in the first month, and in which the delay proved prejudicial to the defense, Stevens thought the question of whether the defendant had been treated unconstitutionally was not an easy one.

In a subsequent case analyzing a claimed denial of right to counsel, United States v. Gouveia (1984), the Court picked up different thread from *Marion*, suggesting again that, as in *Dillingham*, the Sixth Amendment speedy trial guarantee might attach at an earlier point than other Sixth Amendment rights like the right to counsel.

Gouveia was a federal prisoner who was charged with murdering another inmate and placed in administrative detention within the prison where he remained for nineteen months before an indictment was returned. Gouveia moved to dismiss the indictment on speedy trial and due process grounds, because of the delay, and also on the basis that he had the right to counsel during his administrative detention. The court of appeals ruled in his favor on the right to counsel claim and the Supreme Court granted *certiorari* on that issue. In holding that Gouveia had no right to counsel because formal judicial proceedings had not yet been instituted, the Court distinguished cases like *Dillingham,* which held that the Sixth Amendment speedy trial right attaches at the time of arrest. The Court confirmed that the attachment rules for these two Sixth Amendment provisions are different, because they protect different interests: the right to counsel, as previously interpreted by the Court, exists to protect an accused during trial-type proceedings, while the right to speedy trial exists "primarily to protect an individual's liberty interest."

The Court noted that because the speedy trial issue was not before it, it was not addressing the question of whether segregation of an inmate during the pendency of criminal charges was enough like an arrest to implicate the Speedy Trial Clause.

United States v. MacDonald, United States v. Loud Hawk—When the Clock Tolls

Once the Court had established that delay before indictment or arrest did not count in assessing the speed of proceedings for Sixth Amendment purposes, it was inevitable that cases would arise in which it was difficult to say whether delay was pre- or post-indictment because multiple proceedings were involved, one of which had concluded and was therefore no longer pending when the next proceeding involving the same charges began. Once a formal accusation was brought, would the speedy trial clock run continuously until all proceedings involving those charges had been resolved, or would the clock be stopped at the end of the first proceeding and restarted at commencement of the subsequent proceeding?

The first of two highly notorious cases raising this question was the prosecution of Captain Jeffrey MacDonald for the murder of his wife and children. MacDonald's family was living on a military reservation on February 17, 1970, when he called the military police, who arrived at his home to find his pregnant wife and two children dead. MacDonald had multiple stab wounds, most of which were superficial, but one of which was a life-threatening chest wound that caused his lung to collapse. He had been rendered unconscious. MacDonald survived and reported that his family had been victims of a bizarre, ritualistic murder involving a woman wearing a floppy hat, white boots, and a short skirt who was carrying a lit candle and chanting, "Acid is groovy; kill the pigs." Needless to say, this sensational crime received a tremendous amount of attention from the public and press. The Army Criminal Investigation Division (CID) found physical evidence at the scene that appeared to contradict MacDonald's account and charged MacDonald with the murder, under the Code of Military Justice, on May 1, 1970. Press coverage intensified as the question of whether MacDonald was a tragic victim or a heinous murderer fascinated the public. Contradictory evidence supported each position. Following military procedure, an investigating officer held a hearing with fifty-six witnesses and subsequently submitted a report recommending that the charges against MacDonald be dismissed. The recommendation was followed and all charges were dismissed on October 23, 1970. Several months later, MacDonald was granted an honorable discharge on the basis of hardship.

MacDonald's saga did not end there. At the request of the Justice Department, the CID continued its investigation and in June of 1972 submitted a thirteen-volume report recommending further investigation. Additional reports were submitted in November 1972 and August 1973. Following evaluation of the reports, the Justice Department presented the matter to a grand jury in August 1974, and in January 1975, almost five years after the killings, the grand jury returned an indictment charging that MacDonald was the murderer.

MacDonald, not surprisingly, moved to dismiss the indictment on the ground that he had been denied his right to a speedy trial. When the district court denied his pretrial motion, the court of appeals allowed him to take an interlocutory appeal on the theory that if MacDonald's constitutional rights had indeed been violated, the violation would be exacerbated by forcing him to go to trial before allowing him to appeal the speedy trial ruling. The court of appeals then ruled in MacDonald's favor on the speedy trial issue. The Supreme Court granted *certiorari* and reversed the ruling on the ground that it was premature. A criminal defendant may not appeal the denial of a motion to dismiss on speedy trial grounds, the Court ruled, until after the trial has been completed (United States v. MacDonald, 1978). This was a position the government had argued in *Lovasco*, on the ground that whether defendant has been prejudiced by a delay can be better determined after the trial.

MacDonald was then tried and convicted, more than nine years after the initial prosecution. The appellate court again ruled that he had been denied his right to a speedy trial, and the Supreme Court again granted *certiorari*, this time to consider the substance of MacDonald's argument in United States v. MacDonald (1982). The issue of whether to count the period of time between the dismissal of the military charges and the grand jury indictment split the Court five to four. The majority began with *Marion*'s declaration that the Sixth Amendment speedy trial right attaches only when a formal criminal charge is instituted and concluded that the right has no application after the government, acting in good faith, has formally dropped the charges. Because there were no charges pending between October 1970 and January 1975, MacDonald could only bring a due process claim to challenge the five-year pre-indictment delay. The majority found comfort in the fact that most lower courts had concluded that the period of time after initial charges are dropped is not to be included in determining whether there has been a Sixth Amendment violation. Congress, in formulating the Speedy Trial Act of 1974, had agreed with this concept, providing that if charges are dismissed and later reinstated, the period between the dismissal and reinstatement is not to be counted.

Considering whether the functions of the Speedy Trial Clause were implicated, the Court again relied on *Marion*, quoting the statement that delay may impair a defendant's ability to defend himself or herself, but that the "major evils protected against by the speedy trial guarantee exist quite apart from actual or possible prejudice." In *Marion*, this argument was made to show that the commencement of a formal proceeding, which could be expected to cause a defendant anxiety and collateral consequences, was a necessary element of a speedy trial claim and that impairment of the defense was not sufficient in and of itself to make out a speedy trial claim. In *MacDonald*, the Court took this reasoning one step further, declaring that "[t]he Sixth Amendment right to a speedy trial is thus not primarily intended to prevent prejudice to the defense counsel by passage of time; that interest is protected primarily by the Due Process Clause and by statutes of limitations. The speedy trial guarantee is designed to minimize the possibility of lengthy incarceration prior to trial, to reduce the lesser, but nevertheless substantial, impairment of liberty imposed on an accused while released on bail, and to minimize the disruption of life caused by arrest and the presence of unresolved criminal charges." This conclusion is an extension of the reasoning of *Marion*, although Justice Marshall's reasoning in *Lovasco* anticipated this discounting of the possibility of prejudice to the defense in the context of a due process challenge. The majority reasoned that once the charges against MacDonald had been dropped, he, as a former accused, was in the same position as any other subject of an open criminal investigation. Any subject, Chief Justice Burger noted, would suffer anxiety and stress from knowing about a pending investigation, but with no charges outstanding, personal liberty is not impaired to the same degree as after charges are pending. The Court distinguished *Klopfer*, the public trial case in which dismissing charges in a *nolle prosequi* with leave to reinstate was held to be contrary to the Speedy Trial Clause, on the ground that Klopfer's charges had not really been dismissed.

Three dissenting Justices, Marshall, Brennan, and Blackmun, would have found that the original prosecution against MacDonald never really terminated because the CID continued to investigate and work with the Department of Justice and its work became a basis of the indictment. The dissenters also believed that the majority's conclusion that the speedy trial guarantee does not apply to a charge that is dropped and then reinstated was contrary to the language, history, and principles of the Clause. A natural reading of the language of the Speedy Trial Clause, Marshall said, is that it continues to protect someone who has been accused of a crime until the government has completed its attempts to try him for that crime. Marshall also argued that the majority's decision was inconsistent with *Klopfer*, in which the prosecution had been abated but could be reinstated at any time, and also with *Marion*, which had declined to count pre-indictment delay largely because there was no feasible way for a court to determine at what point a prosecution should have been brought. In MacDonald's case, by way of contrast, there was no such difficulty because MacDonald had actually been charged. By the dissenters' count, a majority of lower courts had disagreed with the majority's conclusion.

In functional terms, the dissent noted that MacDonald's anxiety clearly would not have abated when the military charges were dropped but the investigation continued and relocated to the Department of Justice. The dissenters urged a flexible fact-sensitive approach, like the approach Barker v. Wingo (1972) had adopted in formulating criteria to determine speedy trial violations, weighing the government's reason for the delay in a case like MacDonald's instead of dismissing his speedy trial complaint on the formalistic basis that for some period of time no charge was technically pending. The dissenters also disagreed that the alternative due process claim could protect MacDonald's speedy trial interests. That limited remedy does not protect against delay that is not tactical but serves no legitimate purpose. And the protection of a statute of limitations was unavailable to MacDonald because there is no limitation on prosecutions for murder.

Having concluded that MacDonald's Sixth Amendment speedy trial rights were implicated by the delay, the dissenters went on to apply Barker v. Wingo analysis and found the case to be close, but on balance, they agreed with the court of appeals that MacDonald had indeed been denied his Sixth Amendment right to a speedy trial.

John Paul Stevens was the fourth Justice to support the dissenters' conclusion that MacDonald's right to speedy trial was not suspended in the period between dismissal of the military charges and the civilian indictment. Stevens wrote a concurring opinion to agree with the dissenters on that point, but not on the ultimate question of whether MacDonald's right had actually been violated. He also regarded application of Barker v. Wingo to these facts to present a close question, but what tipped the balance for him was the argument proffered by Justice Burger at the end of his opinion—that the government should not be required to make hasty decisions about prosecution.

The Court again had the opportunity to apply the *MacDonald* approach of parsing which periods of pretrial delay counted on the complicated facts of United States v. Loud Hawk (1986). The short version of the facts is that Loud Hawk was indicted on weapons possession charges in November 1975, but when the Supreme Court decided his speedy trial challenge in January 1986, he still had not been tried. Out of this period of more than ten years, forty-six months were consumed by an interlocutory appeal the government took (appealing defendant's victories in a pretrial suppression motion and a motion to dismiss the indictment), and twenty-nine months by another set of interlocutory appeals brought by both the defendant and the government.[67] During this time, the district court twice dismissed the indictment against Loud Hawk, the first time for the government's failure to be ready for trial and the second time on speedy trial grounds. Loud Hawk was reindicted after the government's first interlocutory appeal. The Supreme Court was reversing the trial court's second decision to dismiss the indictment.

As it had in *MacDonald*, the Court first divided up the periods of time involved to decide what part of the ten-year delay counted. The Court concluded that, under the theory of *MacDonald*, the period of time during which the indictment had been dismissed should not count. Reviewing the functions of the Sixth Amendment guarantee, the Court quoted *MacDonald*'s injunction that only "actual" restraints imposed by arrest and being held to answer a criminal charge will engage the protections of the speedy trial guarantee. The Court noted that Loud Hawk had not been incarcerated or even subject to bail conditions during the period when the indictment had been dismissed. Although the government obviously desired to prosecute the defendants, the Court found that their situation was not distinguishable from MacDonald's and that they had been "in the same position as any other subject of a criminal investigation" during the periods while they were not actually under indictment. The Speedy Trial Clause does not purport to protect a defendant against all the adverse effects of pretrial delay, like eliminating stress and some disruption of normal life, the Court said. Even more clearly than in *MacDonald*, the Court announced that the Speedy Trial Clause's core concern was now considered to be impairment of liberty, so "when defendants are not incarcerated or subjected to other substantial restrictions on their liberty, a court should not weigh that time towards a claim under the Speedy Trial Clause."

Much of the delay in this case was caused by the court of appeals being so slow to issue opinions. Citing *Ewell*, the Supreme Court agreed with the defendant that the speedy trial guarantee's safeguards "may be as important to the accused when the delay is occasioned by an unduly long appellate process as when the delay is caused by a lapse between the initial arrest and the drawing of a proper indictment." The Court noted, however, that the public has an interest in government interlocutory appeals, and also that the only relevant interlocutory appeal (brought while an indictment was pending) had been brought by the defendant, and thus was comparable to an appeal after a conviction—the time before a new trial might be prolonged, but at the defendant's behest.

The Court, in an opinion by Justice Lewis Powell, the author of Barker v. Wingo, then applied the four factors listed in that case: the first factor, length of the delay, worked in Loud Hawk's favor, as ninety months before the trial of "these serious charges" was presumptively prejudicial and served to "trigger application of *Barker*'s other factors." The third factor, assertion of the right, worked against him, according to Justice Powell, who compared the claim to Penelope's tapestry.[68] Defendants did repeatedly move for a speedy trial, but that fact alone did not establish that they had appropriately asserted their rights. They also "consumed" six months by filing indisputably frivolous appeals for rehearing and *certiorari* after the Supreme Court had ruled in another case that federal courts were without jurisdiction to hear appeals from denials of motions to dismiss indictments, and had filed "repetitive and unsuccessful motions" in the district court. Like Penelope, who wove her tapestry by day only to rip out her work by night to delay the completion of her task, Loud Hawk demanded a speedy trial except when the government might have been prepared to provide one, at which point he took actions that delayed the trial. Like Barker, he may not have genuinely wanted the pretrial period to end, something that the Court thought significant. Loud Hawk had not made any showing of prejudice, having shown at most the possibility of impairment of a fair trial resulting from absence or loss of memory of witnesses. He had not been incarcerated and so did not suffer loss of freedom. The Court also described delay as a two-edged sword, noting that the government bears the burden of proof at trial and so is more likely to be hurt by evidence dissipating or growing stale with the passage of time.

The second *Barker* factor, reason for the delay, Powell described as "the flag all litigants seek to capture." The government's interlocutory appeal is ordinarily a valid reason for delay, the Court said, given that there are important public interests served by appellate review. Conversely, if the government abused the interlocutory appeal process merely to stall a trial, this factor would weigh in the defendant's favor. To determine the purpose and reasonableness of a particular government interlocutory appeal, the Court thought a number of factors should be evaluated, including the strength of the government's position on the appealed issue, the importance of the issue in the posture of the case, and, in some cases, the seriousness of the crime. Loud Hawk could not show that the government's interlocutory appeal was unreasonable because he could not establish any bad faith or dilatory purpose; the government's position was deemed to have been strong because the government had won; and, despite the seriousness of the charged offenses, the district court did not subject Loud Hawk to restraints during the appeal. So the reason for that forty-six-month delay was not counted in the defendant's favor, although the delay had been caused by the courts' deplorable lack of speed in deciding the appeal. In analyzing this factor, the Supreme Court was more interested in whether the delay was motivated by prosecutorial bad faith than in the fact that the delay was not the defendant's choice.

The twenty-nine months attributed to defendant's interlocutory appeal were also held not to contribute to the weight of the speedy trial claim, because the reason for that delay had been within defendant's control. A defendant who resorts to an interlocutory appeal normally should not be able upon return to the district court to reap the reward of dismissal for failure to receive a speedy trial during that period of time. The Court also found that although defendants' interlocutory appeal had been proper under the law at the time (before the intervening Supreme Court decision), "their position was so lacking in merit that the time consumed by this appeal should not weigh in support of" the speedy trial claim. This remark suggests that the Court would apply the same balancing test in deciding how heavily to weigh a defendant's interlocutory appeal (or perhaps postconviction appeal) as it applied in evaluating the weightiness of the delay for the government's appeal: if the Court had deemed the defendant's position to be strong and the issue raised to be important in the posture of the case, this period of time might have counted in his favor, even though he had brought the appeal. The Court also found that the six months additional delay caused by defendant's petitions for rehearing and *certiorari*, after the intervening adverse Supreme Court ruling, should not count in his favor.

Concluding his comments on the balance of factors in this extraordinary case, Justice Powell once again observed that the delays did not "justify the severe remedy of dismissing the indictment." Once again, the severity of the presumptive remedy may have influenced the Court's evaluation of whether there was a violation of the right.

Both holdings—on the scope of *MacDonald* and on the application of Barker v. Wingo—split the Court five to four. Thurgood Marshall, writing a dissent on behalf of himself and Justices Brennan, Blackmun, and Stevens, argued that the delay following the court's dismissal of the indictment should not have been excluded because the defendant's situation in *MacDonald* was highly distinguishable. In *MacDonald*, the first prosecution, the military proceeding, was actually terminated when MacDonald was exonerated; in *Loud Hawk*, there was always a criminal case pending against the defendant. Dismissal by the government, Marshall contended, is qualitatively different from dismissal by a court, which is subject to reinstatement at the stroke of an appellate pen without any need to involve a grand jury.[69]

Marshall also thought the ruling inconsistent with *Marion* and *Dillingham*, which held that an arrest triggers the protections of the Speedy Trial Clause, even if the defendant in that case had not been incarcerated. Thus the Court had not required a showing that an arrested defendant was suffering prejudice as a precondition to counting the time between arrest and indictment in a Sixth Amendment analysis. The *Loud Hawk* majority had distinguished *Dillingham* on the basis that Loud Hawk was not suffering any "actual restraints," positing that if he had been incarcerated or had to post bond, the period of time following the dismissal of his indictment would not have been subject to the automatic exclusion rule of *MacDonald*. The dissent noted that the only restraint in *Dillingham* had been that the defendant was released on bond after his arrest (as opposed to Loud Hawk's release on his own recognizance), a distinction the dissent thought irrelevant to the speedy trial interests involved.

Marshall also noted that *Marion* had based its conclusion that the Speedy Trial Clause does not address delay between the offense and the charge on the premise that the chief protection of a suspect's general need for swift justice before indictment is the statute of limitations. The statute of limitations no longer protected Loud Hawk once he had been indicted.

The dissent's conclusion that the Speedy Trial Clause applied after arrest, regardless of the court's dismissal of the indictment, was reinforced by noting that Loud Hawk was entitled to another Sixth Amendment right pending his appeal—the right to counsel, on the theory that such an appeal is a critical stage of a criminal prosecution. In contrast, MacDonald would not have had a right to counsel after the military proceeding against him was dismissed. *Gouveia* had held that the speedy trial guarantee is broader in application than the right to counsel; *Loud Hawk* reversed the direction of the greater protection.

The dissenters were just as critical of the second part of the Court's holding, the application of the Barker v. Wingo factors to the remaining periods of delay, although they were not unsympathetic to the majority's skepticism about Loud Hawk's "strategically timed" demands for a speedy trial. But the dissenters thought that the government should bear the responsibility for unreasonable delay in the courts because it is the government as a whole, and not just the prosecution, that should be responsible for ensuring that a defendant receives reasonably swift justice. As the Court had said in *Strunk*, lack of resources is not a good reason for denying a defendant a speedy trial. The dissent's proposed rule was that a nonfrivolous appeal by any party permits a reasonable delay in the proceedings, with the reasonableness of the delay to be assessed in light of the number and complexity of issues on appeal, or the number of parties.

The majority's very different rule, evaluating only whether the government's decision to appeal was reasonable and made in good faith, took another step in the direction of rendering the Speedy Trial Clause a deterrent to prosecutorial misconduct rather than a guarantee that defendants will receive a prompt trial. The majority's other holding, that pretrial delay does not count at any time when the indictment has been dismissed unless the defendant is subject to restraints on his freedom, also limited the purview of the Speedy Trial Clause. And the majority's application of the Barker v. Wingo factors showed that test to be so malleable that if the government was not shown to be acting in bad faith, it could always prevail against the backdrop of the Court's disinclination to afford defendants the "severe remedy of dismissal."

Doggett v. United States—The Rebirth of Speedy Trial?

It might well have seemed after *Loud Hawk* that the Court's ambivalence about the right to a speedy trial had, over the years, turned to grudging antipathy. The *Doggett* case (Doggett v. United States, 1992) came as a surprise.

Marc Doggett was indicted on February 12, 1980, for conspiring to import and distribute cocaine. An agent of the Drug Enforcement Agency (DEA), Douglas Driver, told the U.S. Marshal's Service that the DEA would oversee the apprehension of Doggett. On March 18, 1980, the DEA had two police officers go to the home of Doggett's parents in North Carolina, but Doggett was not there and his parents told the officers that he had gone to Colombia several days earlier. Driver sent out word of the outstanding arrest warrant to U.S. Customs stations and other law enforcement organizations. He also placed Doggett's name in a computer network, although that entry expired not many months later. In September 1981, Driver learned that Doggett had been arrested on drug charges in Panama. He did not file an extradition request, but did ask the Panamanian authorities to "expel" Doggett to the United States when they released him. Although those authorities had agreed to this request, they freed Doggett several months later and allowed him to go to Colombia, where he stayed with an aunt for several months. On September 25, 1982, Doggett returned to the United States, passing unnoticed and unapprehended through customs in New York City, using papers bearing his own name. He then moved to Virginia, married, earned a college degree, found steady work in the computer field, and avoided further legal difficulties.

In 1982, the American Embassy in Panama advised the State Department that Doggett had gone to Colombia, but the DEA was not informed. Driver did not ask anyone in Panama to check Doggett's status; however, when he happened to be assigned to Panama in 1985, he then learned that Doggett had gone to Colombia. He assumed that Doggett had settled there and made no attempt to verify his assumption or to track down Doggett's whereabouts. In September 1988, the Marshal's Service ran a simple credit check on several thousand people subject to outstanding arrest warrants and, within a matter of minutes, found Doggett's home and work addresses within the United States. On September 5, 1988, almost six years after his return to the United States and eight-and-a-half years after his indictment, Doggett was arrested.

Not surprisingly, Doggett moved to dismiss the indictment on speedy trial grounds, arguing that the eight-and-a-half-year delay was so serious that he should prevail even without demonstrating that his ability to defend himself had been compromised. When the district court denied his motion, he entered a conditional plea of guilty so that he could appeal the speedy trial ruling. The court of appeals affirmed the denial, agreeing with the lower court that because Doggett complained only of governmental negligence, the first three *Barker* factors did not weigh heavily enough to make proof of specific prejudice unnecessary.

The Supreme Court again split five to four, ruling in Doggett's favor. Justice Souter's scholarly opinion reviewed the Court's earlier speedy trial law, including Barker v. Wingo. Souter described the first *Barker* factor, length of the delay, as a double inquiry. First, just to trigger a speedy trial analysis, a movant must allege that the interval between accusation and trial has crossed the threshold dividing ordinary from presumptively prejudicial delay. If the length of delay passes that threshold, the court must then consider, as one factor among several, the extent to which the delay goes beyond that bare minimum, because the presumption that delay has prejudiced an accused "intensifies over time." As to the second factor, the reason for the delay, the government contended that it sought Doggett with diligence, an assertion that conflicted with the lower court's finding of fact that the government had been negligent. The Supreme Court deferred to the finding of fact, and so attributed the delay to the government's negligence for more than six years, during which time Doggett could have been found within the United States in a matter of minutes. The government also contested the lower court's finding on the third factor, arguing that Doggett knew of the indictment and therefore could have demanded a speedy trial. The Supreme Court noted that not only had Doggett won that evidentiary battle, but also that the government had stipulated that Doggett was unaware of the indictment. If Doggett was unaware of the indictment, he could not have been expected to have asserted his right and so this factor also worked in his favor.

The government's strongest argument, therefore, was on the fourth factor—that Doggett had shown no prejudice. Doggett had not been incarcerated or subject to any restraints on his freedom, and he had not suffered anxiety or disruption of his life while the indictment was pending, because he had not known it was pending. So the question before the Court was whether a strong showing on the first factor, length of delay, in which the reason for delay was government negligence, was sufficient in the absence of any particular showing of prejudice to make out a claim. The majority held that it was.

The government argued, and three dissenters agreed, that the Speedy Trial Clause did not protect against impairment of one's defense, quoting language from *Marion*, *MacDonald,* and *Loud Hawk* declaring that particular interest to be protected by the Due Process Clause and not within the purview of the Sixth Amendment. Justice Souter rejected this argument on the basis that those cases had addressed the question of whether the Sixth Amendment is triggered by pre-indictment delay, a different question from the one raised in *Doggett*. The earlier opinions' observation responded to the defendants' argument that the ability to self-defend could be prejudiced by pre-indictment as much as by post-indictment delay. The quoted language in *Marion,* and the subsequent cases, established that not every threat to the self-defense interest triggers the Sixth Amendment protection, which applies only after indictment or arrest, and that the Due Process Clause offers those who could not raise a Sixth Amendment claim, because of the relative timing of the delay, a default means of arguing that their trial had been unfair because of delay that did not count under the Sixth Amendment. Once the Sixth Amendment is triggered, Souter noted, the Court had recognized in *Barker* that prevention of unfairness at trial was one of the forms of prejudice to be considered, and actually the most serious "because the inability of a defendant adequately to prepare his case skews the fairness of the entire system" (quoting Barker v. Wingo, 1972). The dissenters characterized that statement in *Barker* as dicta and inconsistent with the premise of *Marion* and therefore declared that the Court had to choose between conflicting lines of authority. But the majority did not believe it needed to choose between *Marion*'s statements and *Barker*'s, and so the Court's list in *Barker*, adopted from the earlier opinions in *Ewell* and *Smith*, of the three functions served by the Speedy Trial Clause continued to include preventing impairment of the defense.

The fact that Doggett could not demonstrate any particular way in which his efforts at self-defense had been hampered by the passage of eight-and-a-half years was also held not to defeat his claim. "Affirmative proof of particularized prejudice is not essential to every speedy trial claim," said the Court. *Barker* had recognized that this is the most difficult form of speedy trial prejudice to prove, precisely because of time's erosion. Time can work against either side, and it is impossible to establish with any certainty which side has been disadvantaged. And so requiring proof of prejudice as a prerequisite to relief would impose an often insurmountable barrier on defendants. Therefore the presumptive prejudice to the defendant, which increases with the length of the delay, remains a part of the mix of factors to be balanced. The government conceded that if the lengthy delay in this case had been intentional or motivated by bad faith, Doggett should prevail. On the other end of the spectrum, had the government been diligent in its efforts to locate Doggett, his speedy trial claim would have failed. The government must be allowed sufficient time to track down both the defendant and witnesses and to prepare for trial, important considerations that can counterbalance and justify delay.

Official negligence, the Court said, occupies a middle ground between these two extremes. "Although negligence is obviously to be weighed more lightly than a deliberate intent to harm the accused's defense, it still falls on the wrong side of the divide between acceptable and unacceptable reasons for delaying a criminal prosecution once it has begun." The government cannot complain if negligent lengthy delays are held against it because persistent neglect shows a certain lack of interest in the prosecution—had the government taken Doggett's case seriously, it presumably would have made more diligent efforts to find him. "Condoning prolonged and unjustifiable delays in prosecution would both penalize many defendants for the state's fault and simply encourage the government to gamble with the interests of criminal suspects assigned a low prosecutorial priority." The length of delay in Doggett's case was "egregious," according to the

Court: eight-and-a-half years between indictment and prosecution, six years of which, between the time when Doggett returned to the country and the actual initiation of the prosecution, counting as the portion attributable to the government's negligence. As the Court described it, this delay was six times as long as that generally sufficient to trigger judicial review of a speedy trial claim. Because the presumptive prejudice was neither extenuated not rebutted by the government, Doggett was entitled to relief in the form of dismissal of the indictment. Although the government had effectively rebutted Doggett's particular assertions of prejudice, the Court said, it did not and probably could not have affirmatively proved that the delay had left his ability to defend himself unimpaired. The Court's approach to presumptive prejudice in this case bears some resemblance to the two-stage process suggested by Brennan in his *Dickey* concurrence, although it may not go so far as to switch the burden of proof to the government to prove lack of prejudice.

Three of the dissenters, Justices Thomas, Rehnquist, and Scalia, would have resolved the case by finding the form of prejudice Doggett wished to assert—potential or even actual impairment of his ability to defend himself—outside the purview of the Speedy Trial Clause, agreeing with the government that the statements in *Marion* and subsequent cases should apply to overrule the "dicta" about prejudice in Barker v Wingo. "[Odd] facts make odd law," said Justice Thomas. Justice O'Connor, writing a separate dissent, did not conclude that preventing impairment of the defense function was not a goal of the Speedy Trial Clause. She simply concluded that the facts Doggett presented did not show any form of prejudice. He had suffered neither incarceration nor anxiety, and the proof he proffered of impact on his self-defense was too speculative to tip the scales. She thought, given that delay is a "two-edged sword," that Doggett's Barker v. Wingo claim should have received the same negative response as Loud Hawk's.

As the other three dissenters saw Doggett's case, it raised two questions of first impression about whether "independent of the core concerns" of the Speedy Trial Clause (said to be prevention of undue and oppressive incarceration and the anxiety and concern accompanying public accusation) the Clause also protects an accused from two additional harms. The first of these was prejudice to his or her ability to defend himself or herself, the chief issue on which the majority and the dissent had differed, taking different views on whether the logic of the *Marion* line of cases (on the issue Brennan had described as attachment of the Speedy Trial Clause) was compatible with the *Barker* line of cases (on the issue of speedy trial criteria). Thomas invoked the case of Moore v. Arizona (1973), in which a defendant had prevailed despite not having shown prejudice to his defense at trial because the Court had assumed that defendants would usually suffer either pretrial incarceration or other restraints on liberty, or anxiety. Doggett was a highly unusual defendant who had suffered neither of those evils. Thomas further argued that it was not necessary to "expand" the range of interests covered by the Speedy Trial Clause to protect the legitimate concerns of a defendant like Doggett in avoiding an unfair prosecution. During the time when Doggett was unaware of the prosecution, his interest in preventing a stale or unfair prosecution was protected by the applicable statute of limitations. Thomas argued that statutes of limitations, fixed by the legislature, do a better and more reliable job of balancing the interests of those accused of a particular crime and the continuing interests of society in seeking to punish criminal behavior. Statutes are more predictable, argued Thomas, and more consistent with democracy than ad hoc decisions made by judges based on the facts of each case. Under a statute of limitations, the presumption that a defendant will suffer prejudice after a certain point is made irrebuttable. That point will vary with the legislature's assessment of the seriousness of the offense. The Due Process Clause provides backup, if within the applicable period of limitations, special circumstances render it unfair to prosecute a particular defendant.

The other asserted evil, "disruption of his life years after the alleged commission of his crime," had also been raised by Doggett but not addressed by the majority (even though the Court had requested supplemental briefing on this issue). Thomas mustered many reasons why the disruption Doggett experienced more than eight years after the crime, when he finally learned that he was facing prosecution, should not be considered relevant to his Sixth Amendment claim. In this section of his opinion, Thomas relied heavily on common law history, making it noticeable that the first section, discussing whether the Speedy Trial Clause protects against prejudice at trial, did not avert to history. Quoting Stephen, Thomas observed that at common law, criminals had no right to repose. American federal and state statutes of limitations provided more protection in criminal cases than would have been available at common law.[70] Thomas also noted that the argument that disruption to the life of an accused should be weighed in the speedy trial balance suffered the same defect as the argument about impairing the defense function—the evil occurs regardless of whether or not the suspect has been formally charged. Had Doggett not been indicted until shortly before his trial, his interest in repose would have been the same, but the speedy trial guarantee, under *Marion*, would not have applied to him. "To recognize a constitutional right to repose is to recognize a right to be tried speedily after the offense."

Thomas concluded by complaining that *Barker*'s factors, which were supposed to have contextualized speedy trial analysis, had "taken on a life of their own," becoming a source of new liberties instead of a means to analyze whether defendants have been deprived of a liberty protected by the Speedy Trial Clause, which he read as protecting a more limited range of interests.

Thomas was certainly right in thinking that the majority's approach to the *Barker* factors, more expansive than in *Loud Hawk*, could be perceived by some lower courts as an invitation to apply the *Barker* criteria more expansively. While the Court had answered the first of Brennan's *Dickey* queries (when the speedy trial right attaches) in a manner pleasing to the conservatives on the Court, the second query (what criteria would apply once the right had attached) was now being answered in a manner Justice Brennan would have been likely to approve.

The Statutory and Rule Front

The Federal Rules; The Interstate Agreement on Detainers

One important reason why the Supreme Court has not decided a constitutional speedy trial case since 1992 is undoubtedly that many claims which might otherwise have been raised under the Constitution have been superseded by the more specific and often more demanding speedy trial standards of an increasingly comprehensive set of federal and state statutes and rules.

In the federal courts, Rule 48(b) of the Federal Rules of Criminal Procedure provides for dismissal of an indictment or information for any "unnecessary delay" by the government in presenting charges to the grand jury, filing the information, or bringing the defendant to trial. The applicability of this rule was limited when the Supreme Court in United States v. Marion (1971), in dicta, interpreted the rule as applying only post-arrest, thus complementing statutes of limitations, which apply before charges are instituted. This rule is considered to be a restatement of the inherent power of the court to dismiss a case for want of prosecution.[71] Rule 50(b) requires district courts to prepare plans for the prompt disposition of criminal cases.

During the 1970s, a few years after *Klopfer* incorporated the Sixth Amendment guarantee to the states, thus requiring the states to meet federal constitutional standards, two comprehensive statutory schemes revolutionized speedy trial law: one an interstate compact and the other federal legislation. In 1970, the Interstate Agreement on Detainers[72] (IAD) was adopted by the United States, the District of Columbia, and all states except Alaska, Mississippi, and Louisiana, providing a cooperative framework for resolving the problem of jurisdictions seeking to obtain custody of another jurisdiction's prisoner for purposes of prosecution. The Agreement provides a speedy trial right and remedy to encourage jurisdictions to cooperate in making their prisoners available to other jurisdictions with outstanding charges against them. If a prisoner against whom a detainer is lodged requests a trial on charges pending in a different jurisdiction, trial must commence within 180 days.[73] The charges must be dismissed if the 180 day limit is not met, although the court may grant reasonable continuances beyond the 180 days for good cause shown. This provision entitles defendants to be tried promptly on demand, and affords them a remedy, providing for presumptive dismissal 180 days after the demand. The IAD prevents the situations the Supreme Court considered in Smith v. Hooey (1969) and Dickey v. Florida (1970) from arising and provides defendants an easier remedy if they do. Thus, it would seem that many cases the courts might otherwise have had to decide on the basis of a Sixth Amendment analysis now simply do not arise.

The Speedy Trial Act of 1974

According to the legislative history, Congress enacted the Speedy Trial Act of 1974[74] more to protect the public's interests in speedy trial than out of concern for languishing criminal defendants. The Act's chief sponsor, Senator Sam Ervin, explained the Act's strategy: "[T]he courts, undermanned, starved for funds, and utilizing 18th century management techniques, simply cannot cope with burgeoning caseloads. The consequence is delay and '[t]he solution is to create initiative within the system to utilize modern management techniques.'"[75] The Act responded to public concerns about preventing crime and controlling dangerous defendants. The premise was that prolonged trials represented a loss of control by the courts and posed a danger that defendants who were free on release might commit other offenses while awaiting trial.[76] The Act gained bipartisan support, satisfying those who were concerned about the interests of criminal defendants, because it represented an alternative to preventive detention as a means of addressing the public's concerns. Representative Abner Mikva, for example, explained the purposes of a precursor act known as the "Pretrial Crime Reduction Act": "[T]he . . . Act is an approach to the problems of crime by defendants released prior to trial which does not rely on jailing criminal defendants before they are found guilty. . . . [I]t ensures that defendants are brought to trial quickly enough that the pretrial controls need be used only for a minimum time."[77]

The Act was preceded by a groundswell of support for a statutory solution by the American Bar Association[78] and various commentators,[79] as well as Justice Powell's remark in Barker v. Wingo that legislatures were better suited than courts to craft rules and timetables. The passage of this legislation may also be taken as reflecting a consensus that the constitutional standards of Barker v. Wingo would not solve the problem of delay in the criminal justice system.

The Act adopts precise time limitations in the manner the Supreme Court found inappropriate to the more general standards of constitutional law. The prosecution is given thirty days from the time of arrest or service of a summons on the defendant to the time of the indictment or information and seventy days between the filing of the indictment/information (or arraignment, if that comes later) and trial. To guard against overly hasty trials, the Act also provides that trial will not begin earlier than thirty days after a defendant's first appearance in court.

Certain periods of time are not counted: one category affords automatic exclusions for the time consumed litigating pretrial motions, or time during which the defendant or key witnesses are unavailable. Because the Act does not establish specific time limitations or even clear standards for determining how long such excluded time periods may last, there is considerable litigation on this issue. The second category of exclusions permits a court to grant a continuance if the "ends of justice served by taking such action outweigh the best interest of the public and the defendant in a speedy trial."[80] This category too requires considerable litigation in application.

If delay before indictment/information or before trial exceeds the limitations set, after subtracting excludable time, the Act mandates dismissal. The court does have the discretion to decide whether the dismissal should be with or without prejudice to future prosecution on the same charge, so the sanction is not as severe as the outright dismissal *Strunk* required for constitutional speedy trial violations. The question of what remedy to provide had occasioned active debate in Congress because the choices—a severe remedy allowing alleged criminals to escape punishment or a remedy with few if any teeth—were not inviting.[81] The Act also provides sanctions against prosecutors who seek to delay criminal proceedings for illegitimate reasons.[82]

The flexibility in the Act's excludable periods has been criticized as undermining the goals of speedy justice and predictability[83] by giving trial judges too much discretion to decide what time periods to exclude.[84] At the same time, other critics have complained that the Act puts too much pressure on prosecutors, defense attorneys, and the courts to try cases before they are ready.[85] Some also question whether proceedings are actually more expeditious after the Act. At least one study has concluded that the Act has not really made the processing of criminal cases speedier because compliance with the Act's time limits stems primarily from frequent and effective use of the Act's excludable periods.[86] Some commentators conclude that the Act has failed to meet Congress's expectation of expediting criminal proceedings, for whatever purpose.[87] At least one Supreme Court Justice, John Paul Stevens, has agreed, describing the Speedy Trial Act as a "hollow guarantee" (United States v. Taylor, 1988).

While it might seem self-evident that the Speedy Trial Act, with its precise and ostensibly demanding timetables, would obviate much constitutional speedy trial litigation, it does not supersede all constitutional claims. Given the open-ended nature of the Act's excludable periods, a trial could be held in compliance with the Speedy Trial Act but still have been so delayed as to amount to a constitutional violation. The Sixth Amendment analysis would not even be triggered by the seventy-day period the statute allows, but that time period will often be exceeded if many or lengthy continuances are granted, or if pretrial litigation takes place. The Supreme Court ruled in Henderson v. United States (1986) that periods of time consumed by pretrial litigation, no matter how lengthy or how unreasonably delayed that litigation, are still excluded under the Act. Reasons a court might find acceptable as the basis for an exclusion to the Act might or might not be problematic under the Barker v. Wingo analysis. The marathon of appellate and other procedures in the *Loud Hawk* case provides a dramatic example of how time periods that can be attributed to pending decision making, and hence excludable under the Act, may nevertheless consume years and become constitutionally suspect. The Sixth Amendment analysis, of course, may also include factors not relevant under the statute.

It is difficult to assess how much impact the Act may have had on the Supreme Court's constitutional speedy trial analysis, other than probably reducing its volume. At least once, in the *Lovasco* case, the Court used the Speedy Trial Act to justify its constitutional ruling, excusing the government's delay in instituting charges. Ironically, the Court was reluctant to find that it was a denial of due process for the government to delay indictment because, once the indictment was filed, the government would have been obliged by the statute to stop delaying the trial. It would be difficult to compare how defendants tried before 1974 would have fared under the Speedy Trial Act because, due to the exclusions, application of the time periods is far from mechanical. What does seem clear is that the Court has reconciled its Sixth Amendment jurisprudence with its interpretations of the Speedy Trial Act. The Court's ruling in *Henderson*, that any period of time attributable to pretrial litigation (no matter how long or how unreasonable) may be excluded under the Act, is consistent with its interpretation of the Sixth Amendment in *Loud Hawk*, which was decided in the same year. In United States v. Taylor (1988), the Court reversed a dismissal with prejudice under the Act, seeming to constrain the trial court's discretion to grant this statutorily available remedy by applying some of the reasoning of its Sixth Amendment cases.[88]

State Constitutions, Statutes, and Rules

State speedy trial legislation and rules, like the federal statute, provide timed limits governing pretrial delay, although in some jurisdictions, speedy trial provisions are only triggered if defendant requests a speedy trial.[89] The Constitutions of every state except Nevada, New York, and North Carolina include speedy trial guarantees, typically identical in language to the Sixth Amendment provision.[90] Most states have interpreted their state constitutional speedy trial provisions consistently with the Supreme Court's case law, using the Barker v. Wingo factors, for example, to determine when a constitutional violation has occurred. Although they are free to do so, the state courts rarely interpret their state constitutional provisions as providing defendants with more protection than the Sixth Amendment. This may be because the speedy trial statutes and rules in virtually every jurisdiction provide more specific and usually more demanding time constraints than the federal constitutional doctrine. The state courts seem to be satisfied that, between the federal constitutional floor and their jurisdiction's rules, both the public and the defendant's interests in speedy trials are adequately protected. States are, of course, free to provide either more or less protection than the federal Speedy Trial Act, which does not apply to them, as long as they do not fall below the level of protection required by the Sixth Amendment.

Areas in which state courts could ratchet up speedy trial protections would include the issues decided adversely to defendants in the five to four decisions in *MacDonald* and *Loud Hawk*. Interpreting its own state constitutional speedy trial guarantee, a state court could decide to count periods of delay toward a constitutional claim even if the Supreme Court would not count them in the federal constitutional calculation. A state court would also have the flexibility to interpret a state constitutional provision as applying before arrest or indictment, contrary to *Marion*, or to refine the Barker v. Wingo analysis, as long as the level of protection for defendants was enhanced and not reduced.

Reflections on the Supreme Court's Speedy Trial Doctrine

Developing a coherent doctrine of speedy trial has been a challenge for the Court in many different respects. The Court has had difficulty defining the range of interests the Sixth Amendment right protects and may have generated a list that is both over- and underinclusive. The Court has settled on the idea that the Sixth Amendment right serves three purposes for defendants—preventing undue restraint on liberty, undue anxiety and disruption of one's life because of pending charges, and undue impairment of the ability to defend against the charges—after fending off a challenge by three of the dissenters in *Doggett* to scratch the third interest off its list. These interests are all instrumental and do not take account of a suspect's dignitary interest.[91] The Court has not yet decided whether to include the right to repose that Doggett claimed, which is in part a dignitary interest and would require the Court to analyze pretrial delay more decidedly from a defendant's point of view. And the Court has not included in its standard list of functions the fourth goal Justice Brennan listed in his *Dickey* concurrence: prevention of prosecutorial misconduct. The Court has acted in some respects as if this is a goal of the speedy trial guarantee, distinguishing the 1957 *Pollard* case from an earlier case finding a speedy trial violation on the ground that the government's delay was not purposeful. *MacDonald* and *Loud Hawk* both allow room to count periods of time not counted in favor of the defendants in those cases in different circumstances, particularly if the government had dismissed the initial prosecution or taken an interlocutory appeal in bad faith. But, as Professor Uviller suggested, a court truly interested in deterring or punishing prosecutorial bad faith would recalibrate the factors in Barker v. Wingo. A finding that the prosecution intentionally delayed a trial to harass a defendant or to interfere with his or her ability to defend himself or herself should not need to be accompanied by strong defense showings on two or three other factors. Although the Court has been attentive to government purpose, it has not required that government action be purposeful to count in a defendant's favor. The *Doggett* case, finding a negligent delay unconstitutional, adopts a broader definition of what government misconduct should be prevented or punished.

The Court has given inconsistent assessments of how the interests it has validated are to be prioritized. Preventing undue incarceration or other loss of liberty is the function with the most impressive historical pedigree, and thus can justify its place as first in the usual litany of purposes. The Court announced in *Barker* and subsequent cases, however, that the third interest, in fairness of the proceedings, is the most important. The three Justices who would delete this third interest from the Sixth Amendment roster presumably also think this interest is important, but by relegating it to the Due Process Clause, with its higher threshold, they reduce the likelihood that the interest will be protected. The remaining Justices may focus on the question of whether a defendant has been prejudiced at trial because in the context in which the Supreme Court hears a case, trial has already occurred, the defendant has been convicted, and the other cognizable harms—pretrial detention of a possibly innocent person and the anxiety and disruption of life accompanying a pending charge—can no longer be prevented. Some Justices might also tend to agree with Akhil Amar's analysis[92] that a defendant who was in fact guilty should not be awarded the windfall of having his prosecution dismissed simply because he or she was incarcerated or anxious before trial. This is partly because any error made in deferring a well-founded prosecution may have turned out to be harmless—the defendant has now been found guilty and may well have been incarcerated for an identical period time as a sentenced convict, and suffered the social consequences of an actual conviction rather than the milder repercussions of a pending, unresolved charge. Because the remedy the Court considers after trial would entail the release of a person found guilty of a crime, the Court may well be inclined to limit the award of such a remedy to defendants who might not have been convicted under potentially different circumstances if the trial had been held promptly. It tends to be dissenters in the Supreme Court cases who would find that defendants prejudiced by lengthy pretrial incarceration and anxiety should be found to have suffered a remediable constitutional violation.

In deciding that the Sixth Amendment right does not attach until a defendant has been arrested or charged, the Court also minimized its protection of the second interest, prevention of undue anxiety or disruption of a suspect's life pending trial. As many have noted, this interest may be just as compromised before formal proceedings have begun as after.[93] The elaborate exercises in subtraction of the *MacDonald* and *Loud Hawk* cases also leave some defendants without a source of redress for their anxiety over unresolved charges, because the due process claim remaining to them requires proof of intentional government misconduct as well as prejudice. It is doubtful that Loud Hawk breathed a sigh of relief, or that prospective employers would have suddenly welcomed him, because a trial judge entered a dismissal order that was in the process of being reviewed on appeal (and was actually reversed).

The Court has also included in its account of the functions of the Sixth Amendment interests the public is said to have in swift prosecution—preventing criminals from remaining free to commit other crimes, deterrence, saving the expense of unnecessary incarceration, and so on. Commentators including Uviller have criticized this choice, noting that the purpose of the Bill of Rights provisions concerning criminal procedure is to protect individual defendants and not to serve the public interest. As Uviller notes, Bill of Rights provisions typically provide for rights that counterbalance, at least to some extent, the interests of the public. There is no historical basis for the conclusion, raised by Justice Brennan in *Dickey*, that the Sixth Amendment speedy trial right, like the federal Speedy Trial Act, was intended as a protection of the public rather than only as a protection for the accused. As was the case with the right to public trial, the Court has taken observations about the possible beneficial consequences for society of speedy justice and has then reified its own observations, shoehorning a new set of interests into the "purposes" of the guarantee. The Court's methodology for deciding what functions to include in its list does not seem to follow any particular theory of constitutional interpretation—it is certainly not originalist, an approach that poses difficulty when there is so little instructive history to consult. It is not a classic

Warren Court approach to protection of the rights of the accused, although Justice Brennan endorsed this addition.

Viewing the right as belonging to defendants and the public in tandem is consistent with how the Court has approached the definition of some of the other rights set out in the Sixth Amendment, although not all. In interpreting the right to public trial, the Court has been split over whether that right belongs only to defendants or includes interests of the public. The Court views the right to jury trial as belonging in part to the public, so defendants are not allowed to choose unilaterally whether to be tried by a jury or a judge (Singer v. United States, 1965). This conclusion may be rooted in the Article III guarantee of a right to jury trial, a structural provision. The subsequently added Bill of Rights provision would be redundant if it simply provides for the same right to jury trial, always presumptively speedy and public, for the benefit of the public. As described above with respect to the right to public trial, the most logical reading of the two provisions together would seem to be that the Sixth Amendment provisions guaranteeing a speedy and public jury trial are reiterated in the Bill of Rights to afford the accused an opportunity to challenge the denial of what is now constructed as a right. Other clauses in the Sixth Amendment, like the right of confrontation, are recognized as personal to a defendant, and not subject to internal balancing on the basis of society's interests.

Although the Court has referred to the speedy trial clause as unique in its double-edged nature, Uviller, among others, has pointed out that this is not true. In the same way that a defendant may or may not want a speedy trial, a defendant may or may not want a public trial, or a jury trial. In the same way that the prosecution may want to bring a reluctant defendant to justice, the prosecution may want to open a trial the defendant would prefer to keep private, or invite a jury to decide a case the defendant would prefer to trust to a judge. The public does have its own constitutionally based interest in attending trials, whose source is in the First Amendment, and its own interest in having its representatives try criminal defendants, whose source (at least in federal cases) is in Article III. There is no independent constitutional source beyond the Sixth Amendment conferring on society a right to a speedy trial.

In constitutional adjudication, society's interests are usually balanced against a defendant's rights in some manner. But one reason to keep the analysis clear is that when society wishes to assert that its own interests outweigh a defendant's rights, the Court must then choose how the two sets of interests are to be weighed. The prototypical approach to such balancing when rights set forth in the Bill of Rights are at stake is to ask whether the government, acting on behalf of society, has a compelling interest and whether the action the government wishes to take is necessary to serve that interest. This ideal is not always realized with respect to rights of the accused, but this weighted balancing is in ample evidence in the First Amendment public trial cases. The very idea of using weighted balancing calibrated to the significance of the right is lost if the analysis becomes an olio of various conflicting interests, all competing in a balancing free for all.

The Court has more accurately referred to the speedy trial right as "relative," allowing consideration of countervailing public interests in prosecution. Some provisions of the Sixth Amendment, like the right to counsel, cannot be balanced away. Even if the public does not think it serves their interests to have a talented defense attorney (like Johnnie Cochran) persuade jurors to acquit a possibly guilty defendant, or if the defense attorney becomes ill and cannot complete a trial, the courts would not tolerate a motion to have a defendant go unrepresented for even a portion of a trial. If a prosecutor wants to delay a trial, on the other hand, because the trial judge has become ill or because an important witness is temporarily unavailable, it is not unfair to require the defendant to wait for some amount of time that might seem excessive if there were no good reason for the delay. This is the essential perception of Barker v. Wingo—that when it comes to the speed of prosecution, what is fair does depend on the circumstances.

The Court also struggled with the question of when the speedy trial right attaches before adopting the formalistic answer that it attaches at the commencement of a criminal prosecution, either when a charging document is filed or when the defendant is arrested. This is a somewhat more generous scope than the Court has provided with respect to the right to counsel, which does not attach on arrest but only on the commencement of formal judicial proceedings—occurring when a charging instrument is filed, upon the defendant's arraignment, or upon presentation of the defendant in court for the notification of charges (Massiah v. United States, 1964), usually a period of no more than forty-eight hours after arrest (Country of Riverside v. McLaughlin, 1991). *Marion* allows defendants who experienced delay before arrest or indictment to raise claims on the basis of the Due Process Clause, which would be a reasonable allocation of claims if the due process test were not so predictably fatal. The impact of this allocation has been maximized by *MacDonald* and *Loud Hawk*, which dissect passing time according to highly formalistic distinctions. Klopfer was denied his Sixth Amendment right because the *nolle prosequi* in his case left his case technically pending and subject to reopening; Loud Hawk lost his Sixth Amendment claim because the period of time between the trial judge's dismissal of his indictment and the reinstatement of the indictment by the appellate court ruling on the government's interlocutory appeal was not counted. Evidently, Loud Hawk's case was not "pending," although it was pending appeal and the government was already engaged in seeking the court's permission to "reopen" it.

The Court did not struggle hard enough in laying out the amorphous and internally contradictory Barker v. Wingo test. As the next section will show, the test has been a source of considerable confusion in the lower courts. The lower courts cannot tell whether to treat the length of delay as anything more than a triggering mechanism. They do not know what the Court meant by its mention of "presumptive prejudice." The *Doggett* case has clarified that negligence weighs against the government, but many lower courts are unsure how to handle delay caused by the courts rather than the prosecutor.

Finally, as to remedy, the Court's dictum in *Strunk* that dismissal is the only possible remedy for a constitutional speedy trial violation discourages such findings. As Anthony Amsterdam pointed out, the statement is misleading. It is true with respect to postconviction claims. Before trial, however, a defendant suffering lengthy pretrial incarceration may be released; an appellate court can issue a mandamus to provide for a prompt trial; a defendant who is suffering adverse consequences (like being considered unemployable) might get relief from a dismissal of the charges without prejudice. The severity of the remedy of dismissal with prejudice after a trial in which the defendant has been found guilty has had a profound impact on the development of speedy trial jurisprudence.

Akhil Amar characterizes the dismissal remedy as the "mother of all upside-down exclusionary rules," because it gives a "windfall" to the guilty defendant and has nothing to offer the innocent.[94] He suggests that, instead of dismissal, defendants who have suffered denials of the right to speedy trial be allowed to bring civil actions for damages against the government. His remedy might work for those defendants who are acquitted after excessive delay, but is unlikely to provide any redress for those found guilty. Imagine a jury agreeing to award Willie Barker, a convicted murderer, money damages because he had to wait before he was convicted of a grisly crime. Amar is willing to countenance this result because he believes that the "deep principle" underlying the Sixth Amendment is protection of the innocent and promotion of discovering the truth at trial. This position has little historical support. As long ago as the thirteenth century, Henry de Bracton referred to the evil of lengthy pretrial incarceration as posing a problem for the guilty as well as the innocent. Will prosecutors be deterred from delaying trials if they know that it is likely they will only be held responsible for oppressing a defendant who is ultimately found to be innocent? Anthony Amsterdam, who first raised the concern that trial judges will not find violations if they think the cure is worse than the disease, nevertheless concluded that dismissal with prejudice is indeed the only possible remedy if it is necessary to effectuate the purposes of the Speedy Trial Clause.

State of the Law Today

Analysis in the Lower Courts

The basic legal doctrine of the Sixth Amendment right to speedy trial, as formulated by the Supreme Court, is easily and quickly stated. The Court has now answered the key questions Justice Brennan posed in *Dickey*: When does the right attach? What are the criteria? And what is the appropriate remedy? The thousands of cases in the lower courts considering constitutional speedy trial claims refine the legal doctrine—for example, pondering whether the speedy trial right attaches when a defendant is indicted if the indictment has been sealed—and apply the *Barker* criteria to the facts of each case. Cases applying the Speedy Trial Act involve matters of statutory interpretation and do not usually raise constitutional questions.

When Does the Right Attach?

The Sixth Amendment provides that, "in all criminal prosecutions," the right to a speedy "trial" belongs to "the accused." Therefore, the right does not apply in proceedings other than criminal trials, even in civil proceedings that might affect an individual's freedom, like commitment proceedings, contempt proceedings, deportation proceedings, or parole or probation revocation proceedings.[95] The right may attach to a corporation, which may be an "accused."[96] Juvenile proceedings are often characterized as civil proceedings, which would render the Sixth Amendment inapplicable, but juveniles may be able to claim a speedy trial right in proceedings that are considered to be sufficiently like criminal proceedings, as a matter of due process.[97] Forfeiture proceedings are not criminal prosecutions, but delays may be judged by similar speedy trial standards.[98]

The Supreme Court made some key decisions about when a person becomes an "accused" within the meaning of the Sixth Amendment. According to United States v. Marion (1971), because the Sixth Amendment speedy trial right only attaches once a person is "accused," it does not cover a period of delay before the institution of criminal charges. Although three years had elapsed between the occurrence of the alleged criminal acts and the filing of an indictment against Marion, the Court held that the Sixth Amendment provides no protection "to those not yet accused, nor would seem to require the Government to discover, investigate, and accuse any person within any particular period of time." The Court's explanation for this result was based on the language of the Sixth Amendment itself, and on the purposes attributed to the speedy trial guarantee as described in several Supreme Court cases, including United States v. Ewell (1966) and Smith v. Hooey (1969).

The first of the three canonical interests generally cited by the Court in these and later cases, preventing undue and oppressive incarceration pretrial, is not implicated until an individual has been arrested and experiences restraint of freedom, although actual incarceration does not seem to be the only form of restraint cognizable. The second interest, minimizing the anxiety and concern accompanying public accusation, is not considered to be implicated until a charge has actually been brought. The third interest, limiting the possibility that long delay will impair the ability of the accused to defend himself or herself, may indeed be compromised by delay before arrest or accusation, but the *Marion* Court thought it adequate that a defendant has the statute of limitations and the Due Process Clause available to vindicate this interest, as more fully described in United States v. Lovasco (1977).

Thus the Sixth Amendment right to speedy trial is triggered once an individual has been formally charged with a crime, whether by indictment, information, or any other document considered sufficient to provide a basis for bringing the accused to trial. The Supreme Court also declared in *Marion* that unlike some other Sixth Amendment provisions, such as the right to counsel, the right to speedy trial is also triggered by arrest, because arrest is a public act that may cause an accused the first two kinds of harm the speedy trial guarantee aims to prevent. *Dillingham* (1975) confirmed that the right attaches on arrest, although the Court did not even mention whether Dillingham had been incarcerated.

What Constitutes an "Arrest"?

Because the Court has clearly identified the predicate for Sixth Amendment speedy trial protection as depending on events that are ordinarily easy to identify—the date of arrest, indictment, or information—the question of when the speedy trial clock begins to run is not a difficult one in most cases. Lower court cases have dealt with a few problem areas in applying the Supreme Court's law to particular facts. When arrest is the event triggering speedy trial protection and an accused has been arrested more than once, questions arise concerning which arrest provides the relevant date. In a case from the Eastern New York District Court (United States v. Gutierrez, 1995), for example, a defendant was arrested and then promptly released without charges having been brought, because of the government's desire to protect an ongoing criminal investigation. The court held that the Sixth Amendment was triggered by the defendant's rearrest pursuant to an outstanding arrest warrant rather than by the original arrest. During the interim, the defendant was not incarcerated and had no charge pending against him and thus was in a position comparable to Marion before he was indicted (and to MacDonald after the initial charge against him was dismissed).

A more common occurrence is for a defendant to be arrested for an offense, to be subsequently charged with a related offense, and to claim a delay in prosecution from the date of the initial arrest. It is easy to reason that not just any arrest will begin the speedy trial clock running on every subsequent charge, no matter how unrelated. It is less easy to determine when the later charge is sufficiently related to the former to justify counting the entire period of time as pretrial delay. As the Seventh Circuit put it, the question is whether the crimes for which the defendant was ultimately prosecuted "really only gild the charge underlying his initial arrest and the different accusatorial dates between them are not really explicable."[99]

When the initial arrest is in a different jurisdiction from the one whose charges the defendant is disputing, the courts have applied a doctrine analogous to the "dual sovereignty" doctrine applied to double jeopardy claims. A defendant might, for example, be arrested by state officials and then turned over to federal officials for prosecution on the same or similar charges. For double jeopardy purposes, charges are permissible in either jurisdiction, or even in both, because the two jurisdictions are different "sovereigns."[100] In cases in which the initial arrest was by a different jurisdiction, the courts generally hold that the original arrest does not count as the beginning of the federal prosecution, even if the charges are based on the same events.[101] This approach is consistent with the Supreme Court's holding in United States v. MacDonald (1978) that an indictment in one jurisdiction does not serve to trigger speedy trial protections in another jurisdiction—in that case, the military courts and the federal courts. In fact, *MacDonald* contains dicta stating that an "arrest or indictment" by one sovereign will not implicate the speedy trial restrictions of another sovereign. Some pre-*MacDonald* cases had suggested that the right to speedy trial might "crystallize" if state authorities promptly ceded authority to federal officials who later prosecuted a defendant[102] or that a delay in bringing a federal prosecution after dismissal of a state prosecution for the same transaction might violate the Sixth Amendment.[103] Even if these holdings are not considered to survive *MacDonald,* there should be an exception (as there is in double jeopardy law)[104] if state and federal officials have been collaborating and thus not acting as discrete sovereigns, in which case the speedy trial clock would start at the date of the initial arrest.[105]

The courts have had some difficulty in deciding when someone who is already a prisoner may be considered to be arrested on a new offense. A prisoner might be said to have been subject to arrest if he escapes from prison and is then apprehended. In an example of this scenario in Nevada, a prisoner escaped, was recaptured, and eleven months later a formal charge was filed charging him with the offense of escape. The state court held that the prisoner had not been "arrested" for purposes of the speedy trial guarantee when he was recaptured, because his recapture merely continued lawful custody on an earlier conviction, and so the speedy trial clock did not begin to run in the escape prosecution until the formal charge was brought.[106] Several other courts confronting similar fact patterns concerning escaped prisoners, or parolees reincarcerated after committing a new offense, have agreed that custody must be attributable to the new charge and not to a preexisting right to incarcerate.

In the more typical case, a prisoner may be subject to arrest for allegedly committing an offense while in prison. In such cases, the prisoner is typically placed in administrative or disciplinary segregation before formal charges are brought. The Supreme Court in United States v. Gouveia (1984) left open the question of whether such confinement might trigger speedy trial protections. *Gouveia* held that prison inmates suspected of committing a murder in prison were not entitled to counsel under the Sixth Amendment, even if they were being held in administrative segregation, because no formal charge had been brought against them and thus judicial proceedings had not commenced. Recognizing that the speedy trial guarantee, unlike the right to counsel, can attach at the time of arrest as well as at the commencement of judicial proceedings, the Court left open the question of whether the speedy trial right might attach when a prisoner is confined in a segregation unit—arguably the jail of a prison. The Court noted that a number of circuits had held, before *Gouveia*, that confinement in a segregation unit was not tantamount to an arrest for speedy trial purposes. Cases decided after *Gouveia* have generally taken the same approach,[107] arguing that the consequences of administrative segregation, in a context in which freedom of movement is already limited, are not severe enough to justify speedy trial protection and that the purpose of the prisoner's confinement may indeed be administrative rather than punitive. One court in Montana suggested that a prisoner might have had a due process claim if he could have shown that administrative segregation was imposed to hinder his ability to assist in preparation of his defense (State v. Griffin, 1993).

The courts have also disagreed about whether an individual's speedy trial rights attach on the issuance of an arrest warrant or only when the defendant is actually arrested. In State v. Utley (1997), the Tennessee Supreme Court considered the case of a defendant who was detained on other charges and was not actually served with an outstanding arrest warrant until five-and-a-half years after its issuance. The defendant claimed that he had been denied his right to a speedy trial even though formal charges had not been brought until after he was served with the warrant. The court described the majority of jurisdictions, including the federal courts, as agreeing with its conclusion that under *Marion* the Sixth Amendment right only attaches on the imposition of "actual restraints" or a formal charge, because the defendant has not yet been subjected to restraints on liberty due to the new charge. But the court also listed a number of states, including Kansas, Minnesota, and Wisconsin, that disagree and would count the arrest warrant as beginning the speedy trial period.[108] Several states have concluded that an arrest warrant, which often follows on a complaint, could serve to trigger speedy trial protections if a defendant could be tried on the basis of that document, because it could then be considered a charging document.[109] While these courts have generally considered whether or not a defendant was being subjected to "actual restraint" because of a pending charge, they have not often considered whether or not a defendant was actually aware of an outstanding warrant, in which case the second category of speedy trial evils (anxiety and oppression) would come into play.

This issue often arises, as in the Tennessee case, in cases involving potential defendants incarcerated on another offense. In Smith v. Hooey (1969), the Supreme Court held that an individual who is incarcerated on another charge may bring a speedy trial claim seeking to dismiss a pending new formal charge. The Court explained that defendants may suffer the anxiety and adverse consequences of the second category of evils despite their lawful incarceration, and the prejudice to their ability to defend themselves of the third category. The Supreme Court has never decided whether awareness of a pending charge that has not yet been formally initiated, as in an arrest warrant or complaint, might also trigger speedy trial protections. *Marion* asked whether a defendant had been formally charged; in *Dillingham*, the defendant was subjected to "actual" restraint after arrest. If a defendant who is arrested and then released on bail or recognizance can invoke the speedy trial right, despite not being physically incarcerated, as the Court suggested in *Marion* and again in *Loud Hawk*, the speedy trial right might also properly be applied to those who are aware that a charge is pending against them. As the New Mexico court said, the term "actual restraints" used by the Court in *Marion* seems to be "sensitive both to deprivations of liberty and other relevant factors including harm to employment, financial resources and association, subjection to public obloquy, and creation of anxiety, all as described by the Supreme Court in *Marion*" (Salandre v. State, 1991).

When Do Formal Proceedings "Commence"?

In cases in which an individual claims that the speedy trial period has begun not because of arrest but because of the commencement of formal judicial proceedings, the courts have had some difficulty determining what charging instruments count. An indictment, like an information, clearly counts as the beginning of a criminal prosecution, but a questionable situation is presented if an indictment is handed down and then sealed. Does the speedy trial period commence on the date of the indictment or only when the indictment is unsealed? The Tennessee court in State v. Wood (1996) listed cases addressing this issue, concluding that a majority of courts counted the date of the indictment, although sealed, as the relevant date. The first two speedy trial functions are not applicable because, first, the accused is not incarcerated due to the charge at issue and, second, the charge is secret and thus the accused does not suffer any public obloquy or anxiety. But the court found that the defendant's third interest, in preserving the opportunity to have a fair trial, still applies regardless of whether the indictment has been sealed. The Second Circuit, in a case disagreeing with this conclusion, observed that the Due Process Clause is available to vindicate the fair trial interest (United States v. Watson, 1979). The Tennessee court seemed to recognize that the Due Process Clause imposes a considerably higher hurdle than the Sixth Amendment speedy trial right and thus does not provide an equivalent protection. That court also relied on the language of *Marion*, which said without qualification that the Sixth Amendment is triggered by a formal accusation. The Supreme Court in *Marion* was willing to relegate those who wanted to claim that delay had impaired the fairness of their trials to a due process claim, if no formal charges had been brought against them. The example of the sealed indictment splits the functions *Marion* found relevant once a defendant has been charged—the defendant may not be suffering anxiety if he or she does not know of the indictment, but the third interest, in the potential fairness of the trial, is still implicated.

Some of these lower court cases were decided before Doggett v. United States (1992), in which the defendant was not aware of the pendency of the charge against him and so did not suffer anxiety, but the Court nevertheless held that he made out a Sixth Amendment speedy trial claim.[110] After *Doggett,* therefore, the mere fact that a defendant is not aware that a formal accusation has been brought against him should not in and of itself rule out speedy trial coverage. In *Doggett*, of course, the accusation was still a matter of public record and so there was some chance that Doggett might have been adversely affected by the pendency of the charge. Although he was unaware of the charge, the reactions of others who might have known of the charge might have had an impact on his life or trial prospects. Whether this potential for adverse impact is great enough to distinguish the sealed indictment cases is an open question.

The facts might also turn the other way: a defendant who has been formally accused in a sealed indictment might become aware before the public does that he or she is being charged with a crime. In one case, a defendant who had been cooperating with federal authorities in another district became aware of a sealed indictment against him. The court held that the speedy trial clock ran from the time the defendant had notice of the indictment and not from the date, a year later, when it was actually unsealed (United States v. Dennard, 1984). From the time this defendant learned of the indictment, he attempted to assert his right to prompt disposition of the charges. Thus, the function of the speedy trial guarantee was implicated in this case regardless of whether or not the indictment had been sealed, and the court heeded the functions of the guarantee in reaching its decision.

How much a defendant's awareness of a proceeding that is pending should matter has proved a vexing question. In a variation on this situation in an Illinois case (People v. Fly, 1993), the defendant, a prisoner serving a sentence on another conviction, was actively prevented from knowing about the pendency of an outstanding arrest warrant by the circuit clerk's office, which mistakenly informed him twice, in response to his inquiry, that no outstanding charges were pending against him. The court noted that Fly had been precluded, because of this mistaken information, from requesting a speedy trial but nevertheless found that his rights had not been violated, after applying the Barker v. Wingo balancing test, on the ground that he had shown no prejudice.

Another question arising in some states has concerned whether some document other than an indictment or information can serve to trigger speedy trial protections. Whether a complaint or other instrument will count for Sixth Amendment purposes will depend on the role of that instrument under the jurisdiction's law.[111] If that document alone is sufficient to provide the court with jurisdiction to go to trial, the document plays the same role as an indictment or information and thus its filing should trigger Sixth Amendment speedy trial protection. In California, for example, filing a complaint will start the speedy trial clock running for a misdemeanor but not for a felony (Serna v. Superior Court, 1985), and this is true even if the defendant is unaware of the pendency of the complaint, because it is a public document. This is because "a pleading does not constitute a 'formal charge' for purposes of attaching the federal Constitution's speedy trial right unless the pleading is a formal accusation upon which a defendant may be brought to trial in the court with jurisdiction over prosecution of the offenses alleged,"[112] and a California complaint serves that function for misdemeanors but not for felonies. Thus, a California complaint in a felony case is not considered to trigger speedy trial protections even though it does suffice to toll the applicable statute of limitations. This is the same functional rule that some state courts have applied in determining whether an arrest warrant counts for speedy trial purposes.[113]

Finally, courts have sometimes found it necessary to fix a "constructive" date for the commencement of formal proceedings. In a Washington State case (State v. Jones, 1995), for example, a summons was returned unclaimed and the defendant failed to appear at his arraignment, the point at which formal judicial proceedings would have commenced. Because, as in *Doggett*, the state had not diligently attempted to locate the missing defendant, the state court considered Jones's speedy trial claim and, to ascertain the length of delay, set a "constructive" arraignment date.

Reinstated and Multiple Proceedings

If formal charges are brought and then concluded or suspended, the speedy trial clock will be tolled during periods when no charge is actively pending. One good example of such a hiatus is the Supreme Court's *MacDonald* case, in which a previously dismissed charge was subsequently prosecuted in another jurisdiction. Another is *Loud Hawk*, in which the indictment was reinstated after the trial judge's order of dismissal was reversed on appeal. The lower courts do not seem to have had any difficulty applying the theory of *MacDonald* and *Loud Hawk*, counting only periods of time when charges have been actively pending no matter how technical the distinction. This rule correlates with the Court's holding in the *Marion* case that pre-indictment delays are not governed by the Sixth Amendment. Lengthy delays in resolving charges that have not been continuously pending over a substantial period of time may still be challenged under the Due Process Clause.

If a superseding indictment is filed, charges can be viewed as pending from the date of the initial indictment as long as the same charges are involved.[114] Overlapping charges pending in multiple jurisdictions have proved more difficult for courts calculating how long a particular charge may be deemed to have been pending.

The lower courts have not had occasion to explore the Supreme Court's dicta in *MacDonald* that a period of time when no charge was technically pending might nevertheless be counted if the government had dismissed the initial charge in bad faith. The government is not permitted to dismiss a charge to stop the clock and then reinstate the same charge at a later date as a means of evading the speedy trial guarantee.

Delayed Verdicts

A trial may begin in an expeditious fashion but then fail to reach a prompt conclusion. The lower courts routinely reject complaints that continuances of a trial have led to a denial of the constitutional right to a prompt resolution of charges, although continuances may amount to a violation of the more specific time periods of speedy trial rules and statutes and, in an extreme case, might pose a constitutional problem. In a trial before a judge rather than a jury, a considerable period of time may elapse between the end of the trial and the announcement of a verdict. The Ninth Circuit considered one case, United States v. Beebe (1970), in which verdict had been delayed, but the court was vague about whether or not such a delay could be considered a denial of the right to a speedy trial.[115] The same court in an earlier case, Campodonico v. United States (1955), had apparently assumed that a fourteen-month delay between trial and verdict could constitute a constitutional violation, but it found that no violation had occurred because the defendant did not press for a verdict.

Sentencing

In Pollard v. United States (1957) the Supreme Court assumed, but did not explicitly decide, that the right to a speedy trial encompasses sentencing. In the case of Burkett v. Cunningham (1987), the Third Circuit addressed delays between verdict and sentencing ranging from "excessive to monumental." Defendant Burkett had been convicted in state court on three different offenses and his sentencing was delayed by two or three years on two of the offenses, and by five-and-a-half years on the third. A federal court, two years previously, had ruled that the state risked violating Burkett's right to a speedy disposition if he were not sentenced on that charge within ninety days. The Third Circuit, like the Supreme Court, had never held but had previously assumed *arguendo* that the Sixth Amendment right would apply to a delay in sentencing. The court, in this case, ruled that the right applies "up through the sentencing phase of prosecution . . . in other words, until one final, pre-appellate determination has been made as to whether and for how long the accused should be incarcerated." Applying the Barker v. Wingo balancing test, the court then found that Burkett had been denied his right to a speedy trial. Other courts have agreed with the conclusion that the speedy trial right includes a prohibition against undue delay in sentencing, either explicitly or as assumption preceding an analysis (and usually rejection) of such a claim.[116] The First Circuit, for example, in United States v. Nelson-Rodriguez (2003), found that a fourteen-month delay between conviction and sentencing was not unconstitutional, assuming the speedy trial right applied, because much of the delay was occasioned by disposition of the defendant's own motions and the defendant was not prejudiced by the delay. The District of Columbia Circuit applied a similar balancing analysis to forgive a seven-and-a-half-year delay between verdict and sentencing in United States v. Gibson (2003). The defendant was found not to have been prejudiced because he had been serving another sentence that carried a ten-year minimum. Cases frequently deny defendants' claims to speedy sentencing if the defendant has not pressed for a speedy sentencing.

In cases in which courts find that a delay in sentencing was unconstitutional, the remedy may be dismissal of the charges, as discussed by the New York Court of Appeals in People v. Drake (1984), or possibly credit toward a defendant's sentence, as the Third Circuit ruled in Burkett v. Fulcomer (1991).

Appeals and Other Proceedings

As shown by the Supreme Court decision in the *Loud Hawk* case, time spent resolving appeals or interlocutory appeals is generally not included for purposes of calculating the length of delay. Time spent resolving an interlocutory appeal by the government might count, if the appeal was of questionable substance or motive. But the clock is tolled by appeals brought by the defendant. Just as a defendant who appeals his conviction may not be heard to complain that a retrial upon reversal of the conviction is double jeopardy, defendants cannot complain that time spent resolving appeals they have decided to bring denies the right to a speedy trial, as held by the District of Columbia Circuit in United States v. Bishton (1972). A number of courts have reasoned that the accepted purposes of the speedy trial guarantee—to prevent undue and oppressive incarceration prior to trial, to minimize anxiety and concern accompanying public accusation, and to limit possibilities that long delay will impair the accused's ability to defend himself—no longer apply after a defendant has been duly convicted. Courts also have reasoned that the Sixth Amendment, which only governs the right to a speedy "trial," does not apply to appeals, which are not constitutionally required as part of the trial process. Commentators have been critical of the conclusion that defendants cannot readily challenge delays in appeals, which are endemic in many jurisdictions and which can compromise defendants' interests as much as delay in an initial trial.[117]

The Fifth Circuit in Rheuark v. Shaw (1980) found that there is, however, a right under the Due Process Clause to a reasonably speedy appellate process when a jurisdiction has provided for appeals of criminal convictions, and that whether this right has been violated by delays in the appeals process should be analyzed by applying the Barker v. Wingo test. Courts generally agree that a due process claim may be raised to challenge such delays, but they are not in complete agreement about whether the Barker v. Wingo test should be applied.[118]

Other post-trial proceedings, including parole or probation revocation hearings, are not part of the trial process and thus are not covered by the Sixth Amendment, but, if unduly delayed, may be subject to challenge under the Due Process Clause.[119]

There is no constitutional right to a speedy extradition hearing under either the Sixth Amendment or the Due Process Clause, so defendants who have been detained in jurisdictions outside the United States cannot force prompt resolution of pending charges.[120]

Applying the Barker v. Wingo Balancing Test

Before the Supreme Court decided Klopfer v. North Carolina (1967), the state courts were free to ignore federal constitutional law with respect to speedy trials; before the Court decided Barker v. Wingo (1972), the state and lower federal courts were free to invent their own approaches to all constitutional speedy trial questions. Before Barker v. Wingo, for example, a number of jurisdictions had adopted a demand-waiver rule, holding that if a defendant did not demand a speedy trial in a timely fashion, he or she would be deemed to have waived that right.[121] Barker v. Wingo superseded those decisions, holding that a defendant is not required to demand a speedy trial, but that whether she or he has asserted that right is one factor to consider in evaluating federal constitutional speedy trial claims. All state and federal courts now apply the Barker v. Wingo test to Sixth Amendment claims, as they are required to do, but this superficial uniformity masks a number of differences in practice.

The complex nature of the Barker v. Wingo balancing test makes it impossible to evaluate the courts' results for consistency. Defendants whose trials have been delayed for equal amounts of time will be distinguished based on their actions or the government's actions during that period of time, and by the impact of the delay on their lives and their trials. Inconsistencies are also masked by the amorphous nature of the balancing test. With four factors to juggle, a court's unusual evaluation of one factor may be mooted by analysis of the other factors. There are also some variations in practical application because the Supreme Court has left unanswered many questions about the interaction of the factors listed. Are all factors to be accorded equal weight? Is length of delay just a triggering mechanism or a factor to be weighed heavily in the ultimate balance?

Some commentators have complained about the courts in particular states defying the Supreme Court by twisting application of the Barker v. Wingo factors—actually treating a defendant's failure to assert the right, or a lack of demonstrable prejudice, as dispositive, for example, despite the fact that the Supreme Court's test precludes treating any one factor as decisive. One author, for example, accused the Maryland Court of Appeals of misinterpreting and misapplying two of the four factors and reaching an incorrect conclusion in the case of Glover v. State (2002).[122] Another criticized the North Carolina Supreme Court for misapprehending three of the four factors and imposing a greater burden on a defendant than the Supreme Court test warrants.[123]

Whether or not some state or lower federal courts have been resistant to the Supreme Court's case law, it is demonstrably true that few constitutional speedy trial claims, either under the Sixth Amendment or under the Due Process Clause, prevail. In fact, in looking at cases decided before the Supreme Court occupied the field of constitutional speedy trial analysis, it appears that a higher percentage of claims were successful in the earlier cases. This may well be because the introduction of more specific statutes and rules has led to resolution of many questionable cases on grounds not involving the Constitution. It may also be a sign that the lower courts are simply reluctant to find constitutional speedy trial violations because the required remedy would usually have to be dismissal of a prosecution, and the manipulable, freewheeling balancing test provides ample cover for reluctance to reach the conclusion that a remedy is required. The lower courts may also have understood the implicit message of *Barker*, *MacDonald*, and *Loud Hawk*: courts should be very hesitant to dismiss the charges against defendants who have been convicted of serious offenses and, therefore, should be reluctant to find a constitutional violation that would require them to do so.[124]

In other areas of constitutional interpretation, state courts often rely on their own state Constitutions to raise the level of protection demanded by the Supreme

Court. In the area of speedy trial, some state and lower courts seem reluctant even to follow the Supreme Court's lead as far as the Court has gone. There are not many examples of state courts relying on their own state Constitution to create more expansive speedy trial rights for criminal defendants, although state statutes and rules do generally set clearer and more demanding time limits than the federal constitutional floor would usually require. The speedy trial dialogue between the Supreme Court and the lower courts over the years has generally cast the Supreme Court in the role of expanding rather than contracting protections for defendants despite the fact that the Supreme Court doctrine gives short shrift to many defendants. *Barker* and other Supreme Court cases like *Dillingham* and *Doggett* required a fair number of lower courts to abandon preclusive doctrines they had developed. The reluctance of courts to use even the Supreme Court's modest doctrinal expansions to rule in favor of defendants can be observed in lower court applications of the four Barker v. Wingo factors. Individual factors are often applied in a limiting manner, sometimes despite contrary Supreme Court dicta. And the interaction of the factors frequently seems to work against defense claims. As a general rule, it seems that if a defendant does not prevail on at least three of the four Barker v. Wingo factors, that defendant will not be found to have suffered a constitutional speedy trial violation, even in cases in which there was extraordinarily lengthy delay.

Length of the Delay

Although this is the first factor courts are supposed to consider in evaluating a Sixth Amendment speedy trial claim, Barker v. Wingo, in the words of Richard Uviller, was "not quite clear" about how courts are supposed to treat the length of delay. The Supreme Court described the length of delay as "to some extent a triggering mechanism." Professor Uviller suggests that the Court probably intended to say that "a claim of denial of speedy trial may be heard after the passage of a period of time which is *prima facie* unreasonable in the circumstances."[125] Once delay has been so long as to trigger further inquiry into the reasons for delay and the other *Barker* factors, should the length of delay continue to count as a factor in the overall balance? Most lower court opinions do not appear to weigh the length of delay together with the remaining factors after finding that a *prima facie* case of delay has been established, thus treating delays of one or of fourteen years as comparably weighty and resting their decisions on the other Barker v. Wingo factors. The better approach, evidently intended by Barker v. Wingo, is to weigh the length of the delay in conjunction with the other factors, so that a lengthier delay will be more difficult to justify. The *Doggett* case confirmed that length of delay serves as more than just a trigger, ruling that presumptive prejudice increases with the length of delay.

Many lower courts try to generalize by quantifying the length of delay that can lead to a successful defense claim, counting the number of days the charge in question has been pending without considering the nature of the offense, or other contextual factors that will vary from case to case. This frequently results in jurisdictions producing a blanket rule about the length of delay that will trigger any speedy trial claim. Exactly what that rule is varies from jurisdiction to jurisdiction. Most jurisdictions agree that, as the Supreme Court itself had suggested in the first footnote of the *Doggett* case, a delay of one year will serve to trigger a speedy trial claim—that is, present a *prima facie* case of undue delay that must then be justified[126]—and that a delay of four or five months will not. In between those numbers, courts disagree. The Ninth Circuit, for example, held in United States v. Simmons (1976) that a six-month delay was sufficiently prejudicial to trigger further inquiry; the District of Columbia Circuit held in United States v. Gerald (1993) that eleven months was insufficient. The LaFave, Israel, and King treatise, canvassing lower federal and state court cases, generalizes that any delay of eight months or longer is usually treated as presumptively prejudicial; any delay of less than five months is insufficiently prejudicial; and there is judicial disagreement about delays of six or seven months, with a majority of courts finding a delay of this length presumptively prejudicial.[127]

This mechanical approach seems inconsistent with the Supreme Court's observations in *Barker* that legislation is better suited than constitutional law to fix concrete timetables for criminal trials. The inclination of so many courts to adopt this rule-like approach might be explained by the fact that courts have become accustomed to applying the more concrete timetables of speedy trial rules and statutes. Or perhaps the courts are seeking ways to standardize their approach to constitutional speedy trial claims in the face of the uncomfortably open-ended and ad hoc Barker v. Wingo test, which offers neither concrete rules nor well-grounded standards.

There is also some confusion as to how to calculate the length of delay. Under the rulings of *Marion*, *MacDonald*, and *Loud Hawk*, any period of time during which the defendant was neither under arrest nor formally charged is not a period of time during which the defendant was an "accused" within the meaning of the Sixth Amendment, so such periods of time should be subtracted from the time elapsed. Subtracting a period of time during which charges were pending but the defendant caused a delay in the proceedings by taking some action, perhaps filing an interlocutory appeal or a motion, would be redundant, because the second factor (reason for the delay) inquires into whether the defendant was responsible for part of the delay.[128]

Reason for the Delay

Before Barker v. Wingo, some lower courts had held that a defendant could only make out a Sixth Amendment speedy trial claim if the delay was "purposeful, oppressive, or prejudicial."[129] This test, similar to the current due process test for evaluating pre-indictment delay, tended to focus on whether the government had acted in bad faith.

Under Barker v. Wingo, government bad faith is not a prerequisite to a Sixth Amendment claim, although it is a factor to consider. Reasons for a delay in prosecution are attributable either to the defendant or to the government. Delay is attributable to the defendant either if the defendant was actively avoiding trial (perhaps even by absconding), or if the defendant made motions or took other actions that could have been expected to delay trial and disposition of the charges. If delay is attributable to the defendant, it may well mean that the defendant did not wish to have a speedy trial and is now opportunistically trying to have it both ways—delaying the trial and claiming a right to dismissal based on that delay. Nevertheless, even if a defendant was partially responsible for deferring a trial, if the other factors combine to show that a lengthy delay has caused prejudice, the defendant might still be able to make out a claim. A delay may also be attributable to a defendant who has not acted voluntarily to delay a trial, as in the case of a defendant who is not competent to stand trial.[130] This is because, under the structure of *Barker*, all delays are attributed to one party or the other, and it is certainly not the government's responsibility if the defendant is unable to stand trial. The scenario of the incompetent defendant shows that this factor is not just a redundant way of asking whether the defendant has waived the speedy trial right or whether the government has acted culpably. Although defendants who purposely stall their trials might also be found to have waived their right or, like Barker, find themselves penalized because they did not seem eager to be tried, a defendant who is not competent to be tried cannot be faulted or found to have waived the right to whatever prompt disposition is possible under the circumstances. Because this is just one of four factors, the fact that the defendant has caused most or even all of the delay, even if purposely, is not deemed to constitute a waiver.

If the defendant is not responsible for the delay, the delay is then attributable to the government. If the government has acted purposefully, with the intent of compromising the defendant's ability to defend against the charge, this factor will weigh "heavily" against the government, according to the Supreme Court. Professor Uviller wonders why the balancing process should continue if the government has acted in bad faith, because the test could be used to deter such government conduct.[131] If, at the other extreme, the government delayed prosecution for valid reasons—locating missing witnesses, for example—then the delay would be regarded as excusable and this factor would work against defendant's claim.

The most difficult questions regarding this factor arise in a third category, when delay is due to what the Supreme Court called "a more neutral reason such as negligence or overcrowded courts." There is a good deal of truth in Uviller's observation that these two examples do not have enough in common with each other to form a category.[132] Negligence is more like government malfeasance, especially if the Speedy Trial Clause is viewed as imposing an obligation on the government rather than simply as an injunction to refrain from intentional misconduct. Even if there had been any doubt after Barker v. Wingo, the *Doggett* case was clear in holding that the government's negligence may lead to a successful defense claim.

All the federal agents had done in that case to cause the delay was to fail to take action to search for Doggett. The generally accepted rule, especially after *Doggett,* is that negligence does count against the government, although probably not as heavily as purposeful opportunistic delay.[133]

Some lower courts have been notably resistant to weighing institutional factors like court congestion against the government.[134] These courts may have been misled by *Barker*'s description of such factors as "neutral" or by *Loud Hawk*'s toleration of an appellate court taking years to decide interlocutory appeals without counting that period of time against the government. The Court in *Loud Hawk* was not evaluating the reason for delay but calculating the length of delay because the indictment against Loud Hawk had actually been dismissed during the government's interlocutory appeal. Nevertheless, the Court seemed uninterested in treating the appellate court as an arm of the government bearing responsibility for implementing the speedy trial guarantee, not even remarking on the exorbitant period of time the appeal remained pending.

Most lower courts recognize that "institutional delays," including delays occasioned by such circumstances as a trial judge's illness, a court's summer recesses, overloaded dockets, vacancies on the bench, and so on, are chargeable against the government, even if they do not weigh as heavily. One author criticized the North Carolina Supreme Court for contradicting the Barker v. Wingo framework by, inter alia, exempting crowded dockets from their inquiry into government fault.[135] Most courts follow Barker v. Wingo's treatment of the government as integral and regard dilatory conduct on the part of either prosecutors or courts as adding heft to a defendant's case.

The willingness of some courts to excuse the government for negligence or for institutional delays seems to reflect a profound difference in approach to the function of the speedy trial guarantee.[136] While the Supreme Court, in cases like *Moore* and *Dickey,* has described the Speedy Trial Clause as imposing an affirmative obligation on the government to make diligent good faith efforts to bring an accused to trial, some courts (and some individual Justices) seem to view the Clause as primarily a negative prohibition on bad faith government actions. It seems clear from the Supreme Court's dicta and its articulation of the purposes of the Speedy Trial Clause that the Clause should be viewed as a protection for defendants, not just a limitation on government bad faith action. Only the *Loud Hawk* case seems to edge in the other direction. Defendants may spend time incarcerated, suffer anxiety, and lose their ability to defend themselves if a prosecution is delayed, no matter how benign the reason. It does not make any practical difference to a defendant who is languishing in jail awaiting trial whether the delay is caused by prosecutorial gamesmanship or budget-induced court congestion. Under the Barker v. Wingo balancing test, the courts can nevertheless excuse a lengthy delay, all other factors being equal, if the government had valid reasons for the delay—like locating a missing witness. If delay not attributable to the defendant is not justified by some legitimate reason, the delay will count against the government.[137]

One court has theorized that another function of this factor is to serve as a proxy or substitute for a showing of prejudice. In the same way that the length of a delay increases the likelihood of prejudice, the reason for delay can also be used to determine whether the defendant was presumptively prejudiced in a case in which the defendant is unable to articulate particular harms caused by the delay.[138] If the government has a good reason for the delay, the defendant is unlikely to prevail; if the government has been dilatory, the defendant is more likely to prevail. This approach, something like Uviller's proposal to treat government bad faith as dispositive, focuses on deterring unnecessary government delay rather than on what a defendant has suffered as a result of the delay, which can be difficult to pinpoint. The tension between viewing the speedy trial guarantee as a limitation on government misconduct, whether purposeful or negligent, and as a means of preventing defendants from suffering harm has not been fully resolved by the Supreme Court and surfaces most clearly in lower court cases involving this factor.

One interesting case displayed a surprising tension between the two forks of the Sixth Amendment right to speedy and public trial. In Hutchinson v. Marshall (1983), a federal district court in Ohio ruled that a defendant was not denied his right to a speedy trial by an eight-month delay caused in large measure by the resolution of a controversy about whether to allow television coverage of the trial.

Defendant's Assertion of the Right

As noted above, courts before Barker v. Wingo had held that defendants must demand a speedy trial or be held to have waived their right. Barker v. Wingo treats defendant's assertion of the right as an important factor but not as one that is dispositive unless the defendant has affirmatively waived the right. There are still echoes of the demand-waiver rule in lower court cases that reject the claims of defendants who do not assert their right to speedy trial promptly and vigorously.[139] A defendant who has not asserted the right may indeed have attempted to avoid a prompt trial. The timeliness, vigor, and frequency of a defendant's requests will all be considered relevant, and last-minute assertions of the right will not be viewed as favorably to the defendant.[140]

This factor too is elusive because it seems to overlap not only the question of waiver but also the reason for delay. If the reason for delay is that a defendant is stalling, an assertion of the right will be regarded as hollow (as was Barker's eleventh-hour demand). If the delay is all chargeable to the government, the assertion will weigh in the defendant's favor, although critics might reasonably wonder why it should matter whether a defendant who has not waived the speedy trial right truly desires a speedy trial. This factor seems to play its most important role in providing defendants with an incentive to put the trial court on notice that delay is becoming a problem, thus making it possible for the court to prevent unconstitutional delay (a solution far preferable to redressing an unconstitutional delay after the fact). The advent of speedy trial statutes has obviated the need for a defendant to alert the court to the passing time in most if not all jurisdictions. The status of this factor in the Court's speedy trial jurisprudence may be a vestige of the fact that Barker v. Wingo was decided before the federal Speedy Trial Act instituted new procedures that, even if they do not result in speedier trials, at least ensure that the trial court and the parties are acutely aware of the passage of time.

Defendants who did not know that charges were pending against them, as the Supreme Court found with respect to Doggett, cannot be blamed for failing to assert the right. The same forgiveness may apply to defendants who were not represented by counsel. The courts have been flexible about what to count as an assertion of the right if a defendant acts in the absence of counsel to press for a prompt disposition.[141]

Some defendants have discovered, to their chagrin, that sending a demand for a speedy trial to the prosecutor may be ineffective. Although some courts have held that a demand for trial made to the prosecutor is as valid as a demand made to the court, others have held that a request to the prosecution is not sufficient to count as an assertion of the right.[142] In another case, a defendant asserted his right to a speedy disposition, but addressed his demand to prosecutorial and court officials of the wrong county because of misinformation he had been given by prison administrators. The officials of the county actually involved did not receive the demand for three years and did not delay instituting proceedings once they had finally learned of his demand. The reviewing court found that the defendant had nonetheless been denied his right to a speedy trial.[143] This case provides a good example of a court choosing a vision of the right to a speedy trial that protects a defendant's interests rather than one aimed only at punishing prosecutors for culpable acts.

Prejudice

Barker v. Wingo clearly stated that prejudice is not an essential prerequisite to a successful speedy trial claim; *Moore*, decided the year after *Barker*, and *Doggett*, the Supreme Court's most recent speedy trial case, confirmed that view. The Supreme Court has also been clear in noting that prejudice can take many forms, of which impairment of the defense is only one (the others are prevention of oppressive pretrial incarceration and minimization of anxiety and concern on the part of the accused). Prejudice may also include such circumstances as loss of employment because of the pendency of criminal charges,[144] psychological damage,[145] loss of the opportunity to be treated as a youthful offender,[146] and adverse impact on parole consideration, eligibility for work release and other prison programs, or conditions of confinement.[147] Proof of prejudice is not necessary for several reasons. First, because it is difficult to establish what impact a delay may have had on the evidence at trial, prejudice is presumed to increase with the length of delay; thus, the defendant will not be forced to bear an impossible burden. Second, if the other forms of prejudice are taken seriously, defendants awaiting trial for a lengthy period of time have almost certainly experienced anxiety and other adverse consequences as a result of the open charges. Not requiring a defendant to prove this form of prejudice could be a recognition that, in all likelihood, most defendants could make such a showing, but that a defendant who has suffered to an unusual degree should be able to have that fact considered. The easiest form of prejudice to demonstrate, lengthy pretrial incarceration, is also the form of prejudice most susceptible to prevention under the Speedy Trial Act, Interstate Agreement on Detainers, and other contemporary statutes. Since the Habeas Corpus Act of 1679, defendants have been encouraged to seek release if their trials are delayed.

Most lower courts have recognized that, if the other three Barker v. Wingo factors weigh heavily in a defendant's favor, the defendant is not required to establish any particular form of prejudice.[148] However, as the Tenth Circuit observed in United States v. Brown (1979), courts are reluctant to find a speedy trial deprivation when there is no prejudice, usually in the form of impairment of the defense at trial. Here, too, critics have accused various courts of misapplying the Barker v. Wingo factors and demanding proof of prejudice in practice, despite the fact that the Supreme Court's test does not require such proof in theory.[149] Correspondingly, those rare cases finding that defendants have suffered a constitutional speedy trial violation tend to involve dramatic examples of prejudice like the death or disappearance of an important defense witness.[150] Courts seem far less inclined to find in favor of defendants who claim forms of prejudice other than impairment of their defense at trial, like suffering anxiety due to unresolved charges. Many courts characterize anxiety, or even periods of incarceration, as typical of the experience of being a criminal defendant. If a defendant would have remained incarcerated because of another conviction, this factor will carry less weight. Even defendants who otherwise would not have been incarcerated and were held for a significant period of time pretrial have not prevailed in their claims if they were unable to show that their trials were compromised.[151]

While some courts treat the four Barker v. Wingo factors as equally weighty, others view a showing of prejudice as being of paramount importance.[152] The Fifth Circuit, in a gloss on the Barker v. Wingo test, has held that a defendant needs to show prejudice unless the other three factors all weigh heavily in his or her favor,[153] articulating an approach that many other courts employ in practice if not in theory. The Ninth Circuit has attempted to quantify what length of delay will absolve defendants from affirmatively showing how they were prejudiced by the delay.[154] This is one specific way in which the length of the delay can reenter the balance, after having served as a trigger for inquiry, and is a twist on *Doggett*'s observation that presumptive prejudice increases with the length of delay.

For a defendant to establish prejudice, as the Supreme Court has recognized, can be a daunting task. It is necessarily speculative to argue that one's trial would have been different if, for example, a particular witness who died in the interim had been available. The lower courts routinely find that a defendant has not shown prejudice if the defendant cannot establish what a missing witness would have said, or if the other proof actually submitted at trial seems sufficiently persuasive.

In one case demonstrating that requiring proof of prejudice can truly be a catch-22, a defendant was held not to have provided adequate support for his claim of prejudice because he could no longer remember the names of the people he would have called as witnesses on his behalf.[155]

Three of the dissenters in the *Doggett* case favored eliminating impairment of the defense as a factor to be considered under the Sixth Amendment rather than the more demanding Due Process Clause. As the composition of the Supreme Court changes, the role of prejudice in the speedy trial inquiry may be subject to revision.

Other Factors

The Supreme Court was clear in Barker v. Wingo that the four factors listed were not meant to be exclusive of other considerations that might appropriately enter the balance. As the Fifth Circuit explained in United States v. Avalos (1976), other factors are implicit in *Barker* like the number and complexity of legal and factual issues involved in the case and the availability of evidence. In addition, consideration of some of the *Barker* factors should entail asking additional questions. Where the government claims that the reason for a delay, for example, was that a witness was unavailable, the court should inquire into the importance of the witness, the efforts the government made to locate the witness, and whether there were any adequate alternative means of presenting that witness's evidence.[156]

The Remedy of Dismissal

According to the Supreme Court in *Strunk*, the only effective remedy for a constitutional speedy trial violation that has already occurred is dismissal of the unduly delayed charge. If a defendant who is incarcerated awaiting trial requests a speedy trial, release from incarceration can provide a remedy for one of the harms the Clause was intended to prevent, although not for the problems of anxiety and possible impairment of the defense function. For a defendant who has not yet been tried, an appellate court can issue a mandamus requiring that trial be held promptly[157] or dismiss the prosecution without prejudice. But for defendants who have been tried and convicted after an undue delay, only reversal of the conviction will come close to unringing the bell.

The reluctance of courts to invoke the "severe remedy" of dismissal[158] unquestionably has an impact on the willingness of courts to find a constitutional violation, contributing to judicial resistance to the Supreme Court's relatively expansive readings of the speedy trial right in some cases. At least one prominent commentator has suggested that it would be advisable to preserve this extreme remedy for only the most egregious cases.[159] The Court was clear, however, in ruling in *Strunk* that, in the context of a post-trial finding of a constitutional violation, already a dramatic result, no other remedy would suffice.

It is unlikely that the Court would have intended this broad statement to apply to pretrial motions to dismiss on speedy trial grounds, because preventive remedies do exist. The government argued in the *Lovasco* case that a speedy trial dismissal should not be available pretrial because prejudice can be measured only after trial. This argument, if intended as a generalization, seems to assume erroneously that a showing of prejudice at trial is a necessary component of any successful claim. In addition, a trial judge might well decide to grant a pretrial motion to dismiss founded in part on the idea that the defendant is likely to be prejudiced at trial because it may not be any easier after the trial to determine how the evidence would have been different.

It might also be argued that being required to undergo a trial will exacerbate the suffering of a defendant who has already waited so long for resolution of pending charges as to be able to prevail under the demanding standards of Barker v. Wingo. The Supreme Court in the *MacDonald* case, however, was not sympathetic to this argument, showing its customary antipathy to interlocutory appeals by holding that Jeffrey MacDonald could not appeal the denial of his speedy trial motion until after his trial. In other cases, the Court reasons that an interlocutory appeal by a defendant who believes the deck has been stacked against him or her at trial is premature because the defendant might be acquitted, which would show that this fear was unfounded. The Court prefers to trust the jury trial process rather than preempting it needlessly. But as the four *MacDonald* dissenters observed, the harm of a speedy trial violation, unlike erroneous evidentiary rulings, is not cured by an acquittal. This is another area in which a state court could consider, under its own state constitutional speedy trial provision, whether the nature of a speedy trial claim is different from other procedural claims of error and could decide to be more generous than *MacDonald* with pretrial determinations and interlocutory appeals.

There is little evidence in the reported cases of trial court decisions granting pretrial motions to dismiss on constitutional speedy trial grounds. But given that not all trial court actions are reported in opinions if they are not appealed, it is difficult to know whether trial courts do find that defendants have suffered such serious speedy trial violations that their prosecutions should be dismissed pretrial. The reported appellate decisions show that the remedy of dismissal is granted in a tiny fraction of the thousands of constitutional speedy trial claims brought every year by defendants who did not prevail on statutory speedy trial claims, but who nevertheless aim for the brass ring of dismissal.

Waiver

The constitutional right to a speedy trial may be waived, but any waiver must be an intentional relinquishment or abandonment of a known right.[160] Failure to demand a speedy trial does not constitute a waiver, although it is one factor to be considered in the Barker v. Wingo balancing test. In the *Doggett* case, the Supreme Court held that Doggett's guilty plea did not waive his speedy trial claim and so he was not precluded from raising and prevailing on his constitutional claim. Doggett took a conditional plea of guilty, which permitted him to appeal the decision denying his speedy trial motion. Defendants who plead guilty may waive their constitutional speedy trial rights if the waiver is explicit.[161] The right to a speedy trial belongs to the defendant personally and so counsel cannot waive the right if the client does not concur.[162]

A defendant may forfeit the ability to raise this claim, however, by not bringing a motion to dismiss charges in a timely fashion, as determined by the jurisdiction's procedural rules.

Plea Bargaining and Speedy Trial

The fact that most criminal cases are resolved by plea bargain and not by trial provides an important perspective on the entire question of speedy trial. When a trial will take place is a not a question that is typically asked during a criminal prosecution. Instead, the common question is what kind of bargain the defendant will be offered by the prosecutor. In this respect, the constitutional right to a speedy trial can be a bargaining chip for either side. If a prosecutor realizes that a delay has been lengthy enough that a defendant might have a viable constitutional speedy trial claim, the prosecutor may be more inclined to offer the defendant a favorable plea bargain. The defendant, possibly incarcerated or increasingly anxious as time passes, may become more inclined to make a deal rather than seek a not guilty verdict at trial. A defendant would be unlikely to plead guilty if she or he was aware that the prosecution was not in compliance with speedy trial legislation or rules. But the constitutional guarantee, amorphous and infrequently implemented, is unlikely to provide defendants with an incentive to hold out for a trial with the prospect of a subsequent appeal on speedy trial grounds in case of conviction.

Conclusion

The five to four split on the Supreme Court in the *Doggett* case, the most recently decided case, shows that the shape of constitutional speedy trial laws could change with the composition of the Court. Although the Speedy Trial Act and its counterpart state legislation were intended to moot constitutional litigation on this subject, the Act has, according to most commentators, been something of a disappointment in that respect. Statutes of limitations cannot do the job of eliminating speedy trial problems because, first, they are drafted with the most extreme cases in mind and may therefore allow a time period that is excessive in other cases. Second, they are subject to revision by the legislature, whereas Bill of Rights provisions offer a check on legislative prerogative just as the common law checked royal prerogative. Finally, statutes of limitations cease to apply once a prosecution has been commenced.

The constitutional speedy trial guarantee will continue to have a role to play, however it is interpreted in the future.

Notes

1. Assize of Clarendon, 12 Henry II, ch. 4 (1166), quoted in Theodore Frank Thomas Plucknett, *A Concise History of the Common Law* (Rochester: The Lawyers Co-operative Publishing Co., 1936), 113.

2. David Charles Douglas and George William Greenaway, *English Historical Documents* 408 (London: Eyre & Spottiswoode, 1953).

3. Daniel Klerman, "Settlement and Decline of Private Prosecution in Thirteenth-Century England" 19 *Law & Hist. Rev.* (2001): 1, 5–8, 10–11.

4. Klerman, "Settlement and Decline of Private Prosecution in Thirteenth-Century England," 15–16.

5. Magna Carta, ch. 29, quoted in Sir Edward Coke, *Institutes of the Laws of England* (London: E.&R. Brooke, 1797), 45.

6. Sir Edward Coke, I *Institutes of the Laws of England,* 55.

7. An example of a commission of gaol delivery is provided in Julius Goebel, *Cases and Materials on the Development of Legal Institutions* (Brattleboro: Vermont Print Co., 1946), 5.

8. I Coke, *Institutes of the Laws of England,* 43.

9. I Coke, *Institutes of the Laws of England,* 56.

10. I Coke, *Institutes of the Laws of England,* 55.

11. I Coke, *Institutes of the Laws of England,* 52–55.

12. I Coke, *Institutes of the Laws of England,* 42. "Though the offence, whereof he was accused, were such, as he was not bayleable by law, yet the law did so highly hate the long imprisonment of any man, though accused of an odious, and heynous crime, that it gave him this writ for his relief."

13. See I Coke, *Institutes of the Laws of England,* 42.

14. I Coke, *Institutes of the Laws of England,* 42.

15. I Coke, *Institutes of the Laws of England,* 315.

16. I Coke, *Institutes of the Laws of England,* 315.

17. I Coke, *Institutes of the Laws of England,* 315.

18. Henry de Bracton, II *On the Laws and Customs of England: 1240–1260,* trans. Samuel E. Thorne (Cambridge: Harvard University Press, 1968), 345.

19. II Bracton, *On the Laws and Customs of England: 1240–1260,* 346.

20. II Bracton, *On the Laws and Customs of England: 1240–1260,* 347.

21. II Bracton, *On the Laws and Customs of England: 1240–1260,* 347.

22. Sir John Fortescue, "In Praise of the Laws of England" in *On the Laws and Governance of England,* ed. Shelley Lockwood, 75–77 (New York: Cambridge University Press, 1997).

23. Fortescue, "In Praise of the Laws of England" in *On the Laws and Governance of England,* 76; see also Frederick Pollock and Frederic W. Maitland, *The History of English Law Before the Time of Edward I* (Cambridge: Cambridge University Press, 1980), 655.

24. Klerman, "Settlement and Decline of Private Prosecution in Thirteenth-Century England," 75.

25. David Bodenhamer, *Fair Trial: Rights of the Accused in American History* (New York: Oxford University Press, 1992), 18.

26. 31 Car. II, ch. 2.

27. Sir William Blackstone, IV *Commentaries on the Laws of England in Four Volumes* (London: Cavendish, 2001), 438.

28. Sir William Searle Holdsworth, IX *A History of English Law* (Boston: Little, Brown, 1932), 117–19 (describing abuses); see William S. Church, *Writ of Habeas Corpus* (San Francisco: Bancroft-Whitney Co., 1893), 16; and Alan L. Schneider, "Note: The Right to a Speedy Trial," 20 *Stan. L. Rev.* (1967–68): 476, 483.

29. See IV Blackstone, *Commentaries* *241 (describing statute of limitations on prosecutions);*277–78 (remarking that felonies are usually tried immediately or soon after arraignment).

30. Sir Matthew Hale, *The History of the Common Law* (Chicago: University of Chicago Press, 1971), 87.

31. See also Bodenhamer, *Fair Trial: Rights of the Accused in American History,* 18 (questioning Coke's accuracy).

32. Bodenhamer, *Fair Trial: Rights of the Accused in American History,* 11, 21–22.

33. Bodenhamer, *Fair Trial: Rights of the Accused in American History,* 15.

34. Reproduced in Bernard Schwartz, *The Bill of Rights: A Documentary History* (New York: Chelsea House Publishers, 1971), 71–81.

35. Schwartz, *The Bill of Rights: A Documentary History,* 72; see Bodenhamer, *Fair Trial: Rights of the Accused in American History,* 16.

36. Schwartz, *The Bill of Rights: A Documentary History,* 76.

37. Schwartz, *The Bill of Rights: A Documentary History,* 141.

38. Schwartz, *The Bill of Rights: A Documentary History,* 162–66 (New York), 53 (Virginia), 62–66 (Connecticut), and 95–107 (Rhode Island and Providence Plantations).

39. Bodenhamer, *Fair Trial: Rights of the Accused in American History,* 14–29.

40. Francis Howard Heller, *The Sixth Amendment to the Constitution of the United States: A Study in Constitutional Development* (Lawrence: University of Kansas Press, 1951), 63.

41. Samuel Adams, "The Rights of Colonists and a List of Infringements and Violations of Rights," in Schwartz, *The Bill of Rights: A Documentary History,* 209–10; see also "Declaration and Resolves of the First Continental Congress, 1774," in Schwartz, *The Bill of Rights: A Documentary History,* 215–18.

42. See Richard Perry and John Cooper, *Sources of Our Liberties* (Chicago: American Bar Foundation, 1959), 267–69; Helen Hill Miller, *The Case for Liberty* (Chapel Hill: University of North Carolina Press, 1965), 164–82 (describing the Gaspee incident, where the Crown announced that the colonists who had set an English ship afire would be sent to

London for trial, but never made good on that threat because the perpetrators were never caught). The Crown also authorized trial of violators of the Stamp Act of 1765 in England. See Brian C. Kalt, "Crossing Eight Mile: Juries of the Vicinage and County-Line Criminal Buffer Statutes," 80 *Wash. L. Rev.* (2005): 271, 299.

43. Schwartz, *The Bill of Rights: A Documentary History,* 235.

44. Schwartz, *The Bill of Rights: A Documentary History,* 265.

45. Schwartz, *The Bill of Rights: A Documentary History,* 278.

46. Schwartz, *The Bill of Rights: A Documentary History,* 282.

47. Schwartz, *The Bill of Rights: A Documentary History,* 323.

48. Ky. Const. of 1792, art. XII.

49. Tenn. Const. of 1796, art. XI, §9.

50. Mass. Const. of 1780, part I, art. XI, see the Massachusetts Supreme Judicial Court in Commonwealth v. Hanley (1958).

51. See Gregory P.N. Joseph, "Speedy Trial Rights in Application," 48 *Fordham L. Rev.* (1979–80): 611, 613 n. 16; see also the Maryland District Court in Petition of Provoo (1955) for an interesting account of early cases interpreting some of these state provisions.

52. See Edward Dumbauld, "State Precedents for the Bill of Rights," 7 *J. Pub. L.* (1958), 323, 335 n. 91.

53. Robert Allen Rutland, *The Birth of the Bill of Rights 1776–1791* (Chapel Hill: University of North Carolina Press for the Institute of Early American History and Culture, 1955), 202.

54. Schwartz, *The Bill of Rights: A Documentary History,* 983.

55. Schwartz, *The Bill of Rights: A Documentary History,* 983; Dumbauld, "State Precedents for the Bill of Rights."

56. Schwartz, *The Bill of Rights: A Documentary History,* 1027.

57. Schwartz, *The Bill of Rights: A Documentary History,* 1114.

58. Schwartz, *The Bill of Rights: A Documentary History,* 1114.

59. A good source for discussion of these early cases is the Maryland District Court's scholarly opinion in Petition of Provoo (1955).

60. His only citation was to the case of Ponzi v. Fessenden (1922).

61. Barker v. Wingo (1972), 522.

62. See Anthony Amsterdam, "Speedy Criminal Trial: Rights and Remedies," 27 *Stan. L. Rev.* (1975): 525, discussed in the bibliographical essay.

63. Akhil Reed Amar has criticized the dismissal remedy as "the mother of all exclusionary rules" in his book *The Constitution and Criminal Procedure* (New Haven: Yale Univ. Press, 1997), 89–116, described in the bibliographical essay. Exclusionary rules adopted to implement Fourth and Fifth Amendment guarantees also may result in the dismissal of a prosecution if the evidence suppressed is critical to the prosecution's case.

64. See Amsterdam, Speedy Criminal Trial: Rights and Remedies, 525.

65. H. Richard Uviller, "*Barker v. Wingo*: Speedy Trial Gets a Fast Shuffle," 72 *Colum. L. Rev.* (1972): 1376.

66. United States v. Lovasco (1977), 796–97.

67. The court of appeals heard argument on October 15, 1976, a divided panel affirmed the district court's decisions in an unreported opinion on July 26, 1977. The government petitioned the court of appeals to rehear the case *en banc* (before the full court), which the court agreed to do. After reargument, the appellate court decided, on March 6, 1978, to remand the case for additional factual findings, retaining jurisdiction over the appeal pending the district court's new findings. The district court issued an opinion with the requested findings on

August 23, 1978, and the case returned to the court of appeals. A year later, the court of appeals reversed the suppression order and directed that some disputed counts of the indictment be reinstated, on August 7, 1979. Defendants petitioned the court for a rehearing, which was denied on October 1, 1979, and then petitioned the Supreme Court for *certiorari*, which was also denied, on March 3, 1980. During these interlocutory proceedings, Loud Hawk was unconditionally released.

68. In *The Odyssey,* Penelope, awaiting the return of her husband, Odysseus, stalled her suitors by promising to choose one of them to marry when she finished weaving a tapestry which she wove by day and secretly ripped out at night so that it would never be finished. Homer, *The Odyssey,* trans. Robert Fitzgerald (New York: Vintage, 1990), lines 90–118.

69. Rule 48(b) of the Federal Rules of Criminal Procedure recognizes this difference.

70. For a history of the adoption of statutes of limitations generally, see "Developments in the Law: Statutes of Limitations," 63 *Harv. L. Rev.* (1950): 1177, 1235–37 (dealing with particular issues in limitations on the prosecution of crimes); "Note: The Statute of Limitations in Criminal Law: A Penetrable Barrier to Prosecution," 102 *U. Pa. L. Rev.* (1953–54): 630.

71. A California District Court made this observation in 1940 in *Ex parte Altman*.

72. Pub. L. No. 91-538, §§1-8, 84 Stat. 1397–1403 (1970), *as amended by* Pub. L. No. 100–690, title VII, §7059, 102 Stat. 4403 (1988), *reprinted in* 18 U.S.C. app. §692 (2000).

73. Id. §2, art. III(a).

74. 18 U.S.C. §§3161-3174 (2000).

75. 120 Cong. Rec. 41618 (1974).

76. See Anthony Partridge, *Legislative History of Title I of the Speedy Trial Act of 1974* (Washington, D.C.: Federal Judicial Center, 1980); Richard S. Frase, "The Speedy Trial Act of 1974," 43 *U. Chi. L. Rev.* (1976): 667.

77. Speedy Trial Act of 1974, Pub. L. No. 93-619, 88 Stat. 2076 (1974).

78. ABA Standards ch. 12.

79. See, e.g., John Godbold, "Speedy Trial Major Surgery For a National Ill," 24 *Ala. L. Rev*. (1972): 265.

80. 18 U.S.C. §3161(h)(8).

81. Partridge, *Legislative History of Title I of the Speedy Trial Act of 1974,* 3–33, cited in United States v. Taylor (1988) (Stevens, J., dissenting).

82. 18 U.S.C. §3162(b).

83. See, e.g., Robert L. Misner, "Delay, Documentation and the Speedy Trial Act," 70 *J. Crim. L. & Criminology* (1979): 214, 226–28.

84. Malcolm Feeley, *Court Reform on Trial* (New York: Basic Books, 1983), 173.

85. Feeley, *Court Reform on Trial,* 224; Linda M. Ariola, Deborah A. DeMasi, Edward D. Loughman III, and Timothy G. Reynolds, "The Speedy Trial Act: An Empirical Study," 47 *Fordham L. Rev.* (1979): 713 (almost all defense attorneys interviewed and many judges complained of the impact of the time limitations).

86. See George S. Bridges, "The Speedy Trial Act of 1974: Effects of Delays in Federal Criminal Litigation," 73 *J. Crim. L. & C.* (1982): 50.

87. See Alfredo Garcia, *The Sixth Amendment in Modern Jurisprudence* (Westport, CT: Greenwood Press, 1992), 158.

88. See Garcia, *The Sixth Amendment in Modern Jurisprudence,* 176.

89. For a fairly recent comprehensive summary of state statutes, see Joseph, "Speedy Trial Rights in Application," 649–55 (Appendix: Extraconstitutional Speedy Trial Provisions). For a more current general overview of the variations in state statutory speedy

trial protections, see Wayne R. LaFave, Jerold H. Israel, and Nancy J. King, *Criminal Procedure* (St. Paul: West Publishing, 1999), section 18.3(c) (updated annually).

90. Joseph, "Speedy Trial Rights in Application," 613 n. 16.

91. See Toni Massaro, "The Dignity Value of Face-to-Face Confrontations," 40 *U. Fla. L. Rev.* (1988): 863.

92. Amar, *The Constitution and Criminal Procedure,* 101–16. Additional aspects of Amar's arguments and responses to this work are described in the bibliographical essay.

93. See Phyllis Goldfarb, "When Judges Abandon Analogy: The Problem of Delay in Commencing Criminal Prosecutions," 31 *Wm. & Mary L. Rev.* (Spring 1990): 607, 630.

94. Amar, *The Constitution and Criminal Procedure,* 89–116.

95. See the Western District of New York Court in Deutsch v. United States (1996) (not applicable to deportation proceedings); the Eleventh Circuit in Yapp v. Reno (1994) (not applicable to extradition proceedings); the Idaho Supreme Court in State v. Warwick (1992) (not applicable to probation revocation proceedings); the Eleventh Circuit in Moultrie v. State of Georgia (1972) (not applicable to parole revocation proceedings); the Mississippi Supreme Court in Mississippi Bar v. An Attorney (1994) (not applicable to attorney disciplinary proceedings).

96. See a Texas Appellate Court in State v. Empak, Inc. (1994); the Eleventh Circuit in United States v. Thevis (1982).

97. The Maryland Court of Appeals found that juveniles have a right to a speedy trial under the Due Process Clause of the U.S. Constitution as opposed to the Sixth Amendment, as well as under the Maryland Declaration of Rights. See the Maryland Court of Appeals in In re Thomas J. (2002); Brenda N. Taylor, "Recent Development: *In re Thomas J.*: Juveniles Have a Constitutional Right to a Speedy Trial under the Due Process Clause of the Fourteenth Amendment and Article 21 of the Maryland Declaration of Rights," 33 *U. Balt. L. F.* (2003): 27. In the Maryland court's description, other states to have considered the issue have agreed (compare the California Appellate Court approach in In re Robert B. (1995) (balancing factors including loss to the people if they cannot bring charges).

98. See United States v. $8,850 (1983).

99. See the Seventh Circuit in United States v. De Tienne (1972).

100. See Bartkus v. Illinois (1959).

101. See, e.g., the Eighth Circuit in United States v. Garner (1994).

102. See the First Circuit in United States v. Cabral (1973) (rejected by the court in *Garner* as inconsistent with *MacDonald*).

103. The Second Circuit in United States v. Lai Ming Tanu (1978).

104. See Bartkus v. Illinois (1959); Susan N. Herman, "Reconstructing the Bill of Rights: A Reply to Amar and Marcus's Triple Play on Double Jeopardy," 95 *Colum. L. Rev.* (1995): 1090, 1097.

105. Compare the Ninth Circuit in United States v. Cordova (1976) (speedy trial right may be violated if the state arrest and prosecution are a mere "temporary device" to restrain a defendant until federal authorities can decide to prosecute). To qualify under this exception, according to the District of Columbia Circuit in United States v. Liddy (1976), the defendant bears a heavy burden of establishing that federal officials are controlling or manipulating state processes and that state officials have little or no independent volition in the state proceedings.

106. The Nevada Supreme Court in State v. Gattuso (1992).

107. See the Ninth Circuit in United States v. Mills (1987).

108. See also an Alabama Appellate Court in Kimbrell v. State (1995).

109. See, e.g., the Idaho Supreme Court in State v. Holtslander (1981) (holding on the basis of its own state constitution that the issuance of a John Doe complaint and arrest warrant constituted the initiation of the prosecution).

110. The Court withstood a challenge from three of the dissenters to excise the third component and thereby shrink Sixth Amendment coverage.

111. See an Illinois Appellate Court in People v. Mitchell (2005) (not any charging instrument is sufficient accusation to begin the speedy trial clock; defendant's right to a speedy trial did not accrue until he or she was arrested, although fourteen years had passed between the date of the complaint for a warrant and the arrest).

112. The California Appellate Court in People v. Martinez (2000).

113. See, e.g., the Maryland Supreme Court in State v. Gee (1984).

114. An example of this occurred in the New Mexico Supreme Court case State v. Talamante (2003), in which a first indictment was dismissed on the same day a second indictment charging the same offenses was filed.

115. "The delay of which he complains occurred after trial and before a decision was announced by the District Court. We note further that that delay did not prejudice appeal and that appellant during this period was at large on bail."

116. For an unusual counterexample, see the Supreme Court of Kansas in State v. Freeman (1984) (Sixth Amendment speedy trial right held not applicable to sentencing proceedings).

117. See Marc M. Arkin, "Speedy Criminal Appeal: A Right without a Remedy," 74 *Minn. L. Rev.* (1990): 437 ("as speedy trial problems were the bane of the 1960s, so appellate delay portends to be the issue of the 1990s"); and Winslow Christian, "Delay in Criminal Appeals: A Functional Analysis of One Court's Work," 23 *Stan. L. Rev.* (1971): 676.

118. See the Third Circuit in Burkett v. Cunningham (1987), in which the court used a balancing test similar to but not identical to Barker v. Wingo; the Ninth Circuit in United States v. Mohawk (1994), in which the Ninth Circuit demanded a showing of prejudice that would not have been required under Barker v. Wingo.

119. See Morrissey v. Brewer (1972). The later case of Moody v. Daggett (1976) suggests, however, that the right of a parolee to a prompt disposition may be overcome by other factors.

120. The Eleventh Circuit in Yapp v. Reno (1994). Some courts have concluded that whether the government makes a good faith effort to obtain jurisdiction over an individual detained by another country is relevant in evaluating the defendant's claim that prosecution of a pending charge has not been speedy within the meaning of the Sixth Amendment, see the Eighth Circuit in United States v. Pomeroy (1987), while others disagree, forgiving the government from seeking extradition from other countries where there is less history of cooperation, see the Ninth Circuit in United States v. Hooker (1979).

121. The Second Circuit in United States v. Lustman (1958).

122. Christopher S. Elmore, "Note: *Glover v. State*: A Misinterpretation and Misapplication of the *Barker* Speedy Trial Balancing Test Results in the Weakening of a Criminal Defendant's Rights to a Prompt Trial," 62 *Md. L. Rev.* (2003): 573.

123. Darren Allen, "Note: The Constitutional Floor Doctrine and the Right to a Speedy Trial," 26 *Campbell L. Rev.* (2004): 101. See also Steven J. Stonitsch, "Recent Developments in New York Law: The Effect of *People v. Vernace* on a Criminal Defendant's Right to Due Process and Speedy Trial in New York," 76 *St. John's L. Rev.* (2002): 657 (criticizing the New York Court of Appeals for improper application of due

process standards in the case of People v. Vernace (2001), in which a trial was held fourteen years after the initial investigation).

124. Garcia, *The Sixth Amendment in Modern American Jurisprudence,* 168.

125. Uviller, *The Process of Criminal Justice: Investigation and Adjudication,* 1385.

126. For one of many examples, see the Fifth Circuit in United States v. Lucien (1995) (Fifth Circuit generally requires a one-year delay to trigger *Barker* analysis).

127. LaFave, Israel, and King, *Criminal Procedure,* section 18.2(b).

128. See Joseph, "Speedy Trial Rights in Application," 623 n. 72.

129. The Fifth Circuit in Sanders v. United States (1969).

130. See the Seventh Circuit in United States ex rel. Little v. Twomey (1973) (what constitutes a reasonable time for incarceration of a defendant who is not competent to stand trial will depend on the gravity of the offense involved).

131. Uviller, *The Process of Criminal Justice: Investigation and Adjudication,* 1385.

132. Professor Uviller also questions why the Court would put government negligence in the same category as "neutral" explanations (like a trial judge's illness), Uviller, *The Process of Criminal Justice: Investigation and Adjudication,* 1386.

133. Strunk v. United States (1973); see also United States v. Carini (1977); the Sixth Circuit in Cain v. Smith (1982). Other courts have been resistant to this idea.

134. See the Ninth Circuit in United States v. Nance (1982) (portion of delay caused by court congestion is not attributable to government for speedy trial analysis); the Sixth Circuit in United States v. Mulligan (1975) (overcrowded docket is of only minimal weight).

135. Allen, "The Constitutional Floor Doctrine and the Right to a Speedy Trial," 111–12.

136. In other areas of constitutional interpretation, particularly involving prisoners rights, the Supreme Court has held that mere government negligence does not deny rights to due process, see Daniels v. Williams (1986); Farmer v. Brennan (1994).

137. One issue some courts have struggled with is how to evaluate a delay caused by an interlocutory appeal brought by the government. The Supreme Court in *Loud Hawk* found that this can be a valid reason for delay, unless the government has abused the appellate process or the appeal took an unreasonably long time.

138. The Sixth Circuit in United States v. Mundt (1994).

139. Allen, "The Constitutional Floor Doctrine and the Right to a Speedy Trial," 112–14 (describing a North Carolina case in which a defendant had demanded a speedy trial pro se, over the objection of his attorney, and the court found that defendant could not be credited with asserting his right because his lawyer had not done so on his behalf).

140. According to the Sixth Circuit in Cain v. Smith (1982). That court also found that a demand for reasonable bail is the functional equivalent of a demand for speedy trial.

141. See District of Columbia Circuit in United States v. Calloway (1974).

142. The Fifth Circuit in Prince v. State of Alabama (1975) held that assertion may be made by communication to either the prosecutor or the court; the Second Circuit, in the pre–Barker v. Wingo case of United States v. Santos (1967) found a request addressed to the prosecutor to be insufficient. This result may be questioned in light of Barker v. Wingo's treatment of this factor.

143. The Ninth Circuit in Chauncey v. Second Judicial Dist. Ct. (1973).

144. The Fifth Circuit in United States v. Netterville (1977).

145. The Third Circuit in United States v. Dreyer (1976).

146. The Second Circuit in United States v. Roberts (1975).

147. The Supreme Court of Alabama in Ex parte Archer (1992). See William L. Pfeifer, Jr. and G. Ray Kolb, Jr., "The Right to a Speedy Trial in Alabama," 65 *Ala. Law* (2004): 102.

148. The Eleventh Circuit in Ringstaff v. Howard (1989).

149. Allen, "The Constitutional Floor Doctrine and the Right to a Speedy Trial," 115.

150. For examples, see the First Circuit in United States v. Fay (1974); the New York Eastern District Court in United States v. Upton (1995); the Illinois Northern District Court in United States v. Alcantar-Lopez (1988); the Florida Southern District Court in United States v. Raffone (1975). Courts usually insist that defendants establish that the alleged witness would actually have been helpful to the defense.

151. See the Georgia Supreme Court in Smith v. State (2002) (nineteen months of pre-trial incarceration described as not "oppressive to a degree beyond that which necessarily attends imprisonment"). The Supreme Court did not express any great concern that the defendant in Barker v. Wingo had been incarcerated for ten months because of the delayed charge.

152. Brian P. Brooks, Comment: "A New Speedy Trial Standard for *Barker v. Wingo*: Reviving a Constitutional Remedy in an Age of Statutes," 61 *U. Chi. L. Rev.* (1994): 587, 588.

153. The Eleventh Circuit in United States v. Mitchell (1985). This case is correctly regarded by some other courts as now-questionable authority.

154. See the Ninth Circuit in United States v. Gregory (2003) (twenty-two-month delay is not long enough to excuse a defendant's failure to prove prejudice). For an example of a court finding a speedy trial violation after presuming prejudice on the basis of a six-year delay in prosecution (where the other factors—reason for the delay and assertion of the right—did not help the government), see the Colorado District Court in United States v. Zapata (2003).

155. The Fifth Circuit in United States v. Beckham (1975).

156. The Sixth Circuit in Redd v. Sowders (1987).

157. See LaFave, Israel, and King, *Criminal Procedure,* section 18.3(c) nn.107-08 for examples of jurisdictions providing these alternative remedies.

158. This was the view of the Sixth Circuit in United States v. Holyfield (1986).

159. Amsterdam, "Speedy Criminal Trial: Rights and Remedies," 535. Amsterdam nevertheless concluded that dismissal with prejudice is the appropriate remedy post trial, and if necessary to effectuate the goals of the Speedy Trial Clause. See Amar, *The Constitution and Criminal Procedure*, 109–16 for a more radical proposal to replace the dismissal remedy with civil tort actions.

160. The Ninth Circuit in United States v. Geelan (1975).

161. For an example of a correct express waiver, see the Eighth Circuit in Cox v. Lockhart (1992).

162. California Supreme Court in Townsend v. Superior Court (1975) (counsel's waiver was "over his client's objections").

Bibliographic Essay

ENGLISH SOURCES

The earliest writing on the right to speedy trial at common law is in the second volume of the encyclopedia of Henry de Bracton, *On the Laws and Customs of England: 1240–1260,* trans. Samuel Thorne (Cambridge: Harvard Univ. Press, 1968), who was considered the most reliable source on English law until Blackstone. Bracton described the procedural options open to a person accused by appeal (private prosecution) to seek release rather than be incarcerated "for a long time." Daniel Klerman's article, "Settlement and Decline of Private Prosecution in Thirteenth-Century England" 19 *Law & Hist. Rev.* (2001): 1, 5–8, 10–11, is a useful source of information about limitations on private prosecutions during the thirteenth century, a key era in which speedy trial remedies were being developed in both private and public prosecutions. Sir John Fortescue's fifteenth-century "In Praise of the Laws of England" in *On the Laws and Governance of England,* ed. Shelley Lockwood (New York: Cambridge University Press, 1997), 75–77, a dialogue between the exiled Prince Edward (son of Henry VI) and Fortescue himself (the chancellor), comments on the intolerance of English law for frivolous and unfruitful delays.

The most important early source on the right to speedy trial in England is undoubtedly Sir Edward Coke, Institutes of the Law of England, because of Coke's familiarity to colonial lawyers. Some critics question the reliability and objectivity of Coke's accounts because he was something of a partisan in the seventeenth century's battles between the Stuart monarchy and Parliament. An antagonist of the monarch, he favored actions taken to constrain royal prerogative and described glowingly comparable measures taken during the thirteenth century, including his expansive reading of the Magna Carta provision described in the text.

Sir Matthew Hale, one of William Blackstone's principal sources, described the role of the Habeas Corpus Act as honored by the British during the seventeenth century in *The History of the Common Law* (Chicago: University of Chicago Press, 1971), 87. Blackstone, who waxed so eloquent about the right to public trial and was such a great influence on the framers of the Constitution in other respects, had little to say about speedy trial beyond expressing his enthusiasm for the Habeas Corpus Act, a few remarks about the existence of statutes of limitations on prosecutions, IV Blackstone, Commentaries, *241; and an observation that felonies were usually tried immediately or soon after arraignment, id. at *277–78. He was uncharacteristically reserved in this perfunctory discussion, neither praising English law on the speediness of trials nor critiquing it.

Jeremy Bentham, writing after the addition of the Sixth Amendment to the Constitution, contributed a utilitarian justification for speedy trials, deterrence of crime, that went beyond the interests of the accused, in his *The Theory of Legislation* (London: K. Paul, Trench, Trubner & Co., Ltd., 1931), 326.

SOURCES ON AMERICAN CONSTITUTIONAL HISTORY

Bernard Schwartz, *The Bill of Rights: A Documentary History* (New York: Chelsea House Publishers, 1971) includes the documentation, limited as it is, of the debates over the drafting of the Sixth Amendment. Joseph Story, whose commentaries are a highly regarded source of discussion in other areas of constitutional interpretation, does not mention speedy trial at all. Speedy trial is only briefly mentioned in other sources of constitutional and even of Sixth Amendment history; see, for example, Francis Howard Heller's book, *The Sixth Amendment* (Lawrence: University of Kansas Press, 1951).

CONTEMPORARY SPEEDY TRIAL SCHOLARSHIP

Treatises

Wayne R. LaFave, Jerold H. Israel, and Nancy J. King's *Criminal Procedure,* 4th ed. (St. Paul: West Publishing, 2004), is an excellent treatise providing case citations, summaries, and some commentary on the subject of speedy trial in Chapter 18, Speedy Trial and Other Prompt Disposition. The treatise is mostly an objective analysis of the law, although it sometimes critiques the results of cases, comments on what the law should be, or agrees or disagrees with various commentators. The treatise is kept up to date through pocket parts and is available online through Westlaw under the citation 4 CRIMPROC s 18.

Charles Alan Wright's *Federal Practice and Procedure* (St. Paul, MN: West Publishing, 1969), sec. 813, provides a shorter version of a treatise approach, with updated pocket parts by Nancy J. King and Susan R. Klein.

The Georgetown Law Journal Annual Review of Criminal Procedure includes a cumulative summary of the federal constitutional and statutory law of speedy trial. See, for example, Brook Dooley, "Thirty-First Annual Review of Criminal Procedure, II Preliminary Proceedings, Speedy Trial," 90 *Geo. L.J.* (2002): 1454. Other books and law review surveys of the law of speedy trial exist, including Robert L. Misner, *Speedy Trial: Federal and State Practice* (Charlottesville, VA:

Michie Co., 1983) and Randall S. Susskind, "Eighth Annual Survey of White Collar Crime Procedural Issues: Right to a Speedy Trial," 30 *Amer. Crim. L. Rev*. (1993): 1239, but they are not updated.

A good source for online research is http://caselaw.lp.findlaw.com/data/constitution/amendment06.

Commentary and Critique

Before the Supreme Court's decision in *Klopfer* applying the speedy trial guarantee to the states, few commentators wrote about this Sixth Amendment right. Contemporary authors still note the paucity of scholarship on speedy trial and on the Sixth Amendment generally, compared with the prolific output on other criminal procedure rights, like Fourth Amendment search and seizure. For the best (mostly anonymous) student notes of the era, see "Note: The Right to a Speedy Criminal Trial," 57 *Colum. L. Rev.* (1957): 846 (sounding many of the themes of subsequent critical discussion, including that speedy trial is a mixed blessing for defendants and that the severity of the normal sanction for a denial of a speedy trial, dismissal, has an inevitable impact on analysis of the right); "Note: Dismissal of the Indictment as a Remedy for Denial of the Right to Speedy Trial," 64 *Yale L.J.* (1955): 1208 (arguing that the use of dismissal as a remedy for speedy trial violations should be curtailed in the interest of public security, because most of those accused are convicted of committing crimes); F.D.L., Jr., "Note: The Lagging Right to Speedy Trial," 51 *Va. L. Rev.* (1965): 1587 (finding the Sixth Amendment right to speedy trial "strangely neglected"); and Alan L. Schneider, "Note: The Right to a Speedy Trial," 20 *Stan. L. Rev.* (1967–68): 476 (written shortly after the decision in *Klopfer* and focusing on issues left open after that decision).

The most trenchant academic commentary on the Supreme Court's current approach to speedy trial is H. Richard Uviller's "*Barker v. Wingo*: Speedy Trial Gets a Fast Shuffle," 72 *Colum. L. Rev*. (1972): 1376, whose chief points were described in the text above following the discussion of Barker v. Wingo.

Uviller repeated some of his commentary and added some observations about what he saw as peculiarities of the Supreme Court's speedy trial law in his book *The Process of Criminal Justice: Investigation and Adjudication* (St. Paul, MN: West Publishing, 1979).

Anthony G. Amsterdam's insightful article, "Speedy Criminal Trial: Rights and Remedies," 27 *Stan. L. Rev*. (1974–75): 525, expressed concern about the Supreme Court dictum in the *Strunk* case that dismissal of charges with prejudice is "the only possible remedy" once a constitutional speedy trial violation has been found, urging the courts to be willing to recognize and remedy violations of the right to a speedy trial during the pretrial phase, when they have greater ability to control the speed of proceedings than before charges are brought or after trial has concluded.

Gregory P. N. Joseph's "Speedy Trial Rights in Application," 48 *Fordham L. Rev.* (1979–80): 611, is an ambitious attempt to canvas extraconstitutional as well as constitutional sources of protection for the right to a speedy trial. This article is an invaluable resource gathering all state constitutional speedy trial provisions (listed in note 16) and all state speedy trial statutes and rules (charted in an appendix) as of 1980. Joseph reports on the case law interpreting these provisions, analyzing how the speedy trial guarantees have been implemented and reconciled.

Subsequent law review articles on the right to a speedy trial usually reacted to changes in the law, either by a particular Supreme Court decision or by speedy trial statutes. Student authors reporting on the *MacDonald* case had mixed reactions to the Court's opinion, for example. Nancy Nowlin Kerr, student author of "Constitutional Law – Speedy Trial – Sixth Amendment Right to Speedy Trial Does Not Apply during Interim between Dismissal of Charges and Subsequent Indictment by Same Sovereign," 14 *St. Mary's L.J.* (1982): 113, complimented the Court for "remaining true to precedent by shielding the investigative stage of a criminal prosecution from the ticking of the speedy trial clock," and described *MacDonald* as part of a trend away from "the sixties' spotlight on the rights of the accused toward a contemporary focus on the needs of society." Another student author, Paul R. Clevenger, in "Narrowing the Scope of the Speedy Trial Right: *United States v. MacDonald*," 36 *Sw. L.J.* (1983): 1213, thought the Court had narrowed rather than remained true to precedents like *Marion* and found the *MacDonald* opinion confusing. Kenneth M. Altman, in "*Doggett v. United States*: Giving the Speedy Trial Claimant a Presumptive Helping Hand," 39 *Loyola L. Rev.* (1993): 213, applauded the *Doggett* decision for effectively preventing prosecutors from substantially delaying a trial without a valid reason and for providing substantial protection to the constitutional rights of the accused, while student author Ronna A. Laidley disagreed, as her title suggests: "Constitutional Law—Speedy Trial—The Filing of an Indictment against a Defendant Activates His Sixth Amendment Right to a Speedy Trial, Notwithstanding the Fact that the Defendant Had No Knowledge of the Indictment Until the Time of His Arrest," 24 *St. Mary's L.J.* (1993): 595.

Student author Brian P. Brooks, in his ambitious comment, "A New Speedy Trial Standard for *Barker v. Wingo*: Reviving a Constitutional Remedy in an Age of Statutes," 61 *U. Chi. L. Rev.* (1994): 587, thought that *Doggett* was insufficient to clear up the confusion about Barker v. Wingo in the lower courts and offered his own analysis and clarifying solution. His commentary is worthwhile reading.

Alfredo Garcia's *The Sixth Amendment in Modern Jurisprudence: A Critical Perspective* (Westport, CT: Greenwood Press, 1992), which did not mention public trial, includes a twenty-five-page section on speedy trial, which is highly critical of Barker v. Wingo and most of the Supreme Court speedy trial decisions of the 1970s and 80s.

Akhil Reed Amar wrote "Sixth Amendment First Principles," 84 *Geo. L.J.* (1996): 641, later incorporated as a section of his book, *The Constitution and Criminal Procedure* (New Haven: Yale Univ. Press, 1997), following his earlier articles setting forth what he viewed as the "first principles" of the Fourth and Fifth Amendments. The "deep principles" he derives from all these amendments are the same—protection of the innocent and pursuit of the truth at trial—and his chief target is the same—constitutionally based exclusionary rules, which exclude reliable evidence from trial. Amar describes dismissal of prosecution for speedy trial violation as "the mother of all upside down exclusionary rules," offering a windfall to guilty defendants and leaving the innocent to suffer because judges confronted with such a draconian remedy will be unwilling to admit that anyone's rights have been violated. Like Anthony Amsterdam, he stresses prevention as the first goal, and release of incarcerated pretrial detainees as a second choice. If prevention does not work and a violation occurs, defendants may bring a civil action for damages after the fact, as Amar would have people do if they have been subjected to Fourth Amendment violations. Responses to Amar mostly focus on his Fourth and Fifth Amendment "first principles," but include some criticism of his less extensive treatment of the Sixth Amendment. See Ronald F. Wright, "Book Review: The Constitution and Criminal Procedure: First Principles," 14 *Const. Commentary* (Winter 1997): 557, 562 n. 12; and George C. Thomas, III, in "Book Review: Remapping the Criminal Procedure Universe," 83 *Va. L. Rev*. (1997): 1819, 1846–47.

State and Statutory Law

A number of speedy trial articles focus on the law of particular states but, because Barker v. Wingo is applicable both to federal and most state constitutional analysis, the authors' observations may be of interest to those outside the state. A few examples are Darren Allen, "Note: The Constitutional Floor Doctrine and the Right to a Speedy Trial," 26 *Campbell L. Rev*. (2004): 101 (criticizing the North Carolina Supreme Court for applying the Barker v. Wingo balancing test in a skewed manner that effectively revived that state's pre-*Barker* demand waiver rule); and Christopher S. Elmore, "Note, *Glover v. State*: A Misinterpretation and Misapplication of the Barker Speedy Trial Balancing Test Results in Weakening of a Criminal Defendant's Right to a Prompt Trial," 62 *Md. L. Rev*. (2003): 573.

Table of Cases

United States Supreme Court

Barber v. Page, 390 U.S. 719 (1968)
Barker v. Wingo, 407 U.S. 514 (1972)
Bartkus v. Illinois, 359 U.S. 121 (1959)
Beavers v. Haubert, 198 U.S. 77 (1905)
Brewer v. Williams, 430 U.S. 387 (1977)
Crawford v. Washington, 541 U.S. 36 (2004)
County of Riverside v. McLaughlin, 500 U.S. 44 (1991)
Daniels v. Williams, 474 U.S. 327 (1986)
Dickey v. Florida, 398 U.S. 30 (1970)
Dillingham v. United States, 423 U.S. 64 (1975)
Doggett v. United States, 505 U.S. 647 (1992)
Farmer v. Brennan, 511 U.S. 825 (1994)
Gannett v. DePasquale, 433 U.S. 368 (1979)
Gideon v. Wainwright, 372 U.S. 335 (1963)
Henderson v. United States, 476 U.S. 321 (1986)
In re Oliver, 333 U.S. 257 (1948)
Kirby v. Illinois, 406 U.S. 682 (1972)
Klopfer v. North Carolina, 386 U.S. 213 (1967)
Massiah v. United States, 377 U.S. 201 (1964)
Miranda v. Arizona, 384 U.S. 436 (1966)
Moody v. Daggett, 429 U.S. 78 (1976)
Moore v. Arizona, 414 U.S. 25 (1973)
Morrissey v. Brewer, 408 U.S. 471 (1972)
Pointer v. Texas, 380 U.S. 400 (1965)
Pollard v. United States, 352 U.S. 354 (1957)
Ponzi v. Fessenden, 258 U.S. 254 (1922)
Singer v. United States, 380 U.S. 24 (1965)
Smith v. Hooey, 393 U.S. 374 (1969)
Smith v. United States, 360 U.S. 1 (1959)
Strunk v. United States, 412 U.S. 434 (1973)
United States v. $8,850, 461 U.S. 555 (1983)

United States v. Ewell, 383 U.S. 116 (1966)
United States v. Gouveia, 467 U.S. 180 (1984)
United States v. Loud Hawk, 474 U.S. 302 (1986)
United States v. Lovasco, 431 U.S. 783 (1977)
United States v. MacDonald, 435 U.S. 850 (1978)
United States v. MacDonald, 456 U.S. 1 (1982)
United States v. Marion, 404 U.S. 307 (1971)
United States v. Taylor, 487 U.S. 326 (1988)

United States Courts of Appeal

Burkett v. Cunningham, 826 F.2d 1208 (3d Cir. 1987)
Burkett v. Fulcomer, 951 F.2d 1431 (3d Cir. 1991)
Cain v. Smith, 686 F.2d 374 (6th Cir. 1982)
Campodonico v. United States, 222 F.2d 310 (9th Cir.1955)
Chauncey v. Second Judicial Dist. Ct., 474 F.2d 1238 (9th Cir. 1973)
Cox v. Lockhart, 970 F.2d 448 (8th Cir. 1992)
Moultrie v. State of Georgia, 464 F.2d 551 (5th Cir. 1972)
Prince v. State of Alabama, 507 F.2d 693 (5th Cir.), cert. denied, 423 U.S. 876 (1975)
Redd v. Sowders, 809 F.2d 1266 (6th Cir. 1987)
Rheuark v. Shaw, 628 F.2d 297 (5th Cir. 1980)
Ringstaff v. Howard, 885 F.2d 1542 (11th Cir.1989), cert. denied, 496 U.S. 927 (1990)
Ross v. United States, 349 F.2d 210 (D.C. Cir. 1965)
Sanders v. United States, 416 F.2d 194 (5th Cir. 1969), cert. denied, 397 U.S. 952 (1970)
United States v. Avalos, 541 F.2d 1100 (5th Cir. 1976), cert. denied, 430 U.S. 970 (1977)
United States v. Beckham, 505 F.2d 1316 (5th Cir.), cert. denied, 421 U.S. 950 (1975)
United States v. Beebe, 431 F.2d 428 (9th Cir. 1970)
United States v. Bishton, 463 F.2d 887 (D.C. Cir. 1972)
United States v. Brown, 600 F.2d 248 (10th Cir.), cert. denied, 444 U.S. 917 (1979)
United States v. Cabral, 475 F.2d 715 (1st Cir. 1973)
United States v. Calloway, 505 F.2d 311 (D.C. Cir. 1974)
United States v. Carini, 562 F.2d 144 (2d Cir. 1977)
United States v. Cordova, 537 F.2d 1073 (9th Cir.), cert. denied, 429 U.S. 960 (1976)
United States v. DeTienne, 468 F.2d 151 (7th Cir. 1972), cert. denied, 410 U.S. 911 (1973)
United States v. Dennard, 722 F.2d 1510 (11th Cir. 1984)
United States v. Dreyer, 533 F.2d 112 (3d Cir. 1976)
United States *ex rel.* Little v. Twomey, 477 F.2d 767 (7th Cir.), cert. denied, 414 U.S. 846 (1973)
United States v. Fay, 505 F.2d 1037 (1st Cir. 1974)
United States v. Garner, 32 F.3d 1305 (8th Cir. 1994), cert. denied, 514 U.S. 1020 (1995)
United States v. Geelan, 520 F.2d 585 (9th Cir. 1975)
United States v. Gerald, 5 F.3d 563 (D.C. Cir. 1993), cert. denied, 511 U.S. 1144 (1994)
United States v. Gibson, 353 F.3d 21 (D.C. Cir. 2003)
United States v. Gregory, 322 F.3d 1157 (9th Cir. 2003)
United States v. Herman, 576 F.2d 1139 (5th Cir. 1978)
United States v. Holyfield, 802 F.2d 846 (6th Cir.1986), cert. denied, 479 U.S. 1090 (1987)
United States v. Hooker, 607 F.2d 286 (9th Cir. 1979), cert. denied, 445 U.S. 905 (1980)
United States v. Lai Ming Tanu, 589 F.2d 82 (2d Cir. 1978)
United States v. Liddy, 542 F.2d 76 (1976)

United States v. Lucien, 61 F.3d 366 (5th Cir. 1995)
United States v. Lustman, 258 F.2d 475 (2d Cir.), cert. denied, 358 U.S. 880 (1958)
United States v. Mills, 810 F.2d 907 (9th Cir.), cert. denied, 484 U.S. 832 (1987)
United States v. Mitchell, 769 F.2d 1544 (11th Cir. 1985), cert. denied, 474 U.S. 1066 (1986)
United States v. Mohawk, 20 F.3d 1480 (9th Cir. 1994)
United States v. Mulligan, 520 F.2d 1327 (6th Cir. 1975), cert. denied, 424 U.S. 919 (1976)
United States v. Mundt, 29 F.3d 233 (6th Cir. 1994)
United States v. Nance, 666 F.2d 353 (9th Cir.), cert. denied, 456 U.S. 918 (1982)
United States v. Nelson-Rodriguez, 319 F.3d 12 (1st Cir.), cert. denied, 539 U.S. 928; 540 U.S. 831 (2003)
United States v. Netterville, 553 F.2d 903 (5th Cir.), cert. denied, 434 U.S. 1009 (1977)
United States v. Pomeroy, 822 F.2d 718 (8th Cir. 1987)
United States v. Roberts, 515 F.2d 642 (2d Cir. 1975)
United States v. Santos, 372 F.2d 177 (2d Cir. 1967)
United States v. Simmons, 536 F.2d 827 (9th Cir.), cert. denied, 429 U.S. 854 (1976)
United States v. Thevis, 665 F.2d 616 (5th Cir.), cert. denied, 456 U.S. 1008; 458 U.S. 1109 (1982)
United States v. Watson, 599 F.2d 1149 (2d Cir.), opinion revised on rehearing, 690 F.2d 15 (1979)
Yapp v. Reno, 26 F.3d 1562 (11th Cir. 1994)

United States District Courts

Deutsch v. United States, 943 F. Supp. 276 (W.D.N.Y. 1996)
Ex parte Altman, 34 F. Supp. 106 (S.D. Cal. 1940)
Hutchinson v. Marshall, 573 F. Supp. 496 (S.D. Ohio 1983), aff'd, 744 F.2d 44 (6th Cir. 1984), cert. denied, 469 U.S. 1221 (1985)
Petition of Provoo, 17 F.R.D. 183 (D. Md.), aff'd mem sub nom United States v. Provoo, 350 U.S. 857 (1955)
United States v. Alcantar-Lopez, 685 F. Supp. 181 (N.D. Ill. 1988)
United States v. Banks, 383 F. Supp. 389 (D.S.D. 1974), app. dismissed sub nom. United States v. Means, 513 F.2d 1329 (8th Cir. 1975)
United States v. Gutierrez, 891 F. Supp. 97 (E.D.N.Y. 1995), aff'd, 112 F.3d 506 (2d Cir. 1996)
United States v. Raffone, 405 F. Supp. 549 (S.D. Fla. 1975)
United States v. Upton, 921 F. Supp. 100 (E.D.N.Y. 1995), aff'd sub nom. United States v. Dragone, 78 F.3d 65 (2d Cir. 1996)
United States v. Zapata, 245 F. Supp. 2d 1165 (D. Colo. 2003)

State High Courts

Commonwealth v. Hanley, 337 Mass. 384, 149 N.E.2d 608, cert. denied, 358 U.S. 850 (1958)
Ex parte Archer, 643 So.2d 601 (Ala. 1992)
Glover v. State, 368 Md. 211, 792 A.2d 1160 (2002)
In re Thomas J., 372 Md. 50, 811 A.2d 310 (2002)
Mississippi Bar v. An Attorney, 636 So.2d 371 (Miss. 1994)
People v. Drake, 61 N.Y.2d 359, 474 N.Y.S.2d 276, 462 N.E.2d 376 (1984)
People v. Vernace, 96 N.Y.2d 886, 730 N.Y.S.2d 778, 756 N.E.2d 66 (2001)
Salandre v. State, 111 N.M. 422, 806 P.2d 562 (1991)
Serna v. Superior Court, 40 Cal. 3d 239, 219 Cal. Rptr. 420, 707 P.2d 793 (1985)
Smith v. State, 275 Ga. 261, 564 S.E.2d 441 (2002)

State v. Freeman, 236 Kan. 274, 689 P.2d 885 (1984)
State v. Gattuso, 108 Nev. 49, 825 P. 2d 569 (1992)
State v. Gee, 298 Md. 565, 471 A.2d 712, cert. denied, 467 U.S. 1244 (1984)
State v. Griffin, 848 S.W.2d 464 (Mo. 1993)
State v. Harriman, 513 N.W.2d 725 (Iowa 1994)
State v. Holtslander, 102 Idaho 306, 629 P.2d 702 (1981)
State v. Talamante, 134 N.M. 539, 80 P.3d 476 (2003)
State v. Utley, 956 S.W.2d 489 (Tenn. 1997)
State v. Wavrick, 123 Idaho 83, 844 P.2d 712 (1992)
State v. Wood, 924 S.W.2d 342 (Tenn. 1996)
Townsend v. Superior Court, 15 Cal. 3d 774, 126 Cal. Rptr. 251, 543 P.2d 619 (1975)

State Appellate Courts

Berryman v. State, 94 Md. App. 414, 617 A.2d 1120 (Md. Ct. Spec. App.), cert. denied, 331 Md. 86, 626 A.2d 370 (1993)
In re Robert B., 46 Cal. Rptr.2d 691, 39 Cal. App. 4th 1816 (Cal. App. Ct. 1995)
Kimbrell v. State, 659 So.2d 1039 (Ala. Crim. App. 1995)
People v. Fly, 249 Ill. App. 3d 730, 189 Ill. Dec. 120, 619 N.E.2d 821 (Ill. App. Ct.), app. denied, 153 Ill. 2d 563, 191 Ill. Dec. 623, 624 N.E.2d 811 (1993)
People v. Martinez, 94 Cal. Rptr. 2d 381, 22 Cal. 4th 750, 996 P.2d 32 (2000)
People v. Mitchell, 356 Ill. App. 3d 158, 292 Ill. Dec. 230, 825 N.E.2d 1241 (Ill. App. Ct. 2005)
State v. Empak, Inc., 889 S.W.2d 618 (Tex. Ct. App. 1994)
State v. Jones, 79 Wash. App. 7, 901 P.2d 1057 (Wash. Ct. App. 1995), review denied, 128 Wash. 2d 1009, 910 P.2d 481 (1996)

Index

About the Author

SUSAN N. HERMAN is Centennial Professor of Law at Brooklyn Law School. She serves as a member of the National Board of Directors and Executive Committee and as General Counsel of the American Civil Liberties Union. She writes extensively on constitutional and criminal procedure topics for legal and nonlegal publications.